D0495180

4-50

The Natural History of the
Mediterranean

TEGWYN HARRIS

Foreword by Oleg Polunin

Illustrated by
Franklin Coombs
Josephine Martin
Malcolm McGregor
Andrew Riley
Gordon Riley
John Thompson
Joyce Tuhill

Pelham Books

First published in Great Britain by
Pelham Books Ltd
44 Bedford Square
London WC1B 3DU
1982

© George Rainbird Ltd 1982

All rights reserved. No part of this
publication may be reproduced, stored in
a retrieval system, or transmitted, in any
form or by any means, electronic,
mechanical, photocopying, recording or
otherwise, without the prior permission
of the copyright owner.

ISBN 0 7207 1391 9

This book was designed and produced by
George Rainbird Ltd,
36 Park Street, London W1Y 4DE
for Pelham Books Ltd

House Editors: David Burnie, Valerie Noel-Finch
Designer: Yvonne Dedman
Indexer: Barbara James
Cartographer: Eugene Fleury
Production: Dee Maple

Colour originated by Bridge Graphics Ltd,
Hull, Humberside
Text filmset by SX Composing Ltd,
Rayleigh, Essex
Printed and bound in Spain by
Printer Industria Gráfica SA, Barcelona
D.L.B. 33318-1981

Cover illustrations by Malcolm McGregor

Contents

Foreword   7

Part I   **HABITAT SECTION**
Introduction   9
The Coastal Lands   10
Rocky Shores   22
Sandy Shores   32
Estuaries   36
The Open Sea   41
Glossary and key to abbreviations   48
Map   50–1

Part II   **FIELD GUIDE**
to representative plants and animals
Seaweeds   52
Flowering Plants   62
Invertebrates   80
Fish   148
Amphibians and Reptiles   164
Birds   168
Mammals   208
Further Reading   212
Acknowledgments   213
Index   214

Foreword

For those of us who live in the northern and western parts of Europe the wildlife of the Mediterranean is quite new and strange. So different are the plants, insects, birds, reptiles and in particular the marine life, that without a comprehensive field guide it is impossible to identify what one sees on that restful sun-drenched holiday by the Mediterranean shore.

For many people a few days of sunbathing is enough; the inquisitive visitor then begins to look around and wanders off inland through the bushy maquis and garrigue, which in early spring is so rich in fascinating orchids and aromatic herbs. Here bee-eaters and rollers glide by in search of food, cicadas call incessantly and there are many different butterflies and moths, lizards and tortoises that await discovery. Or, wandering across the rocky shores, away from the sunbathing multitude, one can search for unusual crabs, sponges, sea-urchins and starfish, while the more adventurous will no doubt don a snorkel and explore the rich underwater life.

This excellent field guide, with its rich collection of paintings of the plants and creatures is undoubtedly just what is required to get one started. Much of the identification will be by direct visual comparison with the very life-like paintings. In addition each organism is given a brief diagnostic description, enabling the reader to distinguish between the thresher shark and the basking shark, or the different brown seaweeds, for example. About 1,000 common living organisms are illustrated and described.

This is certainly the best introduction to Mediterranean wildlife that I have so far seen in any language. I do congratulate Dr Tegwyn Harris on such an enterprise, as well as the artists who have contributed so attractively and accurately to this work. There is no doubt that the visual approach is quite essential to the layman to encourage the study of wildlife of this unique sea.

With the enormous influx of tourism, rapid transport, and the desire to escape from the pressures of contemporary life, the Mediterranean has become one of the most important recreational places in Europe. In consequence of this, and the growth of industry, pollution is a growing problem – the only outlet for polluted water is through the narrow Straits of Gibraltar, into the Atlantic. There is growing evidence that the rich animal and plant life is beginning to suffer irreparable damage, and only by knowing it intimately can one appreciate what is happening.

Everyone interested in wildlife should support their governments, and those of the countries bordering the Mediterranean, to reduce the output of industrial waste and sewerage, otherwise we shall lose the richest heritage of wildlife that we have in the whole of Europe.

OLEG POLUNIN

Introduction

The sea of antiquity

From the Mediterranean Sea's most westerly point, the mountains of the African coast loom up a mere 10 km away across the Strait of Gibraltar, the Mediterranean's only link with the Atlantic Ocean. If the sea level were 400 m lower, a rampart of rock would be visible spanning the strait and connecting Europe to Africa. This submerged bridge is a relic from the times when southern Europe and Africa formed one continuous landmass. Earth movements eventually broke up this continent, and for about 220 million years, during the Mesozoic and Tertiary geological periods, a great ocean extended across the world in a broad east-to-west direction. As water levels fell, this ocean, known as the Tethys Sea, gradually became obliterated and the submerged bridge between Europe and Africa came closer to the surface. But the underwater link between the two continents never quite re-emerged, and the Atlantic Ocean is still tenuously joined to the Mediterranean, a vestige of the ancient Tethys Sea.

All life in the Mediterranean relies on this small but vital connection with the Atlantic. A current travelling at about 4 km/h pours in from the ocean, streaming over the rocky sill of the strait and far across the surface of the Mediterranean. Every second nearly two million cubic metres of water flood eastwards, and although the Mediterranean reciprocates this flow to some extent, it gains far more than it loses. From a hilltop in southern Spain or North Africa there is no indication of this interchange of water, but without it the Mediterranean would simply dry up.

For millions of years the Atlantic has replaced the water that evaporates in the Mediterranean's warm climate. Over this time the wildlife has evolved into many forms, some of which are peculiar to this almost landlocked sea. The Mediterranean also has a unique position in the history of man. It has been at various times an arena for war, a highway for trade and, more recently, a haven for leisure. Its wildlife has provoked interest for centuries. The founders of modern biology, men like Theophrastus, Aristotle, Lucretius and Galen, lived on these shores and examined the animal and plant life of the area which was, to them, the centre of the world.

On land, the climate and proximity of the sea have given rise to vegetation and animal life unlike that of regions further north. Today's rapid methods of travel accentuate these differences: while northern Europe is blanketed in the snow and fog of late winter, around the Mediterranean spring is already underway, with flowers blooming, and cicadas starting their piercing song.

A hardy pine tree clings to a rocky hillside overlooking the Aegean

The Coastal Lands

The arrival of man

The first human inhabitants of the Mediterranean shores were wandering hunters and gatherers, people whose ancestors had moved northwards from East Africa. A fascinating insight into the lives of these early nomads was given when hotel construction workers in Nice uncovered the remains of a campsite 400,000 years old. When the camp was in use the climate was cooler and more moist, and elephants, rhinoceros and deer flourished in the thick vegetation, providing plentiful food for the early hunters. Anthropologists were able to deduce that the people who used the campsite made rough shelters of stones and branches. As well as bringing the produce of their hunts back to the camp, shells that litter the site show that they also collected animals from the shore.

The foundations of Mediterranean agriculture were laid much later – about 8000 years ago. A better area for growing crops can hardly be imagined, and in the ideal climate local and introduced species grew with the minimum of attention. Many of the cultivated plants of those times can still be seen today – the grapevine *Vitis vinifera,* the fig *Ficus carica* and the carob or locust tree *Ceratonia siliqua,* whose deep green leaves stand out against the brown hues of midsummer.

To provide room for farming much of the original vegetation was cleared. The broadleaved or coniferous forests that extended right down to the shores of the almost tideless sea were slowly felled, and when all the available flat land was in use, hillside terraces were laboriously constructed to provide more food for a burgeoning human population. With the introduction of sheep and goats, which nibbled away the saplings vital to the future of the forests, a great change in the landscape was brought to completion. The low scrub that covers much of the Mediterranean's coastline today is the legacy of an unusually long history of human influence.

As civilizations developed, crafts emerged which used wood as a raw material. The slow-growing oaks of the coast burn slowly with a fierce heat, and the Greeks, Etruscans and Romans all made use of wood-fuelled kilns to smelt metals and fire pottery and glass. The great demand for leather at the height of the Roman Empire further increased the consumption of wood as bark was stripped from trees for use in tanning.

Fortunately, not all the native forests were destroyed in this onslaught. Around the coast in inaccessible or protected areas remnants of the early wood cover still remain. Along the shores of Spain, Sardinia and Yugoslavia small groves of the holm oak *Quercus ilex,* the cork oak *Q. suber* and the Aleppo pine *Pinus halepensis* give a tantalizing idea of what the Mediterranean must have looked like in classical times. Today these woods are the stronghold of much of the region's native wildlife.

Woodland wildlife

Few habitats have so much to offer animals as woods or even individual trees. Some animals live directly on the trees themselves, while others make use of their products, perhaps by eating their flowers and fruit, or by burrowing into the moist protective carpet of leaf litter. The isolated coastal woods of the Mediterranean offer shelter from predators in a region which is otherwise exposed and full of danger for small animals. The cover given by the trees is not absolute: some hunters specialize in finding prey in woods, like the goshawk *Accipiter gentilis* which often attacks birds in flight, snatching them in its talons and plummeting to the ground to dismember its prey.

The most voracious leaf-eaters in the Mediterranean woods are the insects. The climate is ideal for them, allowing them to remain active almost throughout the year. As young leaves appear in the early spring, they are attacked by beetles and weevils quick to feed on the new growth before it becomes too tough for their jaws to cut into. As well as leaves, the trees provide food in the form of sap. Thousands of insect species live by this method, many of them small and inconspicuous. The cicada *Cicadetta montana* is a giant in the world of sap-sucking bugs. Cicadas lay their eggs on the parts of plants above ground, but their nymphs lower themselves to the soil on silken threads, then burrow into the earth and feed on roots. After a life of some years underground, they emerge as adults in the warmth of early summer, and once more take to the branches. The mature male cicada announces its presence with a shrill and repetitive call of an intensity quite disproportionate for an insect of its size. The sound is produced by muscles stretching the abdomen. The cicada's body is constructed like an amplifier with a number of cavities and sound-reflecting plates which broadcast the sound. Despite their calls, cicadas are not easy to find. Each insect will interrupt its singing at the slightest sign of danger and remain silent until the threat has passed.

It is not only insects that can be located by sound among the trees. A crackling and rustling overhead may be produced by a hawfinch *Coccothraustes coccothraustes* feeding on fruits and seeds. Its massive beak can break open hard-shelled nuts and fruit stones which other animals find inedible. A similar, if not quite so arduous task faces the jay *Garrulus glandarius*. This species, which although unmelodious, is one of the more colourful birds of the woods, feeds on the fleshy contents of acorns.

Not all the woodland birds feed on the trees directly. The chiffchaff *Phylloscopus collybita* pecks insects and spiders off the bark, and the great spotted woodpecker *Dendrocopos major* is able to probe further, extracting any small animals that have taken refuge in the deeper crevices of branches. Insects on the wing are not safe from attack – many become the victims of birds like the collared flycatcher *Ficedula albicollis* and the nightingale *Luscinia megarhynchos* which dart through the air to snap up their prey.

Underfoot, the leaf litter on a woodland floor is a complex world of animal life in miniature. Even in the hot climate, the shaded ground retains its moisture and supports a varied collection of tiny animals which form the prey of a number of birds and mammals common to woods and thickets all over Europe. The song thrush *Turdus philomelos* feeds on the earthworms that flourish in the damp parts of woodland, and the hedgehog *Erinaceus europaeus* probes for food among the decaying vegetation, guided by its keen sense of smell. The woodland floor also provides food for one of the region's most secretive inhabitants, the wild boar *Sus scrofa*. This much-hunted relative of the domestic pig may sometimes be seen in unfrequented woods on the coasts of France or Spain, unearthing roots with its powerful snout.

The heat and dryness of some parts of the coast, particularly the east, promotes the growth of elegant conifers like the Aleppo pine. Unfortunately for wildlife, pine woods are rarely hospitable habitats. Instead of the light, airy composition of broadleaved woods, they are often sombre and uniform, admitting little light to any plants on the ground. The pines also secrete resin which, though delightful as a scent, decomposes in the soil to produce acids which prevent the growth of many other plants and are an irritant to small animals. But although they lack variety, pine woods are by no means devoid of life. Pine wood is the food of the wood-wasp *Urocerus gigas*. The female of this slender-bodied insect deposits its eggs under the bark of a tree by means of a hollow needle-like ovipositor at the tip of the abdomen. The larva spends all its developmental life in the tree and pupates there, the newly hatched adult finally leaving via a hole in the bark. Wood-wasps can be seen flying between branches within a few metres of the sea where the resilient pines have grown close to the water's edge.

The tangled maquis

Maquis is the type of plant cover that replaced woodland in many areas after the disappearance of the forest. Although maquis is typically found close to the coast it may extend quite far inland, and in Spain, for example, covers a large part of the south of the country. The origin of the name maquis is confusing: it is an adaptation of the Corsican *macchia*, a local name for a species of rock-rose. However, *macchia*, and hence maquis, has come to be applied to all areas similar to the dense scrub in which the rock-rose grows. Typical maquis vegetation is an almost impenetrable tangle of low bushes and shrubs from 2 to 4 m in height, where the slow-growing woody plants are bent and twisted by strong winds. Much of the cover is made up of the strawberry tree *Arbutus unedo*, broom *Genista cinerea* and tree heather *Erica arborea*. The wood of the heather is often so thick and incombustible that it can be used for the bowls of pipes. The maquis is an ideal hiding place for animals and man, a fact that was

Lavender and rock-roses, both plants characteristic of the western Mediterranean, provide a highlight of colour in the maquis of Provence

exploited during the interminable Corsican feuds and, more recently, by the *maquisards* of the Second World War.

A visit to the maquis on a typical summer day often demonstrates that it is a harsh place for plants. Strong winds blow across the ground unimpeded by trees, and its shrubs often receive this continual buffeting in the day-long glare of the sun. This atmosphere quickly dries and cracks unprotected human skin and would have the same effect on the leaves of plants were they not specially adapted to withstand such demanding conditions.

One plant that is common over the maquis is the myrtle *Myrtus communis*. If its leaves are held against the light, tiny translucent spots can be seen scattered over their surfaces. These little spots, barely visible except by careful inspection, are the secret of the myrtle's success in such an unpromising environment. In order to live, the myrtle has to maintain a constant supply of water to its tissues. In winter this presents no problems; water flows up through the roots and evaporates through the leaves in the process of transpiration, but in the summer the plant cannot afford to dissipate water in an uncontrolled way, or its supply would soon be exhausted. Instead, the myrtle can physically prevent excessive water loss: the translucent spots on the leaves are, in fact, tiny glands that bathe the surface of the leaves in a blanket of a heavy oily vapour. This oil does not evaporate as readily as water, and so greatly cuts down the water loss. These aromatic oils, often exquisitely scented, are found in many of the maquis plants. The *macchia* rock-rose *Cistus albidus* survives the summer in the same way, by producing a sticky gum. The gum of some of these rock-roses is produced in such quantities that it oozes from the plants; known as 'ladanum', it is collected for use in perfumery. The scent of the rock-roses is particularly pungent after rain. Napoleon said of his native Corsica that he could recognize it with his eyes shut by scent alone, so typical is the fragrance of the *Cistus*.

The rock-rose parasite *Cytinus hypocistis* is one interesting discovery that can be made in the maquis. This plant attaches itself to the roots of rock-roses and becomes conspicuous only when it flowers since, being parasitic, it has no use for leaves and these are reduced to colourless scales. Its flower is far from colourless, being bright yellow and surrounded by protective red or carmine scales. *Cytinus* is a member of the Rafflesiaceae, a family of mostly tropical parasitic plants, one species of which produces the largest flowers in the world.

Those plants that do not have blankets of oily vapour to guard against water loss have evolved other means of withstanding the summer drought. The leaves of the juniper *Juniperus oxycedrus,* for example, are small, narrow and prickly, so small, in fact, that they have very little surface from which water can evaporate. Also, the leaves have relatively few microscopic pores or stomata through which water can escape – a simple but effective modification shared by many maquis plants.

At first sight several maquis plants do not seem to have leaves at all. In these, the leaves have evolved into spines or stem-like structures that have little in common with the spreading leaves of plants from cooler regions. The broom

Genista cinerea has small, sparse leaves and depends largely on its stems to trap sunlight and thereby produce food. Both the buckthorn *Rhamnus alaternus* and the Christ's thorn *Paliurus spinachristi* have very reduced leaves. It is claimed that the historical crown of thorns was made from the Christ's thorn, although this is also said of a number of Mediterranean species. Most of the plants' tissues, including their thorns, are woody, with no surface pores.

Plants of the garrigue

Plants have a more tenuous grip on the land in the garrigue, an often calcareous rocky zone above the shore where exposure to climatic changes is extreme. This windswept and superficially barren hinterland is found in areas where the tree cover has disappeared, and the difficult terrain has prevented agriculture. Known as the *tomillares* in Spain, the *phrygana* in Greece and the *batha* in the Levant, like the maquis, this harsh environment can only sustain plants that are very frugal with water, and here also the aromatic oil-producing plants are the most abundant. A list of the scented plants of the garrigue – thyme *Thymus vulgaris*, sage *Salvia*, rosemary *Rosmarinus officinalis*, summer savory *Satureia thymbra*, hyssop *Hyssopus officinalis* and rue *Ruta chalepensis* – reads like a page from an exotic cookery book or an old-fashioned herbal. The stems and leaves of these plants have been used as culinary flavourings and for production of ointments and medicines for many centuries. The smooth texture of some of these plants is produced by a felt of fine intertangling hairs on the leaves which traps the aromatic vapours and further reduces water loss.

These hardy plants are visible all the year round as they are able to survive and flower even in the hottest months. The remainder of the garrigue plants, however, are conspicuous only during the spring and early summer. From January to May a vast and varied assembly of flowers transforms this habitat into a sea of brilliant colour. The dominant species of this spring blossoming are the bulb-bearing plants and orchids. Practically all the spring bulb flowers of European gardens grow in the Mediterranean garrigue, together with some of its pot-herbs, like the rose-garlic *Allium roseum*. Many plants produce flowers in strong colours. The bright yellow of the dwarf iris *Iris chamaeiris*, and the orange-yellow of the crocus *Crocus flavus* contrast brilliantly with the white of the star of Bethlehem *Ornithogalum nutans*. Most species are either small or relatively compact, but others, like the white and yellow narcissus *Narcissus tazetta*, and the purple and green fritillary *Fritillaria messanensis*, stand clear of the ground on taller stems.

The orchids of the garrigue are spectacular both in form and colour. Plainest among them are the helleborines, like the white helleborine *Cephalanthera damasonium*, but no-one could describe as plain the mirror orchid *Ophrys speculum*, whose small but complex flowers can be seen on the northern Mediterranean coast and in Algeria. Like many orchids, the mirror orchid relies on a fascinating form of biological deception for its survival. The flowers attract the males of the wasp *Scolia ciliata* by imitating the appearance of the female. So accurate is the resemblance of the shiny surfaces of the flowers to

the female wasp that the visiting male actually attempts to mate with them. During this process the wasp is coated with pollen which is transferred to the next flower that successfully entices it to its insect-like petals.

The blooming of the garrigue is short-lived. A summer visitor sees a very different picture: along the coast from Spain to the Greek islands and Turkey, the hot June sun withers the flowers until all that remains is a tangle of brittle leaves and stems.

Some plants – like the rock-roses – are common to both the garrigue and the maquis, but there is a visible difference in their heights. Few plants of the garrigue reach more than 0.5 m above the ground, and then only where there is shelter. The Kermes oak often reaches a height of 3 m in the maquis, but in the garrigue it is low and spreading and seldom reaches a third of that height.

Visitors from northern Europe may be surprised by the leaves of this diminutive oak tree. Instead of being soft and pliable like those of oaks further north, they are hard and spiny, much more similar in texture, and function, to those of the myrtle. In other plants, such as *Daphne gnidium*, a dull patina over the surface of the leaves indicates that a further barrier – a layer of wax – is being used to conserve the scant water.

Animals of the maquis and garrigue

In contrast to the wildlife of the woods, the wildlife of the garrigue is often 'on show' or easily found. With so little cover and so much open ground, any animal that has been disturbed will probably have to make its escape in full view. The same is often true of the maquis. During the heat of midday, grasshoppers display their brilliant hindwings as they fly away from an intruder, and if their webs are accidentally touched, plumb orb-web spiders haltingly run for cover.

Turning over a rock in these areas can be an exciting experience. Boulders harbour lizards and snakes which bask on them in the sun and scuttle or slip away at speed when surprised. Scorpions also seek refuge in these recesses; females protect their young by carrying them on their backs in the cool darkness. Centipedes may share these crevices, particularly where they are damp. The long-legged centipede *Scutigera coleoptrata* will dash for cover with great alacrity if disturbed; its impressive turns of speed may sometimes also be seen on hotel walls!

The dry stony soil of the garrigue is not entirely without inhabitants. The 'tarantula' spider *Lycosa narbonensis* hides in the safety of a silk-lined subterranean chamber from which it emerges to feed. The digger wasp *Larra anathema* constructs the cells of its nest in a similar situation, and where it is sandy the mole cricket *Gryllotalpa gryllotalpa* burrows through the soil with its armoured body.

The mirror orchid's strangely shaped flowers have evolved their insect-like appearance to attract pollinators

These small but ferocious carnivores prey on other invertebrates that are attracted to the plants and their flowers. Many of the insects undergo a soft-bodied larval stage during their development, forming ideal prey for spiders and mole crickets, and a living meal for the young of many wasps. And everywhere in the maquis and garrigue there are ants, ceaselessly scouring the soil for seeds, leaves and any small invertebrates unfortunate enough to cross their paths.

The shrubs and bushes protect animals that are reluctant to venture out into the open. This is the haunt of the grass snake *Natrix natrix* and Hermann's tortoise *Testudo hermanni*. Although tortoises are well camouflaged, a careful observer in France, Italy or the Mediterranean islands may be rewarded with the sight of one browsing on the leaves, flowers or fruit of low plants, seeking an occasional drink of fresh water, or even picking over rubbish dumps!

Some animals in the bushes require more than a passing glance to be spotted. The hesitant Mediterranean chameleon *Chamaeleo chamaeleon* is a master of disguise whose colour changes with its background. The praying mantis *Mantis religiosa* and the stick insect *Clonopsis gallica* are also denizens of the branches which rely on camouflage for protection, often from the chameleon which relishes such large insects.

The lack of cover in the garrigue makes it an ideal hunting ground for birds of prey. The sparrowhawk *Accipiter nisus*, buzzard *Buteo buteo* and kestrel *Falco tinnunculus* inspect the rocks and shrubs for any signs of movement that could provide a meal. Other birds often form their prey: the grey partridge *Perdix perdix* and the smaller quail *Coturnix coturnix* are instinctively aware of this danger from the air and rarely allow their chicks to wander far into the open. Birds of prey are greatly helped by the persistent coastal winds that sustain their glides or hovering. As well as buzzards and hawks, more dramatic predators may appear, particularly near mountains. A black speck spiralling up a hillside may be a short-toed eagle *Circaetus gallicus* or even an imperial eagle *Aquila heliaca* effortlessly gaining altitude before gliding away down the coast, although identifying them at these distances is never easy.

Bushy maquis is well stocked with small birds that feed on insects. Some of these are familiar in northern European woods, but other more exotic species are rarely found away from the warmth of the Mediterranean. The woodlark *Lullula arborea* and the Dartford warbler *Sylvia undata* are two common inhabitants quickly recognized by their songs. The fine plumage of the bee-eater *Merops apiaster*, the roller *Coracias garrulus* and the hoopoe *Upupa epops* is unmistakable when they are seen in flight. But perhaps one of the most interesting birds of the maquis is the curious wryneck *Jynx torquilla*. This unusual bird spends the winter on the coast after travelling from as far away as Russia. It picks insects off trees in the same way as a woodpecker, often

A chameleon catches an insect. With a flick of its tongue, which can only be seen with a camera, it snatches its unsuspecting prey

twisting its head at strange angles, but it is equally at home on the ground where it snaps up ants with its fine bill, holding its tail up as it does so.

The late evening is a rewarding time for watching the maquis wildlife. In the stillness of twilight, echoing calls identify birds that are still awake. A noise like a badly tuned motorcycle engine is the 'song' of the nightjar *Caprimulgus europaeus*, which scoops up night-flying insects in its wide gaping mouth. The monotonous but musical note of the male scops owl *Otus scops* may be answered by the higher-pitched cry of its mate as they search the shrubs for moths, beetles or small mammals. And in the still warm air many bats take to the wing, twisting and banking noiselessly after their prey.

The maritime steppe

Parts of the coastal region are so exposed that not even the resilient shrubs of the garrigue can maintain a roothold on the scant gravelly soil. This occurs particularly on islands like Malta and Gozo, where there are no reserves of water to sustain the plants in summer, and where the hot *sirocco* blows north from the Sahara. However, even these areas, known as maritime steppe, are not lifeless. One of the features of the Mediterranean climate is that rainfall is concentrated into the winter months, unlike northern Europe where it falls all the year round. Many parts of the Mediterranean coast, which receive only a trace of rainfall in the summer, are inundated during the winter. The problem for plants is how to retain this precious moisture before it runs all too quickly to the sea.

In the barren soil of the maritime steppe, the tall flower of the sea squill *Urginea maritima* indicates that there are some plants at least that have found an answer to this problem. If the stem is followed below ground it will be found to spring from a huge bulb, sometimes up to 15 cm in diameter. This is a living reservoir which stores the water needed to produce the strap-like leaves every year, and in summer the elegant white flowers. Despite its promising appearance, the bulb of the sea squill is not edible – on some Greek islands it has been used for centuries as a natural rat poison. One nineteenth-century English naturalist recalled how he packed the bulb of a squill in a trunk in preparation for his return to England from the French Riviera. The plant stayed in the trunk without water for nearly a year, but on being unwrapped was found to be still alive, having flowered in the confines of the trunk!

Many plants that grow in the maritime steppe survive in the same way by storing water. The asphodel *Asphodelus microcarpus* sends up its tall densely flowered stems from swollen tubers in the most inhospitable of soils, and the Spanish oyster plant *Scolymus hispanicus* grows from a succulent tapering root that is sometimes eaten as a vegetable. A touch of the truly exotic may be given to the vegetation by the prickly pear *Opuntia ficusindica*. This cactus stores water in its flattened fleshy stems which are protected not only by spines but by tufts of highly irritating hairs that can prove much more of a hazard to anyone reaching for their succulent fruit.

By contrast with the few but sometimes prominent plants, animal life is inconspicuous. The problems of survival through a long dry summer are too great for many species. A few reptiles, such as the Spanish sandracer lizard *Psammodromus hispanicus* and the ladder snake *Elaphe scalaris* can cope with these conditions, but they are more than usually tolerant of drought. One animal, however, actually relies on the lack of water. This is the larva of the ant-lion *Myrmeleon plumbeus* which eventually develops into a slender-bodied insect with transparent wings rather like a damselfly. The larva is a plump oval creature which excavates a pit for itself in sandy soil, and buries itself with only its large hollow jaws protruding. Provided that the sand is dry, any ants passing the pit slither down its sides, often assisted by sand thrown at them by the ant-lion larva. Once they have reached the bottom of the pit, the larva quickly sucks out their body juices. A straw touched lightly on the edge of one of these pits immediately alerts the larva in expectation of a meal.

Rocky Shores

The Mediterranean cliffs: a wildlife sanctuary

On many parts of the Mediterranean coast, the sea is surprisingly inaccessible. A map of the coasts of Sardinia, Yugoslavia or the Greek islands, for example, reveals great lengths of shore beyond the reach of roads or tracks. This is not the result of a lack of effort on the part of the inhabitants, but more a reflection of the fact that here cliffs defy human attempts to reach the sea.

The cliffs, particularly along the northern coast, offer a reserve for wildlife thousands of kilometres long. Plants and animals that are unable to tolerate human interference can live undisturbed on the rocky walls. The nature of this habitat means that the smaller plants and animals of the cliffs are often difficult to see. However, more accessible locations, such as the rocky headland *corniches* of the French riviera, support animal and plant life similar to that of remoter cliffs.

The rocks that make up the cliffs vary along the coast. On the Costa Brava of Spain, and in many parts of the coastline further east, the rocks are igneous, having volcanic origins. Their sharp edges make climbing difficult for humans, but they are a valuable retreat for lizards and insects, especially where there are pits and cavities originally formed by volcanic gases. In parts of Italy and Dalmatia, the cliffs are formed of limestone *karst*, a relatively soft rock that has been eroded into smooth surfaces and grottoes by the sea. The softest cliffs are made of sandstone, for example on Corfu and Crete, and the rocks weather quickly under exposure to wind and waves.

For plants and animals to live on cliffs, the rock must be stable. Anyone who has seen the cliffs of Santorin, an island composed of the remnants of a volcanic crater in the Aegean, will be struck by the fact that little lives on the huge walls of crumbling pumice. Yet on the steep limestone cliffs of Capri in the Bay of Naples sturdy plants cling to the rock, bursting into brilliant colour in the spring.

Undoubtedly, the most easily observed and most fascinating inhabitants of the cliffs are birds. On the cliff tops the chough *Pyrrhocorax pyrrhocorax* and the raven *Corvus corax* may be more common than truly maritime birds. The handsome red-legged chough soars with the ease of a gull, performing acrobatic manoeuvres in the air for no obvious reason. Like true sea birds, it nests on cliff ledges. The raven is more of a refugee from its former range. It has not coped effectively with living near man, but among cliffs and mountains on the coast at least, it is able to live undisturbed. The raven is often heard before it is seen, as its short harsh call carries a great distance. It may breed on cliffs, but usually only where there are trees or shrubs on which to build its nest.

Surveying a rocky chasm from a convenient perch, a pair of choughs show the red bills and legs that distinguish them from all other members of the crow family

Some sea birds share with the raven an intolerance of human intrusion. The Manx shearwater *Puffinus puffinus*, the gannet *Sula bassana*, Audouin's gull *Larus audouinii* and the gull-billed tern *Gelochelidon nilotica* are likely to be encountered only on remote island cliffs. Other coastal birds are less particular about their habitats: the Cory's shearwater *Calonectris diomedea*, herring gull *Larus argentatus* and the lesser black-backed gull *L. fusca* are commonly seen foraging in towns where they are quickly attracted to refuse.

One bird that breeds on isolated cliffs is more likely to be seen at sea than on the coast. This is the storm petrel *Hydrobates pelagicus*, a remarkable little bird which nests principally in Corsica, Sardinia and Tunisia. The storm petrel is the smallest European sea bird; it spends most of its time on the wing, often following ships, fluttering over the water's surface, sometimes splashing its weak feet in the sea as it pecks at fish and invertebrates. On the relatively rare occasions when the petrel comes to land, it shuffles about on the whole of its lower legs.

Coastal and inland cliffs are the home of one of the Mediterranean's few surviving large mammals, the mouflon *Ovis ammon musimon*, a wild sheep that was once plentiful in Sardinia and Corsica. Colonies of mouflon can be found in a number of places in Europe today, but they represent only remnants of the original population. Human pressure has forced the mouflon into living on cliffs and crags where they are most active at dusk and after dark. Their wariness quickly distinguishes them from sheep or goats; a mouflon is unlikely to be seen unless it is taken by surprise, at which point it will escape with agile leaps over the rocky terrain.

Of all the terrestrial cliff animals, none is so skilful a mountaineer as the Turkish gecko *Hemidactylus turcicus*. There are over 600 species of these agile lizards in the world, but only four are found in Europe, where they are confined to Spain and the Mediterranean coasts and islands. Geckoes have claws on their toes like all lizards, but, in addition, have foot pads bearing large numbers of branched bristles, which enable the animals to find purchase on any surface irregularities. Some geckoes can actually climb up windows, and the vertical surfaces of cliffs present no problems for the Turkish gecko. The best time to see these reptilian acrobats is in the evening when they emerge to feed on insects. They are not conspicuous, but can sometimes be located by their soft *tic-tac* call.

Although the faces of cliffs provide habitats for a variety of birds, reptiles and invertebrates, few really terrestrial animals are able to survive lower down in the splash zone where the cliffs are regularly soaked by seawater. One air-breathing animal that wanders over the surfaces of damp rocks is the sea-slater *Ligia*, a crustacean resembling a large woodlouse, which lives on decaying organic matter. *Ligia* is found all along European coasts. It hides in crevices during the day, but at night, or when the air is cool, scuttles about just above the water level.

In comparison with their domination of land and air, the insects have fared badly in and around seawater, and the Mediterranean has only a few insect species tolerant of a soaking with saltwater. *Petrobius maritimus* is a wingless bristletail that can be seen on rocks in the splash zone. It shares this habitat with *Anurida maritima*, a springtail that feeds on fine plant debris. Even these tiny animals are not free from predators. The juvenile *Anurida*, which live in rock crevices, are eaten by the pseudoscorpion *Pselaphochernes littoralis*. Although the majority of pseudoscorpions are terrestrial, *Pselaphochernes* survives among the rocks by spinning a silken web across the narrow part of the crevice in which it lives. When the crevice is filled by tide, the web traps a bubble of air enabling the pseudoscorpion to breathe.

Tenacious cliff plants

Paradoxically cliff plants, although living so close to water, grow in conditions of almost constant drought. Any rainwater quickly runs off the rock, and the small pockets of soil are unable to hold much water in the strong coastal winds. Most plants of cliff faces are flat and low, an adaptation to an environment where any spreading branches or flamboyant leaves would shrivel or be snatched away by the wind.

The Hottentot fig *Carpobrotus* is a typical Meditteranean cliff plant. The plant is unrelated to the fig, and is, in fact, a succulent that has spread throughout the Mediterranean after being introduced from South Africa. Entire cliff-faces may be covered by this plant with its brilliant daisy-like flowers which bloom between April and July. Its leaves are covered with waxes that prevent water loss, and its tolerance of difficult conditions makes it a favourite plant for covering gravel around buildings.

Some cliff plants can be recognized by their inland relatives. The stag's horn plantain *Plantago coronopus* belongs to a family of leathery plants, the Plantaginaceae, that are common on roadsides and waste ground throughout Europe. But to cope with cliff-top conditions, it has evolved a low spreading shape, the flowers arching out from the centre of the rosette like the antlers of a deer. Similarly, the rock samphire *Crithmum maritimum*, which is found on cliffs all over Europe, has a flat shape with fleshy leaves quite unlike those of the hogweed and hemlock, two more typical members of the family Umbelliferae.

The cliff top is a less demanding habitat for plants than the rock face itself. Between May and July the bright yellow flowers of the daisy-like *Odontospermum maritimum* open in clusters a few centimetres above the ground. Where the wind is not too strong, the golden samphire *Inula crithmoides* (which is not closely related to the rock samphire), sends up tall stems with clusters of golden flowers in late summer, and the milk or holy thistle *Silybum marianum* produces handsome purple flowers on stems up to 1.5 m high. Both plants are found on cliffs in other parts of Europe where water is in short supply.

The wealth of life on rocky shores

Anyone who has swum in the Mediterranean with a mask and snorkel will quickly learn where to look for marine wildlife. The real finds are to be made not off sandy beaches, or even in the open sea, but close to the shore where cliffs and rocks shelve steeply into deep water. From under the surface, the great variety of wildlife is revealed: masses of seaweeds, sponges, anemones, worms, crustaceans and sea-squirts adorn the rocks, picked over by small fish and other animals that feed on them.

One feature of the Mediterranean that has a considerable effect on the distribution of these plants and animals is tidal amplitude. In northern Europe, the tides cover and expose large areas of shore every day. By contrast, the area between high and low tide in the Mediterranean is small. In the Gulf of Cadiz in the Atlantic, the distance between the extreme spring tides is 4 m. At Gibraltar, this is already reduced to 1.1 m, and along most of the Mediterranean coast, the tidal amplitudes are measured in tens of centimetres; at Leghorn in Italy, for example, it is an average of 22 cm, and on the Syrian coast between 30 and 40 cm. One can imagine the consternation of early Mediterranean seafarers on seeing for the first time the comparatively huge tides of the Atlantic.

Because the tidal range is small, the intertidal zone in which many rocky shore animals live is compact. As a consequence, the animals that live on rocks between high and low tide levels can be found in a narrow band. Most of the plant-eating molluscs are concentrated in the intertidal zone.

The inhabitants of rocky shores have provided man with food for centuries. The Romans were familiar with shellfish, crabs and octopuses, and it is claimed that they even raised ferocious moray eels *Muraena helena* in tanks after extracting them from their rocky lairs. Today, the rocks and grottoes of the coast still support a small fishing industry throughout the region, although more modern fishing methods now concentrate on deeper waters.

The reason for this profusion of wildlife is simple and can be summed up in one word – stability. Although waves pound the rocks above sea level, below it conditions are clement. Seaweeds can grow without being smothered by sand or debris, and the number of species that flourish on rocks is vast. Some of them, like the mermaid's cup *Acetabularia mediterranea*, a silvery green weed often seen in shallow water, have only a minor impact on wildlife. Larger weeds provide indispensible shelter among their fronds and holdfasts for many small animals.

If the fronds of the much-branched large brown seaweeds are carefully parted, a hidden community of invertebrate animals will be exposed. Among the fronds of *Dictyopteris membranacea, Fucus virsoides* and *Cystoseira abrotanifolia,* for example, tiny crabs, sponges and anemones mirror their larger relatives that live outside the security of the seaweed. Close inspection may reveal the slender-bodied sea-spider *Pycnogonum pusillum* clinging to the column of sea-anemones, with its tapering proboscis buried deep in their soft tissues, or sea-squirts being slowly rasped off the rock by the European cowrie *Trivia monacha*. Immobile invertebrates use the fronds of larger weeds for support. The purse sponge *Grantia compressa* clings to red seaweeds, pumping water through its pores and sieving out any organic matter. The polychaete worm *Branchiomma lucullana* attaches its muddy tube to plants, and the soft-bodied sea-slug *Polycera quadrilineata* uses the fronds as a mating ground and a depository for its egg masses.

Feeding with sieves and tentacles

Most of the immobile animals of rocky shores live by a process called filter-feeding. By pumping sea water through sieve-like extensions of their bodies, they collect suspended organic matter which is then eaten. As long as the food supply is sufficient, these animals have no need to move and remain tightly anchored to the rock. The methods by which these animals attach themselves vary.

The common Mediterranean mussel *Mytilus galloprovincialis* fixes itself by means of a number of tough threads that emerge between the paired shells. It is this 'beard' or byssus that has to be scraped from the shells if the mussel is to be cooked. Oysters like the Mediterranean jewelbox *Chama gryphoides* cement one of their shells directly to the rock, forming an inflexible bond. Neither of these two methods, however, shows quite the same total integration as that of the date mussel *Lithophaga lithophaga* and the common piddock *Pholas dactylus*. Both these molluscs use their shells to abrade the rock. The piddock is found in both the Mediterranean and north Atlantic, and it shelters by boring into soft rock or wood. The date mussel is found only in the Mediterranean, particularly in limestone areas. The mussel secretes an acid which slowly dissolves rock, and as the shells grind at the limestone, the mussel's soft body burrows out of reach of predators.

The sponges are another group of filter-feeders common to the Mediterranean shore. By no means all resemble the familiar bath sponge *Spongia*

A Greek sponge diver cleans his catch

officinalis. The crumb-of-bread sponge *Halichondria panicea*, for example, often covers rock surfaces in a thin blanket of living tissue. The pores through which water is expelled are dotted over the sponge like minute volcanic cones. Sponges like this have no marketable value; anyone hoping to recover sponges of real size around the Mediterranean will probably be disappointed. Centuries of fishing has greatly reduced the stocks of large sponges, which are now found only at depths of 50 m or more. But despite the development of synthetic substitutes, the sponge trade still continues, and is centred in the eastern Aegean, particularly around the island of Kalimnos. Sponge fishing is a laborious business, and the methods of preparing the glutinous freshly gathered sponges for market have seen little change since Roman times.

Like filter-feeders, sea-anemones are also sessile. Although they will readily eat dead matter, they also capture live prey with their tentacles which are armed with stinging cells or nematocysts.

Although none of the Mediterranean anemones are seriously harmful to man, some people react strongly to the otherwise imperceptible stings of, for example, *Anemonia viridis*. The beadlet anemone *Actinia equina* is a typical Mediterranean species that also thrives in the colder seas of Europe. This attractive animal is often seen as a brownish-red jelly-like blob when exposed by the tide. The plumose anemone *Metridium senile* is found on rocks in deeper water, and looks very much like an aquatic plant, having a crown of very fine tentacles that resemble a feather duster.

Creeping invertebrates and clinging fish
Not all rock-dwelling invertebrates simply wait for food to be washed within their grasp. Many species wander over the rocks and boulders, grazing on small plants or collecting organic matter. Sea-urchins, for example, whose brittle spines are a hazard to swimmers, rove slowly beneath the water-line, and in places the Mediterranean shore bristles with them; they are particularly tolerant of polluted water and are often found around harbours. The most common species are the black sea-urchin *Arbacia lixula*, the Mediterranean green sea-urchin *Psammechinus microtuberculatus*, and the rock-urchin *Paracentrotus lividus*. This last species, the *oursin* of French cooking, is prized for its delicately flavoured roe, which is often eaten raw. Sea-urchins have a set of five jaws that operate rather like the chuck of a carpenter's drill. These jaws may be found in the shells of dead urchins; they are collectively given the name 'Aristotle's lantern' because of their similarity in shape to an old-fashioned lamp. As the urchin moves over rocks, the jaws pinch off and grind up any food under the shell. Although its progress is slow the urchin can move in any direction, and can even right itself if overturned.

In parts of the Mediterranean coast where the rock is soft, rock-urchins live in small burrows excavated to protect their rather fragile bodies from the waves. Often remaining in these burrows for some years, urchins may eventually become too large to escape through the entrance holes. But as long as sufficient food is swept in, the urchins will continue to survive, secure from the waves and predators in their rocky prisons.

One animal that will be familiar to visitors from northern Europe is the limpet. These molluscs graze on microscopic and young algae in the intertidal zone. Limpets feed by using a tough 'tongue', or radula, equipped with a number of minute but beautifully symmetrical teeth that scrape like a file, leaving a trail of clean rock where the limpet has eaten. Limpets keep down algae on rocks and boulders, which would otherwise quickly smother many rocky shore organisms.

Molluscs frequently fall prey to starfish. The Mediterranean boasts a number of brightly coloured species, including *Luidia ciliaris*, which is bright orange and has seven rather pointed arms, and *Ophidiaster ophidianus* which is purplish-red with five arms. The beautiful feather star *Antedon mediterranea* is much more delicate, and swims by beating its arms; the other starfish are restricted to creeping with the aid of their tube feet. Despite their decorative appearance, most starfish are ferocious predators. On being touched by the exploratory arm of a starfish, a mussel will clamp its shells together, but this is no deterrent for the starfish which simply clasps the shells with its arms and steadily pulls them apart. When the mussel eventually tires and allows its shells to part slightly, the starfish slips its stomach through the aperture and consumes the mussel within its shell.

Probably no animal of the rocky shore has suffered as much from fishing as the lobster, the largest Mediterranean crustacean. They have been lured into baited baskets with such persistence over the years that now they are not easy to find. As well as the true lobster *Homarus gammarus*, which is also found in the Atlantic, North Sea and Baltic, the Mediterranean is home to species which are less common outside its waters. One of the strangest of these is the flapjack lobster *Scyllarides latus*. This very flattened animal has stubby claws and short legs; in France it is known as the *grande cigale*, a reference to the insect-like noise it makes underwater.

The weight of lobsters restricts them to clambering over the rocks and sea bed in search of food. By contrast their smaller relatives the crabs are much more mobile. One species of particular interest is the sponge crab *Dromia vulgaris*. This crab takes advantage not only of the natural shelter of spaces between the rocks, but also of some of the other inhabitants. When the young *Dromia* settles to the bottom after a planktonic larval phase, it tears off a piece of sponge or sea-squirt, and attaches it over its shell by means of a pair of modified legs. This animal fragment grows until it forms a kind of living bonnet which covers the whole of the crab's back, giving it superb camouflage. A discerning eye is needed to see it.

Although open-water fish may swim into rocky shallows, some species never stray far from the shore. One sight that may surprise those unfamiliar with life in rock-pools is that of a little fish jumping into water on being disturbed. This is the rock goby *Gobius paganellus*, which clings to rock surfaces by means of pectoral fins modified into a sucker. The rock goby can survive exposure to air for a considerable time, and may move across rocks from one pool to another.

The ability to cling to rock has been taken to its ultimate development by the Cornish sucker *Lepadogaster lepadogaster*, whose pelvic fins and stomach muscles combine to form a powerful sucker. As the waves pound the rocks, the sucker clings to them and thereby avoids injury.

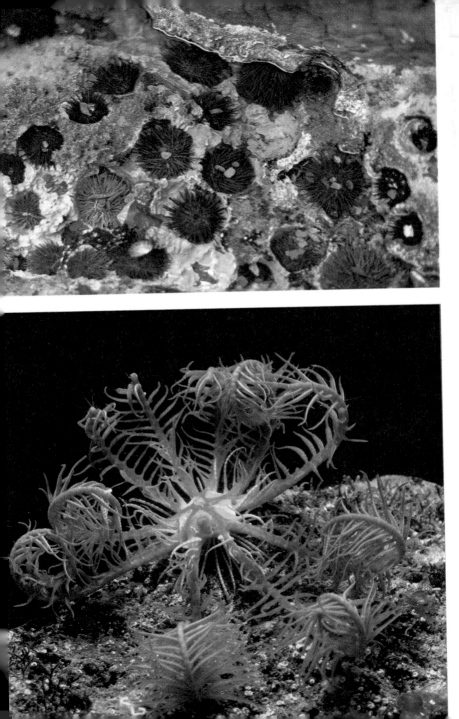

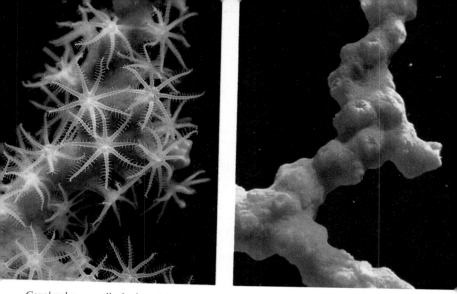

Coral polyps usually feed at night. These photographs show the polyps with their tentacles both extended and withdrawn

Trottoirs: the Mediterranean reefs

In the shallow waters off the coasts of the Golfe du Lion and the Balearic islands, thick bands of what looks like reddish rock can be seen projecting into the water. These formations, known as *trottoirs*, are extensive growths of red algae such as *Lithophyllum tortuosum* which extract lime from seawater and deposit it in their tissues as a hard skeleton – the same process that cements coral reefs. As well as reaching out to sea, the algae form blankets encrusting rocks and boulders in shallow water, sometimes to a thickness of more than a metre.

Like rock, the convoluted and pleated surface of the algae is ideal for invertebrates. They find on the *trottoir* a surface which may be burrowed into with relative ease, a feature which encourages sea-urchins and piddocks. Some animals increase the bulk of the *trottoir*: true corals like *Dendrophyllia ramea* form branching colonies, barnacles and tube-worms similarly thicken the chalky structure. Where fragments of the alga are broken up by waves, the sea floor becomes covered by a granular but stable layer. This is the habitat of the sea-egg *Microcosmus sulcatus*, a large rough-textured sea-squirt which is extensively collected as a delicacy.

OPPOSITE ABOVE *These sea-urchins have bored protective burrows in soft rock. The pebbles that some of them have collected are an additional defence*
OPPOSITE BELOW *A feather star at rest. Its fragile arms unroll and beat rhythmically when swimming*

Sandy Shores

The nature of sand

For many people an extensive sandy beach is essential for an enjoyable holiday. Travel agents are not ignorant of this fact, and brochures designed to attract tourists to the Mediterranean coast often show arcs of almost deserted sand stretching away towards a distant horizon. But if sandy beaches were the only incentive for travel, holiday-makers would do much better to head for the Atlantic or North Sea coasts. Although some parts of the Mediterranean do have large stretches of sand, there are many places where it is almost completely absent. Aggrieved tourists may well ask the reason for the unjust distribution of this sought-after substance.

Sand grains are tiny particles of silica; although they do not float, they are small enough to be carried for some distance by a strong current of water. Accumulations of sand only form where there is a continual source of sand grains, and currents to heap them up. The longest stretches of sand are found on the North African coast east of Cap Bon in Tunisia, and near the estuaries of the Rhône and the Po. Along the North African coast, the beaches have been formed by the interaction of sea currents and the adjacent desert, which, unlike the area further west, is not hidden by a range of coastal mountains. Smaller beaches and sandy coves in rocky areas are formed as a result of local conditions where rock is pounded by the sea and thrown up on the shore.

Sand is a difficult habitat for both plants and animals. Unlike rocky shores, sandy beaches offer no anchorage. Only a small number of species are able to tolerate such unstable conditions. One of the few genuine inhabitants of sandy beaches is the sand-hopper *Talitrus saltator*, a small crustacean that leaps about on the sand. A pebbly shore presents wildlife with similar problems to sand: as pebbles are rolled around by the sea, any animals or plants on them would almost certainly be crushed. The rewards for searching for life on the exposed parts of sandy beaches are few, and on pebble beaches little is to be found except, of course, where the tide has cast debris onto the shore.

Small children are natural experts in those features of sand which have a profound effect on wildlife. They know that sand from one part of the shore is good for building sandcastles, whereas that from another part is useless. They soon discover that sand kicked at the very top of a beach will scatter in all directions, but in the middle of the shore it will go hard underfoot and turn white around the area of contact, and at the lower edge of the shore, when paddled in, it will become liquid and sloppy.

The reasons for these different effects hinge on the shape of the sand grains. Silica is a very hard substance which chips and fractures easily to give the sand grains irregular and sharp-faced facets. Because of their shape, the grains cannot lie in close contact with each other, and any mass of sand contains vast numbers of spaces. This is what gives sand its porosity: water can fill up these spaces or drain away very rapidly, and air will do just the same. But as the relative surface area of the sand grains is so great, it is only under extremes of heat that the surface film of moisture ever dries completely. The hot Mediterranean sun accomplishes this and the sand at the top of the shore becomes dry and loose – an inclement habitat for animals.

Although sand in the mid-region of a beach dries when the tide recedes, it does not lose all its water. When it is squeezed underfoot, the sand grains compact and the water is forced out. It is this process, called dilatancy, that makes the sand a lighter colour and good for building sandcastles. If this sand is dilatant for long during the tidal cycle, it can support few animals. Freely moving organisms would harden the sand as they pushed against it, impeding their progress.

At the bottom of the shore the sand is waterlogged. The water acts as a lubricant and allows the silica particles to glide over each other. When stirred, this sand behaves almost like a thick liquid, reverting to a wet solid when left to settle – a property known as thixotropy. Thixotropic sand is ideal for many burrowing animals. When danger threatens they may bury themselves rapidly, and the sand is an effective lair from which to trap prey.

Sand surface-dwellers

The most striking of the relatively small band of animals that live on the surface of underwater sand are gastropod molluscs which glide over the sandy floor on a single mucus-covered foot. Some are vegetarians; the common cerith *Cerithium vulgatum* grazes in a snail-like fashion on the film of diatoms (microscopically small plants each consisting of a single cell) which covers the sand grains. Where there is enough light and the sea is not too turbulent, they may exist in great numbers, giving the sand a golden-olive tinge. The netted dog whelk *Nassarius reticulatus* and the necklace shell *Natica alderi* are, by contrast, vicious predators. They burrow down into the sand in search of bivalved molluscs on which they feed. This carnivorous life is also shared by one of the Mediterranean's most famous animals, the dye murex *Bolinus brandaris*. It was from this animal that the Phoenicians, and later the Greeks and Romans, extracted a purple dye. This was used to prepare royal purple cloth, which during the Roman era was the perogative of Senators and the Emperor. Such was the scale of the dye industry that until the beginning of this century piles of the *Murex* shells could be seen along parts of the coast of Lebanon.

In some shallows the sandy sea bed may be covered by marine grasses. These underwater 'meadows' are composed of three quite common species of grass which are able to live immersed in seawater – the eel-grasses, *Zostera marina, Cymodocea nodosa* and the Neptune grass *Posidonia oceanica*. Their fibrous roots and branching rhizomes help to bind and stabilize the sand.

Extensive meadows of these grasses may be seen in lagoons, where they appear as black patches against the paler sand. They are often inhabited by the giant tun shell *Dolium galea* and the knobbed helmet *Cassidarea echinophora* which wander in search of sea-urchins. Like other carnivorous gastropods, these secrete acids which assist in attacking the shells of their prey.

Sand burrowers

The great mass of animals that live in sand cannot be seen unless they are actually dug up. As a long streamlined shape is obviously best for moving through sand, it comes as no surprise to find that those burrowing animals that are not actually worms are very worm-like in shape.

Ophelia bicornis is a pinkish polychaete worm that illustrates nicely the kind of adaptations needed for a life in the sand. The worm's body is elongated and sharply pointed at the front. This small snout-like projection can be forced through the sand, parting it to allow the worm to move forward. The pressure of the animal's body fluids, pumped forward by a muscular organ, enable it to use its head like a ram against the sand. Sand is very abrasive and can damage soft-bodied animals as they move through it. To prevent itself literally being worn away, *Ophelia* has a tough skin or cuticle. Its delicate gills are set in a deep groove running along each flank, and fold away during movement.

A short period of digging where the sand has recently been exposed by the fall of the tide will reveal large numbers of worms similar to *Ophelia*. They are particularly abundant where the sand is muddy and the organic content high.

The greater and lesser weever-fish, *Trachinus draco* and *Echiicthys vipera*, show that it is not only invertebrates that have adopted the burrowing life. These fish bury themselves in loose sand with only their eyes, mouths and dorsal fins exposed. Concealed in this way, they wait for their prey to come within striking distance. Weevers are protected from attack by highly venomous spines supporting their dorsal fins, but despite these weapons, they are a popular item in fishmarkets; they are a traditional ingredient of the French *bouillabaisse*. When the fish is cooked the poison, which is a protein, is broken down, rendering the fish harmless. The Mediterranean smooth sand-eel also takes refuge by burrowing. This slender and delicate fish uses its tail muscles to drive its body through the sand at considerable speed.

Many of the shells found on Mediterranean beaches are the remains of bivalved molluscs. These burrowers remain stationary under the sand, filtering food from the seawater or collecting the nutritious debris that settles on the sand's surface. The prickly cockle *Acanthocardia echinata*, a typical example of this group of hidden animals, only constructs a shallow burrow. On the other hand, species like the rayed trough shell *Mactra corallina* and the banded wedge shell *Donax vittatus* burrow more deeply and have slender tubes, or siphons, to maintain their contact with the water.

Cockles and other bivalved molluscs are popular as food for birds as well as man. They have no defences other than inconspicuousness. On the north coast of the Mediterranean the shrill piping of the oystercatcher *Haematopus*

A weever fish stranded on sand above the waterline raises the venomous spines of its dorsal fin

ostralegus resounds over sand and mud flats as it searches out those molluscs unlucky enough to be within the reach of its sensitive bill. The oystercatcher is very successful at this task, as its distribution around the whole of the European coastline indicates.

Digging up an area of sand will reveal that some of its inhabitants actually construct permanent dwellings in their shifting surroundings. The urchin sea-potato *Echinocardium cordatum* buries itself at a depth of several centimetres, maintaining a connection with the surface via a chimney-like channel. It keeps this clear with extensible tube-feet equipped with tiny scraper blades; the tube-feet also spread the mucus which maintains the burrow's shape. The sea-potato's delicate shell, or test, is a heart-shaped, brittle object sometimes found intact on beaches. As an interesting consequence of the sea-potato's burrowing habits, many individuals which have died in the sands have been well preserved as fossils, and may often be seen in the sedimentary rocks around the Mediterranean coasts.

In comparison with the sea-potato's elaborate burrows, the tubular dwellings of many sand animals are more straightforward in their construction. By binding together sand and gravel particles, the sand mason *Lanice conchilega*, for example, makes a protective tube for itself. This tube projects above the surface and is easily visible, but the sand mason adorns it with a ring of false tentacles made of sand and mucus to deceive predatory fish.

Where mud is mixed with sand, worms like *Spirographis spallanzanii* use the finer particles to make rubbery tubes. These tubular homes have an undistinguished appearance, but when inhabited are capped with the worm's exquisite spiral crown of tentacles. The cylinder anemone *Cerianthus membranaceus* fires off vast numbers of stinging threads to make a tube in muddy sand by a different method. The threads are adhesive, and after being released they become entangled and form a felt-like material that houses the anemone like a protective jacket.

Estuaries

The creation of deltas

The estuaries of all the major rivers that empty into the Mediterranean are deltas. The Ebro, Rhône and Po, for example, all flow into the sea by way of great expanses of marshes and lagoons, often studded with thickets of the giant reed *Arundo donax*, whose bamboo-like stems can grow to a height of 5 metres, forming a mass of impenetrable vegetation.

Where the rivers of northern Europe meet the sea, the tide regularly reverses the water flow at the river mouth. As the tide rises silt is swept back up the river for a considerable distance, but when the tide falls the silt is carried out to sea and dispersed. In the Mediterranean the tides are too small to have this washing effect, and material carried to the coast by the rivers tends to remain there. Over long periods of geological time, these mud barrages and sand bars have caused the rivers to diverge, forming extensive deltas as the water meanders sluggishly to the sea.

A vivid illustration of this process can be seen in the estuary of the Rhône. This area, known as the Camargue, is famed for its wildlife, particularly the semi-wild cattle and horses that roam the marshes. In the thirteenth century, the city of Aigues-Mortes was developed as a fortified sea-port and point of departure for a crusade by St Louis. Access to the nearby sea for the fleet was by canal. This canal was to prove the undoing of this splendid city as a commercial venture; within a very short time it became clear that the perpetual silting up of the waterway would be financially disastrous because of the attendant clearing operations, so Aigues-Mortes (the name is appropriately derived from the Latin *aquae mortuae* meaning 'dead waters') ceased to be a port. Today it is separated from the sea by 6 km of sediment.

A similar pattern of silting and delta extension occurs in the other great Mediterranean estuaries. Much of the shore of the northern Adriatic between the River Reno and Gulf of Trieste owes its existence to sediment brought down by rivers, especially the Po. The Adriatic gets its name from the town of Adria, once a thriving port in northern Italy and now, like Aigues-Mortes, an inland town.

The deposition of silt in estuaries is the result of the different chemical properties of seawater and freshwater. When a salt dissolves in water, it splits up into a number of minute electromagnetically charged particles, or ions. Freshwater contains very few dissolved substances, whereas seawater holds vast numbers of particles in solution. The freshwater of rivers does, however, carry mud particles of unbelievably small dimensions in suspension. When the suspended particles meet the ions of seawater in an estuary, a complex process occurs which results in mud particles being attracted to one another. They stick together in clumps, called flocculae, which being too dense to stay afloat, sink to the bottom. This constant deposition builds up mud banks.

Because of their swampy nature, these large areas are relatively free from human interference, and form important overwintering sites for many of Europe's birds. Ducks, waders, fieldfares and redwings all take refuge in these havens until the arrival of spring, and many of the estuaries are internationally known to birdwatchers for these winter gatherings. As well as flocking to the deltas of the Rhône and the Po, birds live in great numbers in the estuary of the Ebro in northern Spain, in the estuaries of the Greek rivers Evros and Nestos and, of course, in the distant delta of the River Nile. Although it actually faces the Atlantic, the Coto Doñana in Spain, which is the estuary of the River Guadalquivir, is a winter home for many birds attracted by its warm climate.

Birds of the estuaries

Estuarine birds are most open to view in the winter when the reeds die back, giving less cover. The shoveler *Anas clypeata* feeds on open lagoons, the males resplendent in their brilliant green, white and orange breeding plumage which develops in autumn. Other ducks prefer the less saline water further from the river mouth. The gadwall *Anas strepera* arrives in western Europe in September after spending summer as far away as Sweden and the Caspian Sea. Many fly south to dabble in river water around the Mediterranean which, unlike that further east, is free of ice. Although in parts of the Mediterranean they are year-round residents, many ferruginous ducks *Aythya nyroca* seek shelter in freshwater lagoons after a summer in central Europe, returning there in the spring. The greylag goose *Anser anser*, a long-distance migrant that travels as far afield as northern Russia, congregates on estuarine marshes to feed on winter grass.

Although the estuaries of the Mediterranean are warm in comparison to the waters of northern Europe, strong winds like the *mistrale* and *bora* will deter all but the most enthusiastic bird-watchers in winter. Summer brings with it a chance to see the glossy ibis *Plegadis falcinellus*, which migrates northwards to the mud and marshes around the coast of Turkey and the southern Mediterranean. The spectacular greater flamingo, *Phoenicopterus ruber* can be seen in the Coto Doñana and Camargue, where it breeds in considerable numbers.

The thickness of the summer vegetation means that many of the birds are visible only when they are actually on the move. Herons are particularly difficult to spot against the background of a reed bed. The purple heron *Ardea purpurea*, for example, which spends the winter in Africa, usually remains close to vegetation. The night heron *Nycticorax nycticorax* and the squacco heron *Ardeola ralloides*, with its curious feathery crest and cape, also have cryptic habits. Although both these summer visitors from the south may be seen feeding during the day, they are generally more active at dawn and dusk. Their relative the white stork *Ciconia ciconia*, which is common around the Mediterranean, will be familiar to visitors from northern Europe where it also breeds.

ABOVE *A flock of greater flamingoes incubate their eggs in closely crowded mud nests on a French lagoon*
LEFT *Although not all the horses of the Camargue are truly wild, most roam free for much of their lives*

Waders are more easily seen than the herons, as their feeding necessitates constant movement instead of patient stealth. The beautiful black-winged stilt *Himantopus himantopus*, with its conspicuous pencil-thin red legs, may be seen in the coastal marshes of Spain and eastern Greece in summer, sometimes in the company of the avocet *Recurvirostra avosetta*. In summer the avocet patrols the coasts of the North Sea and Baltic as well, but in winter it migrates westward. Conditions around the Mediterranean are suitable for it all year round, and on the coasts of Spain, the Camargue and Greece this elegant bird may be seen at any time.

The Ebro delta

The Ebro is one of Spain's major rivers, draining about one-sixth of the country. Its headwaters are in the Cantabrican mountains of Spain's north coast, and from there it flows across the plateau of Zaragoza to empty into the Mediterranean midway between Barcelona and Valencia.

The Ebro delta is typical of those of the region's large rivers. The sediment that the river carries down to the sea is swept along the coast by the same anti-clockwise current that influences the nearby Camargue. It is estimated that in the last two thousand years, the delta has expanded by about 350 square kilometres. The sand spit of Alfacs, home of many of the delta's waders and gulls, is growing steadily as sand is washed southwards, and now extends to a distance of 35 km from the river's main mouth.

At the highest part of the estuary the marshes and ponds created by the river are beyond the influence of saltwater. The vegetation and wildlife are much as would be seen on river banks further inland. The yellow flag *Iris pseudacorus* provides a splash of colour in late spring when the rice crop is sprouting on the fertile alluvial soil. In the backwaters, the marsh or lake frog *Rana ridibunda* can be seen looking for food, and on secluded banks the European pond terrapin *Emys orbicularis* basks in the sun.

Below the point where the river drops to the level of the highest tides, the water becomes brackish. The periodic inundation of salty water permeates the mud, and where water is trapped in pools, the evaporation caused by the sun and wind leaves a crust of dry salt on the ground. In the delta the salt has long been extracted from the seawater in commercial pans or *salinas*.

The salty conditions prevent the growth of many plants, because the concentrated saline water held in the earth actually exerts a pull on the water in plants by the process of osmosis, causing the leaves and stems to lose their rigidity and eventually shrivel. But as the delta's often green banks show, some plants have evolved ways of coping with this problem. The common or herbaceous seablite *Suaeda maritima*, the saltwort *Salsola kali* and the glasswort *Salicornia fruticosa* thrive in the most brackish mud. These curious plants are found in saltmarshes throughout the Mediterranean area, and were at one time valued for the soda in their leaves and stems. When the plants were burned, the soda was collected from the ash and used in the manufacture of glass and soap.

In the oldest parts of the delta, humus has been laid down on the silt, and a wide variety of plants have been able to invade this land regained from the sea. The flat skyline of the delta is interrupted by eucalypts imported from Australasia, palms and the tamarisk *Tamarix gallica*. The tamarisk is among the most resilient of Mediterranean trees, and often grows on quaysides fully exposed to salt spray and storms.

Few animals can live in the brackish mud of the marshes. Deep in the silt, the peppery furrow shell *Scrobicularia plana*, a hardy bivalve found in saltmarshes all over Europe, maintains contact with the surface with siphons up to 25 cm long. Nereid ragworms wriggle through the sediment, and the Mediterranean shore crab *Carcinus mediterraneus* sidles over the mud in search of anything edible. As anyone who visits these marshes will find, this is a 'no-man's land' between river and sea, only thinly inhabited but beautiful in its isolation.

The Open Sea

Profile of a sea

To the Romans, the Mediterranean was the *mare internum*, or 'internal sea', since it was virtually surrounded by land and had only a narrow connection with the Atlantic Ocean guarded by the Pillars of Hercules, two monolithic points known today as Gibraltar and Punta Almina. It is true that the Mediterranean does have some characteristics of a completely landlocked sea, but the effect of the connection with oceanic water at the Strait of Gibraltar is profound.

The Atlantic water which flows in through the Strait passes along the North African coast. This is why the sea off Morocco and Algeria is noticeably cooler than that in, for example, the Adriatic. As the Atlantic water sweeps into the gulfs of Gabes and Sirte in Tunisia and Libya, it sets up subsidiary currents that travel clockwise. Elsewhere, all currents initiated by the Atlantic flow travel in an anticlockwise direction. One encircles the Balearic islands, sweeping past the Camargue and Ebro delta, another travels around the Tyrrhenian sea, and another reaches the Levantine coast. Subsidiary currents circle in the Aegean and Adriatic.

Although both tides and currents are generally weak, in places they produce unusual results, particularly where their flow is impeded by islands. Charybdis, the legendary whirlpool mentioned in Homer's *Odyssey*, for example, still revolves today in the Strait of Messina off Sicily, one of the most turbulent parts of the Mediterranean. The force of the whirlpool has decreased since Homer's time as a result of an earthquake that altered the structure of the sea bed in the late eighteenth century.

The Mediterranean is divided into two unequal parts by the narrow waist between Tunisia and Sicily. The western basin is roughly triangular, the angles being at Gibraltar, Messina and Genoa, while the eastern basin is shaped like an elongated rectangle from which arise two shallow arms – the Aegean and Adriatic Seas. The two basins are dissimilar in many respects, not least of which is their geographical position. The 40th north parallel runs almost through the centre of the western basin but along the northern edge of the eastern basin, the remainder of which extends almost as far as the 30th parallel; as a result there is a great difference in climate between the two basins.

The submarine geography of the two basins is complex. The western basin may be subdivided into three smaller basins, the most westerly of which, the Alboran basin, extends from the Straits of Gibraltar to the island of Alboran and reaches a maximum depth of 1500 m. From Alboran to Sardinia and Corsica the Balearic basin descends to a depth of 3149 m to the west of Sardinia. The third basin is the Tyrrhenian sea, the triangular area bounded by the eastern shores of Corsica and Sardinia, the western coast of Italy and the north of Sicily. The central part of this basin is deeper than 3000 m and, just off the Isole Panziane to the west of Naples, a depth of 3731 m has been plumbed.

Within the eastern basin, the floor drops dramatically from the eastern shores of Sicily and Malta until it reaches the lowest point of the Mediterranean in the Ionian sea, where the Matapan trench drops to a depth of 4400 m. Apart from this area, much of the eastern basin lies over a relatively shallow continental shelf which extends eastward from the Gulf of Gabes in Tunisia.

The surface waters of the Mediterranean, like those of the oceans, vary greatly in temperature throughout the year. However, below about 300 m both temperature and salinity are remarkably high and constant. Three thousand metres below the surface of the western basin, the water is not icy cold like that of the Atlantic at the same depth, but is an almost warm 13°C. This is true of even the deepest parts of the sea. At first sight this might appear to be beneficial to wildlife but, in fact, the opposite is true. Warm salty water cannot hold much dissolved oxygen and consequently few animals are able to live in these depths. As a result, the depths of the Mediterranean are significantly less rich than those of the oceans.

The Mediterranean's almost landlocked position has a noticeable effect on its salinity. Evaporation from the surface is rapid, in fact it has been calculated to reach a rate of 115,000 m^3 of water lost *per second*. In isolation, this huge figure does not mean much, but in the context of an inland sea it is highly significant. This tremendous loss of water tends to make what remains more saline. To offset this, freshwater is added by rain and by the rivers. But of the water entering the Mediterranean, only 21 per cent is derived from rainfall, and 5 per cent contributed by rivers. The remainder of the inflowing water is already salty – 3 per cent from the Black Sea and a massive 71 per cent from the Atlantic. As a result, the Mediterranean has a salinity substantially higher than the Atlantic – 39.5 parts per thousand in the eastern basin in comparison with an average of 35 parts per thousand in the Atlantic.

This high salinity has an interesting effect quite apart from making swimmers more buoyant. Underneath the inflowing Atlantic water at the Strait of Gibraltar a current of Mediterranean water empties into the ocean. Because it carries more salt, it is denser than the Atlantic water and does not mix readily with it. The Mediterranean flow remains intact for hundreds of miles from the Strait, and can be detected even in the North Sea, bringing with it plankton foreign to the cold waters of northern Europe.

The myriad plankton

The organisms that make up the plankton are, to all intents and purposes, moved about passively within the surface waters. Many of them do have organs of movement, but these are often so small that their effects are limited. It is vitally important to the whole marine community that the planktonic plants, or phytoplankton, remain in the upper layers of the sea where the light is strongest. In this zone they can manufacture sugars at the greatest rate. This

Plankton scooped from the surface waters. None of these beautiful animals is more than a centimetre long

process, called primary production, is the ultimate food source for all marine organisms. The phytoplankton show a variety of adaptations for improving their buoyancy, such as trapped gas bubbles, or minute flotation tanks composed of oils or fats. For those that are heavier than water, protruding spines slow down their rate of sinking by increasing their surface area in relation to their bulk.

As well as sunlight, the phytoplankton require a supply of basic minerals in order to produce food. Where nutrients are present in quantity, as in the Golfe du Lion, these microscopic marine plants flourish. But in many parts of the Mediterranean, the supply of nutrients on the surface is poor, and although this often means that the water is strikingly clear, it also indicates that there is not much life in it.

The strange planktonic animals that teem in the open sea comprise many species whose adult stages are quite familiar. But few people would recognize the minute larva of a crab, for instance, with its translucent spines and feathery limbs, or that of the spiny lobster *Palinurus vulgaris* which has a flattened leaf-like body and grotesquely elongated legs. A planktonic phase is essential for the success of many shore-dwelling animals.

Many adult invertebrates have a static existence on rocky shores where they live by filter-feeding. If these animals reproduced so that they were surrounded by immobile offspring, competition for food would become intense and they might all eventually die. Sessile animals avoid this by releasing their eggs into the water to be swept out to sea. The larvae develop in the upper layers of the water, feeding on other planktonic animals and plants, and themselves falling prey to larger animals. Of the thousands of young that begin their lives in this way few will survive, and of those that do even fewer reach a suitable surface on which to develop their adult form. Consequently, in order to survive, sessile animals produce eggs in vast numbers, and their progeny mix with organisms that permanently drift in the sea's upper layers, forming an abundant but almost invisible community of plants and animals.

The culture of oysters and mussels, both of which have planktonic larvae, has been carried out in the coastal waters of the Mediterranean since pre-Roman times. The larvae are allowed to settle on artificial surfaces, such as wooden posts, and when the developing adult animals are about 0.5 cm long they are detached and transferred to wire baskets and trays where they live until maturity. Cultured oysters and mussels do not have to compete with their neighbours for food to the same extent as their wild counterparts because the culturing process ensures that they are carefully spaced out. Consequently, cultured individuals grow quickly to a large size, particularly in lagoons and near estuaries where the water is laden with organic matter.

Many fish also produce planktonic young at a prodigious rate. The level of overproduction that has to be maintained to keep the numbers of adults constant is well illustrated by the sun-fish *Mola mola*. Even a relatively small sun-fish weighing 25 kg may produce 28,000,000 eggs in one season, but despite this, the strangely shaped fish is nowhere common. By comparison, the million eggs produced annually by the flounder *Platichthys flesus* seems moderate!

Surface drifters

Anyone sailing in an open boat in the Mediterranean will have an opportunity to see another group of animals that drift passively in their surroundings. But, unlike the plankton, these species float on the surface where they are propelled not only by water currents but also by wind. Although these animals are few in number, one of them at least, the Portuguese man-o'-war *Physalia physalis*, should be treated with great respect. From above the surface this animal looks like a gelatinous bag tinged with light purple and magenta, but below this gas-filled sail, strings of reproductive and food catching polyps dangle deep into the water. These tentacle-like projections carry powerful stinging cells that can kill fish and severely injure a man. As it drifts, the man-o'-war's sail rhythmically dips in the water to keep it moist. The smaller by-the-wind-sailor *Velella velella* also fishes from the surface, sometimes in small shoals. This species forms the prey of a remarkable mollusc, the purple sea-snail *Ianthina janthina*. This animal is a true sailor, floating on a raft of slimy bubbles of mucus. When the sea-snail comes into contact with the by-the-wind-sailor, it starts to feed immediately. The snails' delicate shells may sometimes be found on Mediterranean beaches; they are a brilliant purple and quite unmistakable.

The sea's harvest

The colourful fishing fleets of the smaller Mediterranean ports present a very different spectacle from the rusting high-prowed trawlers that set out into the North Sea and Atlantic from northern Europe. Few Mediterranean fishermen spend more than a day at sea before returning home, and for this small wooden boats are quite adequate. Some larger craft do venture out into the Atlantic – their produce can be seen in the fishmongers of southern France bearing the label *ocean* to distinguish it from local fish.

For many people, one of the most interesting sights at the quayside is that of the *pêche-à-la-lumière* boats unloading their night's catch. A long time ago in this area it was discovered that fish and other marine animals could be attracted to light. Fishermen have exploited this ever since and today anchovies, sardines, octupuses and squid are lured into nets by lamps that throw pools of yellow light onto the dark water.

But to capture the tunny *Thunnus thynnus* and the swordfish *Xiphias gladius* – the two giants of the Mediterranean fishing industry – more elaborate equipment is required. The tunny is the largest member of the mackerel family, a streamlined and powerful fish found throughout the world's oceans. In early summer the Atlantic tunny migrate into the Mediterranean to spawn, at which time the fishermen are awaiting their arrival with an array of ingenious traps. Off Sicily, shoals of tunny are impounded in nets and gradually ushered into chambers of decreasing size. Eventually their exit route is closed off, and the final part of the *mattanza* begins. Panic seizes the huge fish as they thrash about in the water, while anxious fishermen on barges surrounding the net haul the tunny out of the water with gaffs. A similarly ancient tunny fishery exists in the northern Adriatic around the islands of the Kvarner Gulf. Fishermen perched on ladders overlooking deep water keep a daily watch for the approach of the spawning shoals. When a shoal swims past, the signal is given to raise sunken nets and the fish are pulled ashore.

Swordfish, like tunny, migrate into the Mediterranean to spawn. About 3000 tonnes are landed every year, most being taken off southern Spain. Usually each swordfish is pursued individually from a fast high-masted boat. The boat's controls are on top of the mast, and from this vantage point the captain locates and follows the fast-swimming fish, which is then harpooned and winched aboard. The success of the swordfish and tunny industry depends on sufficient numbers returning to the Mediterranean each year. Recently there have been signs that overfishing in the Atlantic is reducing the catch, and it is possible that the traditional tunny traps might disappear by the end of this century.

One of the fish most popular with Mediterranean cooks is the red mullet *Mullus barbatus*, This brilliantly coloured fish feeds on the sea bed, detecting its prey with two barbels that project from its lower jaw. In Roman times, the popularity of this tasty fish bordered on fanaticism. They were eaten in such quantity that they became increasingly rare and huge sums of money changed hands for specimens of any appreciable size. Prices became so inflated that

eventually a heavy tax on fish was introduced, putting them beyond the reach of most buyers. As the demand for the red mullet declined, its numbers gradually recovered and today it is fairly common.

The problem of pollution

During the holiday season, the population of the already extensively inhabited Mediterranean area swells considerably. As a result, the normally large output of sewage into the sea increases to high levels. This can have serious consequences for marine life. Sewage acts as a fertilizer for bacterial and plant growth, and as plants and animals suddenly flourish in an area the water's oxygen content plummets, eventually killing many of the organisms in the water. This problem is compounded by the untreated nature of much of the sewage. Coastal towns and villages have traditionally disposed of their sewage by the direct and cheap way of piping it into the sea, and these old habits are hard to change.

While, in a sense, sewage may be regarded as a 'natural' inclusion in seawater, however large in volume, the effluent of industrial enterprises certainly is not. Industries have developed all round the Mediterranean and along many of the rivers which empty into it. In addition, Mediterranean sea-ports are obviously well sited for the handling of crude oil. As a result, a great deal of industrial waste is poured continuously into the sea.

The same is, of course, true of the other seas of the world, but the Mediterranean has a special, unique problem in the matter of marine pollution. At Gibraltar surface Atlantic water flows into the surface layers of the Mediterranean and only water from mid- and deep-layers escapes from it. The majority of chemical pollutants are less dense than seawater and so tend to remain on the surface. The outflowing current therefore takes with it, at best, an insignificant quantity of pollutants, while the inflowing current not only traps the offending substances within the Mediterranean basin, but also introduces more pollutants from the Atlantic. Sadly, it is true to say that the Mediterranean is one of the world's most polluted seas.

The situation is not entirely gloomy, however. At last, after many years of futile effort, agreements are beginning to be reached with those who produce the polluting chemicals. This will help to preserve for posterity an area and a sea where it is pleasant to live and which is, biologically, one of the most interesting in the world.

On a beach in Tyre in the Lebanon, local fishermen load their nets before putting to sea

Glossary

abdomen in adult insects, spiders and crustaceans, the body segments behind the thorax (*qv*)

anal fin unpaired fin behind anus of fish

axil angle between stem and leaf

barbel sensory filament protruding beneath lower jaw of some fish

bract modified leaf, in axil (*qv*) of which a flower arises

body whorl in shelled molluscs, largest and most recently formed whorl of shell

bulbil a young bulb, often found attached to parent bulb, stems, leaves or inflorescences

calcareous composed of or containing calcium carbonate (lime)

carapace hard shield covering the head and thorax (*qv*) of spiders and crustaceans; dorsal shell of tortoises and turtles

cephalothorax fused head and thorax (*qv*) of spiders and crustaceans

chelicerae paired jaws of scorpions, spiders and sea-spiders

chlorophyll green pigment present in most plants

cilia minute hair-like cellular processes often used for movement and producing feeding currents by invertebrates (*qv*)

cirri threadlike appendages, often sensory

dichotomous branching by division into two equal parts

disc-floret reduced inner floret (*qv*)

dorsal of, or near, the back (*cf* ventral)

dorsal fin in fish, fin in mid-line of back

elytra hardened wing cases of some insects, esp. beetles

exoskeleton external skeleton encasing body

floret individual flower in a composite inflorescence

garrigue exposed land, often coastal and usually calcareous, dominated by low aromatic plants

invertebrate animal lacking backbone

isopod order of crustaceans including woodlice and sea-slaters

lamina flat blade of a leaf or petal

larva immature animal having characteristics markedly different from adult

littoral area of shore between high and low tides

lophophore feeding organ with semicircle of tentacles

mantle in molluscs, the outer layer of the body wall which secretes the shell

manubrium in jelly-fish, tube-like extension of mouth

maquis vegetation, often coastal, characterized by extensive shrub thickets

medusa bell-shaped body assumed by *eg* jellyfish

nacre constituent of innermost layer of mollusc shell; mother-of-pearl

operculum flap or disc covering an opening *eg* shell cavity of mollusc or gill chamber of fish

osculum opening of sponge through which water is expelled

ostium in sponges, opening through which water is drawn in

ovule part of plant which after fertilization develops into seed

ovipositor in insects an egg-laying tube; modified into a sting in worker bees and wasps

palp sensory mouthpart

papilla in flatworms, a retractile adhesive projection

parapodium a muscular flap extending laterally from the body of worms and some molluscs, usually paired and used for locomotion

pectoral fin paired lateral 'shoulder' fin of fish

pedipalp paired mouthparts of arachnids, sometimes modified into pincers

pelagic living in open water

pelvic fin paired 'hip' fin of fish

perisarc in sea-anemones, a tough outer membrane

pharynx in sea-squirts and lancelet, part of gut into which gill slits open; in many worms the first protrusible part of the gut

polyp usually sedentary aquatic animal with central mouth surrounded by tentacles

proboscis in invertebrates, a tubular mouthpart

rostrum in crustaceans and insects, a pointed 'snout' or beak

ray-floret floret (*qv*) at circumference of composite inflorescence

pupa an immobile resting stage produced by larva (*qv*) of some insects that gives rise to the adult; a chrysalis

sepal usually green petal-like structures forming ring around flower

septum a dividing wall or partition

seta a bristle-like structure of invertebrates

siphon a tube-like structure, often used in feeding or respiration

siphonophore animal similar to jelly-fish composed of numbers of polyps (*qv*) and medusae (*qv*)

spatulate spoon-shaped

spicule microscopic needle-like structure composed of hard mineral

spiracle in cartilaginous fish, a respiratory opening behind the eye

stamen male reproductive organ of a flower

stigma female part of flower on which pollen is received

stridulation production of noise by repeated rubbing together of parts of the body

style structure in flower supporting the stigma (*qv*)

stylet a sharp appendage used for piercing

sublittoral area of shore below level of lowest tides

substrate surface on which or through which organisms move or are attached

telson in crustaceans, the terminal body segment

test in invertebrates, a rigid shell or protective outer covering

thallus a simple plant structure showing no differentiation into stem and leaf

thorax region of body linking head and abdomen, often bearing legs or wings

umbellifer plant bearing flowers in rounded clusters radiating from a central point on stem

umbilicus in some gastropods, navel-like depression in shell at base of spire

umbo (*pl* umbones) oldest part of shell of bivalved mollusc, often beak-like

ventral of, or near, the underside (*cf* dorsal)

vertebrate animal with backbone

MEASUREMENTS

Although the relative sizes of plants and animals have been preserved in the following plates wherever possible, the measurements in the entries themselves should be referred to before making any comparisons.

Abbreviations

D	diameter
H	height
L	length
W	width
WS	wingspan
ad	adult
juv	juvenile
s	summer
w	winter

Symbols

♀	female
♂	male

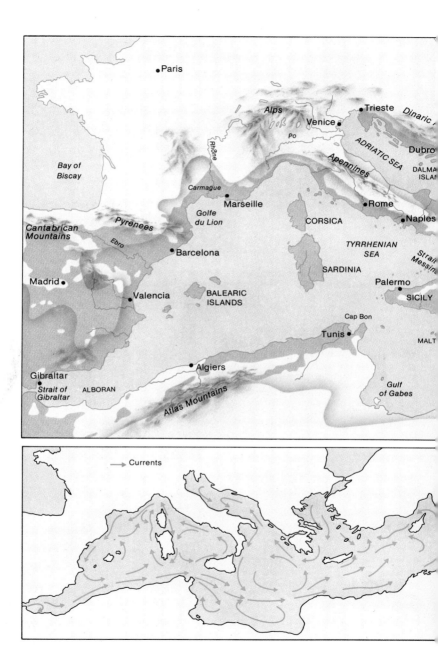

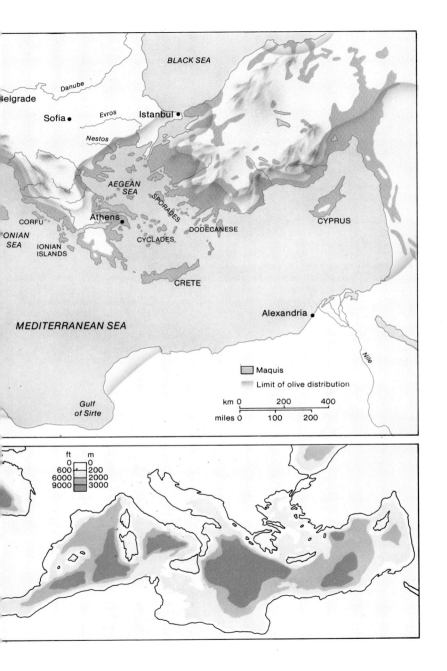

BLACK SEA

Danube

elgrade

Sofia •

Evros

Istanbul •

Nestos

AEGEAN
SEA

SPORADES

CORFU

Athens •

CYPRUS

ONIAN
SEA

IONIAN
ISLANDS

DODECANESE

CYCLADES

CRETE

Alexandria •

MEDITERRANEAN SEA

Nile

Maquis

Limit of olive distribution

km 0   200   400

miles 0   100   200

Gulf
of Sirte

ft   m
0   0
600   200
6000   2000
9000   3000

SEAWEEDS (Algae)
Plants with a simple frond-like stem (thallus), often branched, without roots and attached to substrate by holdfast, or encrusting; contain chlorophyll and manufacture food using sunlight; reproduce by spores.

GREEN SEAWEEDS (Chlorophyceae)
Algae which appear green because their chlorophyll is not masked by secondary red or brown pigments.

green seaweed *Palmophyllum crassum*
TETRASPORACEAE L to 5 cm. Frond rounded, fan-shaped, very thin, wavy or scalloped, folded into concentric waves. Dark green. Encrusting stones and coralline algae. Lower shore to sublittoral. [1]

Sea Lettuce *Ulva lactuca*
ULVACEAE L to 40 cm. Frond very variable but usually wavy and resembling a translucent lettuce leaf; old specimens are more opaque. Attached by a tiny holdfast to solid objects, often in rock-pools. Upper shore to sublittoral. [2]

green seaweed *Enteromorpha intestinalis*
ULVACEAE L to 1 m (or more). Frond tubular, bright green and irregularly constricted so resembling a length of large intestine. In rock-pools and coastal lagoons, including their drainage ditches, often in brackish water. Upper shore. [3]

green seaweed *Cladophora pellucida*
CLADOPHORACEAE L to 5 cm. Frond dark green, filamentous, one stalk-like filament giving rise to finely subdividing branches. Occurs in tufts on solid objects. Upper shore to sublittoral. [4]

green seaweed *Anadyomene stellata*
SIPHONOCLADACEAE L to 4 cm. Frond flattened, leaf-like, undulating; cells that make up the frond are visible as veins through its tissues. On solid objects in shallow water. [5]

green seaweed *Valonia utricularis*
VALONIACEAE L to 3 cm. Frond club-shaped, bulbous, bottle-green, iridescent.

Arising as groups from a common holdfast on solid objects in shallow water. [6]
green seaweed *Dasycladus clavaeformis* is similar but felt-like and dull dark green.

Mermaid's Cup *Acetabularia mediterranea*
DASYCLADALES H to 8 cm. Frond a greenish-white slender stalk which supports a disc of many narrow, petal-like structures, so resembling a thin-stalked fungus. On stones and shells in shallow water, often in very large numbers. [7]

green seaweed *Derbesia lamourouxi*
DERBESIACEAE L to 10 cm. Frond dull, darkish green, threadlike, each thread with a tiny knob-like reproductive organ near the tip. Occurs in tufts on stones and mud, sometimes on other seaweeds. Upper shore to sublittoral. [8]

green seaweed *Bryopsis plumosa*
BRYOPSIDACEAE L to 10 cm. Frond branched, feather-like: ♂ fronds yellowish-green; ♀ fronds dark green. On stones. Mid- to lower shore. [9]
green seaweed *Bryopsis balbisiana* is similar but more straggly, as the feathery part of the frond is smaller and more compact.

green seaweed *Halimeda tuna*
CODIACEAE L to 15 cm. Frond of dull green linked, circular or diamond-shaped segments; branched; extracts calcium carbonate from seawater and deposits it within the tissues as a very hard skeleton. On solid objects, sand and mud. Sublittoral. [10]

green seaweed *Codium dichotomum*
CODIACEAE L to 40 cm. Frond tubular, composed of many filaments, felt-like, dichotomously branched; dark green, but fades with age. Often arising as ample tufts from one holdfast; on solid objects, often in rock-pools and along coastal lagoons; upper shore to sublittoral. [11]

green seaweed *Codium bursa*
CODIACEAE D to 20 cm. Frond globular, composed of many dark green filaments, felt-like and spongy; holdfast of fine filaments, on objects in shallow water. [12]

BROWN SEAWEEDS (Phaeophyceae)
Algae which appear greenish-brown or
brown because their chlorophyll is masked
by the presence of the brown pigment
fucoxanthin; often tough and leathery.

brown seaweed *Ralfsia verrucosa*
RALFSIACEAE L to 10 cm. Thin, encrusting
mass of many rounded dark brown individuals, irregular in surface texture. On solid
objects. Lower shore to sublittoral. [1]

brown seaweed *Halopteris filicina*
SPHACELARIALES H to 10 cm. Frond delicate
and regularly branched, resembling a fern;
several fronds usually arise from a common
source. Olive-brown or dark brown. On
rock, stones and other algae, sometimes
grows in shaded places. Mid-shore to
sublittoral. [2]

brown seaweed *Cladostephus verticillatus*
SPHACELARIALES L to 25 cm. Frond is dull
brown and consists of a main stem from
which arise branches, themselves
branched; secondary branches bear whorls
of tiny, spiny, smaller branches which are
usually absent from the basal part of the
plant. On solid objects and coralline weeds.
Mid- to lower shore. [3]

brown seaweed *Cutleria multifida*
CUTLERIALES L to 40 cm. Frond thin, flat,
gives rise to narrow, ribbon-like dichotomous branches with divided tips; surface
finely spotted. Yellowish-brown. On solid
objects in shallow water. [4]

brown seaweed *Dictyota dichotoma*
DICTYOTALES L to 15 cm. Frond thin, flat,
delicate, dichotomously branched, with
narrow, ribbon-like translucent or even
transparent branches; surface often hairy
due to reproductive structures. Olive-
brown or yellow-brown. On stones. Mid-
to lower shore. [5]

brown seaweed *Dictyopteris membranacea*
DICTYOTALES L to 30 cm. Frond fairly thin,
flattened, dichotomously branched, each
branch with a conspicuous mid-rib, and its

membranous part dotted with numerous
groups of delicate hairs; plant has a
distinctly unpleasant smell when freshly
picked. Mid-brown, young specimens
yellow-brown. On solid objects. Lowest
shore to sublittoral. [6]

Peacock's Tail *Padina pavonia*
DICTYOTALES H to 10 cm. Frond curved,
fan-shaped, often almost funnel-shaped;
surface minutely hairy. Outer surface
olive-green or light brown with brown
bands, inner surface pale olive- or lime-
green, sometimes greyish. On rock surfaces
in shallow water. [7]

brown seaweed *Taonia atomaria*
DICTYOTALES L to 30 cm. Frond flat,
broadening steeply from a narrow base to
give a roughly triangular appearance,
irregularly subdivided into strap-like lobes;
tiny hairs and reproductive organs are
arranged in transverse bands across the
frond, which is brown becoming progres-
sively paler towards the margin. On solid
objects. Lowest shore to sublittoral. [8]

brown seaweed *Punctaria latifolia*
PUNCTARIACEAE L to 40 cm. Frond broad
(to 8 cm), entire, leaf-like, arising from a
short, narrow stalk; surface with numerous
conspicuous small spots and, sometimes,
hairs. Olive-brown. On rocks and shells.
Mid-shore to shallow sublittoral. [9]

brown seaweed *Asperococcus bullosus*
ASPEROCOCCACEAE L to 30 cm. Frond
entire, inflated, arising from a short,
narrow stalk; more or less translucent;
pale olive-brown; young specimens soft
and gelatinous, older specimens thick and
rather tough. Often occurs in groups on
stones and other algae in shallow water.
[10]

brown seaweed *Colpomenia sinuosa*
PUNCTARIACEAE D to 20 cm. Frond thin-
walled, inflated, hollow; surface covered
with conspicuous brown dots. Olive-
brown. On stones and other algae. Mid-
shore to sublittoral. [11]

brown seaweed *Scytosiphon lomentaria*
SCYTOSIPHONACEAE L to 45 cm. Frond tubular, constricted, resembling a string of sausages, arising from a short, narrow stalk. Olive-brown. On solid objects and other algae. Lower shore to shallow water. [1]

kelp *Laminaria rodriguezi*
LAMINARIACEAE L to 1 m. Frond band-like, wrinkled, wavy, arising from a slightly branched holdfast, usually with other fronds. Mid- to olive-brown. On solid objects or gravel. Lowest shore to sublittoral. [2]

brown wrack *Fucus virsoides*
FUCACEAE L to 20 cm. Frond tough, dichotomously branched, with a conspicuous mid-rib; tips of branches paler, swollen and speckled with openings of reproductive bodies. Mid- or olive-brown. On rocks. Mid-shore to shallow water. [3]

brown seaweed *Cystoseira barbata*
SARGASSACEAE L to 40 cm (may sometimes reach 1 m). Frond has substantial main stem from which subdivided branches arise; tips of branches swollen and speckled with the openings of reproductive bodies; stem and branches round in cross-section. Mid-brown or olive-brown. On rocks and stones. Lower shore to sublittoral. [4]
Cystoseira abrotanifolia is similar, but the swollen reproductive bodies occur below branch tips.
Cystoseira adriatica is smaller, spiky and arises from a tufted base.

brown seaweed *Sargassum linifolium*
SARGASSACEAE L to 30 cm. Frond with distinct, irregularly branched main stem bearing leaf-like laminae, spherical bladders and clusters of thickened reproductive bodies. On solid objects. Sublittoral. [5]
brown seaweed *Sargassum vulgare* is similar, but has shorter less strap-like 'leaves' that clothe the main stem more closely, and more globular reproductive bodies.

brown seaweed *Sargassum hornschuchi*
SARGASSACEAE L to 40 cm. Frond has strong main stem and alternate or irregular side branches bearing large leaf-like, crinkled laminae with prominent mid-ribs, spherical bladders and grouped elongated reproductive bodies. On rocks and boulders. Sublittoral. [6]

RED SEAWEEDS (Rhodophyceae)
Algae which appear red or purplish because their chlorophyll is masked by the red pigment phycoerythrin, sometimes calcareous.

Laver *Porphyra leucosticta*
BANGIACEAE B to 30 cm. Frond very thin, in rounded or oval sheets, attached at one point; gelatinous or slimy. Purple, darker when dry. On rocks, sometimes attached to algae. Lower shore to sublittoral. [7]

red seaweed *Nemalion helminthoides*
HELMINTHOCLADIACEAE L to 25 cm. Frond round in cross-section and rubbery; dark brown, worm-like, seems to wriggle when agitated by water; several arise from a common, short, main stem; occasionally branched. On rocks, often in exposed places. Mid-shore to sublittoral. [8]

red seaweed *Peyssonnelia squamaria*
SQUAMARIACEAE D to 10 cm. Frond dark red, of lobed, flattened, leaf-like laminae, spreading out in layers from a fibrous holdfast; darker rings on upper surface. On solid objects and other algae. Lowest shore to sublittoral. [9]

red seaweed *Hildenbrandia prototypus*
HILDENBRANDIACEAE D to 5 cm (but irregular). Frond flat, closely adhering to its support, resembling a thick smear of red paint on rocks; port-wine coloured, smooth and glossy, becoming dull and dark when dry. On solid objects. Mid-shore to sublittoral. [10]

red seaweed *Grateloupia filicina*
GRATELOUPIACEAE H to 12 cm. Frond has tapering main stem, which is round in cross-section, and side branches either opposite or alternate with similarly arranged secondary branches. Dark red or purple-red. On stones, often near freshwater outlets. Mid- to lower shore. [11]

red seaweed *Lithothamnion fruticulosum*
CORALLINACEAE T to 3 cm (extent of thallus
very variable). An encrusting alga which
extracts calcium carbonate from seawater
and deposits it as a hard skeleton within its
tissues; upper surface of thallus granular,
with irregular rounded or slightly pointed
projections. Pink to clear red. On solid
objects. Mid-shore to sublittoral. [1]
red seaweed *Lithothamnion lenormandi* is
similar, but thallus is usually thinner and
less regularly granular, resembling rough,
pink cement.

red seaweed *Pseudolithophyllum expansum*
CORALLINACEAE T to 5 cm (extent of thallus
very variable). Thallus with calcareous
skeleton, forms encrusting layers and
extensive reefs (*trottoirs*) in some places;
upper surface very convoluted. Pink, with
white areas. On solid objects in shallow
water. [2]
Lithophyllum incrustans has less coarse
surface convolutions.
Lithophyllum racemus has a knobbly surface.

Lithophyllum tortuosum occurs as a single
spreading layer.

red seaweed *Corallina officinalis*
CORALLINACEAE H to 8 cm. Lateral branches
arising from main stem are themselves
branched; stems and branches have segmented appearance; stems arise as a tuft
from common base; plant has calcareous
skeleton and is harsh to touch; reproductive bodies at tips of branches. Purple-pink
or red; white skeleton remains after soft
parts decay. On rocks. Mid-shore to sublittoral, often in rock-pools. [3]
Corallina mediterranea is similar but less
coarse; reproductive bodies are slightly
inflated and tipped by a tiny pair of horns.

red seaweed *Gracilaria confervoides*
GRACILARIACEAE L to 50 cm. Frond ap-
proximately round in cross-section,
stringy, with side branches tapering at their
bases and tips, and covered with scattered
wart-like reproductive bodies. Reddish-
brown. On rocks and gravel. Mid- to
lower shore. [4]

red seaweed *Neurocaulon reniforme*
FURCELLARIACEAE L to 10 cm or more.
Frond has rubbery, flexed main stem which
branches irregularly and bears leaf-like
and kidney-shaped laminae. Dark red. On
rocks. Sublittoral. [5]

red seaweed *Phyllophora nervosa*
PHYLLOPHORACEAE L to 20 cm. Frond
strap-like, narrow, irregularly branched,
with a slender, but conspicuous central
rib; margins wavy and crinkled. Dark red.
On solid objects. Sublittoral, sometimes in
shaded places. [6]

red seaweed *Gigartina acicularis*
GIGARTINACEAE L to 10 cm. Frond of
slender, branched threads, pointed at their
tips and rounded in cross-section. Reddish-
purple. On rocks in shallow water. [7]

red seaweed *Botryocladia botryoides*
RHODYMENIACEAE L to 12 cm. Frond of
string-like filaments, several of which
often arise from a common base; infre-
quently branched; spherical reproductive
bodies scattered over surface. Brownish-
red. On solid objects. Sublittoral, in shady
places. [8]

red seaweed *Lomentaria linearis*
LOMENTARIACEAE L to 20 cm. Frond round
in cross-section, dichotomously branched,
composed of segments which resemble
strings of sausages, clear pinkish-red. On
stones and with coralline algae. Lowest
shore to sublittoral. [9]

red seaweed *Asparagopsis armata*
BONNEMAISONIACEAE L to 20 cm. Frond has
main, branching stem from which arise
numerous, delicate, thread-like branchlets,
and occasional branches which bear minute
barbs and resemble diminutive harpoons.
Rose-red. On rocks, frequently in rock-
pools. Lower shore. [10]

red seaweed *Falkenbergia rufolanosa* is a
sexual generation of this species so different that the two generations were originally
thought to be separate species. It resembles
tufts of dark red cotton-wool attached to
the fronds of other seaweeds. [11]

red seaweed *Ceramium rubrum*
CERAMIACEAE L to 15 cm. Frond delicate, much branched, main stem and branches usually cross-banded; tips of branches resemble the curved jaws of pincers when viewed closely. Pink, clear red or brownish-red. On rocks; often in rock-pools and in considerable quantities. Upper shore to sublittoral. [1]

red seaweed *Wrangelia penicillata*
CERAMIACEAE L to 15 cm. A delicate feathery frond of branched stems from which arise tufts of tiny branchlets. Rose-red. On stones and other seaweeds. Sublittoral. [2]

red seaweed *Nitophyllum punctatum*
DELESSERIACEAE L to 50 cm. Frond broad, flat, leaf-like, deeply divided into broad lobes which are further divided into strap-like parts. Reddish-pink. On other seaweeds. Lowest shore to sublittoral. [3]

red seaweed *Polysiphonia sertularioides*
RHODOMELACEAE L to 5 cm. Frond of much-branched, thread-like filaments; often occurs as a dense tuft arising from one holdfast. Dark red. On stones. Lowest shore to sublittoral. [4]
Polysiphonia fruticulosa is similar but secondary branchlets are tufted and arise as distinct groups along the main branches.

red seaweed *Laurencia obtusa*
RHODOMELACEAE L to 15 cm. Frond has main stem and opposite or alternate branches which are round in cross-section and from which arise stubby, almost globular branchlets arranged spirally; texture tough, cartilaginous. Brownish-red, pink or yellowish-brown. On other seaweeds. Lower shore and shallow water. [5]

red seaweed *Vidalia volubilis*
RHODOMELACEAE L to 16 cm. Frond strap-like, serrated, notched or toothed,

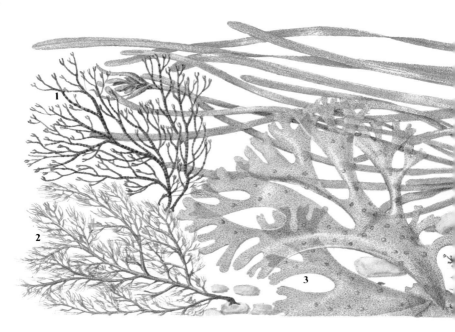

occasionally branched, partly divided into leaf-like regions, slightly twisted; clear mid-rib. Dark red. On stones, sand, gravel or mud. Sublittoral. [6]

EEL-GRASSES (Zosteraceae)

Flowering plants included here and not in their proper, botanical position among other flowering plants (angiosperms) because they occur in similar habitats to the seaweeds – totally submerged by the sea – and resemble some of them in form.

Eel-grass *Zostera marina*

ZOSTERACEAE L to 1 m. Tough, thick underground stems give rise to groups of narrow, bright green, strap-like leaves in which the parallel veins are evenly spaced; flowers grass-like but inconspicuous. In sand and sandy mud. In shallow water. [7] **Narrow-leaved Eel-grass** *Zostera hornemanniana* is similar, but has shorter, narrower leaves in which the parallel veins are arranged as two pairs flanking a central vein.

Neptune Grass *Posidonia oceanica*

ZOSTERACEAE L to 1 m. Tough underground stems give rise to tufts of dark green, strap-like leaves, surrounded at the base by fibrous, shaggy remains of old leaves, which are often washed up on shore; under the influence of wind and water they become rolled up into soft, fibrous sea-balls which often accumulate near the top of the shore. In sand, gravel and muddy sand; often forming dense 'meadows'. In shallow water. [8] [ball 9]

sea-grass *Cymodocea nodosa*

ZOSTERACEAE L to 20 cm. Resembles the eel-grasses, but is smaller and more delicate; leaf-bases have no fibrous sheaths. In similar habitats to *Zostera* and often associated with it. [10]

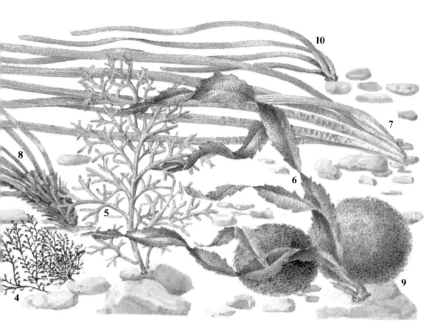

FLOWERING PLANTS (Angiospermae)
Plants that have their ovules contained
within a closed chamber, the ovary, which,
after fertilisation, becomes a fruit containing one or more seeds.

Yellow Horned Poppy *Glaucium flavum*
PAPAVERACEAE H to 90 cm. Branched stem;
bluish-grey leaves deeply lobed, clasping
stem; yellow flowers (D to 9 cm); fruit a
long pod (L to 30 cm), rough but not hairy.
In shingle or coarse sand. Upper shore. [1]

Wild Mignonette *Reseda lutea*
CRUCIFERAE H to 75 cm. Rough, grooved
stem; pale green leaves deeply divided;
greenish-yellow flowers small (D to 6 mm),
on a spike on long stalks. In dry places,
often in sand-dunes and limestone areas. [2]

Virginian Stock *Malcolmia maritima*
CRUCIFERAE H to 40 cm. Low-growing;
branching from base; greyish-green leaves
few, lance-shaped or oval, toothed; flowers
white, pale pink or violet (D to 1.5 cm),
petals notched; fruits stalked, elongated
(L to 6 cm). Often on sea cliffs. [3]
Stock *Malcolmia flexuosa* is similar, but
has larger flowers and fruit stalks.

Sea Stock *Matthiola sinuata*
CRUCIFERAE H to 60 cm. Much branched
and covered with glandular hairs; grey-
green leaves; flowers rosy lilac, petals
toothed (D to 2.5 cm), scented, in loose
heads; fruit a hairy pod (L to 12 cm). In
sandy and rocky places by the sea. [4]

Sweet Alison *Lobularia maritima*
CRUCIFERAE H to 30 cm. Slender, branching;
leaves silvery-white lance-shaped, hairy;
scented, white flowers (D to 5 mm), in
closely packed heads, rounded when
young, elongating with age. In sandy and
rocky places by the sea. [5]

Sea Kale *Crambe maritima*
CRUCIFERAE H to 1 m. Coarse, branching;
leaves greyish-green (L to 30 cm), lower
broad, upper toothed narrow; flowers
green-veined white (D to 1.6 cm); fruit
elongated, dispersed by seawater. On
sand, rocks and cliffs by the sea. [6]

St John's Wort *Hypericum empetrifolium*
HYPERICACEAE H to 30 cm. Low-growing,
shrubby; leaves pale green, narrow, transparent spots on upper surface; flowers
bright yellow. In rocky ground. [7]

Rock-rose *Cistus monspeliensis*
CISTACEAE H to 50 cm. Bushy; leaves lance-
shaped, deep green and glossy. Flowers
small, white (D to 3 cm), sometimes with a
yellow blotch on each petal; aromatic. On
limestone soil in maquis and garrigue. [8]
Rock-rose *Cistus albidus* is similar, but
larger with elliptical leaves. Flowers magenta or rose-red (D to 6 cm), with papery
petals and a central tuft of stamens, sepals
orange.

Annual Rock-rose *Tuberaria guttata*
CISTACEAE H to 30 cm. Delicate, hairy;
leaves lance-shaped with three conspicuous, parallel veins; often dead when plant
in flower; flowers pale yellow compact,
each petal with a red spot at its base. On
dry soils, often on sand; on hillsides. [9]

Tamarisk *Tamarix gallica*
TAMARICACEAE H to 10 m. A woody shrub,
much branched; leaves greyish-green
small, densely clothing twigs; flowers
pink, tiny (D to 2 mm), in elegant spikes.
In sandy soil near the shore. [10]

Tree Mallow *Lavatera arborea*
MALVACEAE H to 3 m. Stout, shrub-like
with woody stem; leaves large, irregular,
often folded; flowers rose-pink with red
veins (D to 5 cm), petals overlapping. Fruits
five-segmented, conspicuous. In sandy and
stony ground near the sea. [11]

Sea Mallow *Lavatera maritima*
MALVACEAE H to 1 m. Bushy, woody; leaves
with greyish-white bloom; flowers pale
pink with a purplish centre (D to 4 cm).
Near the sea. [12]

Sea Spurge *Euphorbia paralias*
EUPHORBIACEAE H to 40 cm. Main stem
short, woody; leaves greyish-green, concave, fleshy, closely clothing stems; flowers
pale green and yellow, tiny, grouped in a
flattish umbel. In sand-dunes. [13]

Flax *Linum campanulatum*
LINACEAE H to 25 cm. Low-growing; main
stem short, woody; leaves lance-shaped,
margin transparent, two brown glands at
base; flowers bright yellow with pale
orange veins; petals fused into a tube. In
limestone soils in garrigue. [1]

Common Storksbill *Erodium cicutarium*
GERANIACEAE H to 60 cm. Delicate, spreading; stem junctions sheathed in papery
stipules; leaves divided, feathery; flowers
rosy purple; fruits with a long (L to 4 cm)
tapering beak. In sandy soils. [2]
Storksbill *Erodium gruinum* is similar, but
lower leaves oval with heart-shaped bases,
upper leaves divided; beak of fruit very
long (L to 11 cm).

Rue *Ruta chalepensis*
RUTACEAE H to 80 cm. Tall, branching;
stems woody; leaves divided, fetid; flowers
yellow, each petal with a conspicuous
fringe of tooth-like hairs. In stony and
rocky ground. [3]

Buckthorn *Rhamnus alaternus*
RHAMNACEAE H to 5 m. A woody shrub;
thornless; leaves evergreen, may be oval or
lance-shaped, toothed or smooth; flowers
greenish-white, tiny, single-sexed, ♀ heads
upright, ♂ heads drooping; fruit red,
turning black. In rocky ground in maquis
and garrigue. [4]

Christ's Thorn *Paliurus spinachristi*
RHAMNACEAE H to 5 m. A woody very
thorny shrub, two unequal spines at the
base of each leaf; leaves oval, asymmetrical; flowers yellow tiny, in groups in leaf
axils; fruit resembles an open umbrella. In
dry soils in maquis and garrigue. [5]

Fig *Ficus carica*
MORACEAE H to 5 m. Rather untidy,
straggling shrub in the wild state, upright
tree when cultivated; leaves dark-green
large, divided, hairy; flowers single-sexed,
completely enclosed within a green pear-
shaped capsule; ♂ and ♀ occur in wild figs,
but ♀ only in the cultivated form. Wild
form in rocky places, woodland, maquis
and garrigue. [6]

Hottentot Fig *Carpobrotus edulis*
AIZOACEAE L to 1 m (stems). Low-growing,
trailing, much branched; stems woody;
leaves linear, fleshy; flowers daisy-like
large (D to 10 cm), pale yellow, yellow,
orange or pale lilac; fruit fleshy, edible. On
cliffs, rocks and sand by the sea. [7]
Hottentot Fig *Carpobrotus acinaciformis* is
similar, but has carmine-red flowers.

Sea Purslane *Halimione portulacoides*
CHENOPODIACEAE H to 1.5 m. A woody
shrub, dense; leaves greyish-green, oval,
downy; flowers tiny, pink-tinged greenish-
yellow in rather open spikes. In saltmarshes, frequently bordering the margins
of creeks and pools. [8]

Glasswort *Salicornia fruticosa*
CHENOPODIACEAE H to 50 cm. Shrubby,
branching, especially from the lower parts;
stems succulent; leaves reduced to pairs of
scales closely adhering to stems; flowers
tiny, in spikes, but insignificant. Entire
plant bright green, lower parts often tinged
red. In saltmarshes, sometimes in the drier
parts. [9]

Common Seablite, Herbaceous Seablite
Suaeda maritima CHENOPODIACEAE
H to 40 cm. Shrubby, prostrate but with
ascending branches; leaves narrow, fleshy;
flowers tiny, in small spikes in the leaf
axils. Entire plant bright green. In saltmarshes and sandy shores. [10]

Saltwort *Salsola kali*
CHENOPODIACEAE H to 60 cm. Shrubby,
spiny, prostrate, leaf-bearing branches
ascending; leaves taper to a spine at the tip;
flowers tiny, whitish, in the leaf axils. On
sandy shores [11]

Bladder Campion *Silene vulgaris*
CARYOPHYLLACEAE H to 90 cm. Bushy,
with numerous flowering stems; leaves
oval, pointed; flowers white, with bladder-
like sepals and deeply cleft petals. In
rocky areas near the sea, shingle. [12]
Bladder Campion *Silene succulenta* is
similar but rather more low-lying, succulent, with hairy, sticky leaves to which sand
often adheres.

Scarlet Pimpernel *Anagallis arvensis*
PRIMULACEAE L to 30 cm. Low, spreading;
stems square; leaves oval, pointed; flowers
star-shaped, pink, scarlet, blue or violet,
spiky sepals projecting beyond and between
the petals. In a variety of soils, but often in
sandy areas near the sea. [1]

Coris monspeliensis PRIMULACEAE
H to 30 cm. Bushy, branching; leaves
numerous, thyme-like, usually with two
to three spines at the base; flower bluish-
purple, with three large upright lobes and
two smaller lips; stamens conspicuous. On
sand near the sea and on stony ground
further inland. [2]

Brookweed *Samolus valerandi*
PRIMULACEAE H to 45 cm. Slender; stem
arises from basal rosette; leaves oval,
sickly green; flowers white (D to 3 mm) in a
loose spike. In moist places near the sea. [3]

Sea Lavender *Limonium sinuatum*
PLUMBAGINACEAE H to 50 cm. Main stem
two- or three-winged, arises from basal
rosette, stem-wings also give rise to leaves;
sepals purple, petals small pale yellow,
insignificant, flowers crowded on branched
flowering heads. At the upper edge of sandy
and stony shores. [4]
Common Sea Lavender *Limonium vulgare* is
similar, but has an unwinged stem and
bright purple petals.

Strawberry Tree *Arbutus unedo*
ERICACEAE H to 10 m. Tree with rough
brown bark, young branches reddish;
leaves lance-shaped, toothed, tough,
glossy; flowers creamy yellow, vase-
shaped, borne in clusters; fruit red, like a
round strawberry with a tough, rough
skin. In maquis. [5]

Tree Heather *Erica arborea*
ERICACEAE H to 3 m (may be taller). A
woody shrub, much branched; leaves tiny,
woolly above; flowers tiny, white or

pale pink, bell-shaped (L to 3 mm),
clustered in dense spikes. In maquis. [6]

Slender Centaury, Lesser Centaury
Centaurium pulchellum GENTIANACEAE
H to 15 cm. Slender; main stem often unbranched, otherwise spreading; leaves
oval; flowers pink, star-like, on long
clustered flower stems clothed with small
leaves. In damp places near the sea. [7]

Yellow-wort *Blackstonia perfoliata*
GENTIANACEAE H to 45 cm. Slender; main
stem arises from basal rosette; leaves grey-
green, oval, bases of stem leaves are joined
around stem; flowers bright yellow, on
leafy flower stalks. In sand-dunes. [8]

Olive *Olea europea*
OLEACEAE H to 10 m. A tree with clearly
furrowed bark, often gnarled; leaves lance-
shaped, greyish-green above, white and
silky beneath; flowers tiny, in loose spikes;
fruit plum-shaped, dull green or black. [9]
The wild olive *Olea europea* var. *oleaster*
occurs in maquis and garrigue.

Wild Jasmine *Jasminum fruticans*
OLEACEAE H to 1 m. An upright shrub with
ridged stems; leaves elongated, dark green;
flowers yellow, with five spreading petals.
Fruit black, glossy. Usually on calcareous
soil; in the garrigue. [10]

Bindweed *Convolvulus althaeoides*
CONVOLVULACEAE L to 1 m. Climbing,
hairy; stems elongated; lower leaves oval,
upper leaves divided; flowers purplish-
pink, trumpet-shaped, papery. Amongst
vegetation near the sea. [11]

Dyer's Alkanet *Alkanna tinctoria*
BORAGINACEAE L to 30 cm. Spreading;
main stem short, woody, surrounded by a
mass of hairy, lance-shaped leaves; flowers
bright blue on spreading, leafy branches.
On the upper parts of sandy shores and on
other calcareous soils. [12]

Purple Viper's Bugloss *Echium lycopsis*
BORAGINACEAE H to 60 cm. Conspicuous with erect or spreading stems; stem and leaves hairy; flowers large (L to 3 cm), blue-violet, with broad throats and five teeth, and conspicuously long stamens. On sandy soils near the sea. [1]

Viper's Bugloss *Echium diffusum*
BORAGINACEAE H to 30 cm. Bushy, branched stem arises from a rosette of yellowish-green leaves; leaves and stem covered in dense, stiff hairs; flowers small (D to 14 mm), red or pinkish-purple with projecting stamens. On sandy soil near the sea. [2]
Viper's Bugloss *Echium italicum* is similar, but larger (H to 1 m), with small flesh-pink or white flowers in a pyramidal head.

Chaste Tree *Vitex agnus-castus*
VERBENACEAE H to 3 m. A woody shrub with branched stems; leaves segmented, lance-shaped, glossy above and covered in a felt of fine hairs beneath; flowers lilac with two lips, hairy on the outside with projecting stamens, borne in a long spike. In damp places by the sea. [3]

Ground-pine *Ajuga chamaepitys*
LABIATAE H to 20 cm. Low-growing, bushy; stem branched, spreading from the base and turning upward at the tips; leaves divided, resinous; flowers yellow, irregular, in pairs in the leaf axils. In dry soils, in the garrigue. [4]

Germander *Teucrium fruticans*
LABIATAE H to 1.5 m. A shrub with branching stems; leaves oval, tough, dark green above with white felt of fine hairs beneath; flowers pale blue, irregular. Among rocks wooded hills by the sea. [5]

Rosemary *Rosmarinus officinalis*
LABIATAE H to 1.5 m. A bushy shrub with branched stems; leaves aromatic, oblong, with white, hairy lower surface; flowers lilac, irregular, with projecting stamens and style. In the maquis and garrigue. [6]

French Lavender *Lavandula stoechas*
LABIATAE H to 60 cm. A low-growing shrub with branching stems; leaves aromatic, oblong, hairy; flowers small, purple, in dense spikes from which project violet, hairy bracts. In the garrigue. [7]

Hyssop *Hyssopus officinalis*
LABIATAE H to 60 cm. A woody shrub with branching stems; leaves aromatic, lance-shaped; flowers bluish-violet, irregular. In the garrigue. [8]

Wild Clary *Salvia verbenaca*
LABIATAE H to 80 cm. A hairy shrubby plant with large and irregular leaves borne on a main stem with few branches. Basal rosette of leaves. Leaves grey-green, elongated, upper surfaces wrinkled. Flowers violet or blue, the upper lip larger than the lower and curved at its tip. In the maquis and garrigue. [9]
Three-lobed Sage *Salvia triloba* is similar, but has branching stems, and irregular violet flowers in erect, sticky spikes.

Summer Savory *Satureia thymbra*
LABIATAE H to 50 cm. A low shrub with much branched stems; leaves dark green, aromatic, oval, with a folded blade, very hairy; flowers pink, irregular. In the garrigue. [10]

Thyme *Thymus vulgaris*
LABIATAE H to 30 cm. A compact shrub with much branched, woody stems; leaves aromatic, tiny, lance-shaped, with glandular spots above, hairy beneath; flowers reddish-purple, irregular, hairy, in a cushion-like head. In the garrigue and other dry habitats. [11]

Mullein *Verbascum undulatum*
SCROPHULARIACEAE H to 1 m. Conspicuous, with spreading stems arising from a basal rosette of large grey-green, hairy leaves; flowers yellow, cup-shaped, in clusters along stem. In dry, rocky places. [12]

Bartsia *Parentucellia latifolia*
SCROPHULARIACEAE H to 20 cm. Slender with stems unbranched or branched from base; leaves reddish-green, hairy, deeply divided; flowers reddish-purple with white inside, small (L to 1 cm), hairy. In dry sandy soil near the sea. [13]

Buckshorn Plantain, Stag's-horn Plantain
Plantago coronopus PLANTAGINACEAE
H to 6 cm (leaf). Low-growing; leaves deeply toothed, variable, in a rosette; flowers light brown, tiny, in a compact head with protruding yellow stamens. In sandy and stony ground, sometimes in rock-clefts, near the sea. [1]

Starry Stonecrop *Sedum stellatum*
CRASSULACEAE H to 15 cm. Creeping; stems erect, stout; leaves egg-shaped, fleshy, toothed; flowers pink, star-like, in the axils of leafy bracts on a forked stem. In dry rocky places. [2]

Carob, Locust Tree *Ceratonia siliqua*
LEGUMINOSAE H to 10 m. A tree with many spreading branches; leaves compound, tough, glossy; flowers tiny, greenish, in groups among the leaves; fruits conspicuous, long (L to 20 cm) leathery pods brown when ripe (the seeds were the original carat weights of jewellers). In rocky places near the sea, but commonly cultivated. [3]

Broom *Genista acanthoclados*
LEGUMINOSAE H to 1 m. A conspicuous shrub; much branched, spiny greyish-white stems; leaves three-segmented, only on young branches; flowers bright yellow, irregular, keel hairy, borne in clusters along the branches. In rocky places, especially in calcareous soil. [4]
Broom *Genista cinerea* is similar, but a low shrub (H to 1 m) with three-segmented leaves; stems lack spines.

Spiny Restharrow *Ononis spinosa*
LEGUMINOSAE H to 20 cm. Low-lying, straggling; stems stiff, spiny, with slender, zig-zagging branches; flowers pink similar in shape to broom. In sandy and stony places by the sea. [5]

Sea Medick *Medicago marina*
LEGUMINOSAE L to 15 cm (or more). Low-lying, spreading; leaves white with woolly hairs; flowers pale yellow, small (L to 8 mm), in rounded heads at the tips of the branches; fruit spirally coiled pod. In sandy places by the sea. [6].

Trefoil *Trifolium uniflorum*
LEGUMINOSAE H to 5 cm (in flower). Low-growing, forming dense mats; leaves typically trefoil-like; flowers pinkish-purple or white, similar to broom. In dry soils, often in sandy places by the sea. [7]

Kidney Vetch *Anthyllis cytisoides*
LEGUMINOSAE H to 80 cm. A rounded shrub; stems and leaves greyish-white; flowers yellow, in clusters in axils of bracts. In dry, stony ground near the sea. [8]

Birdsfoot Trefoil *Lotus creticus*
LEGUMINOSAE L to 40 cm. Low-growing, straggly, spreading; leaves covered with silky hairs; flowers yellow, similar to broom, sometimes single, sometimes in heads of up to eight. In sandy places, also on cliffs near the sea. [9]

Horseshoe Vetch *Hippocrepis unisiliquosa*
LEGUMINOSAE H to 30 cm. Low-growing, spreading; leaves compound; flowers yellow, similar to broom; fruit characteristic, a curved pod with seven to ten horseshoe-like marks. In the maquis and garrigue. [10]

Sainfoin *Onobrychis caput-galli*
LEGUMINOSAE H to 40 cm. Spreading or erect; leaves greyish, hairy; flowers pink, small (L to 6 mm) in compact heads; fruit a flattened, spiny pod with triangular teeth around margin and rounded depressions on each surface. In dry soils, often in sand and stony ground near the sea. [11]

Thorny Burnet *Poterium spinosum*
ROSACEAE H to 50 cm. A compact shrub; stems branched, young branches tipped with a pair of thorns; leaves small, compound; flowers red, in compact heads all of one sex, ♂ yellow stamens, ♀ feathery purple styles. In dry places, garrigue. [12]

Prickly Pear *Opuntia ficus-indica*
CACTACEAE H to 5 m. A typical cactus; stems succulent chains of segments, spiny; leaves tiny falling shortly after their appearance; flowers yellow, showy (D to 7 cm), with numerous petals fused into a tube; fruit yellow, brick-red or purple, edible. In dry stony or rocky places. [13]

Rock-rose parasite *Cytinus hypocistis*
RAFFLESIACEAE H to 8 cm. Parasite on roots of rock-roses, *Cistus* spp; stems with numerous sheathing red scales; leaves absent; flowers bright yellow with four sepals fused into a tube, borne in groups of up to 10 in a compact head. Under rock-roses in the maquis and garrigue. [1]

Myrtle *Myrtus communis*
MYRTACEAE H to 3 m. A woody, evergreen shrub, bushy, with branched stems; leaves privet-like, with translucent glandular spots, aromatic; flowers white with a tuft of long stamens, borne singly, fragrant; fruit an oval or rounded berry, black when ripe. In the maquis and garrigue; cultivated. [2]

Sea Holly *Eryngium maritimum*
UMBELLIFERAE H to 60 cm. Much-branched, stiff; leaves greyish, very spiny, holly-like; flowers blue, tiny with long stamens, borne in compact, cushion-like heads. In sand-dunes and other sandy soils near the sea. [3]

Rock Samphire *Crithmum maritimum*
UMBELLIFERAE H to 30 cm. Low-growing, bushy with much-branched stems; leaves greyish, fleshy; flowers white, tiny, in a flattened, branched head. On sea cliffs. [4]

Thymelaea hirsuta THYMELAEACEAE
H to 1 m. Shrubby with much branched stems; leaves tiny, fleshy, concave, hairy beneath; flowers greenish-yellow with no visible petals, but hairy petal-like sepals. On rocky and sandy soil by the sea. [5]
Thymelaea tartonraira is different; leaves spatulate, hairy and concentrated near tops of stems, lower parts of which are covered in swollen leaf-scars.

Daphne *Daphne gnidium*
THYMELAEACEAE H to 1.25 m. An erect, woody shrub with slender branches; leaves lance-shaped, greyish with pale white spots; flowers greenish-grey, hairy on the outside; fruit a conspicuous red or black berry. In rocky soil, in the garrigue. [6]

Scabious *Scabiosa atropurpurea* var.
maritima DIPSACACEAE
H to 1 m. Slender, branched; leaves
toothed or segmented; flowers pink or pale
violet, small, clustered into a flattened,
compact head; fruiting head cylindrical,
with many projecting spines. In sandy soils
near the sea. [7]

Daisy *Evax pygmaea*
COMPOSITAE H to 4 cm. Small, compact;
leaves in a rosette, white with dense hairs;
flowers yellow, with petal-like bracts. In
sandy soils and garrigue. [8]

Everlasting Flower *Helichrysum stoechas*
COMPOSITAE H to 30 cm. Low-growing,
spreading; leaves greyish-white, strap-like,
densely hairy, smelling strongly of curry;
flowers yellow, tiny, borne in spherical
groups. On sandy and stony coasts. [9]

Pallenis spinosa COMPOSITAE
H to 1 m. Upright, branching; lower leaves
wedge-shaped, upper leaves lance-shaped;
flowers yellow, daisy-like, with spiny
tipped bracts. In rocky soils. [10]

Odontospermum maritimum COMPOSITAE
H to 30 cm. Shrubby, much branched,
spreading; leaves spatulate, hairy; flowers
yellow, daisy-like, large (D to 4 cm). In dry
and rocky soils, near the sea. [11]

Chamomile *Anthemis chia*
COMPOSITAE H to 30 cm. Low-growing,
erect or spreading; leaves divided; flowers
daisy-like (D to 3 cm), with yellow disc
florets and white ray florets. In dry
localities. [12]

Sea Aster *Aster tripolium*
COMPOSITAE H to 1 m. Upright with robust
brownish stems; leaves fleshy, elongated;
flowers daisy-like, with yellow disc florets
and purple or lilac ray florets, borne in
flattened heads. In a variety of soils near
the sea, often in saltmarshes. [13]

Golden Samphire *Inula crithmoides*
COMPOSITAE H to 90 cm. Shrubby, ascending stems and leaves fleshy; flowers daisy-like, with orange disc florets and yellow ray florets. On sea-cliffs and in saltmarshes. [1]

Cottonweed *Otanthus maritimus*
COMPOSITAE H to 40 cm. Low-growing, spreading; whole plant woolly; leaves and stem white; flowers yellow, in rounded heads. In sandy soils by the sea. [2]

Silver Ragwort *Senecio cineraria*
COMPOSITAE H to 60 cm. Shrubby, branched; hairy leaves deeply segmented; flowers yellow in compact heads. In sandy and rocky soils near the sea. [3]

Globe Thistle *Echinops ritro*
COMPOSITAE H to 1 m. Leaves deeply divided, each segment spiny, the lower surface downy; flowers clear blue in spherical heads (D to 5 cm). In stony ground, often near the sea. [4]

Carline Thistle *Carlina corymbosa*
COMPOSITAE H to 40 cm. Strong ascending stems; leaves stiff, dull green; flower-head yellow. In dry ground, in the garrigue. [5]

Milk Thistle, Holy Thistle *Silybum marianum* COMPOSITAE
H to 2 m. Robust ascending stems; leaves dark green, patterned white, broad, deeply cut, spiny; flower-heads purple, large (D to 8 cm), spiny. In rocky ground. [6]

Thistle *Leuzia conifera*
COMPOSITAE H to 30 cm. Upright with little-branched stems; leaves greyish-green, deeply divided; stem and lower leaf surfaces densely hairy, white; flowers resemble pine-cones. In the garrigue. [7]

Sowthistle *Sonchus spinosus*
COMPOSITAE H to 1 m. Erect with stout stems; leaves downy beneath; flowers yellow, dandelion-like, in stalked groups at tips of the stems. In stony ground. [8]

Spanish Oyster Plant *Scolymus hispanicus*
COMPOSITAE H to 1 m. Bushy; stems stout, hairy, with toothed wings; leaves deeply divided spiny; flowers yellow, like untidy daisies, with spiny bracts, borne in the axils of the leaves. In sandy and stony ground, often in wasteland. [9]

Chicory *Cichorium pumilum*
COMPOSITAE H to 1.25 m. Upright, with stiff, branching stems; leaves blue-green, lance-shaped, the lower divided; flowers bright blue, dandelion-like (D to 4 cm), borne in the axils of the upper leaves, the outer bracts very hairy. In sandy and rocky soil near the sea. [10]

Kermes Oak *Quercus coccifera*
FAGACEAE H to 3 m. A woody tree which often occurs as densely branched, shrubby thickets (H to 1 m); leaves holly-like; flowers tiny, only ♂ are conspicuous as tassel-like catkins; acorn cups bristly. In dry soils and especially the garrigue. [11]

Holm Oak *Quercus ilex* is taller, and has hairy branches and leaf under-surfaces, sometimes spiny; acorn cups have scales closely pressed to the cup; not spreading.
Cork Oak *Quercus suber* is a large tree (H to 15 m), with deeply fissured bark (cork); acorn cups conical, hairy, with slightly spreading scales which increase in length toward the rim of the cup.

Asphodel *Asphodelus microcarpus*
LILIACEAE H to 1.5 m. Tall, slender; stem much branched; leaves sword-shaped (L to 1 m); flowers white, borne in conspicuous pyramidal heads; underground potato-like tubers. In rough, dry soil. [12]

Rose Garlic *Allium roseum*
LILIACEAE H to 40 cm. Slender, upright, smelling of garlic; leaves flat, strap-like; flowers rose-pink or pale violet (D to 2.5 cm), in rounded heads; underground bulb surrounded by many small bulbils. Often at the extreme upper shore. [13]

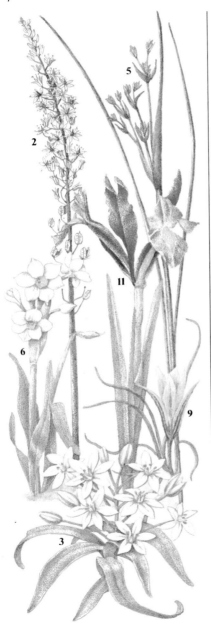

Fritillary *Fritillaria messanensis*
LILIACEAE H to 50 cm. Slender, upright; leaves bluish-green, lance-shaped; flower purple and yellowish-green, bell- or cup-shaped (L to 4 cm), borne singly, usually no more than two per plant. In meadows and damp woods. [1]

Sea Squill *Urginea maritima*
LILIACEAE H to 1.5 m (flowering stem). Conspicuous; leaves lance-shaped, die before flowers appear; flowers green-veined white, star-like with protruding stamens. Plant grows from enormous bulb (D to 15 cm). In sandy and rocky ground, often near the sea. [2]

Star of Bethlehem *Ornithogalum montanum*
LILIACEAE H to 20 cm. Upright, slender, bulbous; leaves lance-shaped; flowers white, with green vein, star-like, clustered into flattened heads of up to 20. In a variety of soils, often in stony ground. [3]

Tassel Hyacinth *Muscari comosum*
LILIACEAE H to 60 cm. Slender, upright; leaves strap-shaped; flowers either blue, in tufts (sterile), or purplish-brown (fertile). In fields and orchards, sometimes in stony ground. [4]
Grape Hyacinth *Muscari commutatum* has a more compact head of rounded fertile dark blue flowers, occasionally topped by very few pale blue sterile flowers.

Sea Rush *Juncus maritimus*
JUNCACEAE H to 1 m. Densely tufted, very tough; stem and leaves wiry; flowers pale green and straw-coloured, small, in an irregular tuft on one side of the flowering stalk. In saltmarshes. [5]
Sharp Rush *Juncus acutus* is similar but may be taller (H to 1.5 m), with fewer leaves; flowers reddish-brown in a more compact tuft. On sandy shores and in dune slacks.
Toad Rush *Juncus bufonius* is small (H to 25 cm), with slender, much-branched stems; flowering head extensive.

Polyanthus Narcissus *Narcissus tazetta*
AMARYLLIDACEAE H to 50 cm. A typical narcissus; leaves strap-shaped with a keel; flowers with a relatively short corona (L to 8 mm). In meadows and in the garrigue in moist localities. [6]

Sea Daffodil *Pancratium maritimum*
AMARYLLIDACEAE H to 40 cm. Often size-able clumps; leaves bluish-green, strap-shaped, spirally twisted; flowers large (L to 15 cm), white with green stripes, borne in groups of up to 12, and scented. In sands near the sea, often in sand-dunes and maritime steppe. [7]

Crocus *Crocus flavus*
IRIDACEAE H to 8 cm (flower). A typical crocus; leaves sword-like; flowers bright orange sometimes lined with pale grey. In rough ground, garrigue [8]

Crocus *Romulea bulbocodium*
IRIDACEAE H to 7 cm (flower). Crocus-like with narrow dark green leaves; flowers lilac, purple, yellow or white, borne either singly or in groups. In sandy areas near the sea, often in sand-dunes. [9]

Dwarf Bearded Iris *Iris chamaeiris*
IRIDACEAE H to 15 cm. Sword-shaped, dark green leaves sheath the stem; flowers purple or pale yellow with sharply reflexed, 'bearded' outer petals. In rocky ground, in the garrigue. [10]

Spanish Iris *Iris xiphium*
IRIDACEAE H to 60 cm. Tapering, chan-nelled leaves; flowers violet-purple, stigmas tongue-like, erect. In grassy places near the sea. [11]

Yellow Flag *Iris pseudacorus*
IRIDACEAE H to 1.5 m. In extensive clumps; leaves mossy green, sword-like, stiff; flowers pale yellow to orange, large (D to 10 cm) with broad, tongue-like outer petals. In swampy ground. [12]

Marram Grass *Ammophila arenaria*
GRAMINEAE H to 1.25 m. Forms large clumps; leaves light green, stiff, sharply pointed; flowers whitish-fawn, tiny, in a thick tuft, like a fox's brush; the fibrous root system is extensive and most effectual in binding mobile sand. In sand-dunes. [1]

Common Reed *Phragmites australis*
GRAMINEAE H to 3 m. Forms thick clumps and extensive beds; leaves broad (w to 20 mm), tapering; flowers purple, small and packed into a long, nodding head (L to 30 cm). In moist places, notably near the margins of streams, in estuaries, along the banks of coastal lagoons. [2]

Giant Reed *Arundo donax*
GRAMINEAE H to 5 m. Forms thickets; stems bamboo-like; leaves strap-like; flowers pale fawn, small, clustered into heads which may be 70 cm long. In wet places, often on the banks of streams and lagoons. [3]

Broad Helleborine, White Helleborine
Cephalanthera damasonium ORCHIDACEAE
H to 60 cm. Slender, upright; stem fairly stiff; leaves dark green, oval; flowers white, tulip-like, in a rather scattered spike. In woods and scrub, always on limestone, often near the sea. [4]

Autumn Lady's Tresses *Spiranthes spiralis*
ORCHIDACEAE H to 12 cm. Delicate leaves in a basal rosette die before flowering stem arises; flowers white, tiny (L to 5 mm) in a dense spiral near the top of the stem. This orchid flowers in late summer or autumn while most others flower in spring. In sand-dunes and dry grassy places near the sea. [5]

Mirror Orchid *Ophrys speculum*
ORCHIDACEAE H to 15 cm. Sturdy, upright; leaves strap-shaped; flower insect-like, green, maroon, blue and yellow. In grassy places, on calcareous soil. This is only one of many insect-like orchids which occur in the region. [6]

Pink Butterfly Orchid *Orchis papilionacea*
ORCHIDACEAE H to 50 cm. Massive; stem thick, stiff; leaves dark-green, oval; flowers reddish- to greenish-violet with frilly lip, scented. In grass, sometimes in dry localities, in garrigue. [7]

Roman Orchid *Dactylorhiza romana*
ORCHIDACEAE H to 35 cm. Slender; leaves strap-like; flowers violet to reddish-purple, sometimes white or yellow, borne in a loose spike. In sandy and rocky soil, in garrigue. [8]

Heart-flowered Tongue Orchid *Serapias cordigera* ORCHIDACEAE
H to 45 cm. Sturdy; leaves green, spotted purple at base, narrow, channelled; flowers reddish-purple, large (L to 4 cm) with a heart-shaped, hairy dark purple lip. In dry, sandy or stony places, in garrigue. [9]
Scarce Tongue Orchid *Serapias parviflora* is much smaller (H to 20 cm) with slightly wavy leaves; flower reddish-violet with a narrow, hairy, rust-red lip. In sandy and stony places near the sea.

Pyramidal Orchid *Anacamptis pyramidalis*
ORCHIDACEAE H to 30 cm. Slender; leaves narrow, keeled; flowers pink and rosy purple, borne in spirally arranged, compact, pyramidal head. In dry soils, often in sand-dunes. [10]

Aleppo Pine *Pinus halepensis*
PINACEAE H to 20 m. A woody tree with silvery bark, branching from the base when young and forming an umbrella from the top when mature; leaves bright green, slender, flexible (L to 10 cm); cones yellowish-brown becoming chestnut brown. In rocky ground near the sea. [11]

Juniper *Juniperus oxycedrus*
CUPRESSACEAE H to 6 m. A bushy, woody shrub; leaves white and green above, dark green below, sharply pointed; cones yellow, rounded, plants usually unisexual; fruits berry-like, in clusters, black when ripe. In dry soils, in garrigue. [12]

SPONGES (Porifera)

Sessile animals; body cavity communicates with outside through one exhalant opening (osculum) and many small inhalant openings (ostia). They are supported by calcareous or siliceous spicules or horny fibres.

sponge *Leucosolenia coriacea*

HOMOCOELIDAE H to 3 cm, W to 10 cm. Lacelike encrustations of branching tubes; upright parts join at tips, sharing a common osculum. White, dirty-white, yellow, brown or brick-red. Under boulders, on shells and among holdfasts of large weeds. Mid-shore to sublittoral. [1]

sponge *Sycon coronatum*

SYCETTIDAE H to 3 cm. Vase-shaped; rough spicules conspicuous around osculum. Yellowish-white or fawn. Attached to solid surfaces. Lower shore to sublittoral. [2]

Purse Sponge *Grantia compressa*

GRANTIIDAE H to 5 cm. Flattened and purselike out of water, rounded when immersed; osculum conspicuous. Off-white or pale yellow. Attached to weeds or rocks; usually in groups. Lower shore. [3]

Leather Sponge *Chondrosia reniformis*

CHONDROSIIDAE D to 10 cm, H to 3 cm. Rounded or kidney-shaped; tough, smooth outer skin; no spicules; internal tissues firm; ostia and oscula tiny. Shiny dark reddish-brown or grey, sometimes speckled with dots. On rocks. Littoral. [4]

sponge *Tethya aurantium*

TETHYIDAE D to 4 cm (D to 10 cm in sublittoral specimens). Globular; surface rough and warty; interior resembles cut orange in cross-section due to long siliceous spicules radiating toward the centre. Pale yellow to deep orange. Under boulders in sheltered places, sometimes in groups. Lower shore to sublittoral. [5]

Sea Orange *Suberites domuncula*

CLAVULIDAE D to 30 cm. Massive, rounded, surface smooth, oscula prominent; firm like tough dough. Grey, sulphur-yellow or dull orange. Commonly encrusts shells

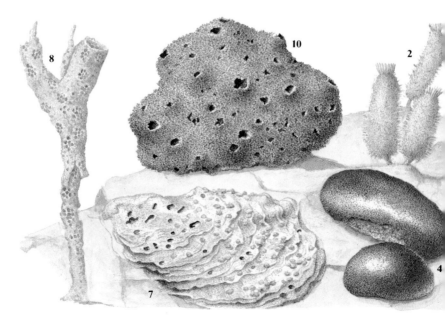

occupied by hermit crabs. Sublittoral. [6]

Boring Sponge *Cliona celata*
CLAVULIDAE W to 1 m (massive form). Two forms. Littoral: bores into bivalve mollusc shells (then visible only as rounded projections; D 2 mm); sometimes covers shell as smooth layer. Sublittoral: may become massive; tough and dough-like, with soft projections bearing the oscula. Sulphur-yellow, sometimes green or bluish. Lower shore to sublittoral. [littoral form **7**]

sponge *Axinella polypoides*
AXINELLIDAE H to 30 cm. Elongated, cylindrical; oscula in groups, like pepper-pots. Yellow or red. Sublittoral. [**8**]
Axinella verrucosa is similar but smaller (H to 20 cm). Much-branched, tubular; oscula small. Pale yellow, orange or rose-red.
Axinella damicornis is smaller still (D to 10 cm). Encrusting, forms pleated layers; sometimes projects as finger-like folds. Golden-yellow. On rocks and weeds. Sublittoral.

Crumb-of-bread Sponge *Halichondria panicea* DESMACIDONIDAE
W to 25 cm, H to 3 cm. Fairly smooth encrustation; large oscula on volcano-like protuberances; very variable. Commonly green but may be yellow, orange or brown. On rocks and solid objects, among holdfasts of weeds. Mid-shore to sublittoral. [**9**]

Bath Sponge *Spongia officinalis*
SPONGIIDAE D to 30 cm. Massive, usually spherical, dark brown or black; may form thick encrustation; surface granular or lacy; oscula large. Skeleton, horny yellow. On solid objects. Usually sublittoral. [**10**]

Golden Sponge *Verongia aerophobia*
SPONGIIDAE H to 20 cm, D to 3 cm. Almost straight-sided tubes arise from thinly encrusting base; osculum large. Bright golden-yellow; turns green, then black in air. On solid supports, in eel-grass *Zostera* 'meadows', sublittorally becomes very large (to 60 cm). Lowest shore to sublittoral. [*not illustrated*]

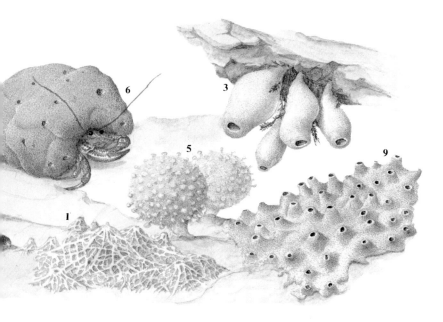

SEA-ANEMONES, CORALS AND JELLY-FISH (Cnidaria)

Hollow-bodied animals having two layers of cells separated by jelly-like layer. Corals: outer surface horny or calcareous. Ring of tentacles around mouth. Possess specialized cells, cnidocytes, containing barbs and stings for food capture.

sea-fir *Tubularia mesembryanthemum*
TUBULARIIDAE H to 15 cm or more. Basally root-like, inconspicuous. Polyp globular with several circlets of tentacles, the outer drooping, white, the inner stiffer pink or red. Reproductive bodies like tiny bunches of grapes. Horny perisarc pale brown, polyps pink, or red and white. On solid objects, especially where water flow strong, often on boat bottoms. Lower shore to sublittoral. [1]

jelly-fish *Neoturris pileata*
PANEIDAE to 7 cm. Elongated transparent medusa narrowing near apex; 90 or more short, slender tentacles; manubrium large, with much-folded margin, bearing pleated brick-red gonads. Radial canals faintly milky-white. In open water, shallows. [2]

siphonophore *Physophora hydrostatica*
PHYSOPHORIDAE L to 10 cm (stinging polyps are extensible and may increase length). Colony consists of small, transparent, elongated float with a double row of muscular swimming bells, and a radiating cluster of feeding, reproductive and trailing stinging polyps. In open water. [3]

Portuguese Man-o'-war *Physalia physalis*
PHYSALIIDAE L to 30 cm (float only). Float elongated, tapering, silvery blue, magenta and purple, with an erect, undulating 'sail'. Suspended below float are numerous blue and purple feeding, reproductive and stinging polyps, the latter extending to over 30 m in length; sting painful, potentially very dangerous. In open water, sometimes washed up on shore. *It should not be touched.* [4]

By-the-wind-sailor *Velella velella*
VELELLIDAE L to 10 cm (float). Float, a flattened oval disc, silvery blue and purple, with a gas-filled central chamber and a horny support forming a sail; suspended is one large feeding polyp surrounded by numerous reproductive and stinging polyps. In open water. [5]

Compass Jellyfish *Chrysaora hysoscella*
PELAGIIDAE D to 30 cm. Umbrella bowl-shaped, biscuit-coloured with brown patches and central spot; margin with 32 lobes and 24 tentacles. In open water. [6]

jelly-fish *Pelagia noctiluca*
PELAGIIDAE D to 15 cm. Umbrella dome-shaped, spotted, milky purple-pink or reddish-brown; phosphorescent; margin lobed, bearing 8 long tentacles. In open water. [7]

jellyfish *Rhizostoma pulmo*
RHIZOSTOMIDAE D to 60 cm at least. Umbrella milky, deeply domed with 96 marginal lobes but no tentacles; leathery; no central mouth, red-marked mouth-lobes fused into bunches containing numerous pores into digestive cavity. In open water, occasionally shallows. [8]

Cylinder Anemone *Cerianthus membranaceus* CERIANTHIDAE
L to 35 cm (body). Violet body with tapering hind end; 130 slender patterned tentacles up to 20 cm long; tube dark brown, thick, felt-like, slimy on inside. Buried in muddy sand. Sublittoral. [9]

sea-anemone *Epizoanthus arenaceus*
EPIZOANTHIDAE H to 1 cm. Colonial, anemone-like greyish polyps arise from a filmy base which encrusts solid objects; each polyp has 24 white tentacles. On stones and mollusc shells. Sublittoral. [10]
sea-anemone *Parazoanthus axinellae* is similar but has up to 36, golden-yellow tentacles per polyp. On rocks and other organisms, often on cave-walls. Sublittoral.

sea-anemone *Peachia hastata*
HALOCLAVIDAE H to 10 cm. Elongated, worm-like, no adhesive basal disc; pinkish-brown, with 12 vertical stripes and 12 pale tentacles. Burrowing in sand, mud and gravel. Lower shore to sublittoral. [11]

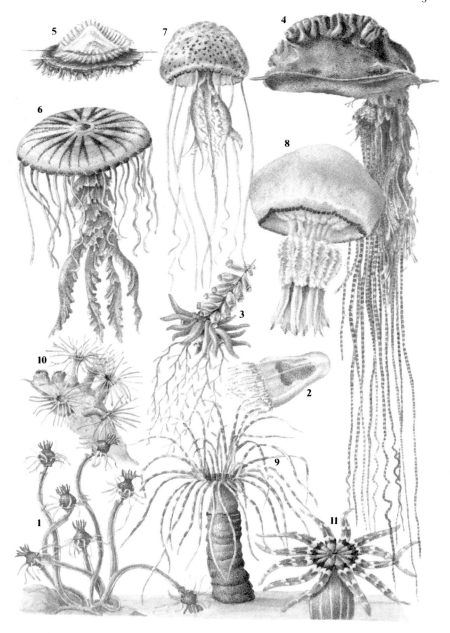

Golden Anemone *Condylactis aurantiaca*
HALOCLAVIDAE H to 40 cm, D to 7.5 cm.
Column whitish or flesh-coloured with
orange-red vertical stripes and white warts;
disc flattened, with numerous greenish,
purple-tipped contractile tentacles; base
sucker-like. Attached to shells and stones
buried in sand so only tentacle disc visible.
Sublittoral.[1]

Beadlet Anemone *Actinia equina*
ACTINIDAE H to 8 cm, D to 6 cm. Smooth;
red, dull green, brown or orange, or red
with green speckles in 'strawberry' form;
base adhesive, with narrow blue band
around margin; 6 circles of 200 tentacles,
24 bright blue spots around disc margin.
On rocks and in crevices. Upper-middle
shore to sublittoral. [2]

Wartlet Anemone, Gem Anemone
Bunodactis verrucosa ACTINIIDAE
H to 5 cm, D to 3 cm. Column pink or
mottled grey-green, with adhesive basal
disc; 6 vertical rows of white adhesive
warts, numerous rows of smaller, greyish
warts; up to 50 banded, greenish tentacles
in 6 circles. Under boulders, in crevices and
in rock-pools. Mid-shore to shallow sublittoral. [3]

Snakelocks Anemone *Anemonia viridis*
ACTINIIDAE H to 10 cm, D to 6 cm. Column
grey, green or light brown, smooth with
weakly adhesive basal disc; up to 6 circles
of purple-tipped, long, sticky, non-retract-
able tentacles. On rocks and large weeds.
Mid-shore to sublittoral. [4]

Trumpet Anemone *Aiptasia mutabilis* var.
couchi AIPTASIIDAE
H to 6 cm, D to 4 cm. Column brown with
minute warts, base weakly adhesive, trumpet-shaped; disc white-lined, with retractile tentacles broad at the base. On rocks.
Lower shore to sublittoral. [5]

'Parasitic' Anemone *Calliactis parasitica*
HORMATHIIDAE H to 10 cm, D to 4 cm.
Column spotted, buff or brown, stiff with
highly adhesive basal disc and about 300
translucent tentacles. Almost always on

gastropod mollusc shell occupied by a
hermit crab. Sublittoral. [6]

Mantle Anemone *Adamsia carcinopados*
HORMATHIIDAE D to about 5 cm. Column
and base wrapped around gastropod shell
occupied by a hermit crab; creamy fawn or
yellowish with magenta or purple spots;
older specimens may replace the shell
entirely, mouth often on underside; about
500 white tentacles. Anemone ejects purple
threads through the body wall when
disturbed. On sandy and muddy substrates.
Sublittoral. [7]

Plumose Anemone *Metridium senile*
METRIDIIDAE H to 10 cm, D to 5 cm.
Column white, fawn, orange, pink or
brown, smooth and slimy, topped by a
conspicuous collar under the broad lobed
oral disc. Tentacles numerous, translucent,
feathery. On solid objects, often under
overhangs. Lowest shore to sublittoral. [8]

Daisy Anemone *Cereus pedunculatus*
SAGARTIIDAE H to 10 cm, D to 4 cm.
Trumpet-shaped column pale grey or
orange with scattered warts, basal disc
highly adhesive; often more than 700 short,
brown-patterned tentacles. In crevices and
sheltered rock-pools, but often attached to
solid objects buried in soft mud; may be
very numerous. Lower shore to sublittoral. [9]

cup coral *Ballanophyllia italica*
EUPSAMMIDAE H to 2.5 cm. Solitary, but
many may be clustered together; skeleton
dirty white, pyramidal, oval at the top;
polyps iridescent, colourless or tinged with
yellow-brown. On rocks. Sublittoral. [10]
cup coral *Caryophyllia clavus* is similar but
skeleton is more tulip shaped, smaller
(H to 1.5 cm) and has smooth septa; polyps
pink or brown.

cup coral *Lophelia pertusa*
OCULINIDAE H to 50 cm. Colonial; skeleton
yellowish-white, irregularly branched with
scattered cups from which the pink polyps
arise. On rocky surfaces. Sublittoral, often
in deep water. Adriatic only. [11]

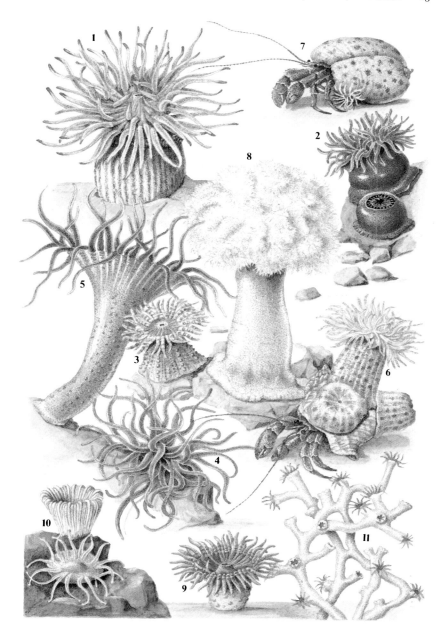

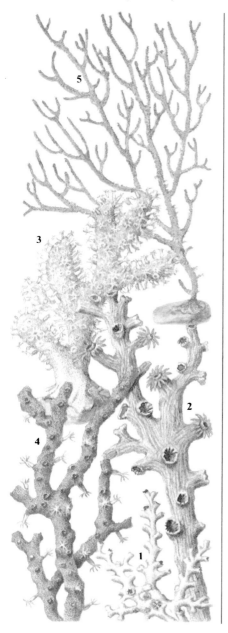

stone coral *Madrepora oculata*
OCULINIDAE H to 40 cm. Colonial; skeleton white, irregularly branched, polyp-cups in zig-zag arrangement, polyps white and orange. On hard surfaces, sometimes forms massive platforms. In deep water (200–1000 m). [1]

Yellow Coral *Dendrophyllia ramea*
OCULINIDAE H to 80 cm. Colonial; skeleton dirty white, irregularly branched, ribbed, often resembling a piece of driftwood; polyps yellow. On hard surfaces. Sublittoral. [2]

Dead Man's Fingers *Alcyonium palmatum*
ALCYONIDAE H to 50 cm. Tough, branching colonies; white, pink, orange, red or brown skeleton composed of rubbery or horny tissue and chalky spicules; huge numbers of small translucent white polyps. On hard surfaces, but occasionally free-standing on firm muddy bottoms. Lowest shore to sublittoral. [3]

Precious Coral *Corallium rubrum*
CORALLIDAE H to 50 cm. Colonial: brick-red, white, pink, brown or black skeleton, much-branched, irregular, ribbed; polyp-cups small, numerous; polyps white. Coral used for jewellery is the polished skeleton. On solid surfaces in shady conditions, often in submarine caves. In deep water (50–200 m). [4]

sea-fan *Eunicella cavolini*
PLEXAURIDAE H to 30 cm. Colonial; red or yellow skeleton irregularly branched like a fan, outer layer soft, inner layer horny; polyp-cups small, numerous, on raised swellings, polyps pale pink. On rocks. Sublittoral. [5]
sea-fan *Eunicella verrucosa* is similar, but skeleton is deep pink or brick-red.

sea-fan *Veretillum cynomorium*
VERETILLIDAE L to 30 cm or more. Body soft, tubular, lower portion modified into a foot for anchorage; polyps protrude directly from body and may be 2 cm long. Pale

pink or flesh-coloured. Anchored in mud or muddy sand. Sublittoral. [6]

Grey Sea-pen *Pteroeides griseum*
PTEROEIDIDAE L to 30 cm. Body soft but firm, pink with greyish lateral branches strengthened with iridescent spines and bearing the polyps; lower part modified into a muscular foot for anchorage. In mud and muddy sand. Sublittoral. [7]

sea-fan *Virgularia mirabilis*
VIRGULARIIDAE L to 50 cm. Body white, pink or flesh-coloured, extremely slender, stiff, with short, paired lateral branches; polyps short; lower part modified for anchorage. In mud or muddy sand. Sublittoral. [8]

COMB JELLIES (Ctenophora)

Animals which superficially resemble jellyfish, but lack stinging cells (cnidoctyes) and swim by means of conspicuous bands of cilia. Some species have trailing tentacles for catching prey.

Sea Gooseberry *Pleurobrachia pileus*
PLEUROBRACHIDAE L to 3 cm. Oval to globular; transparent with 8 rows of ciliary comb-plates; one pair of long, fringed tentacles; pinkish gut; faintly iridescent. Free-swimming in open water, occasionally numerous in coastal water and may be trapped in rock-pools. [9]

Venus's Girdle *Cestus veneris*
CESTIDAE L to 1.5 m. Body transparent, colourless, strap- or belt-shaped; two ciliary bands along each long margin; tentacles reduced; phosphorescent at night. In open water. [10]

comb-jelly *Beroe cucumis*
BEROIDAE L to 10 cm. Tulip-shaped somewhat compressed, transparent, pinkish; wide mouth and large internal cavity; eight conspicuous rows of comb-plates; no tentacles; internal canals visible as veins through body-wall. In open water, sometimes trapped in rock-pools. [11]

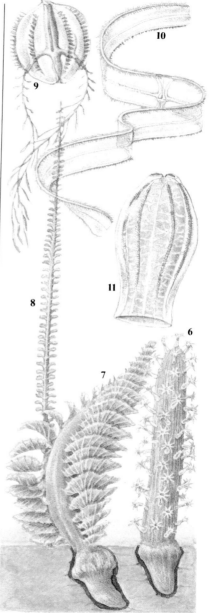

FLATWORMS (Plathyhelminthes)
Flattened, leaf-shaped animals. Mouth opens on underside of body; no separate anus; eyes and sensory tentacles present. Glide through water by means of vast numbers of cilia.

flatworm *Thysanozoon brocchii*
PSEUDOCERIDAE L to 5 cm. Body noticeably thicker in central area than at margins, two stout tentacles; numerous fleshy dorsal papillae. Among seaweeds, mussel beds. Lower shore to sublittoral. [1]

RIBBON WORMS (Nemertini)
Worm-like, but not segmented, usually flattened; may be immensely long. Food captured by extensible blind tube which opens near the mouth and can be discharged rapidly.

ribbon worm *Lineus geniculatus*
LINEIDAE L to 40 cm. Body flattened, greenish-black with conspicuous lateral bands; head blunt and snakelike. Among stones, lower shore. [2]

ribbon worm *Cerebratulus fuscus*
LINEIDAE L to 10 cm. Body flattened, light yellow or fawn, tapering sharply towards both head and tail. 4 to 8 conspicuous eyes. Among weeds and stones. Lower shore to sublittoral. [3]

Pink Ribbon Worm *Amphiporus lactifloreus*
AMPHIPORIDAE L to 8 cm. Body flattened on ventral surface and rounded on dorsal; tail tapers sharply; head trowel-shaped. Among weeds and stones. Lower shore to sublittoral. [4]

POLYCHAETE WORMS (Polychaeta)
Worms with segmented bodies and a true body-cavity. Each body segment bears two flap-like paddles (parapodia) and bunches of bristles (setae) used for movement.

Sea-mouse *Aphrodita aculeata*
APHRODITIDAE L to 12 cm. Dorsal scales hidden beneath a grey or brown felt of long, tangled setae; parapodia hidden by mass of green and gold, iridescent setae. In soft muds. Sublittoral. [5]

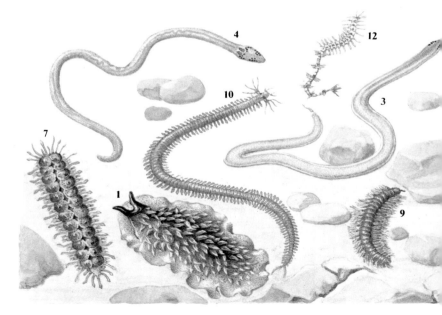

Sea-mouse *Hermonia hystrix*
APHRODITIDAE L to 7 cm. Body elongated, oval; dorsal surface concealed by large, overlapping brown scales; parapodia have long filaments (cirri), setae numerous, long, pale yellow or golden and shimmering; head concealed. In mud, sand and shell-debris. Sublittoral. [6]

scale-worm *Lepidonotus clava*
POLYNOIDAE L to 3 cm. Body brown, flattened; dorsal surface almost hidden beneath 12 pairs of non-overlapping scales; head concealed. Under stones. Mid-shore to sublittoral. [7]

scale-worm *Sthenelais boa*
SIGALIONIDAE L to 30 cm. Dorsal surface covered by overlapping scales. Colour metallic, variable. Under stones, among weeds, in muddy places. Lower shore to sublittoral. [8]

Note: Many species of scale worm may be found on the shore. They are difficult to identify without specialist knowledge.

fire-worm *Euphrosine foliosa*
AMPHINOMIDAE L to 3 cm. Body oval; parapodia elongated; each bearing gills. Under stones. Lowest shore to sublittoral. [9]

Green Leaf Worm *Eulalia viridis*
PHYLLODOCIDAE L to 15 cm. Body rounded; parapodia with trowel-shaped paddles; five antennae. Among encrusting weeds on stones. Mid-shore to sublittoral. [10]

planktonic bristle-worm *Alciopa cantraini*
ALCIOPIDAE L to 11 cm. Body transparent, tapering at hind end, anterior blunt with two very large red eyes. Free-swimming in open water. [11]

bristle-worm *Myrianida pinnigera*
SYLLIDAE L to 4 cm (or longer). Body flattened, pure white with bright orange or yellow patches; chain of reproductive structures at rear; parapodia with flattened, spatulate cirri. Among fibrous seaweeds; in holdfasts. Lower shore to sublittoral. [12]

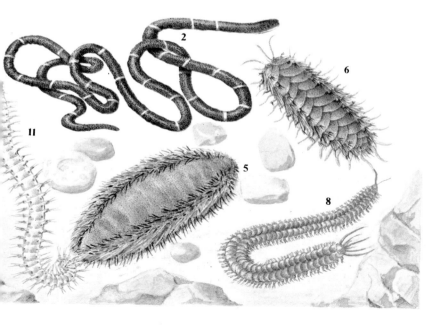

bristle-worm *Glycera convoluta*
GLYCERIDAE L to 10 cm. Body earthworm-like, conspicuously ringed, flesh-coloured; head a conical snout bearing 4 tiny tentacles; pharynx enormous, pear-shaped, armed with four sickle-shaped, black jaws. Burrowing in sand and gravel. Lower shore to sublittoral. [1]

Ragworm *Nereis pelagica*
NEREIDAE L to 20 cm. Body muscular; grey or brown, coppery; parapodia, head appendages and dorsal blood vessel distinct. Among encrustations on boulders, sometimes within a flimsy, membranous tube. Lower shore to sublittoral. [2]

Catworm *Nephtys hombergi*
NEPHTYIDAE L to 20 cm. Body rectangular in cross-section, opalescent; parapodia with closely packed setae; head small, eyes microscopic; one slender filament on tail. In sand. Lower shore to sublittoral. [3]

bristle-worm *Eunice harassii*
EUNICIDAE L to 25 cm. Body rounded, thick; purplish, with white patches on each segment; a pair of comb-like, bright red gills on each segment (except first four); two slender tail filaments. Under stones and in crevices. Lower shore to sublittoral, often in eel grass beds. [4]

tube-worm *Hyalinoecia tubicola*
ONUPHIDAE L to 12 cm. Slender, iridescent, pale pink or yellow; 5 conspicuous tentacles, 3 very long; lives within a horny, straw-coloured tube like a quill. On sandy and gravelly bottoms. Sublittoral. [5]

boring worm *Polydora ciliata*
SPIONIDAE L to 3 cm. Body rounded, slender, yellowish-brown; 5th segment larger with setae; anus surrounded by collar; head blunt with two tentacle-like palps. In U-shaped galleries bored into limestone and shells. Lower shore to sublittoral. [6]

Paddle Worm *Chaetopterus variopedatus*
CHAETOPTERIDAE L to 25 cm. Body off-white or yellow. First 9 segments have triangular parapodia; segment 10 has large, wing-like parapodia; segment 11 a cup-like structure; segments 12 to 14 are modified into semicircular paddles; head flat with long palps. In a membranous U-shaped tube (L to 75 cm) in sand. Lowest shore to sublittoral. [7]

bristle-worm *Ophelia bicornis*
OPHELIIDAE L to 7 cm. Body iridescent, pink-purple, in two parts; anterior segments inflated, rounded; posterior region narrower, deeply grooved ventrally and bearing slender gills; head small, pointed. ♂ white ♀ green at sexual maturity. In well-drained sand. Lower shore. [8]

tube-worm *Flabelligera affinis*
FLABELLIGERIDAE L to 6 cm. Body green, stout, tapering, surrounded by thick, transparent, gelatinous coat; head in cage of very long setae; palps yellow or orange: red stomach visible through body wall. Under stones or among algae. Lower shore to sublittoral. [9]

tube-worm *Lagis koreni*
PECTINARIIDAE L to 5 cm. Body pink, plump, gradually tapering; 2 pairs feathery red gills anteriorly; tail short; knobbed papillae and 2 fans of large, dagger-like setae on head. Tube conical, gently curved, of sand-grains. In sand, lowest shore to sublittoral. [10]

fan-worm *Sabellaria alveolata*
SABELLARIIDAE L to 4 cm. Pinkish-brown, almost rectangular, with conspicuous parapodia, finger-like gills and setae; tail tubular, hooked, so anus points forward; head flattened, crowned with trowel-like setae; tube of cemented sand-grains; tubes often aggregated into reefs. Attached to rocks. Lower shore. [11]

tube-worm *Amphitrite gracilis*
TEREBELLIDAE L to 12 cm. Body plump, pink or yellow-grey; anterior 17–19 segments with distinct setae; numerous sinuous tentacles; tube, when present, a flimsy mucus-lined burrow in sand or mud. Lower shore to sublittoral. [12]

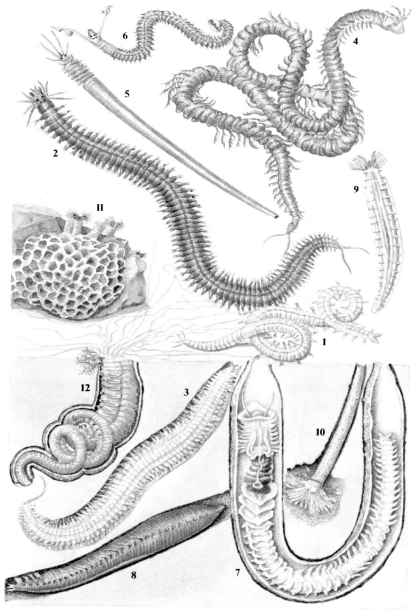

Sand Mason *Lanice conchilega*
TEREBELLIDAE L to 30 cm. Anterior swollen, remainder of body slender; numerous sinuous, pale pink tentacles; tube of sand, gravel and shell-debris, the top bearing a tuft of sandy filaments. In sand. Lower shore to sublittoral. [1]

peacock worm *Sabella penicillus*
SABELLIDAE L to 25 cm. Body slightly flattened; 2 fans of up to 45 long tentacles on head; tube of mud-reinforced mucus. In muddy sand, from which tube protrudes up to 15 cm. Lowest shore to sublittoral. [2]
peacock worm *Branchiomma lucullana* is similar, but much smaller (L to 3 cm), with paired, finger like projections on the tentacles. Tubes attached to seaweeds.

peacock worm *Spirographis spallanzanii*
SABELLIDAE L to 30 cm (or more). Similar to *Sabella*, but with unequal fans of brown- or purple-banded tentacles – one tiny, the other large with numerous tentacles and coiled. In muddy sand, from which the tube protrudes. Sublittoral. [3]

peacock worm *Potamilla reniformis*
SABELLIDAE L to 10 cm. Body slender, flattened, orange or brick-red; distinct setae on grey-green anterior segments; 2 fans of feathery, brown or purple-banded tentacles, some with up to 8 eyespots; tube horny, encrusted with sand. In crevices. Lower shore to sublittoral. [4]

Myzostomum cirriferum MYZOSTOMIDAE
D to 5 mm. Yellow or pale brown, parasitic on Mediterranean feather-star, *Antedon mediterranea*; flattened, circular, on under surface are 5 conical parapodia with few setae, and 4 suckers. Lowest shore to sublittoral. [5]

fanworm *Serpula vermicularis*
SERPULIDAE L to 7 cm. Body orange, pink and green; anterior segments covered by thin membrane forming a funnel-like 'collar'; two fans of white, yellow and orange-banded feathery tentacles, one cone-shaped, tipped by a circle of small projections; tube calcareous, thick-walled, ridged. On stones. Sublittoral. [6]

fanworm *Pomatoceros triqueter*
SERPULIDAE L to 3 cm. As *Serpula vermicularis*, but with one tentacle massive, winged, club-shaped, often with two or more terminal projections. [7]

fanworm *Janua pagenstecheri*
SPIRORBIDAE D to 3 mm (tube). Tiny head tentacles; one tentacle modified for incubating embryos; tube ridged, coiled anticlockwise. On stones and shells. Mid-shore to lower shore. [8]

LEECHES (Hirudinea)
Segmented worms with large anterior and posterior suckers.

fish leech *Pontobdella muricata*
PISCICOLIDAE L to 10 cm. Body warty, brownish-grey. Parasitic on rays and skates, usually attached to the gills. [9]

ECHIURID WORMS (Echiurida)
Superficially worm-like animals with a muscular proboscis, and ventral mouth. Male tiny and parasitic upon female.

echiurid worm *Thalassema gigas*
ECHIURINEA L to 40 cm. Body sac-like, slimy; mouth has two fang-like bristles. Among sediments under boulders and in crevices. Sublittoral. [10]

echiurid worm *Bonellia viridis*
ECHIURINEA L to 15 cm. Body oval, slimy, bright green; proboscis very long (up to 1.5 m), bifurcated into two large flaps. In rock crevices. Sublittoral. [11]

SIPUNCULID WORMS (Sipuncula)
Worm-like, sausage-shaped animals with mouth on a retractile proboscis.

sipunculid worm *Sipunculus nudus*
SIPUNCULIDAE L to 35 cm. Trunk brownish-grey, proboscis with much-pleated lobes. In sand. Sublittoral. [12]

sipunculid worm *Golfingia elongata*
GOLFINGIIDAE L to 15 cm. Trunk smooth, straw-coloured; circle of paired tentacles around mouth. In muddy sand and gravel from lowest shore to sublittoral. [13]

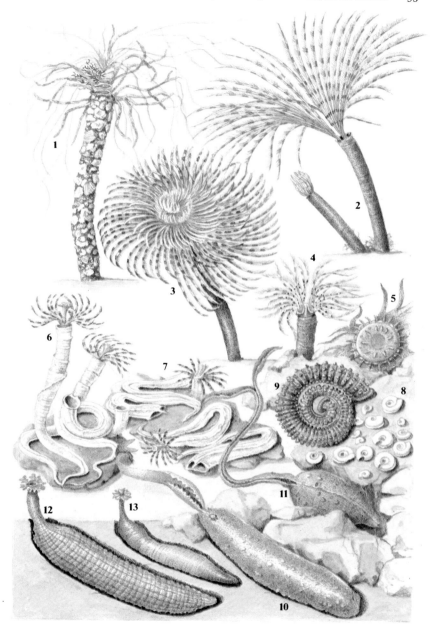

SNAILS, SLUGS AND BIVALVES
(Mollusca)
Invertebrates with well-developed heads and sensory structures; often with shells; free-moving species have a strap-like, abrasive organ – the radula – with which they 'graze' algae or rasp the tissues of their prey. Sessile molluscs are often filter-feeders, collecting food from suspension in the surrounding water.

Coat-of-mail Shell *Lepidopleurus cajetanus*
LEPIDOPLEURIDAE L to 3 cm. A typical chiton with shell of 8 narrow, overlapping, transverse plates; 1 and 8 with conspicuous concentric rings, others with curved ridges on lateral margins. Light brown. On rocks and boulders, under overhanging seaweeds. Middle shore to sublittoral. [1]
Coat-of-mail Shell *Acanthochitona communis* ACANTHOCHITONIDAE is similar, but larger (L to 5 cm); with bristle tufts on lateral plate margins.

Common Ormer *Haliotis lamellosa*
HALIOTIDAE L to 7 cm. Shell oval, creased, flattened asymmetrical spiral, with conspicuous series of lateral holes; often encrusted with sessile organisms. Brown, red and green. On rocks and boulders. Lowest shore to sublittoral. [2]
Green Ormer *Haliotis tuberculata* is similar, but clearly sculptured.

slit limpet *Emarginula elongata*
FISSURELLIDAE L to 1 cm. Shell conical, ribbed, with hooked apex and anterior slit. Yellowish-white. On rocks and stones. Lower shore. [3]

keyhole limpet *Diodora italica*
FISSURELLIDAE L to 4.5 cm. Shell a flattened cone, with elongated hole in apex. Light grey-fawn, with greyish-violet ribs and indistinct ridges. On rocks. Lowest shore to sublittoral. [4]

Mediterranean Limpet *Patella coerulea*
PATELLIDAE L to 4.5 cm. Shell conical, ridged with wavy margin. Brown, red or violet, tinged green; inside striped, with blue nacreous centre. On rocks. Middle to lower shore. [5]

Large Topshell *Gibbula magus*
TROCHIDAE L to 2.5 cm; W to 3 cm. Shell massive, spired, with well-defined whorls, and tubercles; slight keel on lower side. Greyish-white with reddish spots and bands, but upper part almost invariably worn down to nacre. On sand and gravel. Lowest shore to sublittoral. [6]
topshell *Gibbula divaricata* is similar, but less broad with more distinct whorls. Greyish-green with red spots.

Toothed Winkle *Monodonta turbinata*
TROCHIDAE H to 2.5 cm; W to 2.5 cm. Shell conical. body whorl large, with slight tooth on inside at mouth. Base lustrous white, remainder yellowish-white with parallel reddish transverse stripes; apex usually worn to nacre. On rocks and boulders. Lower shore. [7]

topshell *Clanculus cruciatus*
TROCHIDAE H to 1 cm; W to 1 cm. Shell compact, whorled, with spiralling rows of small knobs; one tooth at mouth. Reddish-brown, banded white and brown. On rocks, among algae. Lower shore. [8]

topshell *Cantharidus exasperatus*
TROCHIDAE H to 1 cm; W to 0.6 cm. Shell steeply conical; conspicuous keel at base of each whorl; small umbilicus. Body whorl reddish, remainder greyish-white and yellowish with reddish-brown markings. On rocks, among algae. Lower shore. [9]

Painted Topshell *Calliostoma zizyphinum*
TROCHIDAE H to 3 cm. Shell straight-sided, steeply conical, resembles a spinning top. Mottled greyish-green with red, brown, sometimes purple markings. Under boulders. Lower shore to sublittoral. [10]
Painted Topshell *Calliostoma conulus* is similar, but narrower, with blunt keel along upper margin of each whorl.

Rough Star Shell *Astraea rugosa*
TURBINIDAE H to 5 cm; W to 5 cm. Shell massive, thick, conspicuously ridged; operculum closing shell aperture massive, orange-pink, with a deeply indented spiral. Reddish-brown. On weed-covered rocks. Lowest shore to sublittoral. [11]

Pheasant Shell *Tricolia pullus*
TURBINIDAE H to 0.7 cm. Shell conical, spired; operculum closing shell aperture massive, calcareous, glossy. Off-white with reddish-brown smudges and stripes. Among encrusting organisms on rocks. Lower shore to sublittoral. [1]
Pheasant Shell *Tricolia speciosa* is similar, but aperture longer, giving shell elongated appearance. Rose-coloured patches and 3 tinted bands on body-whorl.

Small Periwinkle *Littorina neritoides*
LITTORINIDAE H to 0.5–1 cm. Shell conical, smooth, with sharply pointed spire; body whorl large. Dark brown, with glossy dark bluish sheen. In rock crevices. Extreme upper to middle shore. [2]

marine snail *Alvania cimex*
RISSOIDAE H to 0.6 cm. Shell a thick-walled spire, with rounded sides and flared aperture; whorls ornamented with 4 rows of rounded knobs. Dark brown, opening white. On weed-covered rocks. Lower shore to sublittoral. [3]

marine snail *Rissoa variabilis*
RISSOIDAE H to 0.8 cm. Shell tall, sharply spired; aperture has smooth margin; whorls ornamented with shallow longitudinal ridges. Milky-white with fine brown spiral bands and speckling. In clumps of fine and filamentous algae. Lower shore to sublittoral. [4]
marine snail *Rissoa ventricosa* is similar, but has straighter sides with less prominently inflated whorls and fainter longitudinal ridges. Yellowish-brown with violet at tip of spire and around aperture.

tower shell *Turritella communis*
TURRITELLIDAE H to 5 cm. Shell elongated, narrow, steeply tapering with many spirally ridged whorls. Reddish-brown. On muddy substrates. Sublittoral. [5]
tower shell *Turritella triplicata* is similar, but each whorl ornamented with a triple, spiralling row of small knobs.

needle shell *Triphora perversa*
TRIPHORIDAE H to 0.3 cm. Shell slender, elongated; whorls numerous, ornamented with spiralling rows of small knobs; shell coils in a left-handed spiral (sinistral) – the majority of gastropod shells coil to the right. Reddish-brown. In rock crevices and among encrusting algae. Lower shore to sublittoral. [6]

Giant Worm Shell *Vermetus gigas*
VERMETIDAE L to 20 cm (difficult to measure due to loose coiling). Shell thin-walled, irregularly coiled, cemented to substratum, so resembling a worm tube. Light grey or dirty white. On a variety of substrates. Lower shore to sublittoral. [7]
worm shell *Vermetus triqueter* is similar, but smaller, often more compactly coiled; shell brittle. White and usually glossy.

needle shell *Bittium reticulatum*
CERITHIIDAE H to 1 cm. Shell steeply and narrowly conical with many sculptured whorls, each demarcated by a groove. Shades of brown. Under boulders. Lower shore to sublittoral. [8]

Common Cerith *Cerithium vulgatum*
CERITHIIDAE H to 5 cm. Shell steeply tapering with many whorls ornamented with knobs and conical projections; aperture flared with pleated margin. Brown and reddish-brown, often marked with white or fawn. In a variety of habitats. Lower shore to sublittoral (chiefly sublittoral). [9]
Rough Cerith *Cerithium rupestre* is similar but smaller (L to 2.5 cm) with more bulging sides, and larger knobs on whorls.

Common Wentletrap *Clathrus clathrus*
SCALIDAE H to 4 cm. Shell steeply conical with round, distinct whorls and projecting transverse ribs. Cream or pale fawn, sometimes with faint brown markings. On sand and solid substrates. Sublittoral but comes onshore in spring. [10]

Purple Sea-snail *Ianthina janthina*
IANTHINIDAE H to 3 cm. Shell fragile, spired, with finely grooved whorls; body whorl large, inflated. Brilliant violet or purple. Pelagic, floating attached to raft of mucus-coated air bubbles. [11]

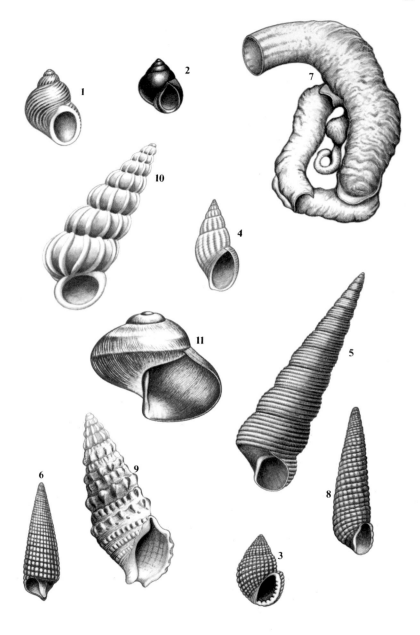

Bonnet Limpet, Hungarian Cap Shell
Capulus ungaricus CAPULIDAE
L to 4 cm. Shell moderately tall, bonnet-shaped with slight evidence of spiralling; apex sharply twisted. Fawn or off-white; outer horny layer green, frilled and layered. On bivalves. Sublittoral – occasionally on rocks of lowest shore. [1]

Chinaman's Hat *Calpytraea chinensis*
CALYPTRAEIDAE D to 2.5 cm. Resembles a shallowly conical limpet with an almost circular margin; apex may show slight spiralling; inside shell is a shelf with a C-shaped margin. White. On stones and shells. Lowest shore to sublittoral. [2]

Slipper Limpet *Crepidula fornicata*
CALYPTRAEIDAE L to 5 cm. Shell oval in outline, apex sharply curved; about half the shell aperture occupied by glossy white shelf with slightly incurved margin. Pink with shades of darker pink or brown. Normally occurs in vertical chains, with females at the base and males uppermost. Males change sex as they age. Lowest shore to sublittoral. [3]

Pelican's Foot Shell *Aporrhais pespelicani*
APORRHAIDAE H to 4 cm. Shell conical with sculptured whorls; margins of aperture expanded, flared and divided; resembles a bird's webbed foot. Yellowish-grey, interior lustrous cream. On sandy mud and gravel. Sublittoral. [4]

sea snail *Carinaria mediterranea*
CARINARIIDAE L to 30 cm. Body elongated, vaguely slug-like with a projecting snout; foot modified into a flattened fin; shell flimsy, reduced to act as gill cover; animal swims upside down. Transparent, colourless or faintly milky-white. Free-swimming. In open water. [5]

sea snail *Pterotrachea coronata*
PTEROTRACHAEIDAE L to 10 cm. Elongated and superficially slug-like; foot modified into flattened fin as in *Carinaria mediterranea*; shell entirely absent. Transparent, colourless. Free-swimming. In open water. [6]

Moon Shell *Polynices guillemini*
NATICIDAE H to 2 cm. Shell rounded; body whorl inflated; spire relatively small; aperture large, flared; umbilicus prominent. Brown with red markings, a reddish-flecked white band along suture line between whorls. On sandy bottoms. Sublittoral. [7]

Necklace Shell *Natica alderi*
NATICIDAE H to 1.5 cm. Shell rounded with short spire; body whorl large. Cream or fawn with distinctive pattern of red-brown spots. In surface layers of sand. Lower shore to sublittoral. [8]
Necklace Shell *Natica millepunctata* is similar, but larger (H to 3.5 cm) and cream with reddish-brown dots.
Necklace Shell *Natica hebraea* is similar, but larger (H to 4.5 cm), with much-enlarged brownish-violet aperture. White or light grey, upper surfaces of whorls yellowish-orange with reddish flecks, shell interior glossy white, umbilicus red. On muddy substrates. Sublittoral.

European Cowrie *Trivia monacha*
ERATOIDAE L to 1.25 cm. A typical cowrie; body whorl envelops all other whorls and is patterned with minute ridges; aperture a longitudinal slit on underneath. Purple-white, with 3 conspicuous black spots, pink near the aperture. Under stones, especially among compound sea-squirts. Lower shore to sublittoral. [9]

Pear Cowrie *Erronea pirum*
CYPRAEIDAE L to 5 cm. Outer surface like porcelain; margins of aperture slightly toothed. Reddish-brown above with darker patterning, light red below. On rocks and boulders, especially when weed-covered. Sublittoral. [10]

Lurid Cowrie *Cypraea lurida*
CYPRAEIDAE L to 4.5 cm. A typical cowrie; outer surface like porcelain; margins of aperture slightly toothed. Brownish-fawn with 3 transverse brown bands and two dark brown spots at each end, white underneath. On solid substrates. Sublittoral. [11]

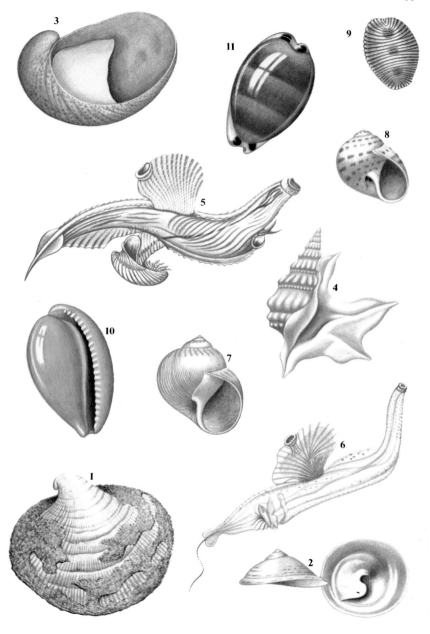

Knobbed Helmet Shell *Cassidaria*
echinophora CASSIDAE
H to 11 cm. Shell massive with large body
whorl and steeply tapering spire; whorls
ornamented with rows of large tubercles;
margins of shell aperture flared and
reflexed. Yellowish-fawn, skirt of aperture
white. On sandy bottoms and eel-grass
'meadows'. Sublittoral. [1]

Giant Tun Shell *Dolium galea*
DOLIIDAE H to 20 cm. A large, rounded
shell, inflated in appearance; upper margin
of each whorl slightly overlaps the next;
whorls prominently sculptured with concentric ribs. Yellowish-brown, inside of
aperture more pale. On sandy substrates.
Sublittoral. Preys on sea-urchins, sea-
cucumbers and bivalves; produces saliva
containing strong concentration of sul-
phuric acid, which dissolves calcareous
exoskeleton of prey. [2]

Dye Murex *Bolinus brandaris*
MURICIDAE H to 9 cm. Body whorl large,
inflated, with very long siphonal canal;
outer surface ornamented with relatively
long spines and spiral ridges. Fawn or light
brownish-grey, interior of aperture orange-
brown. This species was the source of
'imperial purple' dye. On muddy and stony
substrates. Sublittoral. [3]

sea snail *Trophon muricatus*
MURICIDAE H to 1.5 cm. Shell with clearly
defined whorls, giving a distinctly spiralled
effect; siphonal canal at least half length of
shell; external sculpture of wavy ridges
more-or-less confined to the lower sides of
the whorls, whitish grey with tints of
yellow and pink. On hard substrates.
Sublittoral. [4]

Sting Winkle, Oyster Drill *Ocenebra*
erinacea MURICIDAE
H to 6 cm. Shell heavily sculptured with
prominent ribs and stout spiral ridges;
body whorl large; margin of shell aperture
has highly ornamented, flared 'skirt';
siphonal canal short, open in juveniles,
closed in adults. Shades of fawn and
yellow. On rocks. Lower shore to sublittoral. A pest of oyster beds. [5]

Spindle Shell *Fusus rostratus*
FASCIOLARIIDAE H to 4 cm. Shell with clearly
defined whorls, steeply tapered with tall
spire; siphonal canal nearly as long as
shell; broad longitudinal ridges and sharp,
fine spiralling ridges. Reddish-brown. On
sand and mud. Sublittoral. [6]

Mitre Shell *Mitra ebenus*
MITRIDAE H to 2 cm. Shell with elongated
whorl and almost slit-like aperture; spire
of several whorls, the whole effect compact;
central pillar of shell (columella) has 2 or 3
conspicuous ridges. Very dark brown and
glossy, with whitish band round whorls.
On rocks. Lowest shore to sublittoral. [7]

Netted Dog Whelk *Nassarius reticulatus*
NASSIDAE H to 2.5 cm. Shell conical, whorls
slightly flat-sided; sculpture of characteristic criss-crossing ridges. Greyish-
brown. Under stones, often in sand. Lower
shore to sublittoral. [8]

Thick-lipped Dog Whelk *Nassarius*
incrassatus NASSIDAE
H to 1 cm. Shell conical, whorls distinct
with deep sutures between them; strong
sculpture of criss-crossing ridges. Light
brown with black smudge on siphonal
canal. Under stones. Lower shore to
sublittoral. [9]

Mediterranean Cone Shell *Conus*
mediterraneus CONIDAE
H to 5 cm. Body whorl dominant, elongated, tapering toward the base; shell
aperture an elongated slit; spire shallow,
broad-based. Shell patterned in brown,
yellow and green on white. Produces venom
which can cause considerable irritation if
injected into human skin. [10]

bubble shell *Scaphander lignarius*
SCAPHANDRIDAE L to 14 cm. A sea slug with
muscular body, demarcated into broad,
tongue-like central part and two narrower
flanking parts; shell about half body
length, rather simple in form with large
aperture tapering at one end. Soft parts
pinkish-fawn, shell yellowish-fawn patterned with brown. On sandy and muddy
substrates. Sublittoral. [11]

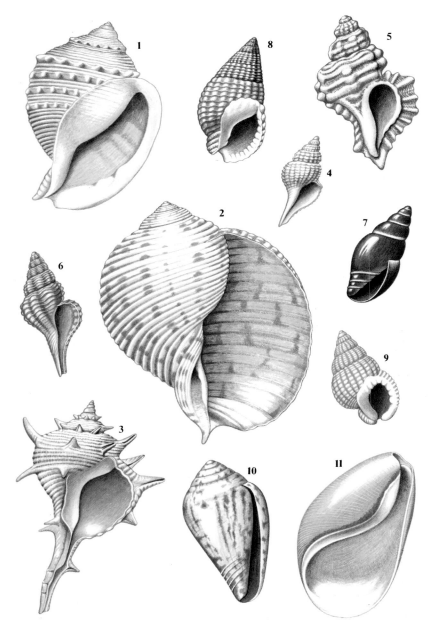

Sea Hare *Aplysia depilans*
APLYSIDAE L to 30 cm. Body elongated, flabby; 4 tentacles; shell internal, flanked by 2 muscular flaps. Greenish-brown, dappled with contrasting spots of white or pale yellow. Among weeds in rock pools. Lower shore to sublittoral. [1]
Sea Hare *Aplysia punctata* is similar, but smaller (L to 20 cm) and more slender; speckled green or brown.

sea slug *Elysia viridis*
ELYSIIDAE L to 4 cm. Body elongated, flattened with 2 wing-like flaps that may be carried upright or flat; 2 tentacles. Green or red (depending upon food-source, more commonly green), with tiny red, blue and green spots. On seaweeds. Middle shore to sublittoral. [2]

sea slug *Berthella aurantiaca*
PLEUROBRANCHIDAE L to 6 cm. Body plump; mantle overhangs foot except at rear; single, feather-like gill under mantle on right side; one pair of tentacles and broad head veil; shell internal. Golden yellow or orange-red. Under stones. Lower shore to sublittoral. [3]

sea slug *Polycera quadrilineata*
POLYCERIDAE L to 2 cm. Slug-like, shell absent; head bears 2 pleated tentacles and 4 yellow-tipped processes; ring of feathery gills, flanked by two yellow-tipped processes. Milky-white with longitudinal yellow stripes and flecks. On weeds. Lower shore to sublittoral. [4]

sea slug *Archidoris tuberculata*
DORIDIDAE L to 11 cm. Body humped, leathery, concealing foot; 2 pleated tentacles; ring of 7 to 9 feathery gills, and scattered globular tubercles on dorsal surface. Yellowish with brown or violet flecks. On a variety of substrates. Lower shore to sublittoral. [5]

sea slug *Tethys leporina*
TETHYIDAE L to 30 cm. Head very broad, almost semicircular, bordered in black or deep blue, with filamentous fringe and 2 fat tentacles; body humped; two rows of

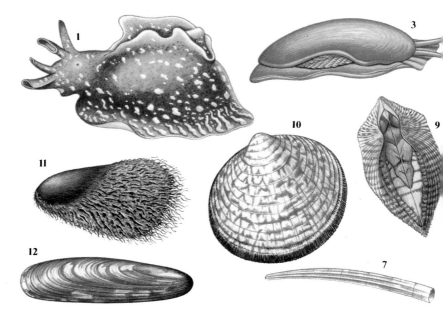

delicate gills at base of leaf-shaped red-splotched papillae. Milky-white. In a variety of habitats. In deep water, occasionally rising to surface and swimming freely. [6]

Tusk Shell *Dentalium vulgare*
DENTALIIDAE L to 6 cm. Shell tubular longitudinally ridged, tapering to rear, from broad end. Dirty white. Burrowing in sand. Lowest shore to sublittoral. [7]

Common Nut Shell *Nucula nucleus*
NUCULIDAE L to 1.25 cm. Shell broadly triangular, ridged, margins curved, finely toothed inside; umbo displaced from centre; small teeth on hinge. Green, yellow or brown. In muddy, sandy and gravelly substrates. Sublittoral. [8]

Noah's Ark Shell *Arca noae*
ARCIDAE L to 8 cm. Shell brown, elongated, boat-shaped, ribbed; umbones in anterior quarter, widely spaced; hinge long, straight with numerous small teeth. Attached to stones. Sublittoral. [9]

ark shell *Arca barbata* is similar but shell ribs interrupted by growth rings.

Dog Cockle *Glycymeris glycymeris*
GLYCYMERIDAE L to 6 cm. Shell almost circular, with crenulate margins and many hinge teeth. Light fawn with characteristic zig-zag brown markings, interior white. In muddy sand and gravel. Lower shore to sublittoral. [10]

Bearded Horse Mussel *Modiolus barbatus*
MYTILIDAE L to 6 cm. Shell broadly 'mussel-shaped' but more rounded and bulky; growth lines coarse; covered with rough hairy layer (periostracum). Brownish-purple. Attached to rocks and algal hold-fasts. Lower shore to sublittoral. [11]

Date Mussel *Lithophaga lithophaga*
MYTILIDAE L to 7 cm. Shell elongated, long edges slightly curved, sculptured with fine concentric lines; like a date stone or fat, blunt cigar. Rich yellowish-brown. Bores into rocks, cliff-faces and coralline structures. In shallow water. [12]

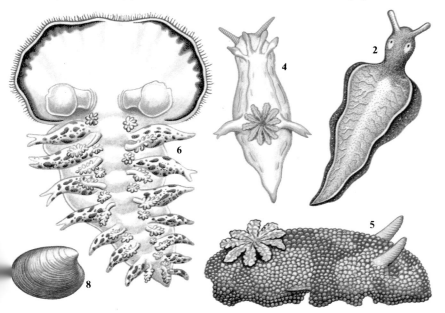

Mediterranean Mussel *Mytilus galloprovincialis*
L to 15 cm (larger when cultured). Typical mussel shape, broad in relation to length; umbo pointed and hooked. Dark blue-brown, mantle margin dark. Attached to solid supports. In shallow water. Extensively cultured. [1]
Common Mussel *Mytilus edulis* is similar but narrower in relation to length; umbo straight; mantle margin yellowish-white.
NB: *Mytilus galloprovincialis* is sometimes regarded as a local race of *Mytilus edulis*.

Fan Mussel *Pinna nobilis*
PINNIDAE L to 45 cm. Shell fan-shaped, tapering toward rear; sculptured with tubercles and wavy ridges. Light brown and fawn, byssus threads golden. Buried in muddy sand, anchored by byssus. Sublittoral. [2]

Winged Oyster *Pteria hirundo*
PTERIIDAE L to 7.5 cm. Shell highly asymmetrical, brittle, lower margin wavy; broadly oyster-shaped, but with one short, round projection and another long, straight projection along the hinge margin. Greyish-fawn, interior nacreous; horny layer covering shell brown. Attached to stones, often in muddy habitats. Sublittoral. [3]

Queen Scallop *Chlamys opercularis*
PECTINIDAE L to 9 cm. Shell broadly fan-shaped, ridged; both valves curved; umbo flanked by ears, the anterior longer and more rounded than the posterior. Varies from white through yellow and brown to red, sometimes striped. On sand and gravel. Lowest shore to sublittoral. [4]

Fan Shell *Pecten jacobaeus*
PECTINIDAE L to 13 cm. Typical scallop shape, with broad square ribs; lower valve saucer-shaped, upper valve flat; umbo flanked by large ears. On sand and gravel. Sublittoral. [5]

Gaping File Shell *Lima hians*
LIMIDAE L to 4 cm. Shell narrow, irregular, asymmetrical with spiny ribs; ears reduced, unequal; thick fringe of orange-red non-retractile tentacles protrude between valves. Off-white or dirty fawn. Among rocks. Lower shore to sublittoral. [6]

Thorny Oyster *Spondylus gaederopus*
SPONDYLIDAE L to 10 cm. Shell oval; ears reduced; lower valve convex with widely spaced, broad spines; upper valve flatter, delicately ribbed, with longer, irregular, sharp spines. Warm brown or brownish-purple. Attached to rocks. Sublittoral. [7]

Saddle Oyster *Anomia ephippium*
ANOMIIDAE L to 6 cm. Shell round, but often distorted; upper valve slightly domed; lower valve much smaller with large aperture off-centre. Light fawn, interior nacreous. On rocks. Lower shore to sublittoral. [8]

Native Oyster, European Oyster *Ostrea edulis* OSTREIDAE
L to 10 cm. Shell circular, or irregular; lower valve saucer-shaped, usually cemented to substrate; upper valve flatter, crenulated. Dirty fawn, inside pearly. On solid substrates. Lowest shore to sublittoral. Extensively cultured. [9]

Portuguese Oyster *Crassostrea angulata*
OSTREIDAE W to 15 cm. Shell elongated, tapering, with layered sculpturing; lower valve trough-like, upper valve flatter, valves latch together at margin. Dirty greyish-white, interior pearly with dark muscle scar. On solid substrates. Sublittoral. Extensively cultured. [10]

Heart Cockle *Glossus humanus*
GLOSSIDAE L to 10 cm. Shell thick, massive, almost circular; resembles a stylized heart when seen from one end; umbones long, coiling away from midline; light brown. Horny tissue covering shell dark brown. In sand and mud. Sublittoral. [11]

Mediterranean Jewelbox *Chama gryphoides* CHAMIDAE
L to 4 cm. Shell almost circular, lower valve dish-like, cemented to substrate, upper valve domed; growth rings conspicuous, often frilled. White; interior violet. Attached to rocks. Sublittoral. [12]

Prickly Cockle *Acanthocardia echinata*
CARDIIDAE L to 7.5 cm. Shell broadly oval, solid, ribbed, spiny; margin crenulated. Off-white or fawn. In sand or mud. Sublittoral. [1]
Spiny Cockle *Acanthocardia aculeata* is similar, but ridges of radiating spines beset with separate, conical spines.

Common Cockle *Cerastoderma edule*
CARDIIDAE L to 5 cm. Shell broadly oval, solid, ribbed, with scale-like spines. Yellow, fawn or light brown. In sand. Middle shore to sublittoral. [2]
Lagoon Cockle *Cerastoderma lamarcki* is similar, but less oval as posterior part of shell drawn out; ridges of lower surface extend almost to umbo.

Venus Shell *Callista chione*
VENERIDAE L to 9 cm. Shell almost oval, thick, heavy; umbo displaced anteriorly. Fawn and light brown, interior white; horny layer covering shell chestnut-brown. In clean sand. Sublittoral. [3]

Smooth Artemis *Dosinia lupinus*
VENERIDAE D to 4 cm. Shell solid, almost circular, with concentric ridges; heart-shaped area (lunule) near umbones. Dirty white, fawn or pinkish-brown; horny layer pale yellow. In sand and sandy gravel. Lowest shore to sublittoral. [4]

Warty Venus *Venus verrucosa*
VENERIDAE D to 6 cm. Shell ridged, with warty spines posteriorly; heart-shaped lunule prominent. Dirty white, yellow or fawn, horny layer brown. In sand or gravel. Lower shore to sublittoral. [5]

Cross-cut Carpet Shell *Venerupis decussata* VENERIDAE
L to 7.5 cm. Shell solid, oval to rectangular, cross-hatched. Light fawn, brown or grey with rayed, blotched or zig-zagged brown patterns. In sand and mud. Lower shore to sublittoral. [6]

Rayed Trough Shell *Mactra corallina*
MACTRIDAE L to 5 cm. Shell broadly tri-

angular, brittle, with delicate concentric sculpture. Cream or pale fawn, streaked brown, purple near umbo, glossy. In sand. Lower shore to sublittoral. [7]

Banded Wedge Shell *Donax vittatus*
DONACIDAE L to 4 cm. Shell wedge-shaped, solid, finely grooved; margin crenulate, rough. Off-white, yellow, pale brown or violet, white or purple inside; horny layer brown or purple, glossy. In sand. Lower shore to sublittoral. [8]

Peppery Furrow Shell *Scrobicularia plana*
SCROBICULARIIDAE L to 6 cm. Shell thin but not fragile, broadly oval; finely ridged and grooved. Off-white, pale grey, light brown or yellow, often stained by substances in its habitat. In mud. Middle shore to sublittoral; chiefly in estuaries and salt-marshes. [9]

Thin Tellin *Tellina tenuis*
TELLINIDAE L to 2 cm. Broadly oval; thin, brittle, ventral margin twisted posteriorly. All shades of pink, rose, orange, yellow and grey. In sand. Lowest shore to sublittoral. [10]
tellin *Tellina balaustina* is similar, but less narrow. White or yellow, external rays pink.

Large Sunset Shell *Gari depressa*
GARIIDAE L to 6.25 cm. Shell oval; umbones central; valves gape posteriorly; growth lines obvious. Pink, interior white-purple; horny layer greenish-brown. In sand. Lowest shore to sublittoral. [11]

Common Otter Shell *Lutraria lutraria*
LUTRARIDAE L to 13 cm. Shell broadly oval, solid with fine concentric grooves. Off-white or yellowish-fawn; horny layer olive-brown. In muddy sand or gravel. Lower shore to sublittoral. [12]

'razor shell' *Pharus legumen*
SOLECURTIDAE L to 13 cm. Shell elongated, narrow, rounded at each end. Light fawn; horny layer greenish, glossy. In sand. Lower shore to sublittoral. [13]

Grooved Razor Shell *Solen marginatus*
SOLENIDAE L to 12.5 cm. Shell thin, elongated, with straight ends; deep vertical groove in each valve parallel to anterior margin. Fawn and yellow; horny layer light brown. In muddy sand. Lowest shore to sublittoral. [1]

Curved Razor Shell *Ensis ensis*
SOLENIDAE L to 13 cm. Shell elongated, curved, both ends shallowly rounded. Creamy fawn with reddish-brown blotches; horny layer olive-green, glossy. In sand. Lower shore to sublittoral. [2]
Pod Razor *Ensis siliqua* is similar, but shell almost rectangular, anterior and posterior margins straight with rounded corners.

Wrinkled Rock-borer *Hiatella arctica*
HIATELLIDAE L to 4 cm. Shell solid, irregular, broadly rectangular with posterior gape, often twisted; ridged. Off-white. Bores in soft rock or free under rocks, attached by byssus threads. Lower shore to sublittoral. [3]

Common Piddock *Pholas dactylus*
PHOLADIDAE L to 15 cm. Shell thin, brittle, elongated; posterior tapering, rounded, ridged; anterior triangular, spiny; antero-ventral gape; accessory shell plates present. White, interior glossy, shows traces of external sculpture. Bores into solid materials. Middle shore to sublittoral. [4]
White Piddock *Barnea candida* is similar, but smaller (L to 6.5 cm); posterior more rounded and anterior less acutely angled.

Shipworm *Teredo navalis*
TEREDINIDAE L to 1 cm (primary shell). Shell brittle, rounded, globular, irregular, notched and grooved; animal superficially worm-like, burrows into wood, secretes a hard, thick-walled, white tube. In wooden structures. Sublittoral. [5]

Common Cuttlefish *Sepia officinalis*
SEPIIDAE L to 40 cm. Body oval, broad, muscular; lateral fins along whole length of flanks; eyes conspicuous; 10 suckered tentacles, 2 long, ending in leaf-shaped pads; shell (cuttlebone) internal, leaf-shaped. Background creamy-white, can rapidly change colour to all shades from reddish-brown to purple-black. Free-swimming, occasionally near shore. [6]
Cuttlefish *Sepia elegans* is similar, but smaller (L to 8 cm), with 2 rows of suckers on narrow tentacles.

Little Cuttle *Sepiola rondeleti*
SEPIOLIDAE L to 5 cm. Body goblet-shaped; lateral fins rounded, set posteriorly, about half length of body; head bulbous; eyes conspicuous; 10 tentacles. Colour variable, capable of rapid change. In shallow water over sand; may burrow into sand. [7]

Long-finned Squid *Loligo vulgaris*
LOLIGINIDAE L to 50 cm. Body slender, tubular, narrowing posteriorly; lateral fins broad-based, almost triangular, about two-thirds body-length; head small; eyes large; 10 suckered tentacles, 2 long; shell internal, horny, pen-like. Colour variable, frequently pinkish-white patterned with pinkish-purple on dorsal surface, ventral surface pale. In open water. [8]

Sagittal Squid *Ommatostrephes sagittatus*
OMMATOSTREPHIDAE L to 60 cm. Body torpedo-shaped; lateral fins triangular, about one-third body length; 2 long non-retractile suckered tentacles. Colour as *Loligo vulgaris*. Free-swimming. [9]

Common Octopus *Octopus vulgaris*
OCTOPODIDAE L to 1 m. Body bag-like; 8 tentacles, each with 2 rows of suckers. Grey-brown or greenish-brown, can change to suit background. In caves, crevices. Sublittoral. [10]
Webbed Octopus *Eledone moschata* is similar, but only one row of suckers on tentacles; adjacent tentacles webbed.

Paper Nautilus *Argonauta argo*
ARGONAUTIDAE L to 20 cm (♀), 1 cm (♂). Similar to *Octopus vulgaris*, but two tentacles in ♀ paddle-shaped, carry fragile, coiled, white shell-like brood chamber; one tentacle in ♂ modified for transference of spermatophore (sperm packet). Colour variable, silvery white, green, violet, grey, red or blue. On sandy bottoms or free-swimming in open water. [11]

CRABS, LOBSTERS AND THEIR ALLIES (Crustacea)

Animals with a hard exoskeleton, typically arranged as a box-like carapace over head and thorax (cephalothorax) and jointed plates over the abdomen; limbs jointed. Mainly aquatic.

stalked barnacle *Scalpellum scalpellum*
SCALPELLIDAE L to 2 cm (shell). Body on a short, muscular, scaly, brownish stalk; enclosed in 14 small, chalky, greyish-white plates. Attached to solid objects, such as hydroids, bryozoans, shells. Usually sublittoral. [1]

Goose Barnacle *Lepas anatifera*
LEPADIDAE L to 5 cm (shell). Body covered by 5 delicate white plates and supported on a tubular, muscular, stalk; animal dark greyish-brown or black. Pelagic, attached to floating objects. [2]

Star Barnacle *Chthamalus stellatus*
CHTHAMALIDAE D to 1.5 cm. Shell conical, of 6 overlapping plates; sculpture of conspicuous grooves; central aperture kite-shaped, lateral sutures of central plates straight. Dirty-white or fawn. On rocks and other solid objects, upper to lower shore. [3]

barnacle *Acasta spongites*
BALANIDAE D to 1.2 cm. Shell of 6 spiny plates arranged like the petals of a tulip; base of barnacle convex. Pale fawn, tinged pink or purple. Always in sponges. Lowest shore to sublittoral. [4]

barnacle *Boscia anglicum*
BALANIDAE D to 1.0 cm. Shell of 6 plates arranged in a steep-sided cone. Pinkish-fawn. Always attached to the cup-coral *Caryophyllia*. Sublittoral. [5]

Mantis Shrimp *Squilla mantis*
STOMATOPODA L to 25 cm. Carapace roughly shield-like; abdomen wider toward the rear; two large black eye spots on tailplate (telson); last joint of second walking legs very spiny and hinged to form a crusher; eyes large; antennae moderately long, divided at the tips, off-white to sand colour. On sand and mud. Sublittoral. [6]

Krill *Meganyctiphanes norvegica*
EUPHAUSIIDAE L to 4 cm. Shrimp-like; no rostral spine; all limbs similar; eyes large, globular. Transparent, or translucent with scattered pigment spots. Planktonic in open water. [7]

opossum shrimp *Siriella clausi*
MYSIDAE L to 1 cm. Slender, with very short carapace and delicately feathery limbs; rostrum slender, pointed; eyes large on conspicuous stalks. Transparent. In open water, but often in groups in shallow inshore water and estuaries. [8]

Sea Slater *Ligia italica*
LIGIIDAE L to 1.5 cm. Resembles a large, greyish-brown woodlouse; eyes very large; antennae long; body terminates abruptly and has two Y-shaped anal projections. Under stones and weeds. Upper shore. [9]

isopod *Idotea balthica*
IDOTEIDAE L to 3 cm. Body an elongated oval, somewhat flattened; telson long with a median point at the tip, flanked by angular shoulders. Colour variable, usually reddish-brown or green. Among weeds, lower shore to sublittoral. [10]

isopod *Anilocra physodes*
CYMOTHOIDAE L to 4 cm. Body woodlouse-like, but with large, shield-like telson, flanked by paired, flap-like limbs; eyes large, stalkless. Whitish-fawn or very pale grey. Parasitic, attached to, or near the eyes of fish. [11]

sand-hopper *Gammarus locusta*
GAMMARIDAE L to 2 cm. Body laterally flattened, curved; upper antenna has small branch; appendages of telson and last 3 segments divided into two; limbs longer towards the rear. Greenish-brown. Under stones, middle to lower shore. [12]

woodlouse *Armadillidium granulatum*
ONISCIDAE L to 2 cm. Oval, clearly segmented body, antennae short. Rolls into ball when disturbed. Grey or brownish-grey. Under stones, near buildings. [13]

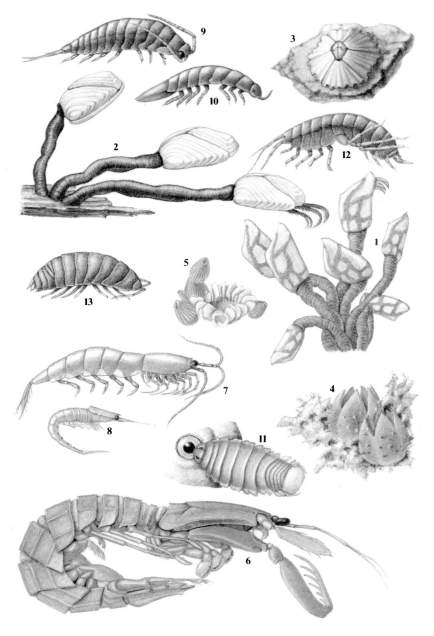

Sand-hopper *Talitrus saltator*
TALITRIDAE L to 1.6 cm. Similar to *Gammarus locusta*, but upper antenna shorter than lower, without branch. Grey-green or greenish-fawn with a dark stripe. In sand, under rotting weed. Upper shore. [1]

Ghost Shrimp *Phtisica marina*
CAPRELLIDAE L to 1.5 cm. Body like a knotted thread; forelimbs have pincers; ♀ has brood-pouch beneath 3rd and 4th segments. Pale brown or red. Among encrusting organisms. Middle shore to sublittoral. [2]

prawn *Penaeus trisulcatus*
PENAEIDAE L to 20 cm. Inner branch of lower antenna paddle-like; carapace ridged; pincers tiny. Sand-coloured. Over sand and mud. Shallow water, estuaries. [3]

Red Prawn *Aristeomorpha foliacea*
PENAEIDAE L to 22 cm. ♀ long, with 5 or 6 teeth, in ♂ shorter, strongly toothed; outer mouth-parts large, fringed. Red. Deep water. Sold in fish markets. [4]

prawn *Athanas nitescens*
ALPHAEIDAE L to 3 cm. Rostrum pointed; pincers of 1st walking legs large. Pink or reddish with white dorsal stripe. Among weeds. Lower shore to sublittoral. [5]

Snapping Prawn *Synalpheus laevimanus*
ALPHAEIDAE L to 2 cm. Upper antenna branched; rostrum flanked on each side by a large tooth; pincers unequal; hinged finger on left pincer can snap shut audibly. Sand-coloured. Among weeds and other encrusting organisms. Sublittoral. [6]

prawn *Spirontocaris cranchi*
HIPPOLYTIDAE L to 2 cm. Abdomen flexed; lower antenna long, slender; rostrum with 3 or 4 dorsal teeth and divided tip. Semi-transparent with orange, black, red and yellow spots, occasionally brownish-green with red stripes. Among algae. Lowest shore to sublittoral. [7]

Sea-grass Prawn *Hippolyte prideauxiana*
HIPPOLYTIDAE L to 4.2 cm. Abdomen flexed; rostrum large, two teeth on lower margin

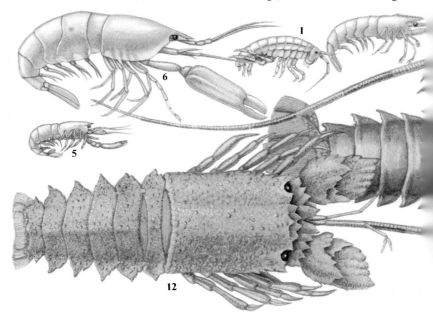

and one at tip; pincers tiny. Often brilliant green, may be brown or crimson, sometimes with white dorsal stripe. Among algae and eel-grasses. Sublittoral. [8]

prawn *Palaemon elegans*
PALAEMONIDAE L to 6.5 cm. Upper antenna in three filaments; lower antenna whiplike; rostrum large, colourless, or red-spotted with 7–9 teeth above and 3 teeth below. Banded yellow-brown. Among weeds, in rock-pools. Lower shore and sublittoral. [9]

Common Prawn *Palaemon serratus* is similar but larger (L to 11 cm); rostrum very large with 6 or 7 teeth above, 4 or 5 below and a bifid tip.

prawn *Typton spongicola*
PALAEMONIDAE L to 2.5 cm. Carapace large, inflated; antennae and rostrum short; large spine over each eye. Orange or yellowish-red. Always inside a clump of compound sponge. Sublittoral. [10]

Guardian Prawn *Pontonia custos* is similar, but carapace is less inflated; rostrum

hooked. Within the mantle cavity of large bivalves, especially the fan mussel *Pinna nobilis*. Sublittoral.

Common Shrimp *Crangon crangon*
CRANGONIDAE L to 5 cm. Body slender; rostrum tiny, pincer of 1st walking leg wrench-like. Pale brown or grey with red spots. In sandy habitats, often in pools. Lower shore to sublittoral. [11]

Flapjack Lobster *Scyllarides latus*
SCYLLARIDAE L to 45 cm. Massive, flattened, with reflexed abdomen; first antennae short, jointed, inner branches of second antennae leaflike. Brown. On rocky and muddy bottoms. Sublittoral. [12]

Flapjack Lobster *Scyllarus arctus* is similar, but smaller (L to 10 cm), with larger eyes.

Spiny Lobster *Palinurus elephas*
PALINURIDAE L to 50 cm. No pincers, except on 5th legs in ♀; outer antennae long, whiplike, very spiny at base; carapace spiny. Brown or rust-coloured. In sheltered places. Sublittoral. [13]

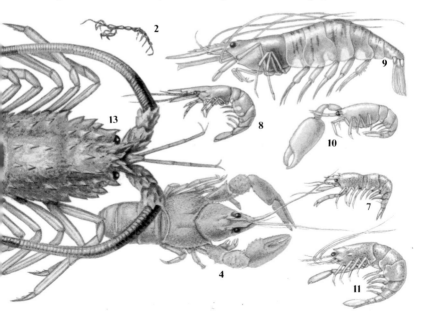

Scampi, Norway Lobster, Dublin Bay Prawn *Nephrops norvegica* NEPHROPSIDAE
L to 30 cm. A slender lobster, pincers of 1st walking legs elongated, sculptured; antennae long; eyes large. Sandy-red. On mud and sand. Sublittoral. [1]

Common Lobster *Homarus gammarus*
NEPHROPSIDAE L to 50 cm. Body broad, slightly flattened; outer antennae longer than body; pincers of 1st walking legs massive. Blue with reddish touches. In sheltered places, caves, crevices. Sublittoral. [2]

burrowing shrimp *Jaxea nocturna*
LAOMEDIIDAE L to 5 cm. Carapace rounded; rostrum short, pointed; abdomen and legs slender; outer antennae long; pincers of 1st walking legs long with slender fingers; white, pink or brown. Burrowing in mud. Sublittoral. [3]

burrowing shrimp *Upogebia littoralis*
CALLIANASSIDAE L to 10 cm. Slender, hairy; carapace narrow; rostrum long concealing the small eyes; movable finger on pincer of 1st walking leg much longer than fixed finger. Whitish or greenish. Burrowing in mud. Lowest shore to sublittoral. [4]

burrowing shrimp *Callianassa subterranea*
CALLIANASSIDAE L to 6 cm. Similar to *Upogebia*, but carapace more inflated with very small rostrum; pincers of normal shape, but unequal size. Burrowing in mud. Lowest shore to sublittoral. [5]

Squat Lobster *Galathea nexa*
GALATHEIDAE L TO 2 cm (body). Flattened; abdomen tucked under carapace; rostrum triangular, 3 small teeth on each side; long pincers on 1st walking legs. Reddish brown or violet-brown. Among stones and boulders. Lowest shore to sublittoral. [6]

Broad-clawed Porcelain Crab *Porcellana platycheles* PORCELLANIDAE
L to 3.5 cm. Body rounded; antennae long; pincers broad, flat, hairy; 5th walking legs very reduced. Greyish-brown. Under boulders. Lower shore to sublittoral. [7]

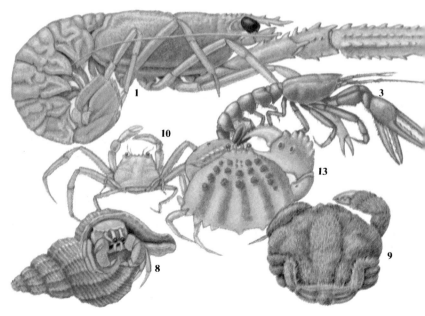

hermit crab *Pagurus arrosor*
PAGURIDAE L to 10 cm. Carapace a truncated pyramid, yellow; pincers red, left one larger; 2nd and 3rd legs red with black claws, 4th and 5th legs reduced. In gastropod shells. Sublittoral. [8]

hermit crab *Paguristes oculatus* is similar but smaller (L to 4 cm); pincers almost equal. Eye-stalks yellow-orange, antennae red, eyes blue, carapace reddish brown, violet spots on 2nd joint of 1st walking legs.

hermit crab *Diogenes pugilator* is similar but smaller (L to 2.5 cm) with hairy antennae and white-tipped pincers.

Sponge Crab *Dromia vulgaris*
DROMIIDAE L to 8 cm (carapace). Slightly broader than long; pincers broad; 4th and 5th legs small, hold a compound sponge on the back; very hairy. Brown, pincer tips bright pink or violet. Among stones. Lower shore to sublittoral. [9]

crab *Dorippe lanata*
DORIPPIDAE L to 3 cm (carapace). Pear-shaped, pinkish-brown, small teeth on front margin; pincer legs short; other legs except 5th much longer, straw-coloured; hairy. On mud. Sublittoral. [10]

crab *Ebalia tuberosa*
LEUCOSIIDAE L to 1.2 cm (carapace). Carapace diamond-shaped, plump; pincers on first walking legs have a knob just below the fixed finger; other legs short. Greyish-brown or yellowish-red. On sand and gravel. Sublittoral. [11]

Nut Crab *Ilia nucleus*
LEUCOSIIDAE L to 3 cm (carapace). Circular with several bumps on posterior carapace margin; pincers long, slender. Yellowish-brown. On mud and stones and among weeds. Sublittoral. [12]

crab *Calappa granulata*
CALAPPIDAE L to 11 cm (carapace). D-shaped carapace with 9 triangular bumps at rear, massive and heavily furrowed; pincered legs massive, sculptured. Red-blotched sandy-grey. On muddy bottoms. Sublittoral. [13]

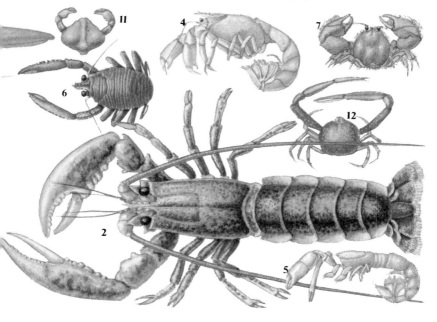

spider crab *Macropodia longirostris*
MAIIDAE L to 2 cm (carapace). Pear-shaped
carapace with short spines on back, 2 long
projections between eyes, which are prominent on long stalks; pincers slender; legs
have spiny joints; usually covered with
weed or sponge. Reddish-brown. Among
weeds. Lower shore to sublittoral. [1]

spider crab *Inachus dorsettensis*
MAIIDAE L to 3 cm (carapace). Similar to
Macropodia, but broader; eyes retractile;
pincers larger; usually covered with weed
or sponge. Light brown. Among weeds.
Lower shore to sublittoral. [2]

Spiny Spider Crab *Maia squinado*
MAIIDAE L to 30 cm (carapace). Pear-
shaped, spiny carapace; 2 spines between
eyes; pincers elongated, slender; other legs
long, hairy. Reddish. Among stones and
on sand. Usually sublittoral. [3]

spider crab *Lambrus angulifrons*
PARTHENOPIDAE L to 2 cm (carapace). Pear-
shaped carapace; pincers short, angled, on
very long legs. Sand-coloured above, pure
white below, inner side of pincers violet;
often covered in sponge. Among rocks and
encrustations. Sublittoral. [4]

Masked Crab *Corystes cassivelaunus*
CORYSTIDAE L to 4 cm (carapace). Oval
carapace, with 2 spines aside eyes, 2 blunt
projections between them; pincers. very
long in ♂, shorter in ♀; antennae hairy,
modified into a long respiratory tube.
Sand-coloured. Burrows into clean sand.
Lower shore to sublittoral. [5]

crab *Atelecyclus rotundatus*
ATELECYCLIDAE L to 6 cm (carapace). Pear-
shaped, hairy carapace, broader anteriorly
with 5 teeth between the eyes; pincers
massive, sculptured. Red, with black-
tipped pincers. On sand. Sublittoral. [6]

Edible Crab *Cancer pagurus*
CANCRIDAE B to 25 cm (carapace). Oval
carapace, much broader than long, with
distinctive pie-crust edge anteriorly, 3
small, blunt teeth between eyes; pincers
massive. Brick-red, pincers tipped dark

brown or black. In sheltered places,
crevices. Lower shore to sublittoral. [7]

Mediterranean Shore Crab *Carcinus*
mediterraneus PORTUNIDAE
B to 10 cm (carapace). Carapace rounded
anteriorly, with 5 sharp saw-teeth to right
and left of eyes and 3 blunt teeth between
them; pincers massive, sharp; other legs
end in claws. Dark green, often mottled
black, juveniles may be sand-coloured with
dark patterns. Among weeds. Middle to
lower shore, often in saltmarshes. [8]

Swimming Crab *Macropipus depurator*
PORTUNIDAE B to 5 cm (carapace). Similar
to *Carcinus*, but 5th walking legs end in
distinctive paddle; surface scaly. Pink or
red. Often pelagic in open water, sometimes among weeds on lowest shore. [9]

Yellow Crab *Eriphia spinifrons*
XANTHIDAE B to 10 cm (carapace). Similar
to *Carcinus*, but with many tiny projections
on front of carapace; pincers large, sharp,
fingers slender; legs hairy. Yellowish-
green, pincers brown-tipped. Among
weeds. Sublittoral. [10]

crab *Goneplax angulata*
GONEPLACIDAE B to 5 cm (carapace).
Almost rectangular; pincers on long legs;
eyes on mobile stalks. Red, purplish-pink
and white. On sand. Sublittoral. [11]

Pea Crab *Pinnotheres pisum*
PINNOTHERIDAE D to 1.5 cm (carapace).
Body almost spherical, inflated, margins
smooth; limbs, including pincers, small,
slender; ♂ much smaller than ♀, and
hairy. Creamy yellow, often with dark
yellow or orange blotches, glossy. Within
the mantle cavity of bivalved molluscs,
frequently in mussel *Mytilus*. [12]

Running Crab *Pachygrapsus marmoratus*
GRAPSIDAE B to 6 cm (carapace). Box-like,
massive carapace with few teeth on margins; eyes and antennae far apart; pincers
massive. Yellowish-green or fawn, with
darker transverse stripes. On rocky shores.
From upper to lower shore, often running
on rocks above the high-tide mark. [13]

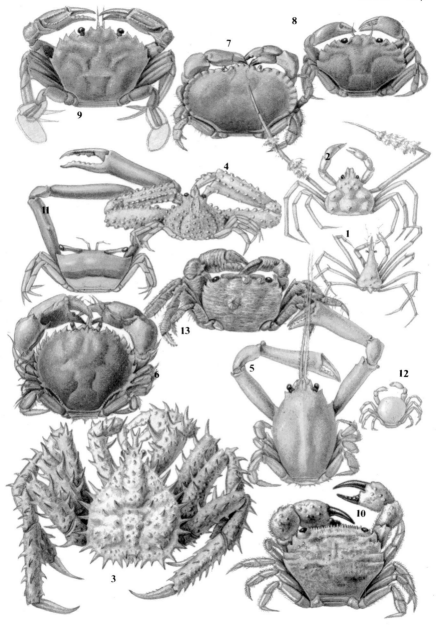

CENTIPEDES AND MILLIPEDES

(Myriapoda)
Terrestrial arthropods, characterized by relatively long bodies bearing many legs. Most need humid environment; live under stones and wood or in soil.

centipede *Scutigera coleoptrata*

SCUTIGERIDAE L to 2.5 cm (body). Body compact; antennae long and slender; 15 pairs of long limbs; the last pair very long, up to three times body length. Grey-brown. In crevices, under boulders, in inhabited buildings. [1]

millipede *Iulis mediterraneus*

IULIDAE L to 4.5 cm. Body rounded in cross-section; glossy, as if varnished; numerous segments, each with two pairs of walking limbs. Brown. In leaf-litter, under moss. [2]

centipede *Scolopendra cingulata*

SCOLOPENDRIDAE L to 9 cm. Body slightly flattened, head and mouthparts distinct; numerous segments, each with one pair of limbs; movement characteristically rippling. Yellow-brown. In dry, stony places, in garrigue. [3]

INSECTS (Insecta)

Arthropods with three pairs of legs as adults; body divided into distinct head, thorax and abdomen; thorax often bears wings. Juvenile or larval stage often very different from adult in appearance and habitat. Insects show greatest variety in form, colour and function of any group of animals.

bristletail *Petrobius maritimus*

MACHILIDAE L to 1.5 cm. Body slender, tapering toward the rear; antennae long, held stiffly in a V-shape, last body segment with three stiff antenna-like processes (cerci). Greyish-brown, metallic. In crevices, under stones. Upper shore. [4]

springtail *Anurida maritima*

LIPURIDAE L to 2.5 mm. Body compact, plump, hairy. Bright grey-blue. In crevices, or floating on the surface of water in pools. Upper to lower shore. [5]

damselfly *Agrion virgo*

AGRIIDAE WS to 7 cm. Body very slender, head conspicuous, especially eyes. Body metallic blue-green; wings in ♂ brown with blue sheen, in ♀ pale brown. In a variety of habitats, but frequent in and near marshy areas, including estuarine saltmarshes. [6]

damselfly *Agrion splendens*

AGRIIDAE WS to 7 cm. Similar to *Agrion virgo*, but wings in ♂ gauzy, with broad blue-green band, in ♀ pale green, transparent. Usually in the vicinity of running water. [7]

Emperor Dragonfly *Anax imperator*

AESCHNIDAE WS to 11 cm. Head and thorax broad, eyes very large, abdomen slender, in ♂ bright blue with dark markings, in ♀ green-blue with brown markings; wings transparent, colourless, lacy. In a wide variety of habitats. Flies strongly and well. [8]

dragonfly *Cordulia aenea*

CORDULIIDAE WS to 7.5 cm. Eyes very large, glowing green; abdomen slender, swelling towards rear. Body metallic green; wings transparent, colourless, lacy. Near fresh and brackish water, in forests. [9]

dragonfly *Libellula quadrimaculata*

LIBELLULIDAE WS to 8.5 cm. Body broad, somewhat flattened, abdomen flat, tapering gradually. Body brown, wings pale brown or fawn, transparent, with four brown spots. Near stagnant water. [10]

praying mantis *Mantis religiosa*

MANTIDAE L to 7.5 cm. Body slender, but abdomen swollen; face triangular, eyes prominent; wings transparent, membranous; first pair of legs modified into spiny grasping organs. Predominantly green, with some brown tinges. Among the leaves of shrubs and bushes. [11]

praying mantis *Empusa pennata*

MANTIDAE L to 6 cm. Similar to *Mantis religiosa*, but with conspicuous helmet-like crest on head; antennae of ♂ feathery. Golden-brown. In warm, usually humid, leafy places. [12]

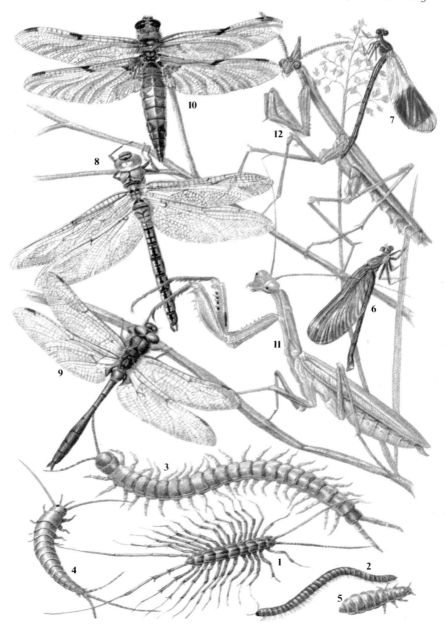

stick insect *Clonopsis gallica*
BACTERIIDAE L to 8 cm. Body extremely slender and elongated, the effect enhanced by the forward-pointing antennae. Leaf green. In leafy places, remains immobile for long periods on like-coloured twigs. [1]

Great Green Bush Cricket *Tettigonia viridissima* TETTIGONIIDAE
L to 4.5 cm. A stout-bodied, grasshopper-like insect with long, slender antennae; terminal part of abdomen spike-like. Green; hindwings colourless and lacy. In meadows and reedbeds. [2]

grasshopper *Acrida mediterranea*
ACRIDIDAE L to 7.5 cm. A typical grasshopper; third pair of walking legs greatly elongated and used for hopping; head conical, with large eyes and relatively short, horn-like antennae. Green with some brown patterning. Does not sing (stridulate) and is not a powerful jumper, but flies well. In bushy places. [3]

Field Cricket *Gryllus campestris*
GRYLLIDAE L to 2.5 cm. Body flattened, broad; antennae long; third pair of walking legs stout and longer than others; abdomen appears to be tipped with four horn-like projections (two are on wings). Brown. In sandy, stony and grassy places, in garrigue. Excavates burrows. [4]

Mole Cricket *Gryllotalpa gryllotalpa*
GRYLLOTALPIDAE L to 5 cm. Body massive, relatively flattened, broad; thorax covered by massive shield; first pair of walking legs massive, toothed and shaped for digging; antennae short. Brown. In a variety of soils, often in dry, stony or sandy places. [5]

False Mantis *Mantispa styriaca*
MANTISPIDAE L to 2.5 cm. Thorax long, slender; abdomen inflated; head not as flat and triangular as true praying mantis *Mantis religiosa*; eyes large, greenish; first legs grasp prey. Light brown; wings colourless. In leafy, bushy places. [6]

Migratory Locust *Locusta migratoria*
ACRIDIDAE L to 6 cm. Grasshopper-like; third pair of walking legs much elongated, used for leaping; antennae short; hindwing membranous, lacy, forewing less so. Usually shades of light brown, sand and fawn, but may have pinkish overtones. Occurs as two 'phases' – inactive sedentary phase (*sedentaria*) and active migratory phase (*gregaria*); the latter is feared as a voracious pest of crops. In a wide variety of habitats from cultivated land to open desert. [7]

Blue-winged Grasshopper *Oedipoda coerulescens* ACRIDIDAE
L to 2.8 cm. Hindwings light, luminous blue, bordered with dark grey band and tipped white or colourless. Body and forewings light brownish-green or olive. In dry areas, garrigue. [8]

striped shield bug *Graphosoma lineata*
PENTATOMIDAE L to 1 cm. Shield-shaped with a somewhat flared hind border; antennae long. Longitudinally striped in black and red. On umbellifers in a variety of habitats. [9]

green shield bug *Palomena viridissima*
PENTATOMIDAE L to 1.5 cm. Shield-shaped, the tips of the membranous under-wings visible near tip of abdomen. Leaf green. On umbellifers and other plants, in a variety of habitats. [10]

ground bug *Lygaeus saxatilis*
LYGAEIDAE L to 1 cm. Body elongated, oval; antennae long, stout. A striking pattern of red on a black background. On a variety of plants, often around the margins of cultivated land. [11]

cicada *Tibicina haematodes*
CICADIDAE L to 4 cm. Body broad, somewhat flattened, massive; head and thorax shield-shaped; tip of abdomen pointed: wings gauzy, transparent with brown veins ♂ produces characteristic 'song'. In wooded places. [12]

cicada *Cicadetta montana*
CICADIDAE L to 3 cm. Similar to *Tibicina haematodes*, but body more slender, not so 'heavy' in appearance. On hillsides covered with bushes and thickets. [13]

Ant-lion *Myrmeleon plumbeus*
MYRMELEONTIDAE WS to 5 cm. Body slender, superficially dragonfly-like with large eyes but short, clubbed antennae; wings leaf-shaped, membranous, delicate. Larva flattened, oval, with a very large pair of curved jaws, excavates pit in sandy soil, lurks at bottom and waits for passing ants and small insects to fall into its clutches. Feeds on body fluids only. Larva in dry, sandy places; adult in a variety of habitats. [1]

tiger beetle *Cicindela littoralis*
CICINDELIDAE L to 1.5 cm. Head and thorax narrower than abdomen, which is shield-shaped with more-or-less straight margins; antennae slender, long; jaws conspicuous. Brownish-green, sometimes bronzy, with a distinctive pattern of white marks. In dry, often sandy places near the upper shore. [2]

ground beetle *Carabus coriaceus*
CARABIDAE L to 4.5 cm. A large, conspicuous beetle with an inflated abdomen. Black, sometimes with very dark grey markings. Does not fly. In a variety of wooded habitats, vineyards, garrigue, often under leaf-litter, old logs, etc. [3]

ground beetle *Agonum dorsale*
CARABIDAE L to 0.75 cm. Abdomen elongated, inflated; elytra bronzy, green-tipped, with fine, longitudinal grooves. Head and thorax metallic green. In dry places often near field margins. [4]

ground beetle *Chlaenius chrysocephalus*
CARABIDAE L to 1 cm. Similar to *Agonum dorsale* but with green, sometimes bluish, elytra, copper-coloured head, thorax and legs, and red feet. In grassy places, sometimes in marshes, including saltmarshes. [5]

rove beetle *Staphylinus caesareus*
STAPHYLINIDAE L to 2.5 cm. Body slender,
elongated; antennae short, obviously segmented; wings and elytra much reduced.
Dark grey-brown overall, with pale grey
markings on abdomen, and copper elytra,
antennae and legs. In hilly places. [6]

Firefly *Lampyris mauritanica*
LAMPYRIDAE L to 1.5 cm. Body slender;
♂ winged, with slender, brown elytra,
♀ wingless, fawn; larvae superficially
worm-like, pale cream-coloured. ♀ and
larvae produce greenish-blue light from an
organ in the abdomen. Light produced by
♀ is strong and is used to attract ♂. In
bushy and grassy places. [♂7]

Checkered Beetle *Trichodes apiarius*
CLERIDAE L to 1.6 cm. Antennae distinctly
clubbed. Body and legs metallic blue, with
alternating transverse bands of deep blue
and bright red on elytra. Larva preys upon
bee larvae. Adult on umbellifers in a
variety of habitats. [8]

Seven-spot Ladybird *Coccinella
septempunctata* COCCINELLIDAE
L to 8 mm. Oval in shape; abdomen
inflated. Head and thorax black with two
pale spots; abdomen red with seven black
spots. Larva slender, tapering, grey with
black spots and yellow smudges. On a
variety of plants in many habitats. [9]

Fourteen-spot Ladybird *Coccinella
quatuordecimpustulata* COCCINELLIDAE
L to 4 mm. Similar to seven-spot ladybird,
but coloration very variable. Usually yellow with 14 black spots, but may be black
with yellow spots, or entirely without
spots. [10]

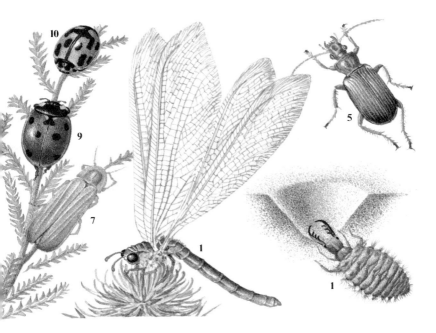

Spanish Fly, Blister beetle *Lytta vesicatoria*
MELOIDAE L to 2 cm. Head roughly
triangular and clearly separated from the
thorax; abdomen tapering, slightly longer
than the elytra; antennae long, segmented.
Green with some bronzy tones. Produces a
pungent and penetrating smell, and contains very large quantities of extremely
poisonous cantharidin. On a number of
different plants, especially ash and privet.
[1]

Stag Beetle *Lucanus cervus*
LUCANIDAE L to 7.5 cm. ♂ probably the
most distinctive beetle of the region with its
very large 'antler'-like jaws; jaws of ♀ not
enlarged; thorax broad and slightly flattened, abdomen shield-shaped. Glossy
black. In wooded and bushy habitats. [2]

Holy Scarab *Scarabaeus sacer*
SCARABAEIDAE L to 3 cm. A rounded oval in
shape, broad and flattened; first walking
legs have broad, conspicuous comb-like
segments; head-shield has wavy margin.
Black, the thorax roughly wrinkled, the
elytra finely grooved. In a wide variety of
habitats, but frequently in leaf-litter. [3]

dung beetle *Scarabaeus semipunctatus*
SCARABAEIDAE L to 3 cm. Similar to holy
scarab *Scarabaeus sacer*, but thorax is matt
black with numerous, widely spaced
points; thorax is also broader than the
abdomen which tapers toward its tip. This
beetle may sometimes be seen rolling
along a ball of dung in which the egg will be
laid. [4]

Musk Beetle *Aromia moschata*
CERAMBYCIDAE L to 3.5 cm. Body long,
narrow; thorax sculptured; antennae
almost twice the length of the body,
segmented, with swollen joints. Usually
greenish-blue, but sometimes almost entirely blue or purplish-red. Gives out a
musky smell. In wooded places. [5]

leaf beetle *Cryptocephalus sericeus*
CHRYSOMELIDAE L to 0.8 cm. Body a flat-
flanked oval; antennae slender; dorsal
surface finely marked. Deep, glowing
green. On a number of different plants
including the yellow daisy-flowered hawk-
weeds, thyme and other scented herbs.
Dry places, hedgerows, garrigue. [6]

weevil *Curculio venosus*
CURCULIONIDAE L to 0.75 cm. Body oval
with long 'snout' which bears elbowed
antennae. Nut-brown, with two fawn
bands on the elytra. On a number of
different oaks. [7]

scorpion-fly *Bittacus italicus*
BITTACIDAE WS to 4 cm. Superficially like a
crane-fly 'daddy-long-legs', being slender
with very long legs, but has two pairs of
wings and head drawn out into a conspicuous 'beak'. Brownish-fawn. In a
variety of habitats, often near freshwater
and on hillsides. [8]

horse-fly *Tabanus bovinus*
TABANIDAE L to 2.5 cm. A very large,
heavy bodied fly. Thorax and abdomen
grey, the latter patterned in red and cream.
♂ feeds on nectar, ♀ sucks blood, but
rarely that of man. In a wide variety of
habitats. [9]

Mediterranean Fruit-fly *Ceratitis capitata*
TEPHRITIDAE L to 6.5 mm. Thorax black
with irregular pattern of whitish stripes;
abdomen plump, banded alternately greyish-blue and reddish-brown; wings transparent, very pale grey with a pattern of
brown blotches. In orchards and gardens
with fruit trees. Larvae are pests of fruit
trees. [10]

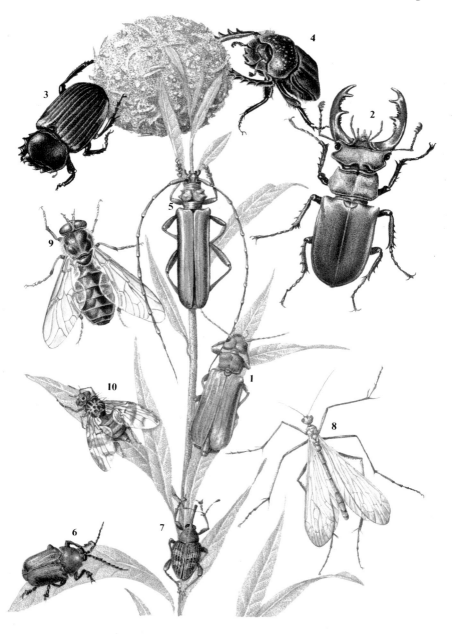

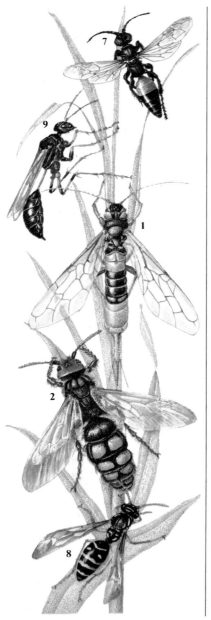

Wood Wasp, Horntail *Urocerus gigas*
SIRICIDAE L to 4 cm. Abdomen cylindrical, expanding toward the tip. ♀ has a powerful stiletto-like ovipositor enclosed in long sheaths, with which it bores into wood to deposit its eggs. ♂ smaller than ♀. Head black and yellow; thorax black; abdomen yellow with a broad central black band. Has no sting. In woodlands. [1]

scoliid wasp *Scolia maculata*
SCOLIIDAE L to 4 cm. Superficially wasp-like, but very large, heavy-looking and impressive. Body predominantly black with partial yellow bands on the abdomen; wings transparent with coloured sheen. Has a sting, but is not aggressive and does not attack man. On a variety of flowering plants. [2]

ant *Cremastogaster sordidula*
FORMICIDAE L to 3 mm. A typical ant; thorax with some sculpturing on the lateral margins. Yellow-brown. In a wide variety of stony places. [3]

Pharaoh's Ant *Monomorium pharaonis*
FORMICIDAE L to 2.3 mm. Notable for its tiny size and habit of moving about in long columns. Brownish-black. In a wide variety of habitats including human habitations and garrigue. [4]

spider wasp *Cryptocheilus annulatus*
POMPILIDAE L to 3 cm. Head broad; abdomen spindle-shaped, separated from thorax by a narrow waist. Antennae and feet orange-yellow, abdomen banded with yellow and black. In dry, stony places, garrigue. [5]

Hornet *Vespa crabro*
VESPIDAE L to 3.5 cm. A large, heavy, wasp-like insect. Head orange-brown, thorax black with brown touches, abdomen yellow

with a black band on the first two segments
and black spots on the others. In a variety
of habitats, often in and near wooded
areas. [6]

digger wasp *Larra anathema*
SPHECIDAE L to 2.5 cm. A long-bodied wasp.
Body predominantly black, but first two
segments of abdomen orange. In a variety
of habitats. [7]

wasp *Polistes gallicus*
VESPIDAE L to 1.6 cm. A typical wasp, with
a narrow waist and black and yellow
striped abdomen. In a variety of habitats.
[8]

digger wasp *Sceliphron destillatorium*
SPHECIDAE L to 3 cm. Waist between
thorax and abdomen narrow, tubular and
elongated, often as long as the thorax.
Predominantly black with orange waist
and black and orange legs. Makes nest of
hardened mud. In a variety of habitats. [9]

bee *Xylocopa violacea*
APOIDEA L to 2.5 cm. A plump, heavy-
bodied bee; legs and parts of body hairy.
Black, glossy; wings brown-violet. Usually
in wooded areas. [10]

Bumble Bee, Humble Bee *Bombus terrestris*
APOIDEA L to 2.8 cm. Body very rounded,
thorax and abdomen plump, hairy. Thorax
black with a transverse yellow band;
abdomen black with a broad transverse
yellow band and a white tip. Nests in the
ground. Chiefly in grassy areas. [11]

Honey Bee *Apis mellifera*
APOIDEA L to 2 cm. A relatively slender-
bodied insect; thorax hairy, abdomen
slightly hairy. Body chiefly dark grey-
black with ochre-coloured hairs. Lives in
large colonies near wooded areas. [12]

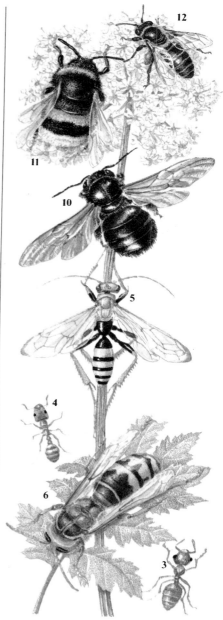

Scarce Swallowtail *Iphiclides podalirius*
PAPILIONIDAE WS to 10 cm. Large-winged, the hindwings with prominent, narrow 'tails'. Background colour pale yellow with very dark grey or black stripes; hindwings have an orange-bordered blue eye-spot and a series of marginal blue scallops edged in black. In hilly limestone areas. [1]

Southern Festoon *Zerynthia polyxena*
PAPILIONIDAE WS to 7 cm. Background colour pale yellow, with black bars, red and black spots on wings, and a scalloped pattern on the wing margins with some orange spotting; undersurface of wings with more red spots and orange and black scalloping. In hot, dry areas. [2]

Green-veined White *Pieris napi*
PIERIDAE WS to 6 cm. A typical 'white' butterfly. Wings chalky-white, slightly spotted with dark grey, forewings tipped with dark grey, veins greenish-grey; undersurface of wings greenish. In fields, gardens, parks, woodland margins. [3]

Orange Tip *Anthocharis cardamines*
PIERIDAE WS to 6 cm. Forewings basically white, but in ♂ have large orange patch and narrow dark grey tip on margin; in ♀ forewings have broader black tip on margin and large central black spot; hindwings in both sexes white with light grey mottling. In gardens, fields, woodland margins and glades. [4]

Provence Orange Tip *Anthocharis eupheno*
PIERIDAE WS to 6 cm. ♂ has pale yellow wings, with orange area on forewings, bordered in black on inner and outer margins; ♀ has basically white wings, with orange, black speckled area on forewings. In gardens, fields, woodland margins, garrigue. [5]

Clouded Yellow *Colias crocea*
PIERIDAE WS to 6 cm. Wings in both sexes buff-yellow, with broad black borders and central black spot on forewings. In fields with leguminous plants which are the food plant of the larva. [6]

Brimstone *Gonepteryx rhamni*
PIERIDAE WS to 6.5 cm. Each wing has a broadly pointed tip and a central vermilion spot; ♂ light sulphur-yellow, ♀ white-cream. In lightly wooded areas, especially those with buckthorn *Rhamnus alaternus* which is the food plant of the larva. [7]
Cleopatra *Gonepteryx cleopatra* is similar, but has an orange patch on each wing.

Purple Hairstreak *Quercusia quercus*
LYCAENIDAE WS to 5 cm. Wings rich velvety brown, with two broad, divergent purple bands on forewings. In oak thickets, oak being the food plant of the larva. [8]

Large Blue *Maculinea arion*
LYCAENIDAE WS to 5 cm. Wings greyish-blue, bordered in grey and marked with elongated spots. In garrigue and other places in which thyme *Thymus vulgaris* is abundant. Larva feeds initially upon thyme and later in ant-hills. [9]

Silver-washed Fritillary *Argynnis paphia*
NYMPHALIDAE WS to 8 cm. Orange-brown overall with a pattern of black lines and spots; undersurface of hindwing greenish with silver spots and border. In heathland, woodland margins, garrigue. [10]

Painted Lady *Vanessa cardui*
NYMPHALIDAE WS to 7 cm. Brown overall with areas of light orange, cream and black; row of spots on hindwing. In a variety of habitats. Larvae feed on nettles, thistles and coltsfoot *Tussilago farfara*. [11]

Red Admiral *Vanessa atalanta*
NYMPHALIDAE WS to 7 cm. Wings velvety
black with brown overtones; forewing
patterned near its tip with a white patch and
spots, below which is a wide band of bright
red; hindwing edged in red. In gardens,
woodland margins. Larvae feed on nettles
and sometimes thistles. [1]

Camberwell Beauty *Nymphalis antiopa*
NYMPHALIDAE WS to 9.5 cm. Wings a deep,
velvety brown, the outer margins creamy
yellow with a line of blue spots on the body
side of the border. In heathland, woodland
margins and clearings. [2]

Large Tortoiseshell *Nymphalis polychloros*
NYMPHALIDAE WS to 7 cm. Predominantly
warm reddish-brown, with black patches
and spots on the forewing and the leading
edge of the hindwing; wing margins with a
complex border of blue spots, edged in
black. In gardens, orchards, woodland
glades. [3]

Small Tortoiseshell *Aglais urticae*
NYMPHALIDAE WS to 6 cm. Coloration
complex, basically reddish-brown with
central areas of dull brown, patches of
black and of pale yellow and borders of
yellow and bright blue spots, edged in
black. Undersurface of wings dull brown
with patches of yellow. In a variety of
habitats, often in waste ground with nettles
which are the food-plant of the larvae. [4]

Peacock Butterfly *Inachis io*
NYMPHALIDAE WS to 7.5 cm. Forewings a
rich, velvety brownish-maroon with black
patches on leading edge; hindwings warm
brown with a dull red patch; fore- and
hindwings have large eye-spots in which
bright blue and yellow predominate. In a
variety of habitats including parks and
gardens; in waste ground with nettles
which are the food-plant of the larvae. [5]

Comma Butterfly *Polygonia c-album*
NYMPHALIDAE WS to 5 cm. Wing margins
irregular, scalloped; butterfly resembles a
dead leaf when sitting with wings folded.
Predominantly warm reddish-brown with
black markings and a distinctive brown
and yellow border. Often found in hiber-
nation behind curtains, pictures and in
cupboards. In a variety of habitats. [6]

Marbled White *Melanargia galathea*
SATYRIDAE WS to 5.5 cm. Background
colour of wings white to pale yellow, over-
laid with a marble-like pattern of dark
brownish-grey; undersurface of wings
generally paler with fawn overlay. In
shrub-covered areas, especially hilly
country, woodland glades and margins,
waste ground. Larvae feed on grasses. [7]

Meadow Brown *Maniola jurtina*
SATYRIDAE WS to 5.5 cm. Basic coloration
nut-brown, the outer parts of the wings
orange or orange-brown; each forewing
has a distinct black and white eye-spot. In
a wide variety of habitats, especially in
grassy areas. Larvae feed on grasses. [8]

Lappet Moth *Gastropacha quercifolia*
LASIOCAMPIDAE WS to 9 cm. Large and
heavy-bodied; wings have a distinctive
'deckle-edge'. Light brown with a pattern
of darker wavy lines on the wings. In
wooded areas, including orchards, parks,
large gardens and wild woodland. [9]

Great Peacock Moth *Saturnia pyri*
SATURNIIDAE WS to 15 cm. Wings large,
velvety. Predominantly brown and purple-
brown with one distinctive central eye-spot
on each wing; wing margins fawn. Antennae of ♂ highly branched, comb-like;
of ♀ unbranched. In woodland, vineyards
and orchards. [10]

Emperor Moth *Saturnia pavonia*
SATURNIIDAE WS to 8.5 cm. Large and
heavy-bodied with velvety wings. In ♂
forewings dark greyish-fawn, patterned
with cream and white patches and bands,
and bearing central yellow and blue eye-
spots, ringed in black; hindwings orange-
brown with central eye-spots and a dark
transverse band; antennae comb-like. In
♀, wings purplish-grey overall, marked
and bordered in white, with central blue
and yellow eye-spot on each wing; antennae
unbranched. In wooded areas, in woodland
glades and margins. [11]

Magpie Moth *Abraxas grossulariata*
GEOMETRIDAE WS to 4.5 cm. Wings creamy white with a distinctive pattern of black spots and orange lines, each wing bordered with black spots; body orange with black spots. In wooded areas; often in orchards and gardens with fruit trees, such as currant and gooseberry, upon which the orange and black larva feeds. [1]

Eyed Hawk Moth *Smerinthus ocellata*
SPHINGIDAE WS to 9.5 cm. Wings narrow, elongated. Forewings mottled grey, fawn and pinkish-grey with darker markings; hindwings bright pink with a conspicuous black-ringed eye-spot. In wooded areas. [2]

Oak Hawk Moth *Marumba quercus*
SPHINGIDAE WS to 11 cm. Pale fawn and yellowish-buff overall; broad central pale bands and distinctive brown spot on trailing edge of forewing; hindwings reddish. In oak woods. [3]

Death's Head Hawk Moth *Acherontia atropos* SPHINGIDAE
WS to 13 cm. Body very large; thorax bears a distinctive pattern which resembles a human skull; abdomen fat, cream and grey with brown stripe. Forewings marbled blue-grey, purple and yellow; hindwings buff with brown bands. Often in agricultural land. [4]

Spurge Hawk Moth *Celerio euphorbiae*
SPHINGIDAE WS to 7 cm. Forewings brown with an irregular yellow longitudinal stripe; hindwings pink with dark brown borders; undersurface of wings entirely pink; antennae white on underside. In a variety of habitats, but often in dry areas with spurges *Euphorbia* which are the food-plants of the larvae. [5]

Oleander Hawk Moth *Daphnis nerii*
SPHINGIDAE WS to 11.5 cm. Wings boldly patterned with marble-like mottling of green, fawn and purple, and wavy white bands; body marbled greenish-fawn. In bushy and wooded areas, especially in vicinity of oleander *Nerium oleander*, the food-plant of the larva. [6]

Privet Hawk Moth *Sphinx ligustri*
SPHINGIDAE WS to 10.5 cm. Wings pinkish-brown with broad dark brown bands. Thorax brown; abdomen with fawn longitudinal stripe and alternate bright pink and brown circular stripes. In parks and gardens, especially in vicinity of privet *Ligustrum vulgare* and lilac *Syringa* bushes. [7]

Elephant Hawk Moth *Deilephila elpenor*
SPHINGIDAE WS to 7 cm. Bright pink overall with bands of pinkish brown; leading edge of hindwings very dark brown. In a variety of habitats, including heathland, parks and gardens. [8]

Puss Moth *Cerura vinula*
NOTODONTIDAE WS to 7.5 cm. A large and heavy-bodied moth with 'furry' appearance. Wings predominantly whitish-grey with complex dark grey and yellow zig-zag patterns on forewings. In a wide variety of habitats, from stony hillsides to parks and gardens. [9]

Garden Tiger Moth *Arctia caja*
ARCTIIDAE WS to 7.5 cm. Very distinctive, although wing pattern variable; forewings basically cream with a pattern of irregular brown patches; hindwings orange with small and large very dark brown-grey spots, ringed in yellow. Thorax rich brown; abdomen orange with dark brown bars. In wooded areas, heathland, garrigue, maquis, parks and gardens. [10]

Old Lady Moth *Mormo maura*
NOCTUIDAE WAS to 7.5 cm. Dull dark brown overall with a pattern of lighter and darker lines; wing margins finely scalloped. In grassy places and heathland. [11]

Burnet *Zygaena carniolica*
ZYGAENIDAE WS to 3.5 cm. Antennae clubbed, tapering toward the tip; wings narrow. Body metallic dark grey, tip of abdomen red; forewings warm grey with yellow-bordered red spots; hindwings red. In a number of different habitats, but usually in limestone areas and garrigue. [12]

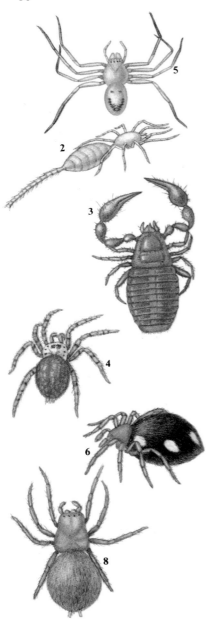

SCORPIONS, SPIDERS AND THEIR ALLIES (Arachnida)

Invertebrates with a hard external skeleton, segmented body and jointed limbs. Head and thorax fused (cephalothorax); 4 pairs of legs; one pair of conspicuous sensory palps (pedipalps); one pair of jaws (chelicerae).

scorpion *Euscorpius flavicaudis*
SCORPIONIDA L to 3.5 cm. Cephalothorax and abdomen continuous without 'waist'; last 5 segments of abdomen curved up over body; venom gland and sting on last segment; pedipalps enlarged into pincers. Brown, last segment fawn. Under stones in dry localities. [1]

palpigrade micro-whip scorpion *Koenenia mirabilis* PALPIGRADI
L to 1 mm. Cephalothorax rounded, separated from oval abdomen by 'waist'; no pincers. White. Beneath stones, often quite deeply buried. [2]

pseudoscorpion *Pselaphochernes littoralis*
PSEUDOSCORPIONIDA L to 6 mm. Superficially spider-like, but with pincers; body elongated oval. Chestnut-brown. Under and among stones, accumulated vegetation and in crevices on shore. [3]

spider *Oecobius annulipes*
OECOBIIDAE L to 2 mm. Flat with lateral legs; makes small, star-shaped web suspended by silken strands. Pale and dark fawn. Under stones. Upper shore. [4]

spider *Olios spongitarsis*
CLUBIONIDAE L to 2 cm. Body rather elongated; long legs held conspicuously at right-angles to the body. Usually fawn or light yellow, but sometimes with pink. In vegetation in garrigue and maquis. [5]

spider *Uroctea durandi*
UROCTEIDAE L to 1.5 cm (body). Cephalothorax and abdomen pentagonal, former short, reddish-brown, latter long, black with 5 yellow spots; anal tubercle very

large. Makes nest like upside down tent, of several sheets of compactly woven silk. Among stones. Upper shore. [6]

Writing Spider *Argiope bruennichi*
ARGIOPIDAE L to 2.5 cm (♀ body). ♀ large, abdomen oval, yellow with black bars; ♂ small, abdomen rectangular, striped. ♀ constructs web in zig-zag pattern. In shrubs, garrigue and maquis. [7]

funnel-web spider *Desidiopsis racovitzae*
AGELENIDAE L to 5.5 cm (body). Cephalothorax broad in front, fawn; abdomen oval, hairy, grey. Spins small web in irregularities of calcareous algae. In tidal shore; submerges as tide rises. [8]

wolf-spider *Lycosa narbonensis*
LYCOSIDAE L to 3 cm (body). Large: abdomen inflated, rounded; chelicerae formidable. Nest cylindrical, excavated in ground, may be 20 cm deep and 5 cm in diameter; spider lurks in burrow and pounces on passing insects. Upper parts brown; undersurface of abdomen black bordered red. In dry areas, often in sand or mud. [9]

SEA-SPIDERS (Pycnogonida)
Invertebrates with exoskeleton, snout-like proboscis; legs very long, digestive and reproductive system extend into them.

sea-spider *Nymphon gracile*
NYMPHONIDAE L to 2.5 cm (leg). Spider-like; extra pair of 'ovigerous' legs beneath body, where ♂ carries egg clutch. Reddish-brown. Among encrusting organisms. Mid- to lower shore [10]

sea-spider *Callipallene brevirostris*
PALLENIDAE L to 6 mm (leg). Similar to *Nymphon gracile*, but proboscis a short, rounded knob. Brown. Among encrusting organisms. Lowest shore to sublittoral. [11]

sea-spider *Pycnogonum pusillum*
PYCNOGONIDAE L to 5 mm. Legs short; ovigerous legs only in ♂. Straw-coloured. Lowest shore to sublittoral. [12]

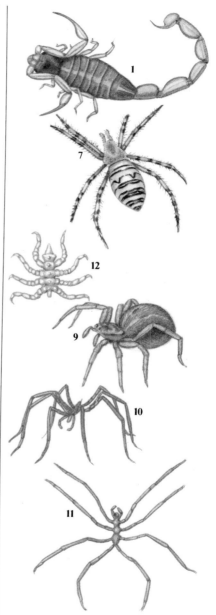

SEAMATS, MOSS ANIMALS
(Bryozoa, Ectoprocta, Polyzoa)
Generally colonial, sessile animals of small size, often mistaken for plants; encased in protective, horny, secreted layer; have specialized food-gathering organ (lophophore) round mouth, with numerous tentacles; feed on suspended matter.

moss animal *Bugula turbinata*
BICELLARIELLIDAE H to 6 cm (colony). Colonial: resembles a finely divided seaweed; individuals arranged in series of whorls about a central 'stem', two sorts – one elongated, box-like with feeding tentacles, the other like a beaked bird's head, the snapping motion of the beak serving to protect the colony. Brown. On solid objects. Sublittoral. [1]

Hornwrack *Flustra foliacea*
FLUSTRIDAE H to 20 cm (colony). Colony branching, like seaweed with broad fronds; horny; individuals close together on both surfaces of frond. Fawn to brown, sometimes yellow, grey or green; fades after exposure to air. On hard surfaces. Sublittoral. [2]

moss animal *Scrupocellaria reptans*
SCRUPOCELLARIIDAE H to 5 cm (colony). Colony like seaweed with narrow, branched fronds; horny; individuals oval. Fawn. In shallow water, usually attached to seaweeds, roots of eel-grasses, etc. [3]

sea-mat *Membranipora membranacea*
MEMBRANIPORIDAE D very variable. Thin, mat-like colony; area variable; margins often rounded, may be irregular; individuals box-like; upright finger-like 'towers' sometimes occur on colony surface. White. On laminarians and other seaweeds. Lower shore to sublittoral. [4]

Lace Coral *Retepora cellulosa*
RETEPORIDAE H to 10 cm (colony). Colony branched, folded, like fine porcelain filigree, very fragile and brittle. Salmon-pink in life, bleaches rapidly after death. Attached to solid surfaces in shaded places, such as grottoes. Sublittoral. [5]

False Coral *Myriozoum truncatum*
MYRIOZOIDAE H to 10 cm (colony). Colony of projecting 'horns', with flat-tipped branches, more-or-less rounded in cross-section. Yellow-red. Attached to solid surfaces, especially in shaded and sheltered places. Sublittoral. [6]

sea-mat *Alcyonidium gelatinosum*
ALCYONIDIIDAE H to 30 cm (colony). Colony branched, gelatinous, spongy, tough; individuals appear as tiny raised, rough spots on surface of mass. Yellow, green, brown or grey. Attached to solid objects. Lowest shore to sublittoral. [7]

moss animal *Bowerbankia imbricata*
VESICULARIIDAE H to 7 cm (colony). Colony of tufted upright stalks with elongated individuals grouped at intervals. Pale brown, buff or grey. Attached to seaweeds. Lowest shore to sublittoral. [8]

PHORONIDS (Phoronidea)
Superficially worm-like animals; they have lophophore with horseshoe-shaped arrangement of tentacles. Manufacture membranous tubes; usually occur in groups; feed on suspended matter.

phoronid *Phoronis muelleri*
PHORONIDAE H to 5 cm. Slender, worm-like, swollen near base; tube sometimes encrusted with sand. Flesh-coloured, the tentacle bases reddish. In muddy deposits. Sublittoral. [9]

LAMP SHELLS (Brachiopoda)
Externally similar to bivalved molluscs, but internally quite different. Possess lophophore with a horseshoe-shaped arrangement of tentacles; feed on suspended matter.

lamp shell *Gryphus vitreus*
TEREBRATULIDAE L to 4 cm. Shell roundish-oval; smooth with concentric growth lines; lower valve has pronounced umbo with conspicuous hole through which peduncle (stalk) protrudes. Greyish-white. Attached to shells, coralline fragments and sea-fans. Sublittoral, in deep water (70–2500m). [10]

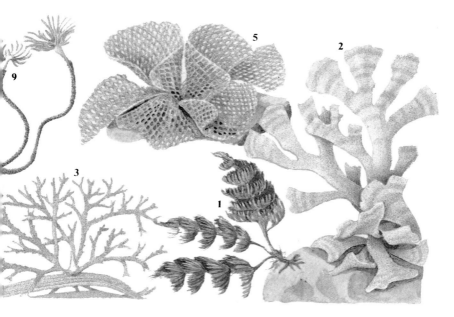

STARFISH, SEA-URCHINS, SEA-CUCUMBERS (Echinodermata)

Animals with radial symmetry; mouth in centre of one side of body, anus on the other, opposite mouth; body may be globular or drawn out into several radiating arms; body wall strengthened by calcareous plates, forms hard 'test' in sea urchins; skin spiny; possess water vascular system, move using 'tube-feet', operated by hydrostatic pressure.

Mediterranean Feather-star *Antedon mediterranea* ANTEDONIDAE

D to 20 cm. Structure clearly visible only underwater. Central disc small; 5 pairs feathery arms and short processes on lower surface for temporary attachment. Animal resembles tangle of knotted string when stranded. Sulphur-yellow, reddish or brown. On boulders and other organisms. Sublittoral. [1]

Seven-armed Starfish *Luidia ciliaris*

LUIDIIDAE D to 45 cm. Typical starfish with 7 broad, flattened arms; tips of tube-feet slightly knobbed. Bright orange above, creamy white below. On sandy bottoms, hiding under seaweeds. Lower shore to sublittoral. [2]

Five-armed Starfish *Luidia sarsi* is similar, but has 5 arms. Yellowish-brown or red above, pale below.

Red Comb-star *Astropecten aurantiacus*

ASTROPECTINIDAE D to 60 cm. Typically star-shaped with 5 stiff arms fringed with 2 layers of spiny plates; 2 or 3 conical spines on each upper plate. Brown with reddish marks above, pale below. Burrowing in sand. Lowest shore to sublittoral. [3]

comb-star *Astropecten irregularis* is similar, but smaller (D to 12 cm), with 1 or 2 small spines on upper marginal plates. Pink, brick-red or brownish above, pale below.

starfish *Ceramaster placenta*

GONIASTERIDAE D to 16 cm. Body flat, pentagonal with slightly curved margins; solid and tough; marginal plates large, conspicuous. A variety of colours from yellow-brown to red. On muddy and sandy substrates. Sublittoral. [4]

starfish *Ophidiaster ophidianus*

OPHIDIASTERIDAE D to 20 cm. Central disc small with 5 radiating, cylindrical blunt-tipped arms; tube-feet suckered and guarded by short spines. Purplish-red. On rocks and boulders. Sublittoral from shallow, inshore water downwards. [5]

starfish *Hacelia attenuata*

OPHIDIASTERIDAE D to 20 cm. Central disc small with 5 radiating, tapering, pointed-tipped arms; tube-feet suckered and guarded by short spines. Brown or red. On rocks and boulders. Sublittoral, from inshore water downwards. [6]

Goose-foot Star *Anseropoda placenta*

ASTERINIDAE D to 15 cm. Flat, pentagonal, with only shallow bays between stubby arms; midline of each arm slightly thickened, producing 'goose-foot' appearance. Colour variable, patterns of orange or red and white above, yellowish below. On mud and sand. Sublittoral. [7]

Cushion Star *Asterina gibbosa*

ASTERINIDAE D to 6 cm. Star-shaped but with stubby, rather rounded arms; thick, leathery, tough. Shades of sandy fawn or greyish-green above, pale below. Under rocks and boulders. Lower shore to sublittoral. [8]

Red Starfish *Echinaster sepositus*

ECHINASTERIDAE D to 20 cm. Central disc small with 5 radiating, gradually tapering arms; skin soft, conspicuously pock-marked on upper surface; tube-feet suckered. Scarlet. On rock, occasionally on sand and mud. Sublittoral. [9]

Spiny Starfish *Marthasterias glacialis*

ASTERIIDAE D to 30 cm (occasionally may be more than 60 cm). Typically star-shaped with 5 long, stiff, very spiny arms. Pale grey with touches of clear blue and bright purple above, pale yellow below. Among boulders. Lower shore to sublittoral. [10]

Blue Starfish *Coscinasterias tenuispina*
ASTERIIDAE D to 15 cm. Central disc fairly
small with 6 to 10 radiating arms, often of
different lengths; surface very spiny.
Colour variable, basically white, purple or
reddish-brown with brown or blue spots.
On rocks and stones. Lowest shore to
sublittoral. [1]

Common Brittle-star *Ophiothrix fragilis*
OPHIOTRICHIDAE D to 2 cm (disc). Disc
pentagonal, with 5 brittle radiating arms
bordered with conspicuous spines. Colour
variable, shades of brownish-red to brownish-purple or fawn, often patterned. Under
boulders and on sand and mud. Middle
shore to sublittoral. [2]

brittle-star *Ophiocomina nigra*
OPHIOCOMIDAE D to 3 cm (disc). Disc almost
round with 5 tapering, fairly flexible arms;
surface spines very tiny, giving almost
velvety texture. Usually matt black, may
be pinkish-brown. Under boulders. Lower
shore to sublittoral. [3]

brittle-star *Acrocnida brachiata*
AMPHIURIDAE D to 1 cm (disc). Disc
pentagonal with 5 very long, very flexible
arms. Sandy fawn. Burrowing in sand.
Lower shore to sublittoral. [4]

Grey Lance-urchin *Cidaris cidaris*
CIDARIDAE D to 7 cm (test). Body roughly
spherical, bearing spines of two sorts −
very long, stout spines, finely grooved on
the outside and often encrusted with
sponges, and numerous very short spines,
clustered around base of larger spines and
arranged along rows of tube-feet. Sandy
fawn. In a wide variety of habitats.
Sublittoral. [5]

Long-spined Sea-urchin *Centrostephanus
longispinus* DIADEMATIDAE
D to 6 cm (test). Body bears large number of
long, hollow, sharply tapering, fragile,
very mobile spines. Reddish-brown, with
brown and white spines. Spines are very
sharp and are liable to penetrate the skin
very painfully; if they snap in the skin they
may poison the wound. In a variety of
habitats. Sublittoral. [6]

Black Sea-urchin *Arbacia lixula*
ARBACIIDAE D to 5 cm (test). Spines solid,
sharp-tipped, up to 3 cm long, black;
when cleaned, test is pink, with very large
oral opening (space occupied by jaws in
life); tube-feet pores marked with distinct
red lines. On boulders, often among
encrusting weeds. Lowest shore to sublittoral. [7]

Rock-urchin *Paracentrotus lividus*
ECHINIDAE D to 6 cm (test). Body globular,
flattened; spines numerous, up to 3 cm
long, pointed, delicately grooved with
fine transverse markings in grooves. Dark
brown, sometimes black, often with dark
green tints. Among rocks with encrusting
weeds; often boring shallowly into suitable
rocks. Lower shore to sublittoral. [8]

Mediterranean Green Sea-urchin
Psammechinus microtuberculatus
ECHINIDAE D to 4 cm (test). Similar to
Paracentrotus lividus, but spines up to 1.5
cm long, delicately grooved, with very fine
granules in grooves, violet. Test green
when cleaned. Under stones, among encrusting organisms. Lower shore to sublittoral. [9]

sea-urchin *Echinus melo*
ECHINIDAE D to 17 cm (test). Body globular;
numerous short spines and occasional
longer ones; 'sockets' of longer spines
may be seen as conspicuous bosses on
cleaned test. Spines green, test brownish-
red. In rocky areas, especially with good
weed cover. Sublittoral. [10]
sea-urchin *Echinus acutus* is very similar,
but test is more conical.

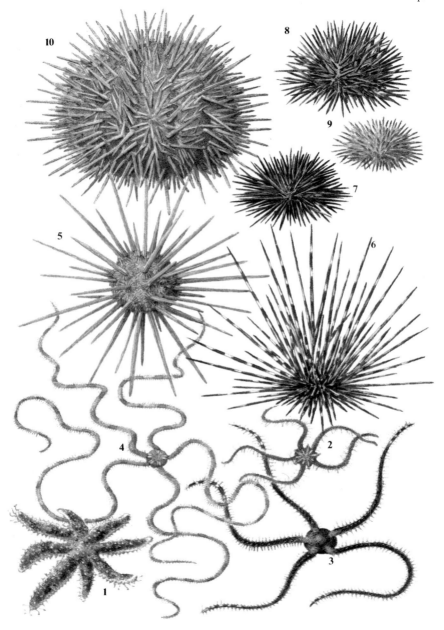

Pea-urchin *Echinocyamus pusillus*
FIBULARIIDAE L to 1.5 cm (test). Body egg-shaped, flattened; spines very short, numerous, giving velvety appearance although animal is harsh to the touch. Pale greenish-grey. Burrows in sand. Lower shore to sublittoral. [1]

Purple Heart-urchin *Spatangus purpureus*
SPATANGIDAE L to 12 cm (test). Body heart-shaped, slightly flattened; spines numerous, relatively short around skirt and on under surface, fewer and longer on dorsal surface. Tube foot apertures arranged in star-like pattern on upper surface, visible only on dead animal. Rich purple. Burrows in sand. Lowest shore to sublittoral. [2]

Heart-urchin, Sea-potato *Echinocardium cordatum* SPATANGIDAE L to 9 cm (test). Body heart-shaped, slightly flattened, deep furrow anteriorly leads almost to mouth; spines numerous, relatively short, longer on underside, flattened, spatulate and curved. Sandy fawn. Burrows in sand. Lower shore to sublittoral. [3]
heart-urchin *Echinocardium pennatifidum* is similar, but anterior groove much less pronounced, and front margin almost without notch.

Lyre-urchin *Brissopsis lyrifera*
SPATANGIDAE L to 7 cm (test). Body heart-shaped, broad; frontal notch shallow; spines very numerous, short, slender, arranged in an irregular manner giving appearance of fur. Reddish-brown. Burrows in sand. Sublittoral. [4]

sea-cucumber *Stichopus regalis*
HOLOTHURIIDAE L to 30 cm. Body massive, cylindrical, flattened on ventral surface into distinct sole with locomotory tube-feet; upper surface warty; mouth opens ventrally. Brownish with pale spots on upper surface, under surface pale, often with golden sheen. On sand and among encrusting organisms. Sublittoral. [5]

sea-cucumber *Holothuria polii*
HOLOTHURIIDAE L to 25 cm. Body cylindrical, slightly flattened on lower surface into a distinct sole bearing the tube-feet; upper surface and sides ornamented with conspicuous pointed outgrowths; feeding tube-feet around mouth branched. Very dark brown, with black overtones, under surface pale. On sand, often in eel-grass. Sublittoral, although often in shallow water. The pearl-fish *Carapus acus* sometimes lives within the body cavity of this species. [6]

sea-cucumber *Ocnus planci*
CUCUMARIIDAE L to 10 cm. Body cylindrical, pentagonal in cross-section, tapering; feeding tube-feet around mouth much branched, arborescent. Greyish-brown. On sand and among encrusting seaweeds. Lower shore to sublittoral. [7]

sea-cucumber *Thyone fusus*
CUCUMARIIDAE L to 20 cm. Body more-or-less oval in cross-section, plump, tapering at both ends; can contract considerably to become lemon-shaped; tube-feet irregularly scattered over surface; 10 branched feeding tube-feet surround mouth. Off-white, dirty pink or shades of pale brown. On sand and mud. Sublittoral. [8]

sea-cucumber *Labidoplax digitata*
SYNAPTIDAE L to 18 cm. Body cylindrical; gut contents visible through semitransparent body wall – looks like polythene tube full of sand; anchor-shaped plates in skin make animal adhesive when touched; tube-feet missing, except for 12 surrounding mouth, each with 4 stubby, finger-like branches. Colourless or very pale pinkish-yellow. Burrows in sand and mud. Lower shore to sublittoral. [9]

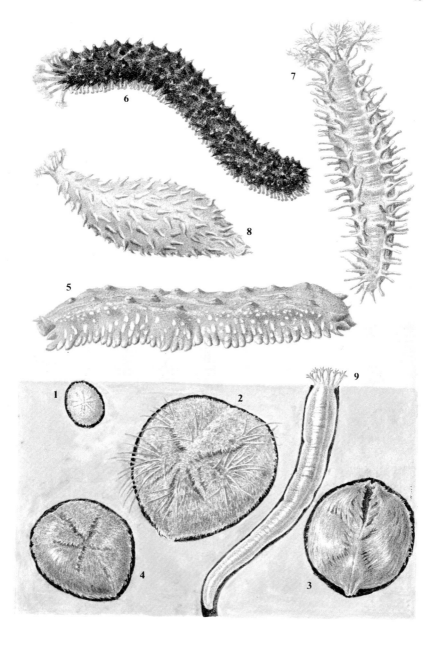

ACORN WORMS (Hemichordata)
Superficially worm-like animals; body divided into three distinct regions – acorn-shaped proboscis, cylindrical collar and partially flattened trunk, pierced by gill slits. Produce prodigious quantities of mucus to lubricate their passage through sand and trap food particles.

acorn worm *Balanoglossus clavigerus*
PTYCHODERIDAE L to 30 cm. Proboscis small, acorn-shaped, yellow; trunk much flattened anteriorly, drawn out into frill-like flaps along each lateral margin. Pale brown. In sand and mud. Sublittoral. [1]

SEA-SQUIRTS AND SALPS
(Urochordata)
Adults cylindrical, possess thick, rubbery outer covering (test). Sea-squirts sessile, often colonial; filter-feed using 2 anterior siphons. Salps solitary or colonial, free-swimming; siphons at each end of body.

sea-squirt *Clavellina lepadiformis*
CLAVELLINIDAE H to 2 cm. Vase-shaped, siphons close together; individuals arise from root-like stolons; test glassy. Internal organs yellow, pink and white. On solid objects. Lower shore to sublittoral. [2]

sea-squirt *Distaplia rosea*
CLAVELLINIDAE H to 3 cm. Colonial, forming rounded aggregations; inhalant siphons encircle central, exhalant opening. Reddish or rose-pink. On solid objects. Lowest shore to sublittoral. [3]

sea-squirt *Distoma adriaticum*
CLAVELLINIDAE H to 9 cm. Colonial, many individuals clustered in massive globular test; each colony usually has broad stalk-like basal portion. Dirty white or light brown. On solid objects. Sublittoral. [4]

sea-squirt *Didemnum maculosum*
DIDEMNIDAE H to 0.2 cm. Colonial, flattened, forming encrustations (D to 4 cm); up to 8 individuals share common exhalant opening. Purple, white or yellow. On stones and seaweeds. Lower shore to sublittoral. [5]

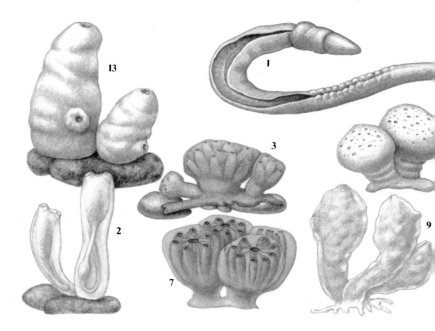

sea-squirt *Aplidium conicum*
POLYCLINIDAE H to 12 cm. Colony massive; openings scattered irregularly over surface. Sulphur-yellow or orange. Usually on solid objects. Sublittoral. [6]

sea-squirt *Aplidium proliferum*
POLYCLINIDAE H to 5 cm. Several colonies together, gelatinous, tough, knobbly, club-shaped. Orange-yellow. On solid objects, including seaweeds. Lower shore to sublittoral. [7]

sea-squirt *Ciona intestinalis*
CIONIDAE H to 12 cm. Solitary; slender; openings orange-spotted, distinct, otherwise semitransparent; highly contractile. On solid objects. Lowest shore to sublittoral. [8]

sea-squirt *Rhopalaea neapolitana*
DIAZONIDAE H to 10 cm. Individuals in small groups; club-shaped, oval upper part contains pharynx, siphons below. Test grey, transparent. Sublittoral, often on coralline ground. [9]

sea-squirt *Diazona violacea*
DIAZONIDAE H to 15 cm. Colonies globular or flattened, massive; siphons and gills protruding. Yellow-green, translucent. On solid supports. Sublittoral. [10]

sea-squirt *Perophora listeri*
PEROPHORIDAE H to 0.5 cm. Colonial; globular individuals arise from much-branched base. Transparent. On seaweeds, eel-grass. Lowest shore to sublittoral. [11]

sea-squirt *Ascidiella aspersa*
ASCIDIIDAE H to 12 cm. Solitary; inhalant opening at top, exhalant opening one-third body length below; test opaque. Brownish-grey. Attached to solid objects, mud. Lower shore to sublittoral. [12]

sea-squirt *Ascidia mentula*
ASCIDIIDAE H to 10 cm. Solitary; upright, plump; test leathery, wrinkled, opaque. Inhalant opening at top, exhalant opening about half-way up body. Greyish-white. On stones and boulders. Lower shore to sublittoral. [13]

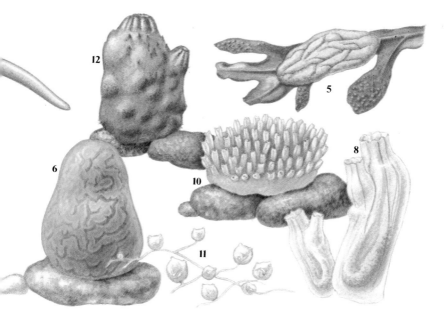

sea-squirt *Phallusia mammillata*
ASCIDIIDAE H to 15 cm. Solitary; upright, massive; test thick, tough, cartilaginous, lumpy, yet fairly smooth to touch. Milky-white, occasionally darker, partly trans-lucent. Attached to solid objects in muddy places. Sublittoral. [1]

sea-squirt *Styela plicata*
STYELIDAE H to 12 cm. Upright, slender, broadening from narrow base; test tough, leathery, with irregular longitudinal creases. Light brown with rosy purple openings. On solid objects, often in large clumps. Lower shore to sublittoral. [2]

sea-squirt *Distomus variolosus*
STYELIDAE H to 1 cm. Colonial; rounded, compact, sometimes slightly flattened; siphons clearly separate but close together; test rough; budding individuals may be present. Brick-red, tinted purple. Under stones, in sheltered places. Lower shore to sublittoral. [3]

Star Ascidian, Star Sea-squirt *Botryllus schlosseri* STYELIDAE
H to 0.5 cm (very variable). Encrusting colony; individuals elongated, grouped around central common exhalant opening, the whole star-shaped. Colour very variable, individual animals often directly contrasting. On stones. Middle shore to sublittoral. [4]

sea-squirt *Botrylloides leachi*
STYELIDAE H to 0.5 cm (very variable). Very similar to *Botryllus schlosseri* but indivi-duals arranged along an elongated com-mon orifice; colony much branched hori-zontally. Colour variable, but mostly grey, orange or yellow. [5]

sea-squirt *Pyura microcosmus*
PYURIDAE H to 2.5 cm. Solitary, plump, resembles Spanish wine flask; inhalant and exhalant siphons with elongated 'necks'; test rough, granular, leathery. Rose-pink longitudinal red lines on siphons. On coralline ground. Sublittoral. [6]

Red Sea-squirt *Halocynthia papillosa*
PYURIDAE H to 10 cm. Solitary; body shaped like an amphora jug, the inhalant opening terminal, the exhalant on the 'shoulder'; 'necks' of siphons relatively long; test tough, firm, rough. Deep reddish-rose. On rock faces in shaded places. Sublittoral. [7]

Sea-egg *Microcosmus sulcatus*
PYURIDAE H to 20 cm. Solitary; massive, test exterior irregular, very creased and pleated, tough; usually encrusted with other sessile organisms. Greyish-brown or dirty fawn. The yellow internal organs have a sour taste and are esteemed as a delicacy. On gravel. Sublittoral. [8]

sea-squirt *Molgula manhattensis*
MOLGULIDAE H to 3 cm. Solitary; body spherical; siphons terminal; test fibrous, often encrusted with small sand grains. Bluish-green. On variety of substrates, sometimes in clumps, but commonly on rocks. Lower shore to sublittoral. [9]

fire-salp *Pyrosoma atlanticum*
PYROSOMIDA L to 25 cm (varies very greatly). Colony conical, the elongated individuals embedded in colony wall; cavity com-municates with water by a common open-ing which may be expanded and contracted to vary speed of movement. Transparent, colourless, luminescent. Free-swimming in open water. [10]

barrel-salp *Doliolum muelleri*
DOLIOLIDA L to 0.5 cm. Body barrel-shaped with 8 muscular bands like cask hoops; inhalant and exhalant openings edged with rounded lobes. Transparent, colourless. Free-swimming in open water. [11]

salp *Salpa democratica*
SALPIDA L to 1.5 cm. Body wedge- or prism-shaped with two conspicuous horn-like projections at the rear. May occur in chains of individuals. Transparent, colourless. Free-swimming in open water. [12]

salp *Salpa maxima*
SALPIDA L to 10 cm. Solitary; body elon-gated, box-like, tapering slightly at rear; muscle bands not completely encircling body. Transparent, colourless. Free-swim-ming in open water. [13]

LANCELETS (Cephalochordata)
Elongated, superficially fish-like animals with a rudimentary spinal cord, but no well-defined head. Filter-feed by means of a complex ciliated sieve.

Lancelet, 'Amphioxus' *Branchiostoma lanceolatum* BRANCHIOSTOMIDAE
L to 5 cm. Anterior fringe of cirri and finned 'tail'; V-shaped muscles conspicuous. Translucent, milky-white to colourless, iridescent. Burrows in coarse gravel, only anterior tip shows above surface. Lowest shore to sublittoral. [1]

JAWLESS FISH (Agnatha)
Superficially fish-like chordates; lack true jaws. Adults feed on blood; mouth may contain strong, horny teeth used to rasp away tissues of prey.

Sea-lamprey *Petromyzon marinus*
PETROMYZONIDAE L to 1 m. Body slender; dorsal fin two-lobed, set near tail; skin scale-less; 7 pairs of circular gill openings; mouth sucker-like, with circlets of numerous teeth around central large, double-pointed tooth. Speckled olive-grey above, silvery beneath. In open water, estuaries; enters rivers for spawning. [2]

Lampern *Lampetra fluviatilis*
PETROMYZONIDAE L to 40 cm. Similar to *Petromyzon marinus*, but outer row of teeth surround two rows of conical teeth flanked by large cusps. Dark olive-green or brown above. Silvery below. In open water; enters rivers to spawn. [3]

CARTILAGINOUS FISH: SHARKS, RAYS AND THEIR ALLIES
(Chondrichthyes)
Vertebrates with true jaws and internal skeleton of cartilage; tail with distinctly unequal lobes; skin covered in backward pointing tooth-like scales. Good swimmers; carnivores or scavengers.

Blue Shark *Prionace glauca*
CARCHARHINIDAE L to 4 m. Snout pointed; teeth serrated, triangular; anterior larger dorsal fin; tail fin upper lobe notched, longer than lower lobe; pectoral fins paddle-like; skin scales tiny. Blue-grey above, white below. In open water. [4]

Smooth Hound *Mustelus mustelus*
TRIAKIDAE L to 1.5 m. Snout pointed; teeth flattened, blunt like diamond-shaped tiles, used for crushing; posterior dorsal fin larger; tail fin notched. Dark grey above, silvery grey beneath. Usually near sea bottom over mud and sand. [5]

Hammerhead *Sphyrna zygaena*
SPHYRNIDAE L to 4 m. Unmistakable; body shark-like, but head drawn out each side in 'hammer-head' shape, with eyes on its extremities and mouth beneath. Slate-grey, paler beneath. In open water. [6]

Large-spotted Dogfish *Scyliorhinus stellaris*
SCYLIORHINIDAE L to 1.5 m. Shark-like; snout rounded; teeth small, triangular, serrated; nostrils form W-shape. Light or greyish-brown above with darker, mottling, paler beneath. On or near sandy and muddy bottoms from shallow to deep water. [7]

Porbeagle, Mackerel-shark *Lamna nasus*
LAMNIDAE L to 3.5 m. Body deep; snout pointed; triangular notched teeth. Dark grey above, pale cream beneath. In open water. [8]

White Shark, Maneater *Carcharodon carcharias* LAMNIDAE
L to 12 m. Snout blunt, head deeper than *Lamna nasus*; teeth large, triangular, serrated; pectoral fins large. Dark grey above, silvery-grey beneath. In open water. [9]

Thresher Shark *Alopias vulpinus*
ALOPIDAE L to 3 m. Upper part of tail exaggerated, arching upwards from body axis. Dark grey above, silvery grey below. In open water. [10]

Basking Shark *Cetorhinus maximus*
LAMNIDAE L to 15 m. Mouth with enormous gape; teeth tiny; gill slits almost encircle body. Elephant grey. In open water, occasionally strays into shallows; feeds in surface waters on plankton strained through gill-rakers. [11]

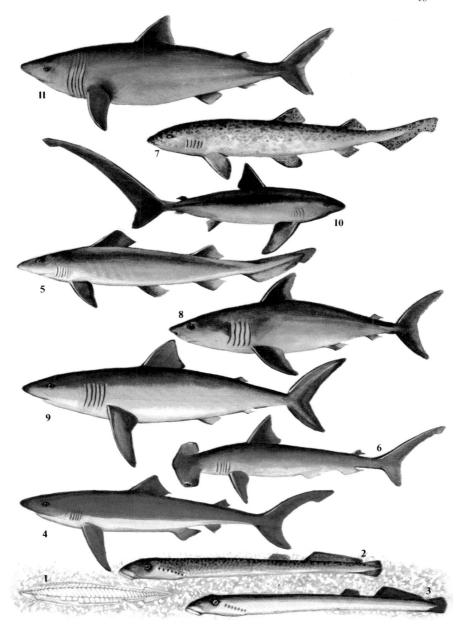

Spurdog, Spiny Dogfish *Squalus acanthias*
SQUALIDAE L to 1.2 m. Shark-like; snout pointed, flattened; eyes relatively large; long, sharp spine in front of both dorsal fins. Grey with white spots, silvery grey beneath. Near the bottom over a variety of substrates. [1]

Humantin *Oxynotus centrina*
OXYNOTIDAE L to 1 m. Thickset; long spines set into anterior of dorsal fins; sexes different in shape. ♀ has very deep body and large anterior dorsal fin extending almost to forehead; gill slits in both sexes very small. Greyish-brown, paler beneath. Near the bottom over sand and mud. [2]

Tope *Galeorhinus galeus*
CARCHARHINIDAE L to 2 m. Snout conical, pointed; teeth pointed with smaller lateral accessory points; tail fin notched. Grey, silvery beneath. In open water. [3]

Monkfish, Angel Fish *Squatina squatina*
SQUATINIDAE L to 2 m. Body flattened dorsoventrally; head broad; pectoral and pelvic fins wing-like; snout blunt; eyes dorsal with large spiracles behind them. Sandy brown above with some greyish-brown mottling, whitish beneath. On sand and gravel, sometimes partly buried. [4]

Electric Ray *Torpedo marmorata*
TORPEDINIDAE L to 60 cm. Body flattened dorsoventrally, head merging almost imperceptibly with broad, semi-circular pectoral fins to give anterior circular outline; eyes dorsal, small, with small spiracles behind them; skin scaleless, smooth; possesses electric organs and can give violent shock if touched. Mottled sandy brown above, pale beneath. On sand, often partly buried. [5]

Thornback Ray *Raja clavata*
RAJIDAE L to 80 cm. Body flattened dorsoventrally, diamond-shaped; head and snout pointed, triangular, merging with pectoral fins; eyes dorsal with large spiracles behind them; skin very rough, many conspicuous spines on dorsal surface and tail. Dull brown with darker mottling above, pale beneath. On sand and mud. [6]

Starry Ray *Raja asterias* is similar, but has fewer, smaller spines and conspicuous, rounded black and yellowish spots on dorsal surface.

Long-nosed Skate *Raja oxyrinchus*
RAJIDAE L to 1.5 m. Body flattened dorsoventrally; front edge of 'wings' slightly concave; snout very long and pointed; no large spines. Greyish-brown or chocolate-brown above; paler beneath with small black spots and stripes. On sand and mud, sometimes half-buried. [7]

Stingray *Dasyatis pastinaca*
DASYATIDAE L to 2.3 m. Superficially like a skate, but no dorsal fins; long, tapering tail, has one, sometimes two, large, serrated, very sharp spines on dorsal surface. Greyish-brown above, paler beneath. On sand and mud, often partly buried. [8]

Eagle Ray *Myliobatis aquila*
MYLIOBATIDAE L to 2 m. Body flattened, diamond-shaped; head broad, with convex snout; pectoral fins huge, triangular, wing-like; tail long, whip-like with large, serrated spine; small dorsal fin just in front of tail spine. Greenish-grey or brown above, paler beneath. In open water and on soft substrates in deep water. [9]

Devil Ray *Mobula mobular*
MOBULIDAE L to 6 m. Body flattened with enormous wing-like, triangular fins and short whip-like tail; dorsal fin small near base of tail; head broad with two horn-like projections; can generate so much speed it sometimes leaves the water. Dark greenish-grey above, pale below. In open water. [10]

Rabbit-fish *Chimaera monstrosa*
CHIMAERIDAE L to 1 m. Body heavy and thick in front tapering towards tail which terminates in long filament; anterior part of dorsal fin triangular, with spine, posterior part long and narrow; pectoral fins triangular, wing-like; head blunt; 6 crushing tooth-plates in mouth, those at front not unlike rabbit teeth; ♂ has curious club-shaped structure on head. Greenish-fawn with brown freckling above, paler below. In deep water. [11]

BONY FISH (Osteichthyes)
Fish with bony internal skeleton and true jaws; body generally covered with scales; paired pectoral and pelvic fins; unpaired fins on back (dorsal) and underneath tail (anal); gills covered by operculum.

Sturgeon *Acipenser sturio*
ACIPENSERIDAE L to 4 m (usually less). Heavy-bodied, snout sharply conical, pointed; 4 barbels beneath round, sucker-like mouth; upper tail-lobe large; 5 longitudinal rows of large, bony plates on body. Grey or greenish above, pale below. On sand and mud, often in brackish water; enters rivers to spawn. [1]

Sprat *Sprattus sprattus*
CLUPEIDAE L to 15 cm. Operculum without radial ridges; pelvic fins just anterior to dorsal fin; tail forked; belly has rough keel formed by ridged scales. Greenish above, silvery below. In open surface water. [2]

Pilchard, Sardine *Sardina pilchardus*
CLUPEIDAE L to 26 cm. Operculum with radiating ridges; pelvic fins below centre of dorsal fin; last rays of anal fin long, protruding; no belly keel. Greenish above, silvery below. In open surface water. [3]

Anchovy *Engraulis encrasicholus*
ENGRAULIDAE L to 20 cm. Slender; mouth huge; lower jaw shorter than upper; pelvic fins just anterior to dorsal fin. Greenish above, silvery below. In open surface water. [4]

Hatchet-fish *Argyropelecus hemigymnus*
STERNOPTYCHIDAE L to 6 cm. Body very deep, rather angular with slender tail; eyes telescopic and upward-pointing; mouth a deep, acute-angled cleft; light organs along belly; several gleaming, silvery plates along sides. Brown above, silvery below. In deep water, sometimes stranded. [5]

Pearlside *Maurolicus muelleri*
GONOSTOMATIDAE L to 7 cm. Slender with rather deeper head; a low adipose fleshy fin behind dorsal fin; light organs along belly and on operculum. Grey above with silvery flanks and belly. In deep water, sometimes stranded in large numbers. [6]

Lantern-fish *Myctophum punctatum* MYCTOPHIDAE is similar, but larger (L to 15 cm), with rounder head; pearl-like light organs extend from lower jaw to tail with short rows on flanks.

Conger Eel *Conger conger*
ANGUILLIDAE L to 2.5 m. A robust and powerful eel which can be aggressive if provoked. Lacks scales and pelvic fins; the jaws are equipped with small but sharp closely packed teeth. Dark brown on the back, and lighter brown or yellow underneath. Among rocks in shallow water, beneath piers. [7]

Common Eel *Anguilla anguilla* is similar, but smaller (L to 1.5 m). Grey-silver to brown-yellow. In coastal waters, estuaries and rivers.

Moray Eel *Muraena helena*
MURAENIDAE L to 1.3 m. Body robust, elongated, jaws moderate length; no pectoral or pelvic fins; dorsal fin continuous with tail and anal fins; no scales. Brown with yellow blotches. Among rocks, in crevices, in fairly open water. [8]

Garfish, Garpike, Greenbone *Belone belone*
BELONIDAE L to 80 cm. Slender, tapering; narrow, forceps-like jaws, upper shorter than lower; dorsal and anal fins just anterior to tail; bones bright green. Green above, silvery below. In open, surface water. [9]

Saury Pike, Skipper *Scomberesox saurus*
SCOMBERESOCIDAE L to 50 cm. Similar to *Belone belone*, but 6 small finlets behind dorsal and anal fins. Bluish-green above with belly silver, bluish spot at base of pectoral fin. In open surface waters. [10]

Flying-fish *Cheilopogon heterurus*
EXOCOETIDAE L to 40 cm. Pectoral fins enormous, wing-like; pelvic fins large, triangular; lower lobe of tail fin larger than upper. Can leave water and glide up to 40 m. Back steel-blue, flanks and belly silvery, pectoral fins blue-grey with transparent tips. In open surface water. [11]

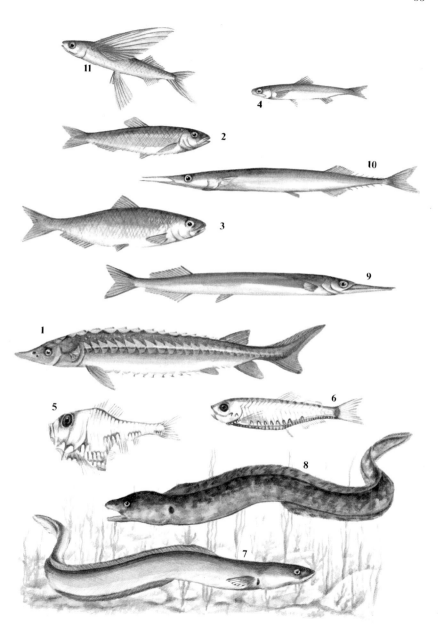

Poor Cod *Trisopterus minutus*
GADIDAE L to 20 cm. Fairly deep-bodied; upper jaw longer than lower; barbel on chin; 3 dorsal fins, the first triangular; 2 anal fins; pelvic fins in front of pectorals. Brown or brownish-grey above, belly silvery, black spot at base of pectoral fin. Often in shallow water around submerged rocks, harbour walls, piers, etc. [1]

Blue Whiting *Micromesistius poutassou*
GADIDAE L to 40 cm. Slender-bodied; lower jaw slightly longer than upper; no barbel; 3 dorsal fins, first 2 triangular. Bluish-grey or brown above, belly silvery, throat black. In open water, sometimes inshore. [2]

Pollack *Pollachius pollachius*
GADIDAE L to 1.2 m. Fairly deep-bodied; lower jaw longer than upper; no barbel; 3 dorsal fins, first triangular, second long-based; lateral line conspicuous, curving over pectoral fin to mid-flank. Brown and green above, underparts silvery. Often in shallow water among rocks, near harbour walls, piers, etc. [3]

Hake *Merluccius merluccius*
MERLUCCIIDAE L to 80 cm. Fairly deep-bodied; lower jaw longer than upper; no barbel; 2 dorsal fins, anterior triangular, posterior elongated, rounded; anal fin similar to posterior dorsal. Back pearly grey, belly silvery. In open water. [4]

Shore Rockling, Three-bearded Rockling
Gaidropsarus mediterraneus GADIDAE
L to 25 cm. Body elongated, slender; 2 barbels on upper jaw, 1 barbel on edges of nostrils; anterior dorsal fin small, with long first fin-ray; posterior dorsal fin and anal fin similar, elongated, rounded. Brownish with large, darker spots above, paler beneath. Among rocks, in rock-pools, also in deeper water. [5]

Trumpet Fish, Snipefish *Macroramphosus scolopax* MACRORAMPHOSIDAE
L to 15 cm. Body laterally flattened, fairly deep in mid-region; snout long and tubular; long serrated spine in front of dorsal fin; body encased in rough-edged scales. Back red-brown, belly silvery white. Deep water, sometimes over sand. [6]

Broad-nosed Pipefish *Syngnathus typhle*
SYNGNATHIDAE L to 35 cm. Slender, round-bodied, worm-like but rather stiff; body ringed; head elongated with broad, laterally flattened snout. Fawn or light brown. In shallow water, often among algae, sometimes in brackish water. [7]
Greater Pipefish *Syngnathus acus* is similar, but has slender, tubular snout and small hump over operculum.
Straight-nosed Pipefish *Nerophis ophidion* is similar, but has 2 ridges along upper surface of snout and no pectoral or tail fins.

Sea Horse *Hippocampus ramulosus*
SYNGNATHIDAE L to 15 cm. Head 'horse-like' with short snout; body plump in mid-region, tapering to slender, prehensile tail; ♂ incubates young in brood sac. Fawn and sandy brown. Among eel-grasses. [8]

Long-nosed Sea Horse *Hippocampus guttulatus* SYNGNATHIDAE
L to 15 cm. Similar to *Hippocampus ramulosus*, but has longer snout and 'mane' of finger-like projections on back above dorsal fin. ♂ incubates young in brood-sac. Among algae, eel-grasses. [9]

John Dory *Zeus faber*
ZEIDAE L to 40 cm. Very deep, laterally compressed body; eyes high on head, mouth highly extensible, set low producing a doleful expression; 2 dorsal fins, anterior with very long rays and spiny scales on each side; pelvic fins long. Greyish-green with a large black spot on the flank. In open water. [10]

Red Boarfish *Capros aper*
CAPROIDAE L to 16 cm. Deep, laterally compressed body; 9 strong spines in anterior dorsal fin, 3 in anal fin; snout conical, pouting; mouth highly extensible. Deep pink. Over muddy habitats in water of medium depth. [11]

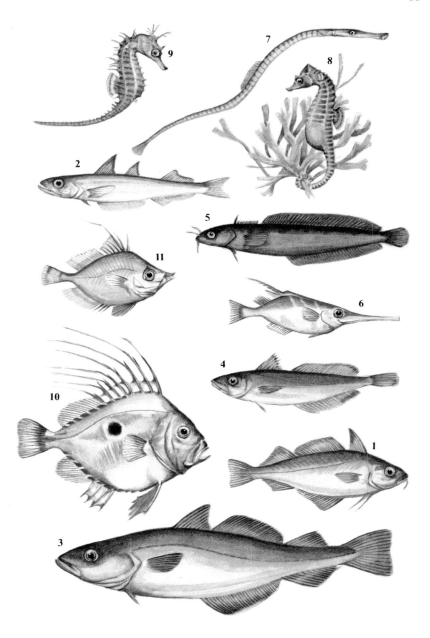

Barracuda *Sphyraena sphyraena*
SPHYRAENIDAE L to 1 m. Body elongated, slender; long, strong teeth; 2 dorsal fins, widely-separated.   Back   greenish-grey, banded, underparts silvery white. A fast predatory fish of open water. [1]

Bass *Dicentrarchus labrax*
PERCICHTHYIDAE L to 80 cm. Body slender; edge of front element of gill cover serrated, 2 spines and conspicuous black smudge on main element; anterior dorsal fin and first ray of posterior spiny. Silvery grey. Over rocks, sand and shingle from shallow to deep water [2]

Wreckfish, Stone Bass *Polyprion americanus* PERCICHTHYIDAE
L to 2 m. Massive; front part of elongated dorsal fin spiny; edge of front element of gill cover serrated, bony ridge on main element. Dark grey or brown with darker blotches. Among boulders, old wrecks, from shallow to deep water. [3]

Dusky Perch, Grouper *Epinephelus guaza*
SERRANIDAE L to 1.4 m. Similar to *Polyprion americanus*; 3 small spines on main element of operculum. Dark brown, mottled dorsal fin tipped orange. Among rocks, in caves. Shallow to deep water. [4]

Comber *Serranus cabrilla*
SERRANIDAE L to 20 cm. Resembling *Epinephelus guaza*, but snout longer; 2 spines on main element of operculum. Light brown banded with dark brown, blue patch above anal fin and red on head and operculum and along sides. Among eel-grasses and algae in shallow water. [5]

Cardinal-fish *Apogon imberbis*
APOGONIDAE L to 15 cm. Body deep; tail region narrower; mouth and eyes very large; fins small, rather spiny. Bright red with darker shading, especially on fin tips; 2 dark bands across eye. In shaded, sheltered places, such as caves, from shallow to deeper water. [6]

Annular Bream *Diplodus annularis*
SPARIDAE L to 18 cm. Deep-bodied with steeply sloping forehead; long dorsal fin spiny in front; teeth protuberant. Goldenbrown with greenish pattern above; blackish-brown band at base of tail. In shallow water. [7]

Saupe *Sarpa salpa*
SPARIDAE L to 30 cm. Distinctly spindleshaped; teeth notched in upper jaw, triangular and saw-edged in lower jaw; long dorsal fins, spiny in front. Green, with golden-yellow bands, and dark smudge at base of pectoral fin. Among rocks and algae in shallow water. [8]
Bogue *Boops boops* is similar, but more slender. Yellowish or yellowish-green with dark longitudinal bands.

Gilthead *Sparus aurata*
SPARIDAE L to 70 cm. Body deep with steep forehead; long dorsal fin, spiny in front. Back olive green, flanks greyish-yellow with dark grey-violet bands, golden bar across forehead, large dark smudge near operculum. Among rocks in shallow water, sometimes in brackish water. [9]

Golden Grey Mullet *Liza aurata*
MUGILIDAE L to 70 cm (often less). Body spindle-shaped; mouth small with fleshy lips; two dorsal fins set widely apart. Back dark silvery-grey, pale yellow line along sides. [10]
Thick-lipped Grey Mullet *Chelon labrosus* is similar, but has 3 rows of wart-like papillae on upper lip.
Thin-lipped Grey Mullet *Liza ramada* is similar, but mouth lacks fleshy lips.

Red Mullet *Mullus barbatus*
MULLIDAE L to 30 cm. Slender; forehead almost vertical; 2 barbels on lower jaw; 3 conspicuous scales extend from end of jaw to below eye; dorsal fins spiny. Reddish-brown, belly white, some yellow banding on flanks. Among rocks in shallow water, sometimes in brackish water. [11]

Striped Mullet *Mullus surmuletus*
MULLIDAE L to 30 cm. Similar to *Mullus barbatus*, but forehead less steep; 2 conspicuous scales from base of jaw to eye. Reddish-brown with yellow bands on flank. Among rocks in shallow water, sometimes in brackish water. [1]

Scad, Horse-mackerel *Trachurus trachurus*
CARANGIDAE L to 35 cm. Slender; mouth angular; 2 spines in front of anal fin; large keeled scales along lateral line, become sharp keel near tail. Silvery grey overall, back greyish-green. In open water. [2]

Pilotfish *Naucrates ductor*
CARANGIDAE L to 40 cm. Deep-bodied; head and forehead rounded; anterior dorsal fin reduced to few spines; 2 spines in front of anal fin; lateral line scales present as keels at base of deeply cleft tail. Silvery grey with broad brownish-grey bands. In open water, often accompanying large fish, such as sharks. [3]

Dolphin (fish) *Coryphaena hippurus*
CORYPHAENIDAE L to 1 m. Head and shoulders very deep; tail narrow, deeply cleft; mouth large; dorsal fin very long; anal fin almost half body length. Bluish-green above, flanks golden, belly white, spotted overall; dorsal fin blue; other fins orange-brown. In open water, follows ships and chases shoals of flying-fish. [4]

Red Band-fish *Cepola rubescens*
CEPOLIDAE L to 50 cm. Slender, elongated, ribbon-like; dorsal and anal fins very long; tail fin reduced, fan-like. Bright pink, colour fading after death. In open water. Burrows in muddy sand. [5]

Demoiselle *Chromis chromis*
POMACENTRIDAE L to 15 cm. Deep-bodied; snout pointed; anterior of dorsal fin spiny, posterior part with longer closer rays; tail deeply forked; scales coarse. Adult, dark brown; juvenile bright blue. In rocky areas in shallow water. [6]

Ballan Wrasse *Labrus bergylta*
LABRIDAE L to 40 cm. Thick and deep-bodied; snout long; thick-lipped mouth; forehead slightly humped; dorsal fin long; tail fin fan-shaped; scales coarse with pale centres and darker hind margins. Can vary its colour. Among weed-covered rocks in shallow water, often coastal. [7]

Rainbow Wrasse *Coris julis*
LABRIDAE L to 20 cm. This species is female when first sexually mature, later becoming male. Slender, shallow-bodied with tapering snout; dorsal fin long, first few rays spiny; tail fin fan-shaped. ♀ phase rust-coloured with yellow flank band and blue spot on operculum; ♂ phase brown overall, flanks blue-green with zig-zag orange band; black spot on spiny part of dorsal fin and centre of flank. Among weed-covered rocks in shallow water. [8]

Axillary Wrasse *Crenilabrus mediterraneus*
LABRIDAE L to 15 cm. Similar to ballan wrasse *Labrus bergylta*, but front element of operculum toothed. Red-brown, dorsal and anal fins blue-tipped; dark spot near base of tail and pectoral fin – the latter dark blue and gold in ♂, brown in ♀. In sandy areas amongst eel-grasses. [9]
Corkwing Wrasse *Crenilabrus melops* is similar, but variable in colour, usually brown and green.

Rock Cook *Ctenolabrus exoletus*
LABRIDAE L to 15 cm. Similar to axillary wrasse *Crenilabrus mediterraneus*, but with dark band across tail fin. Colour variable, usually green, with red and orange patterns on head when sexually active. Among weed-covered rocks in shallow water. [10]
Goldsinny *Ctenolabrus rupestris* is similar, but more shallow-bodied. Reddish-brown with dorsal, dark spot at base of tail and sometimes at front of dorsal fin.

Parrot-fish *Sparisoma cretense*
SCARIDAE L to 40 cm. Solid; snout long; dorsal fin long; teeth fused into sharp crushing plates; scales large and coarse. Reddish-brown or purple, flanks and tail fin violet, the latter white-edged, pectoral and pelvic fins orange. In shallow water, feeds on coralline growths. [11]

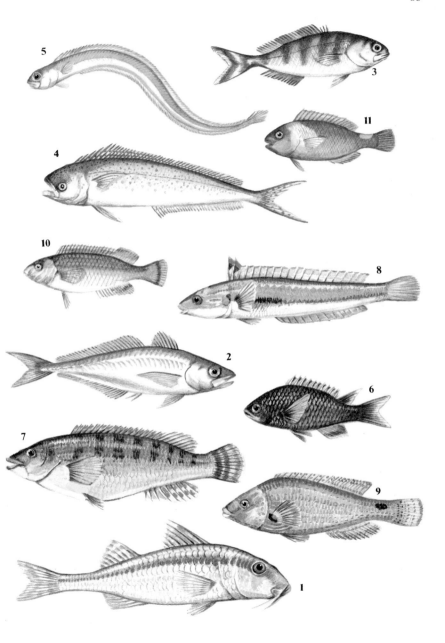

Greater Weever *Trachinus draco*
TRACHINIDAE L to 35 cm. Eyes on top of head, with 2 small spines at top of eye socket; several strong, erectile venomous spines on anterior dorsal fin, one on operculum; pectoral fin notched. Greenish-yellow with grey bands on flanks; black spot near front of anterior dorsal fin. In sandy areas, often partly buried; in moderately deep water. [1]
Lesser Weever *Echiichthys vipera* is similar, smaller (L to 12 cm), lacks spines on eye-socket and pectoral fin notch. Paler anterior dorsal fin black.
weever-fish *Trachinus radiatus* is similar to greater weever, but has a distinctive pattern of spots on the back.

Stargazer *Uranoscopus scaber*
URANOSCOPIDAE L to 25 cm. Solid, muscular; eyes on top of broad head; small projection on lower jaw; operculum heavily sculptured, with one large venom spine; anterior dorsal fin spiny, erectile, venomous. Brown, with some mottling. In sandy areas, often partly buried, in shallow water. [2]

Mackerel *Scomber scombrus*
SCOMBRIDAE L to 40 cm. Long, elegantly tapered toward tail; dorsal fins triangular, widely separated; tail fin forked; row of small finlets behind posterior dorsal and anal fins. Feathery 'mackerel' pattern of light and dark blue-green and black on back, belly silvery. In open surface water. [3]

Spanish Mackerel *Scomber japonicus*
SCOMBRIDAE L to 30 cm. Very similar to Mackerel *Scomber scombrus*, but eyes very large. Greener above with many blue-black lines forming criss-cross pattern on nape, and dark dots on flank within marbled or yellow band. In open water. [4]

Tunny *Thunnus thynnus*
SCOMBRIDAE L to 2 m. Mackerel-shaped, but massive; anterior dorsal fin abruptly tapering; tail fin scimitar-like. Blue-black and greenish above, with blue sheen on flanks, pale below, posterior dorsal fin reddish-yellow. In open water. [5]

Swordfish *Xiphias gladius*
XIPHIIDAE L to 4 m. Highly streamlined; upper jaw a slender, tapering 'sword', up to one-third body length; leading part of dorsal fin is much taller than remainder; tail fin deeply forked. Blue above; silvery beneath. In open water. [6]

Common Dragonet *Callionymus lyra*
CALLIONYMIDAE L to 25 cm. Slender; head broad, flattened; mouth large, thick-lipped; eyes protuberant; dorsal fins larger in ♂. ♀ brown with darker spots; ♂ back brown, otherwise brightly striped blue-green and yellow. On sand and mud in shallow water. [7]

Mediterranean Smooth Sand-eel
Gymnammodytes cicerellus AMMODYTIDAE L to 18 cm. Slender, elongated; edges of dorsal and anal fins undulating; dorsal fin from tail to shoulders, anal fin half this length. Olive-green above, with lustrous blue spots on head and silvery flanks. In sand. Lowest shore to sublittoral. [8]

Tompot Blenny *Parablennius gattorugine*
BLENNIIDAE L to 25 cm. Deep-bodied, especially anteriorly; head massive; eyes high on forehead, with fringed tentacle above each; anterior part of long dorsal fin spiny. Brown overall, with darker bands and green tinges. Among boulders and weeds. Lowest shore to sublittoral. [9]
Note: this is one of many species of blenny common in the Mediterranean.

Pearl-fish *Carapus acus*
CARAPIDAE L to 20 cm. Slender; tapers markedly toward tail; dorsal and anal fins, continuous around tail. Yellowish with reddish spots and some obscure flecking; translucent. Lives within the body cavity of large sea-cucumbers. [10]

Rock Goby *Gobius paganellus*
GOBIIDAE L to 12 cm. Thickset; head flattened, mouth thick-lipped; pelvic fins united to form sucker just behind throat. Brown, mottled, orange band on anterior dorsal fin. Among weed-covered rocks, especially in rock-pools. Lowest shore to sublittoral. [11]

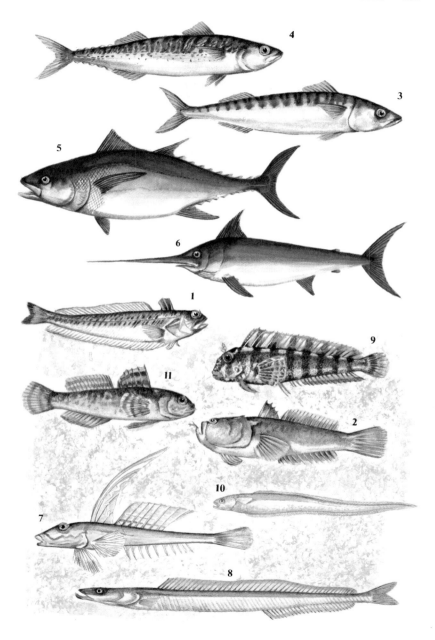

Black Goby *Gobius niger*
GOBIIDAE L to 15 cm. Similar to rock goby *Gobius paganellus*; anterior dorsal fin crest-like in ♂. Brown with darker markings. Among eel-grasses, in shallows. [1]
Giant Goby *Gobius cobitis* is similar, but larger (L to 27 cm); pelvic fins have conspicuous lateral lobe on each side. Basic colour grey, green and yellow with dark blotches above; flanks yellow, white or reddish; ♂ darker.

Red Scorpion-fish *Scorpaena scrofa*
SCORPAENIDAE L to 40 cm. Deep-bodied, muscular; head large, spiny; tentacle over each large eye; small projections beneath lower jaw; anterior part of dorsal fin and operculum have venomous spines. Brownish-red mottled. Among rocks in shallow water. [2]

Striped Gurnard *Trigloporus lastoviza*
TRIGLIDAE L to 35 cm. Head massive, angular; snout blunt; anterior dorsal fin triangular, spiny; three enlarged rays of pectoral fin used as feelers on sea floor. Red with darker flecking, pectoral fins reddish-violet with blue spots. On sand and gravel in shallow water. [3]

Armed Gurnard *Peristedion cataphractum*
PERISTEDIIDAE L to 30 cm. Body covered with armoured scales; snout long, terminates in U-shaped process; numerous fringe-like barbels beneath lower jaw; 2 'feelers' on pectoral fin. Rose-red above, silvery beneath. On sandy substrates in deep water. [4]

Remora, Sucking Fish *Remora remora*
ECHENEIDAE L to 25 cm. Body spindle-shaped; forehead and top of head modified into oval sucker. Brown, fins edged in violet. Attached by sucker to moving objects, such as sharks and turtles. [5]

Plaice *Pleuronectes platessa*
PLEURONECTIDAE L to 55 cm. Head and body flattened, rounded diamond shape, lying permanently on left side; left eye migrates during development to lie high on forehead on right side. Right (upper) side brown or grey-brown with bright orange spots, capable of much colour-change, left side white. On sand in shallow water. [6]
Flounder *Platichthys flesus* is similar, but smaller (L to 20 cm); right side dull brown. Often in brackish water.

Common Sole *Solea solea*
SOLEIDAE L to 35 cm. Asymmetrically flattened, oval, lying permanently on left side; head and tail fin rounded. Brownish-green or brownish-grey with darker markings. On sand in shallow water, sometimes near river mouths. [7]
Solenette *Buglossidium luteum* is similar, but smaller (L to 10 cm); right side with dark uniform spots, and some dark dorsal and ventral fin-rays.

Trigger-fish *Balistes carolinensis*
BALISTIDAE L to 40 cm. Body compressed, diamond-shaped; snout conical, with small mouth at apex; rays of anterior dorsal fin very strong erectile spines; pelvic fin modified into single erectile spine. Pale grey or yellowish-grey with blue or pale yellow flecks and spots. Among boulders in shallow water. [8]

Sunfish *Mola mola*
MOLIDAE L to 2.5 m. Massive; body compressed laterally; dorsal and anal fins elongated triangles, continuous with arc-shaped tail fin. Greyish brown. In open water. [9]

Cornish Sucker *Lepadogaster lepadogaster*
GOBIESOCIDAE L to 7 cm. Body flattened; dorsal, anal and tail fins continuous; pelvic fins and part of flat ventral surface modified into powerful sucker. Deep red, reddish-brown and green above yellowish-white beneath. Clinging to stones. Lowest shore to sublittoral. [10]

Common Angler *Lophius piscatorius*
LOPHIIDAE L to 1.5 m. Body flattened; head very large, spiny, immense gape; lower jaw fringed with small barbels; pectoral fins fleshy; individual rays of anterior part of dorsal fin stand erect along forehead, long front ray is tipped with fringed tuft and used as fishing lure. Dark brown above, white beneath. In shallow water. [11]

AMPHIBIANS (Amphibia)
Cold-blooded vertebrates with smooth, moist skin, usually live close to water; have aquatic larvae – tadpoles (frogs, toads) or miniature versions of adults (newts, salamanders). Often brightly coloured and capable of colour change.

Fire Salamander *Salamandra salamandra*
SALAMANDRIDAE L to 28 cm. Body elongated, robust, tail short; eyes protuberant. Generally black with large scattered bright yellow, orange or red spots, but may be yellow with black stripes. In wooded, hilly areas close to water. Nocturnal. [1]

Natterjack Toad *Bufo calamita*
BUFONIDAE L to 10 cm. Robust, short-limbed; skin warty; conspicuous swelling just behind eye. Brown, green or grey with darker markings, yellow dorsal stripe, eye silvery gold. In a wide variety of habitats; may breed in brackish water. Nocturnal. [2]

Western Spadefoot Toad *Pelobates cultripes* PELOBATIDAE L to 10 cm. Body plump, large; few scattered warts; prominent 'spade' on hind foot. Grey, white or yellow with dark brown or greenish blotches, eye large, greenish or silvery. In sandy areas; dig themselves into sand during day and periods of drought. Nocturnal. [3]

Common Tree-frog *Hyla arborea*
HYLIDAE L to 5 cm. Small-bodied; adhesive pads at tips of fingers and toes; skin smooth. Usually leaf green, but may be yellow or brown with darker blotches, brown flank stripe; ♂ has brown vocal sac beneath chin, spherical when inflated. In bushy places, including reed-beds; active climber. Chiefly nocturnal. [4]

Marsh or Lake Frog *Rana ridibunda*
RANIDAE L to 15 cm. Slim-waisted; robust; skin slightly warty; snout pointed. Olive or green with darker blotches. In water; gregarious; may sit on lily-pads or float among aquatic vegetation with only head showing. More active by night but sings during day and night. [5]

REPTILES (Reptilia)
Cold-blooded vertebrates with dry scaly skins. Turtles and tortoises have bony 'shell' or carapace. Typically long-bodied and short-legged. Lay shelled eggs or give birth to live young; young resemble adults.

Leathery Turtle *Dermochelys coriacea*
DERMOCHELYIDAE L to 1.8 m (carapace). Body massive; carapace ridged, leathery, tapers markedly toward tail; 2 tooth-like points at front of upper jaw. Dark grey or greyish-brown, with lighter flecks. Swims in open seawater where it feeds upon jelly-fish and salps. [6]

Loggerhead Turtle *Caretta caretta*
CHELONIDAE L to 1.1 m (carapace). Carapace oval, long; dorsal plates smooth in adult, 'saw-toothed' in juveniles. Reddish-brown. In open water, but may come inshore to feed on crabs, sea-urchins and molluscs. [7]
Green Turtle *Chelonia mydas* is similar, but has different arrangement of plates in carapace. Brown or olive with darker mottling.

Hermann's Tortoise *Testudo hermanni*
TESTUDINIDAE L to 20 cm (carapace). Carapace domed, often lumpy; large scale on tail tip. Yellow, orange and brown, sometimes greenish, with darker overlay. In a variety of habitats, including wooded and bushy areas, dunes and rubbish-dumps. [8]

Moorish Gecko *Tarentola mauritanica*
GEKKONIDAE L to 15 cm. Body robust, flattened; conspicuous adhesive pads on fingers and toes; only 3rd and 4th toes with claws; skin spiny, with prominent tubercles. Brownish with dark bands on tail. In hot coastal areas. Diurnal. [9]

Turkish Gecko *Hemidactylus turcicus*
GEKKONIDAE L to 10 cm. Body slender; skin with many tubercles; adhesive pads on fingers and toes. Brown with darker markings and tail bands, appearance pale, translucent. In hot coastal areas, often on cliffs and boulders. Nocturnal. [10]

European Pond Terrapin *Emys orbicularis*
EMYDIDAE L TO 20 cm. Carapace oval,
flattened; neck, and legs scaly; tail long,
pointed. Black, dark grey or greyish-
brown, usually with yellowish spots and
streaks on head, neck and margins of
carapace. In still, or slow-flowing water
with good weed growth; sometimes in
brackish water. [1]

Mediterranean Chameleon *Chamaeleo
chamaeleon* CHAMAELEONTIDAE
L to 30 cm. Body flattened laterally, head
massive with neck 'frill'; eyes large, on
conical supports, highly mobile; tail prehensile; movements very slow and delibe-
rate. Basically green, but capable of rapid
change from pale shades to black; often
pale at night. In bushes, but often in dry
places. [2]

Three-toed Skink *Chalcides chalcides*
SCINCIDAE L to 40 cm. Body snake-like;
tail as long as body; limbs tiny, each with
three toes. Olive, grey brown, bronze or

sandy, usually metallic, sometimes with
longitudinal stripe. In damp places with
fairly dense vegetation. [3]

Green Lizard *Lacerta viridis*
LACERTIDAE L to 13 cm (body). Body
slender; tail up to twice body length; head
short. ♂ green with fine black stippling,
head darker with paler stippling; ♀ green
or brown, blotched or striped; belly of
both sexes yellow, throat blue, especially
in ♂. In and around areas with dense
vegetation. [4]

Jewelled Lizard *Lacerta lepida* is larger and
flatter. Often has prominent blue spots
on flanks or black-rimmed white spots on
back.

Wall Lizard *Podarcis muralis* is smaller (L
to 7.5 cm). Colour and pattern very
variable, usually grey or brown with
darker streaks and stripes.

Spanish Sandracer *Psammodromus
hispanicus* LACERTIDAE
L to 5 cm (body). Body slender; tail very

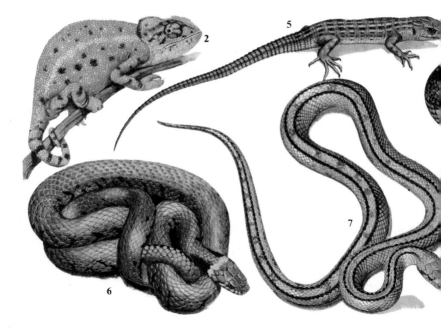

long, may be twice body length; scales large, keeled, overlapping. Colour variable, grey, metallic brown, olive or deep yellow, sometimes striped or barred. In dry, open country, often with scattered shrubs. [5]

Grass Snake *Natrix natrix*
COLUBRIDAE L to 2 m (often less). Body thick; head well-defined, rounded; dorsal scales keeled. Greenish, olive-grey, brown or steel-grey with dark blotches and occasional pale stripes; neck collar yellow, white, orange or red, bordered black. Usually in damp places, woods and hedgerows. [6]
Viperine Water-snake *Natrix maura* is similar, but shorter. Usually has distinctive series of diamond-shaped dark blotches or zig-zag stripe.

Ladder Snake *Elaphe scalaris*
COLUBRIDAE L to 1.6 m. Slender-bodied; scales smooth; snout pointed, overhanging. Yellow-grey or mid-brown with two dark dorsal stripes; juveniles have distinctive 'ladder' pattern of dark bands. In sunny, often stony places, vineyards, abandoned buildings. [7]

Southern Smooth Snake *Coronella girondica* COLUBRIDAE
L to 80 cm (usually less). Body slender, cylindrical; neck poorly defined; snout rounded, with saddle-shaped pattern. Brown, grey or yellow, often pinkish above, with bold, irregular, dark bars and dark line from side of throat to eye, underparts yellow, orange or red, often with darker patterns. Usually in dry habitats. [8]

Montpelier Snake *Malpolon monspessulanus* COLUBRIDAE
L to 2 m. Body slender, rather stiff; head with distinct eyebrow ridges, snout overhangs lower jaw. Grey, reddish-brown, olive, greenish or nearly black, sometimes with scattered light or dark spots. Usually in dry habitats with plant cover; sometimes in sandy areas near the sea. [9]

BIRDS (Aves)

Fore-limbs modified as wings. Special adaptations of wing-feathers permit soaring, gliding, hovering. The horny bill shows a great variety of modifications for different foods and feeding methods.

Dabchick, Little Grebe *Tachybaptus ruficollis* PODICIPEDIDAE

L to 27 cm. Compact; in summer cheeks and neck chestnut-brown, back dark brown, pale patch at base of bill; in winter overall greyish-fawn; ♀ duller than ♂. Resident throughout in freshwater, sometimes in estuaries. Trilling song. Food: small fish, invertebrates. [s1] [w2]

Great Crested Grebe *Podiceps cristatus*

PODICIPEDIDAE L to 48 cm. Large, long-necked; back brown, otherwise white, crown of head with two feathery horns and frills (absent in winter). Resident or winter visitor throughout on rivers, lakes, estuaries. Harsh barking call. Elaborate displays. Food: mainly small fish. [s3] [w4]

Black-necked Grebe *Podiceps nigricollis*

PODICIPEDIDAE L to 30 cm. Long-necked; in winter black above, otherwise white, merging on cheeks with dark crown, bill slightly upturned; golden summer 'ear' tufts. Resident or winter visitor to freshwater, sometimes estuaries. Food: small fish, invertebrates. [5]

Cory's Shearwater *Calonectris diomedea*

PROCELLARIIDAE L to 46 cm. A bird of open ocean; uniformly brown above, underparts and patch on upper tail white, bill yellow. Breeds on rocky islands and cliffs. Colonies produce a raucous cacophony. Food: fish and crustaceans. [6]

Manx Shearwater *Puffinus puffinus*

PROCELLARIIDAE L to 35 cm. Typically, very dark grey above with sharply contrasting white underparts, bill dark grey; western Mediterranean race has greyish underparts, eastern race has brownish upper parts. Call, a raucous cooing. In open water, breeds on rocky islands, noisy by night. Food: fish. [7]

Storm Petrel, Mother Cary's Chicken

Hydrobates pelagicus HYDROBATIDAE L to 15 cm. Region's smallest open-water bird; uniformly black except for white rump patch and pale line beneath wings. Breeds in excavated burrows and cliff crevices; purring 'song' by night. Food: plankton, fish, floating debris, algae. [8]

Gannet, Solan Goose *Sula bassana*

SULIDAE L to 90 cm. A large bird which plunges, dart-like, into the water from great heights; predominantly white with buff head and black wing-tips. Immature plumage dark. Winter visitor to W. Mediterranean. Food: fish, offal. [9]

Cormorant, Great Cormorant

Phalacrocorax carbo PHALACROCORACIDAE L to 90 cm. Wings and tail bronze-green, otherwise blue-black, white patch on face and, in summer, on thigh; bill large, hooked, yellow; older birds, especially of North African races, have face and neck mostly white when breeding. Typical stance with wings extended when drying wing-feathers. Mainly winter visitor. Food: fish. [10]

Shag *Phalacrocorax aristotelis* is similar to cormorant, but slighter (L to 76 cm). Black with greenish sheen; curved crest in breeding season. Scattered colonies throughout on islands. Food: mainly fish.

Pygmy Cormorant *Phalacrocorax pygmeus*

PHALACROCORACIDAE L to 48 cm. Head shorter than cormorant and red-brown when breeding. Scarce resident in east on freshwater. Food: small fish. [11]

Dalmatian Pelican *Pelecanus crispus*

PELECANIDAE L to 1.8 m. Large, with long, pouched bill; white with grey shading, bill-pouch orange. In estuaries and lagoons in east. Food: fish. [12]

White Pelican *Pelecanus onocrotalus*

PELECANIDAE L to 1.8 m. White with pink shading, yellow chest patch, black area on under-surface of wings, bill-pouch pink or yellow. In large shallow lakes, lagoons, estuaries in east of region. Food: fish. [13]

Bittern *Botaurus stellaris*
ARDEIDAE L to 76 cm. A large, heavy bird with extensible neck; brownish-buff, heavily flecked with dark brown and black, crown black. Resident in reed-beds in north and west. Song, a resonant booming. Food: mainly fish. Very shy. [1]

Little Bittern *Ixobrychus minutus*
ARDEIDAE L to 35 cm. When perching appears compact; ♂ black upper parts, buff underparts with conspicuous white section on wing (clearly visible in flight), ♀, juvenile dark brown and black above, flecked brownish-buff below. Summer visitor to reedbeds in most of region. Various croaking calls. Food: fish and other water-dwellers. [♂2]

Night Heron, Black-crowned Night Heron
Nycticorax nycticorax ARDEIDAE
L to 61 cm. Habitual hunched-up posture; crown and back black, long, slender, white crest, breast and underparts white, wings grey, eyes red. Summer or passage visitor in wet habitats. Nocturnal. Croaking call. Food: fish and other water animals. [3]

Squacco Heron *Ardeola ralloides*
ARDEIDAE L to 46 cm. Predominantly buff, wings and tail white; mature bird has long crest, blue bill with black tip. Summer or passage visitor to marshes, riversides, reedbeds. Harsh, high-pitched call. Food: fish and other water-dwellers. [4]

Cattle Egret *Bubulcus ibis*
ARDEIDAE L to 51 cm. A compact bird; crown, back and breast buff, otherwise white, legs red. Scarce, but increasing resident in south. Guttural calls. Food: invertebrates flushed by cattle which it accompanies. [5]

Little Egret *Egretta garzetta*
ARDEIDAE L to 56 cm. Slender; entirely white, bill and legs black, feet bright yellow; adult has long, crest and plumes on neck and wings. Resident, winter or passage visitor to marshes, lagoons. Barking call. Food: fish and aquatic invertebrates. [6]

Grey Heron *Ardea cinerea*
ARDEIDAE L to 90 cm. A tall, stately bird; predominantly grey and white, slender black crest, legs yellow. Resident, especially in east, winter and passage visitor to shallow fresh and coastal waters. Call *'fraaank'*. Food: aquatic animals. [7]

Purple Heron *Ardea purpurea*
ARDEIDAE L to 79 cm. Slender; crown, belly and slender crest black, neck rust-coloured, breast chestnut-brown, both with black and white stripes and black flecks, otherwise dark grey. Summer or passage visitor to reedbeds; very shy. Call and food as grey heron. [8]

White Stork *Ciconia ciconia*
CICONIIDAE L to 1 m. Tall, massive; white, wings black with white patch on the inner part; bill and legs red. Scarce summer and passage visitor to marshes and farmland. Hisses and clatters bill. Food: rodents, frogs and invertebrates. [9]

Glossy Ibis *Plegadis falcinellus*
THRESKIORNITHIDAE L to 56 cm. A slender-looking bird, especially when extending its head to feed; bill long, curved; purplish-brown or deep maroon overall. Juvenile dark grey above, paler below. Scarce summer and passage visitor to shallow fresh and salt waters in east of region. Food: fish and other water-dwellers. [10]

Spoonbill *Platalea leucorodia*
THRESKIORNITHIDAE L to 90 cm. Large with spatulate bill; all-white but for yellow-tipped black bill, black legs and yellow collar. Breeds in south and east in dense reedbeds, passage elsewhere. Food: fish, invertebrates. [11]

Greater Flamingo *Phoenicopterus ruber*
PHOENICOPTERIDAE L to 1.25 m. Tall long-legged with a distinctively hooked, massive bill; pale pink with bright pink and black wings (visible only in flight), bill bright pink with black tip, legs bright pink. Winter visitor to lagoons but a few breeding colonies. Call, a harsh honk. Food: aquatic invertebrates. [12]

White-fronted Goose *Anser albifrons*
ANATIDAE L to 76 cm. Large, with white band across the sides of the face and the forehead; underparts heavily barred black, bill pink, legs orange. Winter visitor to marshes in east where it grazes. Honking in flight. [1]

Greylag Goose *Anser anser*
ANATIDAE L to 90 cm. A heavy, ponderous bird; grey; paler barring on wings, trailing margins black (visible in flight), bill orange, legs pink. Winter visitor to grazing marshes; pink-billed race resident in east. Loud honking in flight. [2]

Shelduck *Tadorna tadorna*
ANATIDAE L to 60 cm. A large, goose-like duck; head dark green, neck and underparts mostly white with some black markings, chestnut breast band extends around front of body; wings black with green speculum, bill red, legs flesh-pink. Mainly winter visitor to muddy shores. ♀ quacks rapidly in flight; ♂ hisses. Food: mainly marine invertebrates. [♂3]

Wigeon *Anas penelope*
ANATIDAE L to 46 cm. ♂ very distinctive; head and breast reddish-chestnut, crown buff; otherwise grey, but forewing white, speculum green, tail black; ♀ predominantly brown. Winter visitor in flocks to estuaries and shallows. ♂ whistles, ♀ purrs. Food: vegetation. [♂4] [♀5]

Gadwall *Anas strepera*
ANATIDAE L to 51 cm. Both sexes dull; ♂ chiefly grey, leading edge of wing chestnut, tail black, belly white; ♀ mainly brown, belly white. Winter visitor to grazing marshes. ♂ grunts, ♀ quacks. [♂6] [♀7]

Teal *Anas crecca*
ANATIDAE L to 35 cm. ♂ has chestnut-brown head with white-bordered green stripe, neck brownish, breast white, otherwise grey, tail darker, with buff patch; ♀ speckled brown with black and green speculum. Winter visitor in flocks to marshes and estuaries. ♂ has croaking whistle; ♀ quacks. Food: vegetation. [♂8] [♀9]

Mallard *Anas platyrhynchos*
ANATIDAE L to 58 cm. Commonest duck of the region; ♂ has lustrous green head, narrow white collar, chestnut or purple-brown breast, black and white tail, speculum electric-blue; ♀ mottled brown. Resident in north, winter visitor in south. Food: vegetation. [*not illustrated*]

Pintail *Anas acuta*
ANATIDAE L to 66 cm. Rather slender; ♂ mainly grey with head rich brown, neck and breast white, a streak extending up side of head, tail very long and narrow, speculum bronzy; ♀ speckled brown, tail shorter. Winter visitor to estuaries; breeds occasionally. Food: mainly vegetation. ♂ calls nasally; ♀ quacks. [♂10] [♀11]

Garganey *Anas querquedula*
ANATIDAE L to 38 cm. A small, slender duck; ♂ has brown head with conspicuous white stripe from above eye down side of neck, brown breast, blue-grey forewing, greyish-white flanks, green speculum, scapular feathers of wing long and curved, overhanging rest of wing; ♀ mottled brown with blue-grey forewing and green speculum. Mainly summer and passage visitor to marshes, estuaries. Food: mainly vegetation. ♂ has distinctive 'croaking' call; ♀ quacks. [♂12] [♀13]

Shoveler *Anas clypeata*
ANATIDAE L to 50 cm. Distinctive broad bill with shovel-like tip; ♂ lustrous green head, white breast, chestnut-brown flanks, pale blue forewing, green speculum; ♀ speckled brown with pale blue forewing and green speculum. Mainly winter visitor to fresh and brackish waters. ♂ grunts; ♀ quacks. [♂14] [♀15]

Marbled Duck *Marmaronetta angustirostris* ANATIDAE
L to 80 cm. Distinctive coloration common to ♂ and ♀; from a distance grey, although colour actually marbled grey on a lighter background; long dark line passes through the eye region, crown shaggy rather than crested. Resident, visitor to south. ♂ squeaks; ♀ whistles. Food: aquatic invertebrates, vegetation. [16]

Red-crested Pochard *Netta rufina*
ANATIDAE L to 56 cm. ♂ has bright red head, bill and legs, otherwise black and brown with white flanks, head has a distinctive fuzzy crest; ♀ brown plumage, pale cheeks and, like ♂, broad white wing-bars (visible in flight). Mainly resident in north, winter visitor to south, on brackish and freshwater lagoons, in reedbeds. Food: mainly vegetation. [♂1] [♀2]

Pochard *Aythya ferina*
ANATIDAE L to 46 cm. ♂ grey above with chestnut-brown head, black breast and tail, grey back and flanks; ♀ brown head, neck and breast, otherwise greyish-brown; bill in ♂ and ♀ blue-grey with black tip and base. Mainly winter visitor but resident Balkans; on fresh and brackish waters. Food: vegetation and seeds, sometimes invertebrates. [♂3] [♀4]

Ferruginous Duck *Aythya nyroca*
ANATIDAE L to 40 cm. ♂ overall warm chestnut-brown with a broad white wing-bar (visible in flight) and sharply contrasting white area beneath tail; ♀ dull brown overall, with same white wing-bar and area beneath tail; bill in ♂ and ♀ blackish. Resident on fresh and brackish waters to north of region; also winter visitor. Food: chiefly vegetation collected underwater, some invertebrates. [♂5]

Tufted Duck *Aythya fuligula*
ANATIDAE L to 43 cm. Both sexes crested; ♂ more conspicuous, drooping crest predominantly black, but flanks, belly and wing-bar white; ♀ mainly brown; both sexes have yellow eyes and grey-blue bill. Winter visitor to fresh waters, breeding occasionally. ♂ whistles; ♀ growls. Food: invertebrates, occasionally some plant material. [♂6] [♀7]

Goldeneye *Bucephala clangula*
ANATIDAE L to 46 cm. Recognisable by the almost triangular shape of the head due to the peaked crest; ♂ has a black head with green sheen and conspicuous white patch between eye and bill, body and wings black, underparts and hindwing predominantly white; ♀ chiefly grey with brown head and no white patch. Wings audible in flight. Winter visitor to coastal waters in north of region. Food: invertebrates and fish, sometimes vegetation. [♂8] [♀9]

Smew *Mergus albellus*
ANATIDAE L to 41 cm. ♂ white except for a black eye-patch and lines on wings, wingtips black, tail grey; ♀ chestnut cap, white throat, otherwise grey, with a white wingbar. Winter visitor to estuaries in north and east of region. ♀ calls harshly. Food: aquatic invertebrates. [♂10] [♀11]

Red-breasted Merganser *Mergus serrator*
ANATIDAE L to 58 cm. Both sexes have elongated slightly hooked bills and conspicuous double crests; ♂ dark green head, crest and back, otherwise chestnut and white, with black wing-tips, grey flanks and tail; ♀ chestnut head and neck, grey upper parts, white underparts. Winter visitor to coastal waters. ♀ calls harshly. Food: invertebrates and fish. [♂12] [♀13]

White-headed Duck *Oxyura leucocephala*
ANATIDAE L to 46 cm. Both sexes heavy-headed: ♂ head white with black crown and neck, otherwise dark brown with a rusty tinge, bill bright blue; ♀ greyer with a conspicuous pale cheek band; bill blue-grey. Tail pointed, often carried upright when swimming. Resident on shallow brackish and freshwater lagoons, mainly in west of region. Food: aquatic invertebrates. [♂14] [♀15]

Honey Buzzard *Pernis apivorus*
ACCIPITRIDAE L to 58 cm. Mainly brown above with variable amounts of brown and white below, a double broad dark bar near base of tail, underwing pale with double dark bands, bill hooked, black with yellow cere. Soars on flat wings, but droops wings when gliding. Summer visitor to woods in north of region; on passage elsewhere. Mewing calls. Carnivorous, often robs the nests of bees and wasps on the ground. [1]

Black Kite *Milvus migrans*
ACCIPITRIDAE L to 56 cm. Tail wedge-shaped with a slight fork; mainly darkish brown with paler head and reddish under-parts, bill hooked, grey-black, cere yellow. Mainly summer visitor to varied habitats, including towns and often by water. Shrill call. Food: carrion and small mammals. [2]

Red Kite *Milvus milvus*
ACCIPITRIDAE L to 61 cm. Tail wedge-shaped, deeply forked; plumage reddish-brown, head pale, flecked, a pale patch under the wing visible in flight, bill hooked, grey-black, cere yellow. Resident or summer visitor to north and west of region, in woods or maquis. Shrill mewing call. Food: chiefly small mammals. [3]

White-tailed Eagle, Sea Eagle *Haliaeetus albicilla* ACCIPITRIDAE
L to 90 cm. A massive bird with very broad wings; dark brown, tail wedge-shaped, white; bill massive, hooked, yellow; cere yellow. Resident on rocky coasts in north-east. Food: fish, caught by plucking from the water with the talons, rarely dives. [4]

Egyptian Vulture *Neophron percnopterus*
ACCIPITRIDAE L to 66 cm. Predominantly white, face and throat naked, yellow; shaggy, yellow ruff, outer wing feathers black; juvenile all-black; bill long, yellow with a black hooked tip. Summer visitor throughout region to open country and near habitations. Food: carrion. [5]

Griffon Vulture *Gyps fulvus*
ACCIPITRIDAE L to 1 m. Large with head and neck appearing naked, but actually covered in fine, white down; overall light brown, with white ruff; bill massive, hooked, yellow. Mainly resident throughout region in open mountainous country. May soar at great height. Food: carrion. [6]

Black Vulture, Cinereous Vulture
Aegypius monachus ACCIPITRIDAE
L to 1.1 m. The largest vulture of the region, similar in shape to griffon vulture, but with a longer and more wedge-shaped tail; head black with bare blue-grey skin extending over neck, otherwise very dark brown, neck-ruff black. Broken distribution as resident mainly in north and east of region, in open country. Calls varied. Food: carrion. [7]

Short-toed Eagle *Circaetus gallicus*
ACCIPITRIDAE L to 69 cm. A small eagle with large, rounded head like an owl; brown, head paler, underparts almost white, barred brown; bill hooked, blue-grey, legs heavily scaled. Summer visitor to open wooded country and maquis. Mewing calls. Food: largely snakes. [8]

Marsh Harrier *Circus aeruginosus*
ACCIPITRIDAE L to 56 cm. A large bird with broad wings; chiefly brown, face and throat paler, belly reddish, wings of ♂ grey, black-tipped, of ♀ brown, bill hooked, black. Resident throughout region except south-east in marshes, reedbeds. ♂ and ♀ have distinctive calls. Food: small mammals, birds, amphibians, snakes. [♂9] [♀10]

Hen Harrier *Circus cyaneus*
ACCIPITRIDAE L to 51 cm. ♂ grey with prominent white rump and black wing-tips; ♀ brown with barred tail and white rump, bill hooked, black. Mainly winter visitor to coastal marshes, reedbeds, dunes. Call a repeated *kek*. Food: small mammals, birds, eggs. [♂11] [♀12]

Pallid Harrier *Circus macrourus*
ACCIPITRIDAE L to 48 cm. Very similar to hen harrier, but ♂ paler grey with less black on wing-tips and no white rump patch; ♀ more slender with less clearly defined tail-bars and narrower rump patch. Winter visitor to open country in south and east. Food: small birds. [♂13]

Goshawk *Accipiter gentilis*
ACCIPITRIDAE L to 61 cm. Short, broad wings; upper parts brown, underparts pale, barred, tail barred, blue-black. Resident in forests in north. Loud repeated alarm call. Food: small mammals, birds, reptiles. [♀1]

Sparrowhawk *Accipiter nisus*
ACCIPITRIDAE L to ♂ 28 cm, ♀ 38 cm. ♂ slate-grey above, reddish, barred beneath; ♀ grey-brown above, tail barred. Resident in wooded country in north and west. Repeated alarm call. Food: small birds, mammals, insects. [♀2]

Buzzard *Buteo buteo*
ACCIPITRIDAE L to 56 cm. Broad-winged, colour variable; may be very pale, dark or reddish. Resident in wooded country; winter visitor to south and east. Gull-like call. Food: small mammals, invertebrates. [3]

Imperial Eagle *Aquila heliaca*
ACCIPITRIDAE L to 84 cm. Distinctive deep brown, with paler head and neck and pale area on tail, shoulders white. Resident in scrubby forest, maquis, marshes. Food: carrion, mammals, snakes and birds. [4]

Golden Eagle *Aquila chrysaetos*
ACCIPITRIDAE L to 88 cm. Dark brown with golden head, tail brown with some white. Resident in mountains throughout region. Call a whistling bark. Food: varied, but chiefly relatively large mammals and birds. [5]

Booted Eagle *Hieraaetus pennatus*
ACCIPITRIDAE L to 53 cm. More common paler form has tawny-brown upper parts with dark mottling; dark form has dark brown upper parts and reddish-brown underparts. Summer visitor or passage migrant in wooded hill country. Food: birds, small mammals and reptiles. [*pale form* 6]

Bonelli's Eagle *Hieraaetus fasciatus*
ACCIPITRIDAE L to 74 cm. Similar to booted eagle but distinguished by pale, speckled underparts and broad black band on wings. Resident in mountainous country; musical call. Food: birds, small mammals and reptiles. [7]

Osprey *Pandion haliaetus*
PANDIONIDAE L to 58 cm. Upper parts brown, underparts predominantly speckled white; wings long and broad. Passage migrant to coasts, lakes, but resident in west of region. Insignificant yelping call. Food: fish captured by diving. [8]

Lesser Kestrel *Falco naumanni*
FALCONIDAE L to 30 cm. ♂ grey, tawny, and reddish-brown with no flecking, wing-tips and tip of tail black; ♀ reddish-brown, with distinctive flecking. In open country. Repeated alarm call. Nests colonially. Food: insects, small mammals. [♂9]

Kestrel *Falco tinnunculus*
FALCONIDAE L to 34 cm. Similar to lesser kestrel, but ♂ spotted mantle; hovers with rapidly vibrating wing-tips and splayed tail. Resident throughout in open country and near human habitation. Shrill repeated alarm call. Food: small mammals and insects. [♂10]

Hobby *Falco subbuteo*
FALCONIDAE L to 36 cm. ♂ grey above, underparts fawn, streaked thighs russet; ♀ browner. Summer visitor to open wooded country. Call like kestrel. Spectacular mating flight. Food: birds, insects taken on the wing. [11]

Eleonora's Falcon *Falco eleonorae*
FALCONIDAE L to 38 cm. Very long tail and wings which reach to tip of tail when at rest; light form has dark brown upper parts; dark form blackish-brown. Summer visitor to coast. [*light form* 12]

Peregrine Falcon *Falco peregrinus*
FALCONIDAE L to 48 cm. Coloration very variable, from light to dark grey above with barred buff underparts. Characteristic anchor shape in flight. Resident throughout north and west. Wailing call. Food: mainly birds. [13]

Rock Partridge *Alectoris graeca*
PHASIANIDAE L to 33 cm. Compact; upper parts and breast violet-grey, belly reddish-buff; legs red. Resident in northeast on rocky and thinly grassed hillsides, in vineyards. Calls distinctive and various. Food: insects, leaves, seeds. [1]

Red-legged Partridge *Alectoris rufa*
PHASIANIDAE L to 34 cm. Upper parts predominantly violet-grey, belly reddish-buff; legs red. Resident in west in open country, garrigue, sand-dunes, semidesert. Calls *chuck-chikar*. Food: insects, leaves and seeds. [2]

Barbary Partridge *Alectoris barbara*
PHASIANIDAE L to 33 cm. Overall violet-grey, head pale grey with darker crown and buff stripe behind eye, breast-band chestnut with white speckles; legs red. A North African species; rocky hillsides, scrub and desert. Calls *chukar*. Food: mainly leaves, shoots, seeds. [3]

Grey Partridge *Perdix perdix*
PHASIANIDAE L to 30 cm. Lower breast pale grey with conspicuous dark horseshoe mark, back and tail violet-brown, legs grey. Resident in north in open country, heaths, sand-dunes. Call typically *kee-rick*. Food: insects, seeds, leaves. [4]

Quail *Coturnix coturnix*
PHASIANIDAE L to 18 cm. Reddish-brown with stripes and speckles, ♂ has black-white-black band on throat. Summer visitor to north, resident or passage migrant elsewhere, in farmland, open grassland. Typical call *'wet-my-lips'*. Food: insects, seeds, leaves. [5]

Water Rail *Rallus aquaticus*
RALLIDAE L to 28 cm. Slender with long, tapering bill; upper parts rich brown, underparts and face, grey, flanks barred black and white. Resident in marshes. Loud squeaking calls. Food: insects, molluscs, seeds, small plants. [6]

Moorhen, Common Gallinule *Gallinula chloropus* RALLIDAE

L to 33 cm. Black overall with white along flank and beneath tail, forehead and bill bright red. Resident almost throughout region on fresh water. Loud *kurruck* call. Food: mainly vegetation, some invertebrates. [*not illustrated*]

Purple Gallinule, Purple Swamphen *Porphyrio porphyrio* RALLIDAE

L to 48 cm. A large, heavy bird with purplish-blue plumage, white patch under tail, forehead and bill bright red. Scarce resident in swamps. Loud calls from thick cover. Food: vegetation, invertebrates. [**7**]

Coot *Fulica atra*

RALLIDAE L to 38 cm. Black overall, forehead and beak white. Resident in fresh water; winter visitor to N. Africa. One typical call rendered *ky-owk*. Food: vegetation and seeds, some invertebrates. [*not illustrated*]

Little Bustard *Tetrax tetrax*

OTIDIDAE L to 43 cm. A long-legged, long-necked bird; upper parts speckled yellow brown, underparts paler; ♂ has black neck. Resident in parts of north and west on open farmland and grassy plains. Grunting alarm calls. Food: mainly vegetation and invertebrates. [♂**8**] [♀**9**]

Stone Curlew *Burhinus oedicnemus*

BURHINIDAE L to 41 cm. Tall with short straight bill and large, staring eyes; overall light brown. Resident or summer visitor to open dry country, heaths, semidesert. Curlew-like calls. Food: invertebrates. [**10**]

Collared Pratincole *Glareola pratincola*

GLAREOLIDAE L to 25 cm. A small, long-legged bird; swallow-like in shape and flight with sharply forked tail and swept-back wings. Summer visitor to open country and mud-flats. Also passage migrant. Gregarious; chattering calls. Food: mainly insects hawked in air. [**11**]

Oystercatcher *Haematopus ostralegus*
HAEMATOPODIDAE L to 43 cm. Chiefly black
with white underparts; white throat-band
in winter; bill long, orange-red; legs long,
pink. Mainly winter visitor to coasts, but
resident in parts of north on suitable sandy
shores. Call, *kleep, pic, pic, pic* and
piping chorus. Food: mainly bivalved
molluscs for which it probes with its long
bill. [1]

Black-winged Stilt *Himantopus himantopus*
RECURVIROSTRIDAE L to 38 cm. A slender
bird with extremely long legs; both sexes
have black back and bill, white underparts and face; legs red. ♂ crown and nape
black, white in ♀. Summer visitor in north,
resident and winter visitor in south of
region to marshes and lagoons. Call *kik-
kik-kik*. Food: aquatic invertebrates. [2]

Avocet *Recurvirostra avosetta*
RECURVIROSTRIDAE L to 43 cm. Unmistakable; body white, with two broad black
stripes along back; seen from below in
flight bird appears entirely white with
black wing-tips; bill upcurved, black, used
in side-to-side sweeping manner to collect
food. Resident or winter visitor almost
throughout to lagoons and estuaries. Call,
kluit. Food: invertebrates. [3]

Little Ringed Plover *Charadrius dubius*
CHARADRIIDAE L to 15 cm. Small, active
bird; crown, dull brown above, neck and
underparts white, black bands through eye
and encircling upper breast, wing-tips
black; legs pale yellow; bill short, dark.
Summer visitor to north, resident in south
on sand and shingle margins of freshwater.
Calls, *piu, kip kip kip*. Food: aquatic
invertebrates. [4]

Kentish Plover *Charadrius alexandrinus*
CHARADRIIDAE L to 16 cm. ♂ dull-brown
upperparts, white underparts and face,
black eye-stripe and incomplete forehead
stripe, black breast-band incomplete, bill
and legs blackish. ♀ dull grey above, white
beneath with trace of breast-band and eye-
stripe. Resident in south, summer visitor
in north on sand and shingle seashores.

Call, quiet *choo-ee*. Food: aquatic invertebrates. [♂5]

Lapwing *Vanellus vanellus*
CHARADRIIDAE L to 30 cm. Striking;
crested; predominantly black with reddish-purple patch on wings, cheeks and
belly white, orange patch under tail; legs
pink. Winter visitor to estuaries and sandy
shores, resident part of Spain. Call, varia-
tions on *pee-wit*. Food: invertebrates. [6]

Snipe *Gallinago gallinago*
SCOLOPACIDAE L to 27 cm. Easily recognised by very long bill, zig-zag flight, harsh
cry and habit of diving at an angle of 45°;
chiefly shades of brown. Winter visitor
throughout, mainly to marshes. Calls *whist*
on rising. Food: invertebrates. [7]

Curlew *Numenius arquata*
SCOLOPACIDAE L to 58 cm. A tall, fairly
long-necked bird with a very long, curved
bill; light brown; flecked with black, face
paler, belly white; tail wedge-shaped.
Winter visitor to muddy shores and
estuaries. *Whaup* and *coorlee* calls. Food:
invertebrates, some vegetation. [8]

Redshank *Tringa totanus*
SCOLOPACIDAE L to 28 cm. Overall grey,
but with conspicuous white hindwing and
rump; bill long, slender, orange-red; legs
bright orange-red. Mainly winter visitor
to brackish marshes and estuaries. Calls
include *tewi tewi tewi*. Food: burrowing
invertebrates. [9]

Common Sandpiper *Actitis hypoleucos*
SCOLOPACIDAE L to 20 cm. A small, 'neat'
bird which flies low over the water; grey-
brown with underparts and wing bars
white. Mainly winter visitor but resident in
parts of north-west, by sheltered fresh
waters. Usually solitary. Loud triple call.
Food: chiefly small insects. [10]

Note: Many species of greyish or brownish
waders may be found on the seashore and
in estuaries. They are very difficult to
identify due to the similarity of their
plumage and habits.

Mediterranean Gull *Larus melanocephalus*
LARIDAE L to 39 cm. Head black, upper parts grey, otherwise white; bill and legs red. Loses black cap in winter. Around coasts in winter, breeding in east, in coastal marshes. Various harsh calls. Food: small aquatic animals; also scavenges. [s1, w2]

Little Gull *Larus minutus*
LARIDAE L to 28 cm. Grey above, head black, wing under-surface dark grey; bill and legs red. Loses black cap in winter. Winter visitor to coasts. Laughing calls. Food: small aquatic animals. [s3]

Black-headed Gull *Larus ridibundus*
LARIDAE L to 38 cm. Head dark brown. Loses brown cap in winter. Mainly winter visitor to coasts but resident southern France. Penetrating call. Food: small aquatic animals but also scavenges. [s4, w5]

Slender-billed Gull *Larus genei*
LARIDAE L to 43 cm. Rather long-necked; bill and legs red, bill yellow in winter; white plumage pinkish when breeding. Resident and winter visitor to a few areas; also passage migrant, mainly coastal lagoons. Variety of loud calls. Food: small fish. [6]

Audouin's Gull *Larus audouinii*
LARIDAE L to 50 cm. White, upper parts grey, wing-tips black; bill red with yellow tip; legs blackish-green. Confined to Mediterranean, with a few breeding stations, on rocky islands. Various sharp calls. Food: marine organisms. [7]

Lesser Black-backed Gull *Larus fuscus*
LARIDAE L to 56 cm. Entirely white, except for grey to black back and upper wings. Winter visitor to coasts. Call, similar to herring gull. Food, marine organisms, also scavenges. [8]
Great Black-backed Gull *Larus marinus* is similar, but larger (L to 79 cm).

Herring Gull *Larus argentatus*
LARIDAE L to 56 cm. Head and underparts white, upper parts grey; bill yellow with a bright orange-red spot. Resident or winter visitor throughout. Strident calls. Omnivorous. [9]

Gull-billed Tern *Gelochelidon nilotica*
LARIDAE L to 38 cm. Crown and nape black, otherwise white and grey. Local summer visitor and passage migrant. Distinctive quacking calls. Food mainly taken on land: small animals. [s10]

Sandwich Tern *Sterna sandvicensis*
LARIDAE L to 41 cm. White and grey with black crown (white in winter). Mainly winter or passage visitor to sandy coasts. Far-carrying call: *kirrick*. Food: small fish, especially sand-eels. [s11]

Common Tern *Sterna hirundo*
LARIDAE L to 35 cm. Crown and nape black, bill slender, vermilion with black tip; legs red. Summer visitor and passage migrant to most of region on both fresh and salt water. Calls, *kee-rah* and '*kik-kik-kik*'. Food: insects and small fish. [s12, w13]

Little Tern *Sterna albifrons*
LARIDAE L to 24 cm. Crown and nape black; bill yellow with black tip; legs yellow-orange. Summer visitor to sandy and shingle shores over most of region. Calls, *kik-kik*, plaintive *ke-er*. Food: small fish. [14]

Whiskered Tern *Chlidonias hybridus*
LARIDAE L to 24 cm. Predominantly dark and light grey, crown black, bill and legs red; tail forked. In winter, pale grey and white, bill black. Summer visitor mainly in west, passage elsewhere. Harsh calls. Food: aquatic animals from insects to small fish and frogs. [s15]

Black Tern *Chlidonias niger*
LARIDAE L to 24 cm. Predominantly dark, wings paler, their under surfaces light grey and white; legs blackish-red. In winter, entire under-surface is white and grey with black patch on side of breast; bill black. Local summer visitor to north; passage migrant elsewhere. Breeds freshwater marshes and lagoons. Sharp *keek* calls. Food: invertebrates, occasionally small fish. [s16, w17]

Black-bellied Sandgrouse *Pterocles orientalis* PTEROCLIDIDAE
L to 34 cm. A heavy, relatively short-tailed bird; ♂ yellow-brown above with grey, white and black banded underparts; ♀ mottled and streaked, upper breast yellow. Resident in N. Africa; summer visitor Asia Minor. Food: leaves and seeds. [1]

Pin-tailed Sandgrouse *Pterocles alchata* PTEROCLIDIDAE L to 37 cm. Slender, long-tailed; ♂ greenish-brown above with brick-red breast, belly and underwings white; ♀ white underparts, otherwise sandy. Resident dry open country in west and south. Flocks call in flight. Food: leaves and seeds. [2]

Rock Dove *Columba livia*
COLUMBIDAE L to 33 cm. Grey overall with two black wing-bars. Resident inland and coastal cliffs throughout region. Call as domestic pigeon. Food: seeds and small fruits. [*not illustrated*]

Woodpigeon *Columba palumbus*
COLUMBIDAE L to 41 cm. Plumage predominantly shades of grey with white wing-bars. Resident in woods, parks and gardens except in south-east. Call, *coo-coo-coo-coorou*. Food; seeds, small fruits, foliage. [*not illustrated*]

Collared Dove *Streptopelia decaocto*
COLUMBIDAE L to 32 cm. Warm grey above, head and underparts pink or pinkish-fawn; conspicuous black and white collar. Resident north and east of region. Persistent triple *coo* and loud shriek. Food: fruit, seeds, leaves. [3]

Turtle Dove *Streptopelia turtur*
COLUMBIDAE L to 27 cm. Generally similar to collared dove, but mottled upper parts, and black and white throat patches. Summer visitor throughout in wooded country, parks and gardens. Purring call. Food: fruits and seeds. [4]

Great Spotted Cuckoo *Clamator glandarius*
CUCULIDAE L to 39 cm. Large with conspicuous crest, long tail and curved, tapering bill; black and grey above, underparts buff. Summer visitor to open woods, olive groves, maquis. Harsh calls. Food: insects. [5]

Cuckoo *Cuculus canorus*
CUCULIDAE L to 33 cm. Sombre grey above with pale buff, transversely barred breast and belly. Summer visitor to various habitats, except parts of N. Africa. ♂ *cuckoo* call; ♀ babbles. Food: insects, especially hairy larvae. [6]

Scops Owl *Otus scops*
STRIGIDAE L to 19 cm. Small, chiefly nocturnal; mottled brown overall, ear-tufts conspicuous only at close quarters. Resident or summer visitor to varied wooded habitats, even into towns. Call, a monotonous, repeated *piu*. Food: large insects, small mammals. [7]

Little Owl *Athene noctua*
STRIGIDAE L to 22 cm. Very small, partly diurnal; dull brown with white flecking. Characteristically perches, bobs and weaves head, turning it through 180°; bounding flight. Resident throughout region in open country with scattered cover. Call, a plaintive *kiew*. Food: small rodents, birds, insects. [8]

Note: several other species of owl occur in the region but are rarely seen.

Nightjar *Caprimulgus europaeus*
CAPRIMULGIDAE L to 27 cm. A shy, retiring bird, overall brown with dark and light flecking, partial white collar. Mouth flanked by bristle-like 'moustache', gape enormous. Summer visitor in open woodland, heath, maquis and garrigue. Call, a soft *cu-ic*, churring, and clapping made by bringing the wings sharply together. Food: insects caught on the wing. [♂9]

Red-necked Nightjar *Caprimulgus ruficollis*
CAPRIMULGIDAE L to 31 cm. Similar to nightjar, but larger, reddish. Summer visitor in west to dry, open country. Call a repeated double note. Food: insects caught on wing. [10]

Swift *Apus apus*
APODIDAE L to 16.5 cm. A small, compact bird with backwardly swept, scythe-like wings; tail short, forked; dark brown overall, throat paler. Summer visitor to most of region in both open country and towns. Call, a harsh scream. Food: airborne insects. [1]

Pallid Swift *Apus pallidus*
APODIDAE L to 16.5 cm. Very similar to swift, but lighter, throat patch paler and more conspicuous, head rather broader. Summer visitor to most of region. Call, food and habitat much as swift. [2]

Alpine swift *Apus melba*
APODIDAE L to 22 cm. Similar to swift, but larger; light brown, underparts conspicuously white. Summer visitor to region. Loud, musical calls in flight. Food and habitats as swift. [3]

Kingfisher *Alcedo atthis*
ALCEDINIDAE L to 16.5 cm. A small, long-billed and brilliantly coloured bird; upper parts blue-green, underparts reddish-chestnut. Resident over most of region; winter visitor in south-east. Along rivers; by lakes, estuaries and coast in winter. Shrill flight call. Food: dives for fish. [4]

Bee-eater *Merops apiaster*
MEROPIDAE L to 28 cm. Compact, long-billed; crown predominantly chestnut above, wings green and chestnut, tail green with the two long central feathers. Summer visitor to most of region, to open country with scattered trees and bushes, maquis, garrigue. Usual call *quilp*. Food: flying insects. [5]

Roller *Coracias garrulus*
CORACIIDAE L to 31 cm. A crow-like bird with a strong hooked bill, head, underparts and wing-patch clear blue, back chestnut. Summer visitor to much of region in all kinds of country. Call, harsh, crow-like. Food: insects, small reptiles. [6]

Hoopoe *Upupa epops*
UPUPIDAE L to 28 cm. Unmistakable with long, curved bill and conspicuous erectile crest; predominantly pinkish-cinnamon, with broad, transverse black-and-white bars above. Summer visitor throughout in wooded country. Call, abrupt *hoo-hoo-hoo*. Food: insects. [7]

Wryneck *Jynx torquilla*
PICIDAE L to 16.5 cm. A very unwood-peckerlike woodpecker, with short bill and long tail; brownish above, much flecked and barred, underparts paler with more conspicuous barring. Summer visitor to north of region to open wooded country, parks and gardens. On passage in south. Call, *kew-kew-kew-kew-kew*. Food: insects, especially ants. [8]

Green Woodpecker *Picus viridis*
PICIDAE L to 32 cm. A typical woodpecker with rather wedge-shaped tail used for bracing against tree-trunks; bright green overall, but cap and nape red, rump yellow-green, wing-tips and tail-feathers brownish, mottled. Resident in wooded areas. Call, laughing *yaffle*. Food: insects, especially ants. [♂9]

Great Spotted Woodpecker, Pied Woodpecker *Dendrocopos major* PICIDAE L to 23 cm. A compact bird with medium length bill; overall black with white cheeks which are interrupted by a narrow, black bar, wing-patches and chin, brilliant red under the tail in both sexes, and on nape in ♂. Resident in wooded areas of region. Usual call, *chick*. Food: insects. [♂10]

Syrian Woodpecker *Dendrocopos syriacus*
PICIDAE L to 23 cm. Very similar to great spotted woodpecker, but no black band on cheek patches, and breast has a faint red band. Resident, spreading in north-east of region. Usual call, a repeated *chick*. [♂11]

Lesser Spotted Woodpecker, Barred Woodpecker *Dendrocopos minor* PICIDAE L to 14.5 cm. Predominantly black and white, the upper parts strongly barred, the underparts flecked; narrow black moustaches; ♂ black-bordered red crown, ♀ black crown. Resident in north and west of region, in wooded areas. Call, *pee-pee-pee-pee*. Food: insects. [♂12]

Hoopoe Lark, Bifasciated Lark *Alaemon alaudipes* ALAUDIDAE
L to 19 cm. A rather long-legged bird with a long, curved bill resembling that of a hoopoe; tawny brown above, underparts pale, black flecking on breast. Resident in south and south-east of region in open, stony country, desert. Sings on ground or wing. Food: insect larvae, seeds. [1]

Calandra Lark *Melanocorypha calandra*
ALAUDIDAE L to 19 cm. A plump, large-billed bird; brown above, underparts white, large black patch on each side of neck, upper breast fawnish, speckled; trailing margin of wings and outer margins of tail white (visible in flight). Resident throughout most of region in various habitats, including cultivated and dry stony areas. Song like skylark, but mimics other birds. Food: seeds; insects. [2]

Short-toed Lark *Calandrella brachydactyla*
ALAUDIDAE L to 14 cm. A small, pale, short-billed lark; dull brown above, underparts pale, streaked, dark smudge on each side of breast. Summer visitor throughout to bare dry areas, semidesert and sand-dunes. Calls include sparrow-like chirping. Food: small insects and seeds. [3]
Lesser Short-toed Lark *Calandrella rufescens* is difficult to distinguish from the preceding species, but lacks the breast-smudges.

Crested Lark *Galerida cristata*
ALAUDIDAE L to 17 cm. Brown above, flecked; underparts white, breast pale fawn with conspicuous flecking, prominent erect crest. Resident throughout, except Corsica, Sardinia, in many different habitats, often near or in towns. Song less sustained than skylark. Melodious triple call. Food: chiefly seeds, some insects. [4]

Woodlark *Lullula arborea*
ALAUDIDAE L to 15 cm. Similar to crested lark, but crest reduced. Resident in most of region; winter visitor or absent south-east, in very open wooded country. Call, melodious *tit-looit*; song like crested lark. Food: insects and seeds. [5]

Skylark *Alauda arvensis*
ALAUDIDAE L to 18 cm. Similar to crested lark, but crest reduced. Resident in open country of all types, throughout north; winter visitor in south. Famous sustained song in air, while ascending, descending and hovering. Food: chiefly seeds, some invertebrates. [6]

Sand Martin *Riparia riparia*
HIRUNDINIDAE L to 12 cm. Small, scythe-winged bird; uniformly brown above, underparts white with conspicuous brown breast-band. Summer visitor near riverbanks where it excavates nest-hole. Twittering song on wing. Food: small flying insects. [7]

Crag Martin *Ptyonoprogne rupestris*
HIRUNDINIDAE L to 14 cm. Similar to sand martin, but tail more slightly forked; underparts light brown with characteristic white marks halfway along tail. Summer visitor to cliffs inland and on the coast, occasionally towns. Twittering song. Food: insects taken on wing. [8]

Swallow, Barn Swallow *Hirundo rustica*
HIRUNDINIDAE L to 19 cm. Scythe-winged, with deeply forked tail; blue-black above, underparts cream to pinkish-buff, lower face, throat and forehead chestnut. Summer visitor throughout, most frequently in the vicinity of buildings, often feeding over water. Sharp calls and twittering song. Food: flying insects. [9]

Red-rumped Swallow *Hirundo daurica*
HIRUNDINIDAE L to 18 cm. Similar to swallow, but tail-forks shorter; upper face, nape and rump reddish-orange. Summer visitor to west and east, near buildings. Wailing call unlike swallow's. Food: insects taken on wing. [10]

House Martin *Delichon urbica*
HIRUNDINIDAE L to 12.5 cm. A small bird with shallowly forked tail; upper parts blue-black, rump and underparts white. Summer visitor throughout, nesting near human habitations. Chirruping call and song. Food: insects taken on wing, [11]

Tawny Pipit *Anthus campestris*
MOTACILLIDAE L to 16.5 cm. Sandy-brown, underparts pale, prominent buff eye-stripe. Summer visitor throughout, except south where passage migrant, to dry, open country, heathland, garrigue, sand-dunes. Simple song; variety of calls. Food: insects. [1]

Tree Pipit *Anthus trivialis*
MOTACILLIDAE L to 15 cm. Similar to tawny pipit, but underparts heavily flecked. Summer visitor to north, on passage elsewhere, to heathland. Call, rather harsh *zee*. Food: insects. [2]

Meadow Pipit *Anthus pratensis*
MOTACILLIDAE L to 14.5 cm. Very similar to tree pipit, most readily distinguished by call, *tsip*. Winter visitor throughout region to open habitats. Food: mainly insects. [3]

Yellow Wagtail *Motacilla flava iberiae*
MOTACILLIDAE L to 16.5 cm. Slender bird with long tail; ♂ has upper parts greenish and cheeks black; ♀ lacks distinctive head pattern. This race, which breeds in S. France and Spain is one of many races of yellow wagtail which are very difficult to distinguish. A summer visitor to most of region, on grassland, saltmarshes. Call, a sibilant *seep*. Food: insects. [♂4] [♀5]

Grey Wagtail *Motacilla cinerea*
MOTACILLIDAE L to 18 cm. Similar to yellow wagtail, but tail longer and ♂ has grey head and mantle. Resident in north, winter visitor in south. Breeds by fast-flowing water. Calls, *zit; see-see-see*. Food: insects. [♂6]

White Wagtail *Motacilla alba alba*
MOTACILLIDAE L to 18 cm. Small, very long-tailed; crown, chin, breast and tail black; mantle and rump grey; wings pied; forehead, cheeks and belly white. Resident in north, winter visitor to south in open country, often near human habitation. Calls, *chick, chizzick*. Food: insects. [♂7] [♀8]

Common Bulbul *Pycnonotus barbatus*
PYCNONOTIDAE L to 19 cm. A long-tailed, slender bird; plumage grey-brown above and on throat, belly, greyish-white. Resident in gardens, orchards, palm groves and bushy areas in North Africa and the Middle East. Sings melodiously. Food: predominantly insects and seeds. [9]

Wren *Troglodytes troglodytes*
TROGLODYTIDAE L to 9.5 cm. Tiny; warm brown above, fawn below, barred; tail often cocked. Resident throughout region except parts of south. Explosive song and rapid *tic* calls. Food: small insects and spiders. [*not illustrated*]

Dunnock, Hedge Sparrow *Prunella modularis* PRUNELLIDAE
L to 14.5 cm. Small; head and underparts grey, flanks conspicuously flecked, upper parts brown, flecked. Resident or winter visitor, absent in south; in montane scrub, maquis. Penetrating call note. Food: insects, seeds. [10]

Rufous Bush Robin, Rufous Bushchat *Cercotrichas galactotes* TURDIDAE
L to 15 cm. Slender, long tail often carried upright; upper parts nut-brown, tail reddish, tips of tail-feathers spotted black and white (visible when fanned); underparts light fawn. Summer visitor to west, south and east in scrub, gardens, vineyards, olive groves and semidesert. Pleasant song, but harsh call note. Food: insects, worms. [11]

Robin *Erithacus rubecula*
TURDIDAE L to 14 cm. A plump, inquisitive bird; brown above, face and breast orange-red, belly whitish. Resident in most of region, winter visitor to south-east; in wooded and scrubby areas. Sings almost throughout year; calls, rapid *tic* and drawn-out *tsee*. Food: insects and other invertebrates, fruits and seeds. [*not illustrated*]

Nightingale *Luscinia megarhynchos*
TURDIDAE L to 16.5 cm. Upper parts nut-brown, tail reddish; underparts pale nut-brown. Summer visitor to woodland, thickets, large gardens. Famous melodic song by night or day. Harsh call. Food: insects and other invertebrates, berries. [12]

Black Redstart *Phoenicurus ochruros*
TURDIDAE L to 14 cm. ♂ black with white wing-patch and reddish tail; ♀ warm grey, without wing-patch. Resident or summer visitor in north, winter visitor in south on rocky hillsides. Rattling song; variety of call notes. Food: invertebrates. [♂1]

Redstart *Phoenicurus phoenicurus*
TURDIDAE L to 14 cm. ♂ black face and throat, fiery reddish-orange breast and tail; ♀ dull brown above and fawn beneath. Summer visitor to north and east; on passage elsewhere; in wooded country, near rivers. Short song; *hwee tuc tuc* of alarm. Food: invertebrates. [♂2] [♀3]

Moussier's Redstart *Phoenicurus moussieri*
TURDIDAE L to 12 cm. ♂ black above, with white wing-patch and banded head; ♀ dull brown above, and muted orange breast. Resident in forests and hilly places in North Africa. Call similar to redstart. Food: insects. [♂4]

Whinchat *Saxicola rubetra*
TURDIDAE L to 12.5 cm. Distinctively mottled above, buff 'eyebrow' line above eye, underparts light chestnut; ♀ paler. Summer visitor to north of region, on heath and open areas. Simple song: alarm call, *utick*. Food: invertebrates. [♂5]

Stonechat *Saxicola torquata*
TURDIDAE L to 12.5 cm. Similar to whinchat, but lacks buff eyebrow; ♂ darker especially on head and throat. Resident in much of region, except south-east, on heaths and maquis. Simple song; loud call like stones knocked together. Food: insects and their larvae, some other invertebrates. [♂6] [♀7]

Wheatear *Oenanthe oenanthe*
TURDIDAE L to 15 cm. ♂ grey above, white tail with bar at the tip, triangular black cheek-patch, breast buff; ♀ brown above. Summer visitor to north of region, in open country. Wheeling song. Food: insects and other invertebrates. [♂8] [♀9]

Black-eared Wheatear *Oenanthe hispanica*
TURDIDAE L to 14.5 cm. ♂ occurs in three colour forms: 1) reddish brown with black wings, tip and central black bar to tail, and triangular patch on cheeks; 2) black throat continuous with cheek-patch; 3) in breeding ♂, reddish-brown replaced by white or creamy white; ♀ is overall brown. Summer visitor, except south-east, in semidesert with scrub. Song resembles wheatear's. Food: insects. [♂10]

Black Wheatear *Oenanthe leucura*
TURDIDAE L to 18 cm. Black with white rump and under-tail patch; ♀ browner. Resident in west in rocky areas. Melodious song; plaintive call. Food: insects. [11]

Rock Thrush *Monticola saxatilis*
TURDIDAE L to 19 cm. ♂'s head, throat and back striking blue, wings grey, tail, breast and belly orange-chestnut; ♀ mottled fawny brown. Summer visitor, in rocky, open areas, sometimes in ruins. Loud song and *chac* calls. Food: insects. [♂12]

Blue Rock Thrush *Monticola solitarius*
TURDIDAE L to 20 cm. ♂ blue with dark grey wings and tail; ♀ dull, dark brown with paler mottling. Resident throughout, except south-east, in rocky areas and in towns. Mellow song and variety of calls. Food: mainly insects. [♂13]

Blackbird *Turdus merula*
TURDIDAE L to 25 cm. ♂ black with yellow bill; ♀ dark brown. Resident throughout except south-east where winter visitor. From woodland to towns. Fluting song and loud explosive call: *chook*. Food: invertebrates, fruit and berries. [*not illustrated*]

Song Thrush *Turdus philomelos*
TURDIDAE L to 23 cm. Head and upper parts warm nut-brown, breast cream, spotted with brown. Mainly winter visitor though resident in north, in wooded areas, often in towns. Loud, repetitive song. Food: invertebrates, fruits and berries. [14]

Cetti's Warbler *Cettia cetti*
SYLVIIDAE L to 14 cm. Very shy, retiring bird most easily recognised by its song; sombre brown above with dark brown tail. Resident throughout, except in south, in dense vegetation by freshwater. Loud bursts of song ending abruptly; several call notes, sharp or churring. Food: invertebrates. [1]

Fan-tailed Warbler *Cisticola juncidis*
SYLVIIDAE L to 10 cm. A tiny, shy bird; upper parts brown with longitudinal dark stripes, underparts cream-fawn, tail edged black and white, fan-shaped in flight. Resident throughout except south, in freshwater margins, reedbeds, marshes. Loud but brief song in flight; *tip tip tip tew*. Food: insects. [2]

Moustached Warbler *Acrocephalus melanopogon* SYLVIIDAE
L to 13 cm. Upper parts rich brown, crown dark, with almost black longitudinal stripes, white superciliary stripe. Resident in west, winter visitor in east, absent from south of region, in reedbanks near freshwater. Song musical, call soft. Food: insects and their larvae. [3]

Sedge Warbler *Acrocephalus schoenobaenus* SYLVIIDAE
L to 13 cm. Similar to moustached warbler, but paler. Summer visitor to north-east of region, in thick vegetation beside freshwater; on passage elsewhere. 'Jazzy' song in flight often imitating other birds; harsh calls. Food: insects. [4]

Great Reed Warbler *Acrocephalus arundinaceus* SYLVIIDAE
L to 19 cm. A large bird; upper parts rich brown, whitish eye-stripe, underparts cream-fawn. Summer visitor to much of region; passage migrant in south; generally in reedbeds. Boisterous song *karra karra karra kut*, with frog-like croaks. Food: insects. [5]
Reed warbler *Acrocephalus scirpaceus* is similar, but smaller (L to 12.5 cm), with redder plumage, and similar distribution. Song a repeated *chirk chirk chirk, chirrup, chirrup, chirrup*. Almost always in reedbeds.

Olivaceous Warbler *Hippolais pallida*
SYLVIIDAE L to 13.5 cm. Upper parts brownish-grey or olive brown, unmarked except for pale eye-stripe, underparts cream or pale fawn. Summer visitor, except north, in bushy and wooded areas, including town parks. Various sharp calls. Food: insects. [6]

Melodious Warbler *Hippolais polyglotta*
SYLVIIDAE L to 13 cm. Upper parts yellowish-brown, yellow underparts. Summer visitor to west along river-banks, in wooded areas, gardens. Song musical; distinctive call notes. Food: insects. [7]

Marmora's Warbler *Sylvia sarda*
SYLVIIDAE L to 12 cm. Tail almost as long as body and carried at an angle; dark grey overall, underparts lighter, especially in ♀. Very local resident in open scrub and maquis in west; winter visitor N. Africa. Song like Dartford warbler, but call distinctive. Food: insects and their larvae, spiders. [♂8]

Dartford Warbler *Sylvia undata*
SYLVIIDAE L to 12.5 cm. Similar to Marmora's warbler, but underparts warm, reddish-brown, cheek-patch bluish-grey, throat spotted white. Resident in thick scrub and maquis in west to Italy. Simple, musical song and quiet churring call. Food: insects and their larvae, spiders. [♂9]

Spectacled Warbler *Sylvia conspicillata*
SYLVIIDAE L to 12.5 cm. Upper parts grey, wings striped reddish-brown, white 'spectacle' round eye, throat white, underparts pinkish, paler under tail; ♀ paler. Summer visitor to north-west, resident in south, in dry open scrubland. Attractive song and rattling alarm call. Food: insects. [♂10]

Subalpine Warbler *Sylvia cantillans*
SYLVIIDAE L to 12 cm. Upper parts of ♂ grey, throat and breast reddish-orange-brown, outer tail-feathers, belly and 'moustache' white; ♀ paler with chestnut wings. Summer visitor to west and north of region; or passage elsewhere; in scrub and maquis. Musical song in flight, distinctive call notes. Food: insects. [♂11]

Sardinian Warbler *Sylvia melanocephala*
SYLVIIDAE L to 13.5 cm. ♂ black head, dark
grey above, chin, upper throat and tail edge
white, breast and belly greyish, eye ringed
in red; ♀ paler with cap same colour as
upper parts. Resident over most of region,
in scrub, open woodland, parks and
gardens. Song and scolding call rather like
whitethroat. Food: insects and their
larvae. [♂1]

Cyprus Warbler *Sylvia melanothorax*
SYLVIIDAE L to 13.5 cm. Resembles Sardinian warbler, but eye-ring paler, underparts
strongly marked in black; legs reddish. In
scrub in Cyprus. [♂2]

Orphean Warbler *Sylvia hortensis*
SYLVIIDAE L to 15 cm. Large, stout bird;
sombre brown above, crown and cheeks
black, outer tail-feathers, throat and eye-
ring white, underparts of ♂ pinkish-fawn,
of ♀ very pale fawn. Summer visitor to most
of region, except south where passage
migrant; in open woodland, parks and
gardens, scrub. Warbling song and harsh

call. Food: insects and their larvae;
fruit. [♂3]

Whitethroat *Sylvia communis*
SYLVIIDAE L to 14 cm. Crown and cheeks
grey in ♂, nut-brown in ♀, wings reddish-
brown, back and tail nut-brown, throat
white, underparts pale fawn, pinkish in ♂.
Summer visitor to scrub and maquis
except in south-east. Song: *wichity wichity*;
harsh alarm call. Food: insects and their
larvae, spiders, berries. [♂4]

Garden Warbler *Sylvia borin*
SYLVIIDAE L to 14 cm. Uniformly grey
above, paler below, becoming off-white
under tail. Mainly a passage migrant, but
summer visitor in parts of north, in thickets
and woodland. Even, warbling song and
tack tack of alarm. Food: insects. [5]

Blackcap *Sylvia atricapilla*
SYLVIIDAE L to 14 cm. Crown of ♂ glossy
black, of ♀ red-brown, upper parts dull
brown. Resident in west and north in open
woodland, scrub, parks and gardens.

Winter visitor or on passage elsewhere. Loud song with abrupt end, often mimicking. Food: insects, larvae, berries, occasionally worms. [♂6] [♀7]

Bonelli's Warbler *Phylloscopus bonelli*
SYLVIIDAE L to 11.5 cm. Head and back grey, yellow patch on rump, yellow areas on wings and tail. Summer visitor to woods in hilly country; on passage in south-east of region. Short trilling song and plaintive call. Food: insects. [8]

Wood Warbler *Phylloscopus sibilatrix*
SYLVIIDAE L to 12.5 cm. Upper parts yellow-brown, superciliary stripe and front yellow, belly white. Summer visitor to woodland in north on passage elsewhere. Song explosive trill or long drawn-out *piu, piu, piu*. Food: insects and larvae, occasionally berries. [9]

Chiffchaff *Phylloscopus collybita*
SYLVIIDAE L to 11 cm. Dull brown, tinged with yellow; legs dark brown. Resident in north, winter visitor in south to open woodland. Song repeats own name. Call note plaintive *hooet*. Food: insects and spiders. [10]

Willow warbler *Phylloscopus trochilus* is very similar, but more yellow with a green tinge above; legs flesh-coloured. Song, a distinctive cadence.

Firecrest *Regulus ignicapillus*
SYLVIIDAE L to 9 cm. Predominantly greenish above, wings barred dark and white, underparts pale whitish-grey, crown of ♂ fiery orange, of ♀ yellow, bordered black in both sexes, eye-stripe black, cheeks grey, a bronzy patch on each side of throat. Resident in north and west in woodland including coniferous forest. Song differs in form from that of goldcrest, call note lower pitched. Food: insects and their larvae. [11]

Goldcrest *Regulus regulus* is very similar; ♂ crest orange, face grey, no eye-stripes or throat patch. Resident or winter visitor, mainly to coniferous woodland. 'Screepy' song and 'needling' call. Food: similar to firecrest.

Spotted Flycatcher *Muscicapa striata*
MUSCICAPIDAE L to 14 cm. Upper parts grey-brown, underparts pale. Summer visitor to most of region; on passage in south; in orchards, parks, gardens, forest margins, maquis. Simple squeaking song and loud call: *huee tuck tuck*. Food: insects mostly caught on wing. [1]

Collared Flycatcher *Ficedula albicollis*
MUSCICAPIDAE L to 12.5 cm. Upper parts of ♂ black, underparts, collar, white; ♀ grey above with faint trace of collar. Summer visitor from Italy eastwards; on passage in south-east, to open woodland. Song, like that of pied flycatcher *tchee tchee tchee cher cher*; call note a sharp *zit*. Food: insects taken on wing. [♂2] [♀3]
Pied Flycatcher *Ficedula hypoleuca* is similar, but ♂ lacks white collar and rump. Song like that of collared flycatcher.

Bearded Tit *Panurus biarmicus*
TIMALIIDAE L to 16.5 cm. A colourful, long-tailed bird; upper parts reddish-orange with black and white wing-bars, ♂ has blue-grey crown, black 'moustaches' and tail patch. Resident in reedbeds in north. Penetrating call: *ping ping – tick*. Food: invertebrates. [♂4]

Long-tailed Tit *Aegithalos caudatus*
AEGITHALIDAE L to 14 cm. A small-bodied, very long-tailed bird; pale pink overall, but crown often pale grey, broad eye-stripe, mantle and tail black, wings black-and-white with reddish bar. Resident throughout north in woodland and scrub. Calls, a mouse-like *zee zee zee* and distinctive *zupp*. Food: chiefly small insects. [5]

Sombre Tit *Parus lugubris*
PARIDAE L to 14 cm. Crown and throat black, back drab brown, wing-tips and tail dull grey, belly white. Resident in rocky, wooded areas in east. Vocabulary resembles great tit's. Food: chiefly small insects. [6]
Marsh tit *Parus palustris* is similar, but black areas confined to crown and chin, wings less grey. Resident in north of region in woodland. Song repeated *tschippi*; *pitchoo* is distinctive call.

Crested Tit *Parus cristatus*
PARIDAE L to 11.5 cm. Head white with black chin, nape and eye-stripe and black-and-white mottled crest; upper parts brown, underparts whitish buff. Resident in woodland in west of region and Balkans. Distinctive purring call and sharp *zee zee zee*. Food: chiefly insects. [7]

Coal Tit *Parus ater*
PARIDAE L to 11.5 cm. Head black with white nape-patch and triangular cheek-patch; upper parts grey with white markings. Resident in woodlands, especially conifers. Loud song: *cher-tu, cher-tee*; call a thin *zee*. Food: chiefly insects. [8]

Blue Tit *Parus caeruleus*
PARIDAE L to 11.5 cm. Grey-blue and blue above, yellow below; face white, bordered in black with a black eye-stripe; North African race has dark blue crown and bluer mantle. Resident throughout region except south-east in variety of wooded habitats. Usual call scolding *tsee tsee tsit*. Food: insects and seeds. [9]
Great Tit *Parus major* is similar, but larger (L to 14 cm), with a black head and bib from chin to tail, and white cheeks. Resident in woodlands throughout region.

Corsican Nuthatch *Sitta whiteheadi*
SITTIDAE L to 12 cm. A stub-tailed bird with a prominent bill; upper parts grey; underparts whitish-buff; ♂ crown and eye-stripe black with white stripe between; ♀ crest and eye-stripe grey. Resident confined to pine forests of Corsica. Quieter than nuthatch but has 'nasal' call. Food: small invertebrates, nuts and seeds. [10]

Rock Nuthatch *Sitta neumayer*
SITTIDAE L to 14 cm. Similar to Corsican nuthatch but no white superciliary stripe. Resident in rocky areas in north-east of region. Varied vocabulary like nuthatch. Food: invertebrates and seeds. [11]
Nuthatch *Sitta europaea* is similar, but underparts deep orange-buff. Resident in woodlands in north of region. Loud call: *wit wit wit*, also repeated *chuchuck*, and singing *pee pee pee* to announce its presence.

Wallcreeper *Tichodroma muraria*
TICHODROMADIDAE L to 16.5 cm. Conspicuously curved, slender bill; head and mantle grey; throat black; underparts dark grey, spotted white; inside wings bright red. Resident in mountainous areas in north. On coasts in winter. Song resembles treecreeper's. Food: insects. [1]

Short-toed Treecreeper *Certhia brachydactyla* CERTHIIDAE
L to 12.5 cm. Relatively short, curved bill; upper parts brown; underparts white. Resident in woodlands throughout except south-east. Explosive song and call-note. Food: chiefly insects. [2]
Treecreeper *Certhia familiaris* is similar, but has no brown on flanks. Resident in coniferous forests in north and east.

Penduline Tit *Remiz pendulinus*
REMIZIDAE L to 11 cm. Overall grey above and white below, with black cheek-patch, and chestnut mantle. Resident near freshwater throughout north. Repeated rather sibilant call. Food: insects, spiders, seeds. [3]

Golden Oriole *Oriolus oriolus*
ORIOLIDAE L to 24 cm. ♂ bright yellow with black wings and centre of tail; ♀ greenish-grey. Summer visitor to most of region, but on passage in south. Fluting song *ori-ole*, and cat-like screeches. Food: invertebrates, fruit. [♂4] [♀5]

Starling *Sturnus vulgaris*
STURNIDAE L to 21.5 cm. Black with iridescent green and purple sheen, conspicuously speckled in winter. Resident in various habitats, especially towns in north and east, winter visitor elsewhere. Song, a mixture of whistles, clicks and imitations of other birds. Very harsh alarm call. Food: insects and other invertebrates. [*not illustrated*]

Spanish Sparrow *Passer hispaniolensis*
PASSERIDAE L to 14.5 cm. ♂ predominantly nut-brown with black cheeks and white belly. Resident throughout in scrub, olive groves, scattered trees. Deep varied *tchup* call. Food: insects and seeds. [6]

House sparrow *Passer domesticus* is similar, but lacks black streaking; ♀ brown, paler beneath. Resident throughout region.

Rock Sparrow *Petronia petronia*
PASSERIDAE L to 14 cm. Basically shades of brown with stripes; throat has pale yellow patch. Resident throughout, except south-east, on rocky ground, near old buildings. Distinctive call notes. Food: insects and seeds. [7]

Chaffinch *Fringilla coelebs*
FRINGILLIDAE L to 15 cm. ♂ blue-grey head, brown back, black-and-white wings, brick-red to pinky-brown underparts; ♀ brown with lighter underparts. Resident in wooded habitats throughout, except south-east, where winter visitor. Short, powerful song. Well-known *pink* call of alarm. Food: mainly seeds. [♂8]

Brambling *Fringilla montifringilla*
FRINGILLIDAE L to 14.5 cm. Breast and shoulder orange-buff, wings black and white, tail black, rump conspicuously white, head black in ♂, brown in ♀. Winter visitor to north, in wooded areas, especially beech. Metallic call, *scrape*. Food: seeds, beech mast. [*not illustrated*]

Serin *Serinus serinus*
FRINGILLIDAE L to 11.5 cm. Greenish-yellow with grey patches above. Resident in open woodland, orchards, parks and gardens; winter visitor in south-east. Jingly song and trilling call note. Food: seeds. [9]

Greenfinch *Carduelis chloris*
FRINGILLIDAE L to 14.5 cm. Predominantly greenish-grey; bill stout; flesh-coloured. Resident in woodland edges, parks and gardens; winter visitor in south-east. Drawn-out *jeee* is distinctive call. Food: chiefly seeds, some insects. [10]

Goldfinch *Carduelis carduelis*
FRINGILLIDAE L to 12 cm. Face bright red, otherwise white, black and brown above with yellow on wings. Resident in woods, parks and gardens throughout, except south-east where winter visitor. Musical tinkling song and calls. Food: seeds. [11]

Linnet *Carduelis cannabina*
FRINGILLIDAE L to 13.5 cm. Brown with some black and white; ♂ red breast and forehead. Resident throughout in scrub and maquis, except south-east where winter visitor. Sustained musical song and twittering calls. Food: seeds. [♂1]

Trumpeter Finch *Bucanetes githagineus*
FRINGILLIDAE L to 12.5 cm. Brown with an overall pink tinge, more pronounced in mature ♂ which also has a bright pink bill and forehead. Resident in N. African deserts and rocky hills. Named from trumpeting call. Food: seeds. [♂2]

Bullfinch *Pyrrhula pyrrhula*
FRINGILLIDAE L to 16 cm. Predominantly black and grey above with white wing-bar and rump; breast and belly bright rose-coloured in ♂, greyish-pink in ♀. Resident or winter visitor in north, in woodlands, parks and gardens. Plaintive call-note. Food: seeds, fruits and buds. [♂3]

Hawfinch *Coccothraustes coccothraustes*
FRINGILLIDAE L to 18 cm. Bill massive, blue-grey in summer, yellow in winter; predominantly chestnut-brown, with white and blue-green areas on wings and black throat patch. Resident in north of region and in west N. Africa, in woodlands, orchards and gardens. Distinctive call-note: *tzik*. Food: seeds, fruits, nuts. [♂4]

Cirl Bunting *Emberiza cirlus*
EMBERIZIDAE L to 16.5 cm. Predominantly brown and grey, with olive-green rump and yellow cheeks, breast and belly; ♂ has dark grey crown and nape, black eye-stripe, cheek-stripe and chin-patch, broad green band on breast; ♀ has no distinctive breast-band. Resident over most of region except south and east, in heathland, farmland with scattered trees and bushes. Song, a brief rattle; call, a sharp *zit*. Food: grain, seeds; some insects. [♂5]
Yellowhammer *Emberiza citrinella* is similar, but has a chestnut rump; ♂ has less black on face and no grey-green breast-band. Resident or winter visitor to north of region.

Rock Bunting *Emberiza cia*
EMBERIZIDAE L to 16 cm. Basically brown and black; ♂ has white stripe above black eye-stripe, black cheek-stripe and moustache, grey throat, chestnut breast; ♀ browner, more flecked on breast. Resident over much of region, except south, on hillsides, vineyards and gardens; descending in winter. Buzzing song and sharp call-note. Food: chiefly seeds. [♂6]
House Bunting, Striped Bunting *Emberiza striolata* is similar, but browner; head, nape and throat grey and flecked. Local resident N. Africa.

Ortolan Bunting *Emberiza hortulana*
EMBERIZIDAE L to 16.5 cm. Predominantly pinkish-brown with darker markings above; ♂ greyish-green head with yellow throat-patch. Summer visitor to open country in north of region; on passage in south. Song variable; several call notes. Food: mainly seeds, some insects. [♂7]
Cretzschmar's Bunting *Emberiza caesia* is similar, but ♂ has grey head with orange-brown throat-patch.

Reed Bunting *Emberiza schoeniclus*
EMBERIZIDAE L to 15 cm. Upper parts brown, flecked black; underparts and moustache white. ♂ has black head and throat with white collar. Resident or winter visitor to wetlands in much of region. Song a variable *chi chi chi chitty*; call, a drawn-out *zeee*. Food: mainly seeds, some insects. [♂8] [♀9]

Black-headed Bunting *Emberiza melanocephala* EMBERIZIDAE
L to 16.5 cm. Upper parts dull brown and black; ♂ chestnut mantle, black head, bright yellow underparts; ♀ paler. Summer visitor to north-east of region, in scrub, olive groves. Quite musical song; several call notes. Food: seeds and insects. [♂10]

Corn Bunting *Miliaria calandra*
EMBERIZIDAE L to 18 cm. Brown with black streaks. Resident except in south-east where winter visitor, in open farmland. Simple song, like jangling keys, and call note, *tsripp*. Food: mainly seeds. [11]

Red-backed Shrike *Lanius collurio*
LANIIDAE L to 17 cm. Bill powerful, sharply hooked; predominantly rich brown above, pinkish-fawn below; ♂ has grey crown and nape, broad black eye-stripe, wing-tips and tail and pale throat; ♀ has more flecking on underparts. Summer visitor to north of region, on passage in west and east, in scrubby habitats. Chattering, warbling, imitative song and harsh alarm notes. Food: large invertebrates and small vertebrates. [♂1] [♀2]

Lesser Grey Shrike *Lanius minor*
LANIIDAE L to 20 cm. Upper parts grey, with broad black forehead stripe, wings and tail; underparts pale pink. Summer visitor to north and east, on passage in south-east, in open woodland and scrub. Harsh double or triple call. Food: chiefly larger insects. [3]
Great Grey Shrike *Lanius excubitor* is similar, but has greyish-white underparts and lacks continuous black band about beak. Resident over much of region but winter visitor in east.

Woodchat Shrike *Lanius senator*
LANIIDAE L to 17 cm. ♂ similar to lesser grey shrike, but has distinctive chestnut crown and nape; ♀ speckled brown. Summer visitor to much of region in scrubby habitats; on passage in south-east. Musical song interspersed with harsh notes; also harsh calls. Food: small birds and insects. [ad4] [juv5]

Masked Shrike *Lanius nubicus*
LANIIDAE L to 17 cm. Upper parts black, forehead, wing-bars and tail margins white, flanks reddish; ♀ grey-brown above. Summer visitor to north-east of region, on passage in south-east, in open wooded country, scrub, olive groves. Warbler-like song and harsh calls. Food: insects. [6]

Jay *Garrulus glandarius*
CORVIDAE L to 34 cm. Plumage variable, basically pink with black moustache, tail and wing-patches, blue wing-patch; white rump. Resident in woodland habitats over much of region except south-east. Harsh scream and cat-like mew most usual calls.

Jumbled song with imitations of other birds. Food: typically acorns, but varied, including small birds and eggs. [7]

Magpie *Pica pica*
CORVIDAE L to 46 cm. Black with distinctive white wing-bars and belly, and long tail. Resident in wooded habitats and scrub except in south-east. Harsh, chattering call. Food varied: mainly insect grubs. [8]

Chough, Red-billed Chough *Pyrrhocorax pyrrhocorax* CORVIDAE
L to 40 cm. Black; tail short; bill long, curved, red. Legs reddish. Resident in mountainous areas, including coasts. Twanging calls distinct from jackdaw's. Food: insect larvae and worms. [9]

Jackdaw *Corvus monedula*
CORVIDAE L to 33 cm. The smallest crow of the region; black with a conspicuous grey nape. Resident in rocky areas, towns and villages, except in south-east. Repeated call, *check*, and musical *kyow*. Food: varied, but largely small invertebrates. [10]

Rook *Corvus frugilegus*
CORVIDAE L to 46 cm. Glossy blue-black; face of adult bare and pale at base of long bill; thigh feathers resemble badly fitting trousers. Winter visitor in north and east to farmland and grassland, but absent in south of region. Typical cawing call, but many other notes. Food: insect larvae, grain, refuse. [*not illustrated*]

Hooded Crow *Corvus corone cornix*
CORVIDAE L to 47 cm. Grey with black head, wings and tail. Resident in varied habitats in east of region, replaced in west by all-black race, the carrion crow. Usual call deep *caw*, distinct from that of rook. Food: omnivorous. [11]

Raven *Corvus corax*
CORVIDAE L to 64 cm. The largest passerine bird; glossy with a faint bluish sheen; bill massive, black. Resident in most of region except south-east, in hilly country, sometimes near towns and sea-cliffs. Call, a deep *cronnk*. Food: varied but much carrion. [*not illustrated*]

MAMMALS (Mammalia)
Warm-blooded vertebrates with skin covered in fur or hair, except in whales. Fertilization and gestation internal; young are suckled on milk. In whales body streamlined, limbs modified into fins.

Hedgehog *Erinaceus europaeus*
ERINACEIDAE L to 29 cm. Body round, plump, snout pointed; coat of hair mixed with prickly spines; can curl up into tight ball when threatened. Brown above, belly brown or whitish. In a wide variety of habitats, usually with good vegetation cover. [*not illustrated*]

Scilly Shrew, Lesser White-toothed Shrew
Crocidura suaveolens SORICIDAE
L to 7 cm. Body compact, plump; snout long, pointed; whiskers prominent; teeth white; tail with occasional long hairs. Greyish-brown, belly paler. In open habitats, moves into cover (including houses) in winter. [1]

Savi's Pygmy Shrew, Etruscan Shrew
Suncus etruscus SORICIDAE
L to 4.5 cm. Tiny, usually weighing no more than 2 g; snout tapering; ears large; tail has occasional long hairs. Pale brownish-grey. In dry places with scrubby plant cover. [2]

Great Horseshoe Bat *Rhinolophus ferrumequinum* RHINOLOPHIDAE
L to 9 cm. Conspicuous leaf-like structures on nose, the lower one horseshoe-shaped; nostrils trumpet-shaped. Brown or brownish-grey. In caves and other sheltered places. [3]

Large Mouse-eared Bat *Myotis myotis*
VESPERTILIONIDAE L to 8 cm. Snout fairly pointed; ears large, membranous, translucent. Brownish-grey. In sheltered places, such as caves, cellars and lofts. [4]

Common Pipistrelle *Pipistrellus pipistrellus* VESPERTILIONIDAE
L to 4.5 cm. Snout short, rounded; ears conspicuous, but not large. Brown or greyish-brown. In sheltered places. [5]

Rabbit *Oryctolagus cuniculus*
LEPORIDAE L to 45 cm. Hindlegs much longer than forelegs; ears long. Brown or brownish-grey, no black markings on ears, tail white below. In a variety of habitats, crepuscular. [*not illustrated*]

Brown Hare *Lepus capensis*
LEPORIDAE L to 65 cm. Long-bodied with fairly long forelegs and long hindlegs; ears long. Yellowish-brown, with black-tipped ears and black stripe on dorsal surface of tail. Does not burrow. Chiefly in grasslands and agricultural areas. [6]

Wood-mouse, Long-tailed Field-mouse
Apodemus sylvaticus MURIDAE
L to 11 cm (body). Eyes large, black; ears prominent, rounded; tail long (L to 10 cm), slender. Grey-brown to golden-brown above, buff beneath. In wooded areas. [7]

Wild Boar *Sus scrofa*
SUIDAE L to 1.8 m. Bristly; snout long, usually with prominent tusks. Dark greyish-brown; juveniles fawn with brown and reddish-brown stripes. In forests, but like to wallow in shallow water and mud. [8]

Fox *Vulpes vulpes*
CANIDAE L to 76 cm (body). Dog-like but slender; ears erect; brush long (L to 44 cm), very thick. Rich reddish-brown, tips of ears and paws very dark, underparts and tip of brush white. In wooded or bushy areas. Chiefly nocturnal. [9]

Mouflon *Ovis ammon musimon*
BOVIDAE L to 1.3 m. Sheep-like; ♂ handsomely-horned. Light to mid-brown, often with irregular white patches above; belly white. In a variety of habitats, but especially in rocky areas; indigenous to Sardinia and Corsica. [10]

Barbary Ape *Macaca sylvanus*
CERCOPITHECIDAE L to 70 cm. Actually a monkey, but resembles apes in being virtually tail-less; thick-set; hair relatively short, coarse. Brown, sometimes reddish. In rocky, wooded areas; confined to North Africa and Gibraltar. [11]

Mediterranean Seal, Monk Seal
Monachus monachus PHOCIDAE
L to 1.8 m. The relatively short head, with its rounded muzzle bearing conspicuous whiskers, looks a little like that of a large dog when protruding above the water. Upper parts of body are brown, sometimes brownish-grey, underparts have an irregular white patch and some indistinct flecking; pups are initially uniformly black. On sheltered coasts of remote rocky islands. This is the region's only seal and is extremely rare. [1]

Common Dolphin *Delphinus delphis*
DELPHINIDAE L to 2 m. Although superficially fish-like, has horizontal tail-flukes; body elegantly streamlined; head with pronounced and clearly-defined 'beak', the jaws long and well-armed with sharp, fang-like teeth; skin smooth; one triangular dorsal fin with curved margins. Dorsal surface black, ventral surface pale, flanks with a complex pattern, usually outlined in a dark grey or black and enclosing a yellow or yellow-brown area. In open water, usually in schools, and often within sight of shore. [2]

Bottle-nosed Dolphin *Tursiops truncatus* is similar, but larger (L to 4 m), with a shorter beak and almost uniform grey colour. Dorsal fin large, conspicuous and prominently recurved.

White-beaked Dolphin *Lagenorhynchus albirostris* is similar, but has a short, white beak and a very large dorsal fin. The flank is grey and this colour extends forward as a narrow band as far as the nape of the neck.

Killer Whale *Orcinus orca*
DELPHINIDAE L to 9 m. A boldly coloured whale typified by the large, triangular dorsal fin; head is relatively short and bluntly conical; mouth armed with sharp

teeth. Upper parts and flanks are strikingly piebald with black, grey and white; under-surface white. In open water, where they usually occur in small schools. This is the only whale which regularly preys upon marine mammals as well as upon large fish; sometimes gather in large numbers near the breeding sites of seals. [3]

Common Porpoise *Phocoena phocoena*
PHOCOENIDAE L to 1.8 m. Head has no beak, the snout being broadly and roundly conical; outline of back between head and the dorsal fin is more rounded than in any dolphin; dorsal fin small with a broad base. Upper parts black or very dark bluish-grey, underparts white, a dark line usually extends from the eye to the flipper. In open water, usually in small schools; frequently enter estuaries or even rivers. Porpoises do not leap from the water as actively nor as frequently as dolphins. [4]

Sperm Whale *Physeter catodon*
PHYSETERIDAE L to 18 m (♂) 10 m (♀). The largest toothed whale; unmistakable flat-topped head resembles enormous, almost rectangular tank. Only the narrow lower jaw has teeth. Usually dark grey. Feed on fish, squid and octopus, often diving to great depths to find prey. May stay sub-merged for up to an hour before surfacing to breathe. The commonest large whale in the Mediterranean. [5]

Blue Whale *Balaenoptera musculus*
BALAENOPTERIDAE L to 30 m. The largest mammal ever to exist. Head long, enor-mous mouth toothless, upper jaw carries fringed baleen plates between which water is passed to sieve planktonic food. Skin of throat and chest deeply pleated as far as navel. Upper parts dark grey, underparts off-white, may be yellow due to presence of diatom film. In open water. [6]

Further Reading

General

The Naturalist's Riviera, A. N. Brangham
(Phoenix House, 1962, London)

Mediterranean – Portrait of a Sea,
E. Bradford (Hodder and Stoughton,
1971, London)

The Naturalist in Majorca, J. D. Parrack
(David and Charles, 1973, Newton Abbott)

Camargue – Soul of a Wilderness, K. Weber,
L. Hoffman (Harrap, 1971, London)

Identification guides – plants

Flowers of Europe, O. Polunin (Oxford
University Press, 1969, London)

Flowers of South-West Europe, O. Polunin
and B. E. Smythies (Oxford University
Press, 1974, London)

Trees and Bushes of Europe, O. Polunin
and B. Everard (Oxford University Press,
1976, London)

Flowers of Greece and the Aegean,
O. Polunin and A. Huxley (Chatto &
Windus, 1978, London)

*A Field Guide to the Orchids of Britain and
Europe*, J. G. Williams, A. E. Williams,
N. Arlott (Collins, 1978, London)

Wild Flowers of the Western Mediterranean,
R. Jones (Jarrold, 1978, Norwich)

Trees and Shrubs of the Mediterranean,
H. Vedel (Penguin, 1978, London)

Identification guides – seashore wildlife

Fauna und Flora der Adria, R. Riedl (Paul
Parey, 1963, Hamburg)

*A Field Guide to the Mediterranean Sea
Shore*, W. Luther and K. Fiedler (Collins,
1976, London)

A Guide to the Seashore, R. Ingle (Hamlyn,
1978, London)

*The Hamlyn Guide to the Seashore and
Shallow Seas of Britain and Europe*,
A. C. Campbell (Hamlyn, 1980, London)

Collins Handguide to the Sea Coast,
D. Ovenden and J. Barrett (Collins, 1981,
London)

Identification guides and reference – animals

Les Insectes, P. Robert (Delachaux &
Niestlé, 1946, Paris)

Insects, J. H. Fabre (David Black ed.)
(Paul Elek, 1979, London)

*A Field Guide to the Butterflies of Britain
and Europe*, L. G. Higgins and N. D. Riley
(Collins, 1970, London)

The Life of Fishes, N. B. Marshall
(Weidenfeld and Nicholson, 1965,
London)

Key to the Fishes of Northern Europe,
A. Wheeler (Warne, 1978, London)

*Fishes of British and Northern European
Seas*, J. Møller Christenson
(Penguin, 1978, London)

British and European Fishes,
(Chatto & Windus, 1979, London)

Fishes of the World, A. Wheeler (Ferndale
Editions, 1979, London)

Guide des Poissons Marins d'Europe,
M. L. Bauchot and A. Pras (Delachaux &
Niestlé, 1980, Paris)

*A Guide to the Reptiles and Amphibians of
Britain and Europe*, E. N. Arnold, J. A.
Burton and D. W. Ovenden (Collins, 1980,
London)

Acknowledgments

The Birds of Britain and Europe, H. Heinzel, R. Fitter and J. Parslow (Collins, 1979, London)

The Hamlyn Guide to the Birds of Britain and Europe, B. Bruun (Hamlyn, 1978, London)

Birds of Britain and Europe, N. Hammond and M. Everett (Pan, 1980, London)

A Field Guide to the Mammals of Britain and Europe, F. H. van den Brink (Collins, 1979, London)

Photographs

8 Klaus Franke/Bruce Coleman
13 Pilloud/Jacana
16 Sean Morris/Oxford Scientific Films
19 J. Andrada/Bruce Coleman
23 Günter Ziesler/Bruce Coleman
27 Maurice and Sally Landre/Colorific
30 *top:* T. P. Crimes/Travel Photo International
   bottom: Dr G. Mazza
31 Dr G. Mazza
35 Dubois/Jacana
38 Hans Reinhard/Bruce Coleman
39 A. Fatras/Ardea
43 Carré/Jacana
46 Paolo Koch/Vision International

Plates

Joyce Tuhill
Seaweeds, flowering plants, invertebrates (pages 80–93, 119–133, 136–143)

Gordon Riley
Invertebrates (pages 95–103)

Andrew Riley/Garden Studio
Invertebrates (pages 105–109)

Josephine Martin/Garden Studio
Invertebrates (pages 111–117, 134–135, 144–147)

John Thompson/John Martin & Artists Ltd
Fish

Malcolm McGregor
Amphibians, reptiles, mammals

Franklin Coombs
Birds

Index

Page references in **bold** refer
to illustrations

Abraxas grossulariata 132, **133**
Acanthocardia aculeata 106
— *echinata* **106**
Acanthochitona communis 94
Acasta spongites 110, **111**
Accipter gentilis 11, 178, **179**
— *nisus* 18, 178, **179**
Acetabularia mediterranea 26, 52, **53**
Acherontia atropos 132, **133**
Acipenser sturio 152, **153**
Acrida mediterranea 120, **121**
Acrocephalus arundinaceus 196, **197**
— *melanopogon* 196, **197**
— *schoenobaenus* 196, **197**
— *scirpaceus* 196
Acrocnida brachiata 140, **141**
Actinia equina 28, 84, **85**
Actitis hypoleucos 182, **183**
admiral, red 130, **131**
Aegithalos caudatus 200, **201**
Aegypius monachus 176, **177**
Aglais urticae 130, **131**
Agonum dorsale 122
Agrion splendens 118, **119**
— *virgo* 118, **119**
Aiptasia mutabilis var *couchi* 84, **85**
Ajuga chamaepitys 68, **69**
Alaemon alaudipes 190, **191**
Alauda arvensis 190, **191**
Alcedo atthis 188, **189**
Alciopa cantraini **89**
Alcyonidium gelatinosum **137**
Alcyonium palmatum **86**
Alectoris barbara **180**
— *graeca* **180**
— *rufa* **180**
alga 31
— red 31
alison, sweet 62, **63**
alkanet, dyer's 66, **67**
Alkanna tinctoria 66, 67
Allium roseum 15, **75**
Alopias vulpinus 148, **149**
Alvania cimex 96, **97**
Ammophila arenaria 78, **79**
amphibians 164
'amphioxus' *see* lancelet
Amphiporus lactifloreus 88, **89**
Amphitrite gracilis 90, **91**
Anacamptis pyramidalis 78, **79**
Anadyomene stellata 52, **53**
Anagallis arvensis 64, **65**
Anas acuta 172, **173**

— *clypeata* 37, 172, **173**
— *crecca* 172, **173**
— *penelope* 172, **173**
— *platyrhyncos* 172
— *querquedula* 172, **173**
— *strepera* 37, 172, **173**
Anax imperator 118, **119**
anchovies 45
anchovy 152, **153**
anemone, beadlet 28, 84, **85**
— cylinder 35, 82, **83**
— daisy 84, **85**
— gem *see* anemone, wartlet
— golden 84, **85**
— mantle 84, **85**
— 'parasitic' 84, **85**
— plumose 28, 84, **85**
— snakelocks 84, **85**
— trumpet 84, **85**
— wartlet 84, **85**
anemones, sea 25, 26, 28, 82–5, **83**
Anemonia viridis 28, 84, **85**
angler, common 162, **163**
Anguilla anguilla 152
Anilocra physodes 110, **111**
animal, moss **136**, **137**
Anomia ephippium 104, **105**
Anser albifrons 172, **173**
— *anser* 37, 172, **173**
Anseropoda placenta 138, **139**
ant, **126**
— pharaoh's 126, **127**
Antedon mediterranea 29, 92, 138,
139
Anthemis chia **73**
Anthocharis cardamines 128, **129**
— *eupheno* 128, **129**
Anthus campestris 192, **193**
— *pratensis* 192, **193**
— *trivialis* 192, **193**
Anthyllis cytisoides 70, **71**
ant-lion 21, **122**
Anurida maritima 24, 118, **119**
ape, Barbary 208, **209**
Aphrodita aculeata **88**
Apis mellifera **127**
Aplidium conicum **145**
— *proliferum* **145**
Aplysia depilans 102, **103**
— *punctata* 102
Apodemus sylvaticus 208, **209**
Apogon imberbis 156, **157**
Aporrhais pespelicani 98, **99**
Apus apus 188, **189**
— *melba* 188, **189**
— *pallidus* 188, **189**
Aquila chrysaetos 178, **179**

— *heliaca* 18, 178, **179**
Arbacia lixula 28, 140, **141**
Arbutus unedo 12, 66, **67**
Arca noae 102, **103**
— *barbata* 102
Archidoris tuberculata 102, **103**
Arctia caja 132, **133**
Ardea cinerea 170, **171**
— *purpurea* 37, 170, **171**
Ardeola ralloides 37, 170, **171**
Argonauta argo 108, **109**
Argynnis paphia 128, **129**
Argyropelecus hemigymnus 152, **153**
Aristeomorpha foliacea **112**
Armadillidium granulatum 110, **111**
Aromia moschata 124, **125**
artemis, smooth **106**
Arundo donax 36, 78, **79**
Ascidia mentula **145**
Ascidiella aspersa **145**
Asparagopsis armata **59**
Asperococcus bullosus 54, **55**
asphodel 20, **75**
Asphodelus microcarpus 20, **75**
aster, sea **73**
Aster tripolium **73**
Asterina gibbosa 138, **139**
Astraea rugosa 94, **95**
Astropecten aurantiacus 138, **139**
— *irregularis* 138, **139**
Atelecyclus rotundatus 116, **117**
Athanas nitescens **112**
Athene noctua 186, **187**
avocet, 39, 182, **183**
Axinella damicornis **81**
— *polypoides* **81**
— *verrucosa* **81**
Aythya ferina 174, **175**
— *fuligula* 174, **175**
— *nyroca* 37, 174, **175**

Balaenoptera musculus **211**
Balanoglossus clavigerus **144**
Balistes carolinensis 162, **163**
Ballanophyllia italica 84, **85**
band-fish, red 158, **159**
barnacle 110, **111**
— goose 110, **111**
— star, 110, **111**
— stalked 110, **111**
barnacles 31
Barnea candida 108
barracuda 156, **157**
barrel-salp 146, **147**
bartsia 68, **69**
bass 156, **157**
bass, stone *see* wreckfish

bat, greater horseshoe 208, **209**
— large mouse-eared 208, **209**
beauty, Camberwell 130, **131**
bee **127**
— bumble **127**
— honey **127**
— humble *see* bee, bumble
bee-eater 18, 188, **189**
beetle, blister *see* fly, Spanish
— checkered **123**
— dung 124, **125**
— ground **122**
— leaf 124, **125**
— musk 124, **125**
— rove **123**
— stag 124, **125**
— tiger, **122**
beetles 11, 20, 122–5
Belone belone 152, **153**
Beroë cucumis **87**
Berthella aurantiaca 102, **103**
Bethlehem, star of 15, **76**
bindweed 66, **67**
birds, 22, 23, 24, 37–9, 168–207
Bittacus italicus 124, **125**
bittern 170, **171**
— little 170, **171**
Bittium reticulatum 96, **97**
bivalves 94–109
blackbird 194
blackcap **198**
Blackstonia perfoliata 66, **67**
blenny, tompot 160, **161**
blue, large 128, **129**
boar, wild 208, **209**
boarfish, red 154, **155**
bogue 156
Bolinus brandaris 33, 100, **101**
Bombus terrestris **127**
Bonellia viridis 92, **93**
Boops boops 156
Boscia anglica 110, **111**
Botaurus stellaris 170, **171**
Botrylloides leachi 146, **147**
Botryllus schlosseri 146, **147**
Botryocladia botryocladia **59**
Bowerbankia imbricata **137**
brambling 202, **203**
Branchiomma lucullana 26
Branchiostoma lanceolatum 148, **149**
bream, annular 156, **157**
brimstone 128, **129**
Brissopsis lyrifera 142, **143**
bristletail 24, 118, **119**
bristle-worm 88, **89**, 90, **91**
— planktonic **89**
brittle-star 140, **141**
— common 140, **141**
brookweed 66, **67**
broom 12, 14, 70, **71**
brown, meadow 130, **131**
Bryopsis plumosa 52, **53**
— *balbisiana* 52, **53**
Bulbulcus ibis 170, **171**
Bucanetes githagineus 204, **205**
Bucephala clangula 174, **175**
buckthorn 15, 64, **65**
Bufo calamita 164, **165**

bug, green shield 120, **121**
— ground 120, **121**
— striped shield 120, **121**
bugloss, viper's 68, **69**
— purple 68, **69**
Bugula turbinata **136**
bulbul, common 192, **193**
bullfinch 204, **205**
Bunodactis verrucosa 84, **85**
bunting, black-headed 204, **205**
— cirl 204, **205**
— corn 204, **205**
— house 204
— ortolan **205**
— reed 204, **205**
— rock 204, **205**
Burhinus oedicnemus 181, **181**
burnet 132, **133**
— thorny 70, **71**
bushchat, rufous, *see* robin, rufous bush
bustard, little **181**
Buteo buteo 18, 178, **179**
butterfly, comma 130, **131**
— peacock 130, **131**
butterflies 128–31
buzzard 18, 178, **179**
— honey 176, **177**
by-the-wind-sailor 44, 82, **83**

Calandrella brachydactyla 190, **191**
— *rufescens* 190
Calappa granulata **115**
Callianassa subterranea **114**
Callionymus lyra 160, **161**
Calliostoma conulus 94
— *zizyphinum* 94, **95**
Callipallene brevirostris **135**
Callista chione **106**
Calonectris diomedea 23, 168, **169**
Calyptrea chinensis 98, **99**
campion, bladder 64, **65**
Cancer pagurus 116, **117**
Cantharidus exasperatus 94, **95**
Caprimulgus europaeus 20, 186, **187**
— *ruficollis* 186, **187**
Capulus ungaricus 98, **99**
Carabus coriacens **122**
Carapus acus 142, 160, **161**
Carcharodon carcharias 148, **149**
Carcinus mediterraneus 40, 116, **117**
cardinal-fish 156, **157**
Carduelis cannabina 204, **205**
— *carduelis* 202, **203**
— *chloris* 202, **203**
Caretta caretta 164, **165**
Carinaria mediterranea 98, **99**
carob 10, 70, **71**
Carpobrotus 24
— *acinaciformis* 64
— *edulis* 64, **65**
Cassidaria echinophora 34, 100, **101**
cattle 36
catworm 90, **91**
Celerio euphorbiae 132, **133**
Centaurium pulchellum 66, **67**
centaury, lesser *see* centaury, slender

— slender 66, **67**
centipede 118, **119**
— long-legged 17
centipedes 17, 118
Centrolabrus exoletus 158, **159**
Centrostephanus longispinus 140, **141**
Cephalanthera damasonium 15, 78, **79**
Cepola rubescens 158, **159**
Ceramaster placenta 138, **139**
Ceramium rubrum **60**
Cerastoderma edule **106**
— *lamarcki* 106
Ceratitis capitata 124, **125**
Ceratonia siliqua 10, 70, **71**
Cercotriches galactotes 192, **193**
Cerebratulus fuscus **88**
Cereus pedunculatus 84, **85**
Cerianthus membranaceus 35, 82, **83**
cerith, common 33, 96, **97**
— rough 96
Cerithium rupestre 96
— *vulgatum* 33, 96, **97**
Certhia brachydactyla 202, **203**
— *familiaris* 202
Cerura vinula 132, **133**
Cestus veneris 86, **87**
Cetorhinus maximus 148, **149**
Cettia cetti 196, **197**
Chaetopterus variopedatus 90, **91**
chaffinch 202, **203**
Chalcides chalcides **166**
Chama gryphoides 26, 104, **105**
Chamaeleo chamaeleon **166**
chameleon **19**
— Mediterranean 18, **166**
chamomile **73**
Charadrius alexandrinus 182, **183**
— *dubius* 182, **183**
Cheilopogon heterurus 152, **153**
Chelon labrorus 156
chicken, Mother Cary's *see* petrel, storm
chicory **75**
chiffchaff **199**
Chilidonias hybridus 184, **185**
— *niger* 184, **185**
Chimaera monstrosa 150, **151**
Chlaenius chrysocephalus **122**
Chlamys opercularis 104, **105**
Chondrosia reniformis **80**
Clonopsis gallica 18
chough 22, 23, 206, **207**
— red-billed *see* chough
Chromis chromis 158, **159**
Chrysaora hysoscella 82, **83**
Chthamalus stellatus 110, **111**
cicada 11, 120, **121**
Cicadetta montana 11, 120, **121**
Cichorium pumilum **75**
— *spinosum* 75
Cicindela littoralis **122**
Ciconia ciconia 37
Cidaris cidaris 140, **141**
Ciona intestinalis 144, **145**
Circaetus gallicus 18, 176, **177**
Circus aeruginosus 176, **177**

— *cyaneus* 176, **177**
— *macrourus* 176, **177**
Cisticola juncidis 196, **197**
Cistus albidus 14, 62, **63**
— *monspeliensis* 62
Cladophora 102
— *pellucida* 52, **53**
Cladostephus verticellatus 54, **55**
Clamator glandarius 186, **187**
Clanculus cruciatus 94, **95**
clary, wild 68
Clathrus clathrus 96, **97**
Clavellina lepadiformis **144**
cleopatra 128, **129**
Cliona celata **81**
clovers, star 70
Coccinella quatuordecimpustulata **123**
— *septempunctata* **123**
Coccothraustes coccothraustes 11, 204, **205**
cockle, common **106**
— dog 102, **103**
— heart 104, **105**
— lagoon 106
— prickly 34, **106**
— spiny 106
cockles 34, 102–106
cod, poor 154, **155**
Codium 102
— *bursa* 52, **53**
— *dichotomum* 52, **53**
Colias crocea 128, **129**
Colpomenia sinuosa 54
Columba livia 186
— *palumbus* 186, **187**
comber, painted 156, **157**
comb-star 138, **139**
— red 138, **139**
Condylactis aurantiaca 84, **85**
Conger conger 152, **153**
conifers 12
Conus mediterraneus 100, **101**
Convolvulus althaeoides 66, **67**
cook, rock 158, **159**
coot 181
Coracias garrulus 18, 188, **189**
coral, cup 84, **85**
— lace **136**
— false **137**
— precious **86**
— stone 84, **85**
— yellow **86**
Corallina mediterranea **58**
— *officinalis* 58
Corallium rubrum **86**
corals **31**, 82–7
Cordulia aenia 118, **119**
Coris julis 158, **159**
Coris monspeliensis 66, **67**
cormorant 168, **169**
— great *see* cormorant
— pygmy 168, **169**
Coronella girondica **167**
Corvus corax 22, 206, **207**
— *corone cornix* 206, **207**
— *corone corone* 206
— *frugilegus* 206, **207**

— *monedula* 206, **207**
Coryphaena hippurus 158, **159**
Corystes cassivelaunus 116, **117**
Coscinasterias tenuispina 140, **144**
cottonweed **74**
Coturnix coturnix 18, **180**
cowrie, European 26, 98, **99**
— lurid 98, **99**
— pear 98, **99**
sowthistle 74, **74**
crab,
— broad-clawed porcelain **114**
— edible 116, **117**
— hermit **115**
— masked 116, **117**
— Mediterranean shore 40, 116, **117**
— nut **115**
— pea 116, **117**
— running 116, **117**
— spider, 116, **117**
— spiny spider 116, **117**
— sponge 29, **115**
— swimming, 116, **117**
— yellow 116, **117**
crabs 25, 26, 29, 43, 110–17
Crambe maritima 62, **63**
Crangon crangon **113**
Crassostrea angulata 104, **105**
Cremastogaster sordidula **126**
Crenilabrus mediterraneus 158, **159**
— *melops* 158
Crepidula fornicata 98, **99**
cricket, field 120, **121**
— great green bush 120, **121**
— mole 17, 18, 120, **121**
Crithmum maritimum 25, 72, **72**
Crocidura suaveolens 208, **209**
crocus 15, 77
Crocus flavus 15, **77**
crustaceans 24, 25, 29, 32, 110–17
Cryptocephalus cericeus 124, **125**
Cryptochelus annulatus 126
Ctenolabrus exoletus 158, **159**
cuckoo 186, **187**
— great spotted 186, **187**
Cuculus canorus 186, **187**
cup, mermaid's 26, 52, **53**
Curculio venosus 124, **125**
curlew 182, **183**
— stone **181**
Cutleria multifida 54, **55**
cuttle, little 108, **109**
cuttlefish 108
— common 108, **109**
Cypraea lurida 98, **99**
Cymodocea nodosa 33, **61**
Cystoseira abrotanifolia 25, 56
— *adriatica* 56
— *barbata* 56, **57**
Cytinus hypocistis 14, 72, **72**

dabchick 168, **169**
Dactylorhiza romana 78, **79**
daffodil, sea **77**
daisy **73**
damselfly 118, **119**
daphne 72, **73**
Daphne gnidium 17, 72, **73**

Daphnis nerii 132, **133**
Dasyatis pastinaca 150, **151**
Dasycladus clavaeformis 52
deer 10
Deilephila elpenor 132, **133**
Delichon urbica 190, **191**
Delphinus delphis **210**
demoiselle 158, **159**
Dendrocopos major 11, 188, **189**
— *minor* 188, **189**
— *syriacus* 188, **189**
Dendrophyllia ramea 31, **86**
Dentalium vulgare 102, **103**
Derbesia lamourouxi 52, **53**
Dermochelys coriacea 164, **165**
Desidiopsis racovitzae **135**
diatoms 33
Diazona violacea **145**
Dicentrarchus labrax 156, **157**
Dictyopteris membranacea 26, 54, **55**
Dictyonota dichotoma 54, **55**
Didemnum maculosum **144**
Diodora italica 94, **95**
Diogenes pugilator 115
Diplodus annularis 156, **157**
Distalpia rosea **144**
Distoma adriaticum **144**
Distomus variolosus 146, **147**
dogfish, large-spotted 148, **149**
— spiny 150, **151**
Doliolum muelleri 146, **147**
Dolium galea 34, 100, **101**
dolphin, bottle-nosed 210
— common **210**
— white-beaked 210
dolphinfish 158, **159**
Donax vittatus **107**
Dorippe lanata **115**
Dory, John 154, **155**
Dosinia lupinus **106**
dove, collared 186, **187**
— rock 186, **187**
dragonet, common 160, **161**
dragonfly 118, **119**
— emperor 118, **119**
drill, oyster *see* winkle, sting
Dromia vulgaris 29, **115**
duck, ferruginous 37, 174, **175**
— marbled 172, **173**
— tufted 174, **175**
— white-headed 174, 175
ducks 37, 172–75
dunnock 192, **193**

eagle, Bonelli's 178, **179**
— booted 178, **179**
— golden 178, **179**
— imperial 18, 178, **179**
— sea *see* eagle, white-tailed
— short-toed 18, 176, **177**
— white-tailed 176, **177**
earthworms 12
Ebalia tuberosa 115
Echiichtys vipera 34
Echinaster sepositus 138, **139**
Echinocardium cordatum 35, 142, **143**
— *pennatifidum* 142, **143**
Echinocyamus pusillus 142, **143**

Echinus acutus 140, **141**
— *melo* 140, **141**
Echium diffusum 68
— *italicum* 68, **69**
— *lycopsis* 68, **69**
eel, common 152, 153
— conger 152, **153**
— moray 25, 152, **153**
eel-grass 61, **61**
— narrow-leaved 61
eel-grasses 33, 61
egret, cattle 170, **171**
— little 170, **171**
Egretta garzetta 170, **171**
Elaphe scalaris 21, **167**
Eledone moschata 108
elephant 10
Emarginula elongata 94, **95**
Emberiza cia 204, **205**
— *cirlus* 204, **205**
— *citrinella* 204
— *hortulana* 204, **205**
— *melanocephala* 204, **205**
— *schoeniclus* 204, **205**
— *striolata* 204
Empusa pennata 118, **119**
Emys orbicularis **166**
Engraulis encrasicholus 152, **153**
Ensis ensis 108, **109**
— *siliqua* 108
Enteromorpha intestinalis 52, **53**
Epinephelus guaza 156, **157**
Epizoanthus arenaceus 82, **83**
Erica arborea 12, 66, **67**
Erinaceus europaeus 12, 208, **209**
Eriphia spinifrons 116, **117**
Erithacus rubecula 192, **193**
Erodium cicutarium 64, **65**
— *gruinum* 64
Erronea pirum 98, **99**
Eryngium maritimum **72**
Eulalia viridis **89**
Eunice harassi 90, **91**
Eunicella cavolini 86
— *verrucosa* **86**
Euphorbia 132
— *paralias* 62, **63**
Euphrosne foliosa **89**
Euscorpius flavicaudis **134**
Evax pygmaea **73**

Falco eleonorae 178, **179**
— *naumanni* 178, **179**
— *peregrinus* 178, **179**
— *subbuteo* 178, **179**
— *tinnunculus* 18, 178, **179**
falcon, Eleonora's 178, **179**
— peregrine 178, **179**
Falkenbergia rufolanosa 59
fan-worm 90, **91**, 92, **93**
feather-star, Mediterranean 138, **139**
festoon, southern 128, **129**
Ficedula albicollis 11, 200, **201**
Ficus carica 10, 64, **65**
fieldfare 37
field-mouse, long-tailed *see* wood-mouse

fig 10, 24, 64, **65**
— Hottentot 24, 64, **65**
finch, trumpeter 204, **205**
fingers, deadman's **86**
firecrest **199**
fire-salp 146, **147**
fire-worm **89**
fish, angel *see* monkfish
— bony 152–63
— cartilaginous 148–51
— jawless 148, **149**
— sucking *see* remora
— trumpet 154, **155**
fishes 25, 28, 29, 34, 44, 148–63
Flabelligera affinis 90, **91**
flag, yellow 40, **77**
flamingo, greater 37, **39**, 170, **171**
flatworms **88**
flax 64, **65**
flounder 44, **162**
flower, everlasting **73**
Flustra foliacea **136**
fly, Spanish 124, **125**
flycatcher, collared 11, 200, **201**
— spotted 200, **201**
flying-fish 152, **153**
fox 208, **209**
Fringilla coelebs 202, **203**
— *montifringilla* 202, **203**
Fritillaria messanensis 15, **76**
fritillary 15, **76**
— silver-washed 128, **129**
frog, lake *see* frog, marsh
— marsh 40, 164, **165**
fruit-fly, Mediterranean 124, **125**
Fucus virsoides 26, 56, **57**
Fulica atra 181
Fusus rostratus 100, **101**

gadwall 37, 172, **173**
Gaidropsarus mediterraneus 154, **155**
Galathea nexa **114**
Galeorhinus galeus 150, **151**
Galerida cristata 190, **191**
Gallinago gallinago 182, **183**
Gallinula chloropus 181
gallinule, common *see* moorhen
— greenbacked *see* gallinule, purple
— purple 181
Gammarus locusta 110, **111**, 112
gannet 23, 168, **169**
garfish 152, **153**
garganey 172, **173**
Gari depressa **107**
garpike *see* garfish
Garrulus glandarius 11, 206, **207**
Gastropacha quercifolia 130, **131**
gastropods 33, 34
gecko, Moorish 164, **165**
— Turkish 24, 164, **165**
geckoes 24, 164–5
Gelochelidon nilotica 23
Genista acanthoclados 70
— *cinerea* 12, 15, 70, **71**
germander 68, **69**
Gibbula divaricata 94

— *magus* 94, **95**
Gigartina acicularis **59**
gilthead 156, **157**
girdle, Venus's **87**
Glareola pratincola **181**
glasswort 40, 64, **65**
Glaucium flavum 62, **63**
Glossus humanus 104, **105**
Glycera convoluta 90, **91**
Glycymeris glycymeris 102, **103**
goats 10, 23
Gobius cobitis 162
— *niger* 162, **163**
— *paganellus* 29, 160, **161**
goby, blue 162, **163**
— giant 162
— rock 29, 160, **161**
goldcrest **199**
goldeneye 174, **175**
goldfinch 202, **203**
goldsinny 158
Golfingia elongata 92, **93**
Goneplax angulata 116, **117**
Gonepteryx cleopatra 128, **129**
— *rhamni* 128, **129**
goose, greylag 37, 172, **173**
— solan *see* gannet
— white-fronted 172, **173**
gooseberry, sea **87**
goshawk 11, 178, **179**
Gracilaria confervoides **58**
grand cigale *see* lobster, flapjack
Grantia compressa 26, **80**
grapevine 10
Graphosoma lineata 120, **121**
grass, marram 78, **79**
— Neptune 33, **61**
grasses, marine 33
grasshopper, 120, **121**
— blue-winged 120, **121**
grasshoppers 17, 120–1
Grateloupia filicina 56, **57**
grebe, black-necked 168, **169**
— great-crested 168, **169**
— little *see* dabchick
greenbone *see* garfish
greenfinch 202, **203**
ground-pine 68, **69**
grouper *see* perch, dusky
Gryllotalpa gryllotalpa 17, 120, **121**
Gryllus campestris 120, **121**
Gryphus vitreus **137**
gull, Audouin's 23, 184, **185**
— black-headed 184, **185**
— great black-backed 184, **185**
— herring 23, 184, **185**
— lesser black-backed 23, 184, **185**
— little 184, **185**
— slender-billed 184, **185**
gurnard, armed 162, **163**
— striped 162, **163**
Gymnammodytes cicerellius 160, **161**
Gyps fulvus 176, **177**

Hacelia attenuata 138, **139**
Haematopus ostralegus 35, 182, **183**
hairstreak, purple 128, **129**

hake 154, 155
Haliaeetus albicilla 176, 177
Halichondria panicea 27, **81**
Halimeda tuna 52, 53
Halimione portulacoides 64, **65**
Halocynthia papillosa 146, **147**
Halopteris filicina 54
hammerhead-shark 148, **149**
hare, brown 208, **209**
— sea 102, **103**
harrier, hen 176, **177**
— marsh 176, **177**
— pallid 176, **177**
hat chinaman's 98, **99**
hatchet-fish 152, **153**
hawfinch 11, 204, **205**
hawks 18
heart-urchin 142, **143**
— purple 142, **143**
heather, tree 12, 66, **67**
hedgehog 12, 208, **209**
Helichrysum stoechas **73**
helleborine, broad 15, 78, **79**
— white *see* helleborine, broad
helleborines 15, 78–9
helmet, knobbed 34
Hemidactylus turcicus 24, 164, **165**
hemlock 25
Hermonia hystrix **89**
heron, black-crowned night *see*
  heron, night
— grey 170, **171**
— night 37, 170, **171**
— purple 37, 170, **171**
— squacco 37, 170, **171**
herons 37–9, 170–1
Hiatella arctica 108, **109**
Hieraaetus fasciatus 178, **179**
— *pennatus* 178, **179**
Hildenbrandia prototypus 56, **57**
Himantopus himantopus 39, 182, **183**
Hippocampus guttulatus 154, **155**
— *ramulosus* 154, **155**
Hippocrepis unisiliquosa 70, **71**
Hippolais pallida 196, **197**
— *polyglotta* 196, **197**
Hippolyte prideauxiana 112
Hippospongia communis 81
Hirundo daurica 190, **191**
— *rustica* 190, **191**
hobby 178, **179**
hogweed 25
holly, sea 72, 73
Holothuria polii 142, **143**
Homarus gammarus 29, **114**
hoopoe 18, 188, **189**
Hormiphora plumosa 87
hornet **126**
horntail *see* wasp, wood
hornwrack **136**
horse, long-nosed sea 154, **155**
— sea 154, **155**
horse-fly 124, **125**
horse-mackerel *see* shad
horses 36, **39**
hound, smooth 148, **149**
humantin 150, **151**
hyacinth, grape 76

— tassel **76**
Hyalinoecia tubicola 90, **91**
Hydrobates pelagicus 23, 168, **169**
Hypericum empetrifolium 62, **63**
hyssop 15, 68, **69**
Hyssopus officinalis 15, 68, **69**

Ianthina janthina 44, 96, **97**
ibis, glossy 37, 170, **171**
Idotea balthica 110, **111**
Ilia nucleus **115**
Inachis io 130, **131**
Inachus dorsettensis 116, **117**
insect, stick 18, 120, **121**
insects 11, 18, 22, 24, 118–35
Inula crithmoides 25, **74**
— *viscosa* 74
Iphiclides podalirius 128, **129**
Iris chamaeiris 15, **77**
— *pseudacorus* 40, **77**
— *xiphium* 70, **77**
iris, dwarf 15, **77**
— Spanish **77**
isopod 110, **111**
Iulis mediterraneus 118, **119**
Ixobrychus minutus 170, **171**

jackdaw 206, **207**
Janua pagenstecheri 92, **93**
jasmine 66, **67**
Jasminum fruticus 66, **67**
jay 206, **207**
jelly, comb **87**
jelly-fish 82–7, 82, **83**
— compass 82, **83**
jewelbox, Mediterranean 26, 104,
  105
Juncus acutus **76**
— *bufonius* **76**
— *maritimus* **76**
juniper 14, 78, **79**
Juniperus oxycedrus 14, 78, **79**
Jynx torquilla 18, 188, **189**

kale, sea 62, **63**
kelp 56, **57**
kestrel 18, 178, **179**
kingfisher 188, **189**
kite, black 176, **177**
— red 176, **177**
Koenenia mirabilis **134**
krill 110, **111**

Labidoplax digitata 142, **143**
Labrus bergylta 158, **159**
Lacerta lepida 166
— *virdis* **166**
lady, painted 128, **129**
ladybird, fourteen-spot 123
— seven-spot 123
Lagenorhynchus albirostris 210
Lagis koreni 90, **91**
Lambrus angulifrons 116, **117**
Laminaria rodriguezi 56, **57**
Lamna nasus 148, **149**
Lampetra fluviatilis 148, **149**
Lampyris mauritanica **123**
lancelet 148, **149**

lance-urchin, grey 140, **141**
Lanice conchilega 35
Lanius collurio 206, **207**
— *excubitor* 206
— *minor* 206, **207**
— *rubicus* 206, **207**
— *senator* 206, **207**
lantern-fish 152
lapwing 182, **183**
lark, bifasciated *see* lark, hoopoe
— calandra 190, **191**
— crested 190, **191**
— hoopoe 190, **191**
— lesser short-toed 190
— short-toed 190, **191**
Larra anathema 17 **127**
Larus argentatus 23, 184, **185**
— *audouinii* 23, 184, **185**
— *fuscus* 23, 184, **185**
— *genei* 184, **185**
— *marinus* 184, **185**
— *melanocephalus* 184, **185**
— *minutus* 184, **185**
— *ridibundus* 184, **185**
Laurencia obtusa 60
Lavandula stoechas 68, **69**
Lavatera arborea 62, **63**
— *maritima* 62, **63**
lavender 13
— common, sea 66
— French 68, **69**
— sea 66, **67**
laver 56, **57**
leech, fish 92, **93**
leeches 92–3
Lepadogaster lepadogaster 29, 162,
  163
Lepas anatifera 110, **111**
Lepidonotus clava **89**
Lepidopleurus cajetanus 94, **95**
Lepus capensis 208, **209**
lettuce, sea 52, **53**
Leucosolenia botryoides 80
— *coriacea* **80**
Libellula maculata 118, **119**
Ligia 24
— *italica* 110, **111**
Ligustrum vulgare 132
Lima hians 104, **105**
Limonium sinuatum 66, **67**
limpet, bonnet **98**
— keyhole 94, **95**
— Mediterranean 94, **95**
— slit 94, **95**
— slipper 98, **99**
limpets 28–9, 94–8
Lineus geniculatus **88**
linnet 204, **205**
Linum campanulatum 64, **65**
Lithophaga lithophaga 26, 102, **103**
Lithophyllum incrustans 58
— *racemus* 58
— *tortuosum* 29, **58**
Lithothamnion fruticulosum **58**
— *lenormandi* 58
Littorina neritoides 96, **97**
Liza aurata 156, **157**
— *ramada* 156

lizard, green **166**
— jewelled 166
— Spanish sandracer 21
— wall 166
lizards 17, 22, 24, 166
lobster,
— common **114**
— flapjack 29, **113**
— Norway **114**
— spiny 43, **113**
— squat **114**
lobsters 29, 43, 110–17
locust, migratory 120, **121**
Locusta migratoria 120, **121**
Loligo vulgaris 108, **109**
Lomentaria linearis **59**
Lophelia pertusa 84, **85**
Lophius piscatorius 162, **163**
Lotus creticus 70, **71**
Lucanus cervus 124, **125**
Luidia ciliaris 29, 138, **139**
— *sarsia* 138, **139**
Lullula arborea 18, 190, **191**
Luscinia megarhynchos 11, 192, **193**
Lutraria lutraria **107**
Lycosa narbonensis 17, **135**
Lygaeus saxatilis 120, **121**
lyre-urchin 142, **143**
Lytta vesicatoria 124, **125**

macchia 12
mackerel 45, 160, **161**
— Spanish 160, **161**
mackerel-shark *see* porbeagle
Macropipus depurator 116
Macropodia longirostris 116, **117**
Macroramphus scolopax 154, **155**
Mactra corallina 34, **106**
Maculinea arion 128, **129**
Madrepora oculata 84, **85**
magpie 206, **207**
Maia squinado 116, **117**
Malcolmia maritima 62, **63**
mallard 172
mallow, tree 62, **63**
— lesser tree 62
— sea 62, **63**
Malpolon monspessulanus 167, **167**
mammals 20, 208–11
maneater *see* shark, white
Maniola jurtina 130, **131**
man-o'-war, Portuguese 44, 82, **83**
mantis, false 120, **121**
— praying 18, 118, **119**, 120
Mantis religiosa 18, 118, **119**, 120
Mantispa styriaca 120, **121**
Marmaronetta angustirostris 172, **173**
Marthasterias glacialis 138, **139**
martin, crag 190, **191**
— house 190, **191**
— sand 190, **191**
Marumba quercus 132, **133**
mason, sand 35, 92, **93**
Matthiola sinuata 62, **63**
Maurolicus muelleri 152, **153**
Medicago marina 70, **71**
medick, sea 70, **71**

Meganyctiphanes norvegica 110, **111**
Melanargia galathea 130, **131**
Melanocorypha calandra 190, **191**
Membranipora membranacea **136**
merganser, red-breasted 174, **175**
Mergus albellus 174, **175**
— *serrator* 174, **175**
Merluccius merluccius 154, **155**
Merops apiaster 18, 188, **189**
Metridium senile 28, 84, **85**
Microcosmus sulcatus 31, 146, **147**
Micromesistius poutassou 144, **155**
mignonette, wild 62, **63**
millipede 118, **119**
Milvus migrans 176, **177**
— *milvus* 176, **177**
Mitra ebenus 100, **101**
Mobula mobular 150, **151**
Modiolus barbatus 102, **103**
Mola mola 44, 162, **163**
Molgula manhattensis 146, **147**
molluscs 25, 26, 28, 29, 33, 34, 44, 94–109
Monachus monachus **210**
monkfish 150, **151**
Monodonta turbinata 94, **95**
Monomorium pharaonis **126**
Monticola saxatilis 194, **195**
— *solitarius* 194, **195**
moorhen **181**
Mormo maura 132, **133**
Motacilla alba alba 192, **193**
— *cinerea* 192, **193**
— *flava iberiae* 192, **193**
moth, death's head hawk 132, **133**
— elephant hawk 132, **133**
— emperor 130, **131**
— eyed hawk 132, **133**
— garden tiger 132, **133**
— great peacock 130, **131**
— lappet 130, **131**
— magpie 132, **133**
— oak hawk 132, **133**
— old lady 132, **133**
— oleander hawk 132, **133**
— privet hawk 132, **133**
— puss 132, **133**
— spurge hawk 132, **133**
moths 20, 130–33
mouflon 23, 208, **209**
mullein 68, **69**
mullet, golden grey 156, **157**
— red 45, 156, **157**
— striped 158, **159**
— thick-lipped 156
— thin-lipped 156
Mullus barbatus 45, 156, **157**
— *surmuletus* 158, **159**
Muraena helena 25, 152, **153**
murex, dye 33, 100, **101**
Muscari commutatum 76
Muscicapa striata 200, **201**
mussel, bearded horse 102, **103**
— common 104
— date 26, 102, **103**
— fan 104, **105**
— Mediterranean 26, 104, **105**
mussels 26, 29, 44, 102–5

Mustelus mustelus 148, **149**
Myctophum punctatum 152
Myliobatis aquila 150, **151**
Myotis myotis 208, **209**
Myrianida pinnigera **89**
Myriozoum iruncatum **137**
Myrmeleon plumbeus 21, **120**
myrtle 14, 17, **72**
Myrtus communis 14, **72**
Mytilus edulis 104
— *galloprovincialis* 26, 104, **105**
Myzostomum cirriferum 92, **93**

narcissus 15
— polyanthus **76**
Narcissus tazetta 15, **76**
Nassarius incrassatus 100, **101**
— *reticulatus* 33, 100, **101**
Natica alderi 33, 98, **99**
— *hebraea* 98
— *millepunctata* 98
Natrix maura 167
— *natrix* 18, **167**
Naucrates ductor 158, **159**
nautilus, paper 108, **109**
Nemalion helminthoides 56, **57**
Neophron percnopterus 176, **177**
Neoturris pileata 82, **83**
Nephrops norvegica **114**
Nephtys hombergi 90, 91
Nereis pelagica 90, **91**
Nerium oleander 132
Nerophis ophidion 154
Netta rufina 174, **175**
Neurocaulon reniforme **59**
nightingale 11, 192, **193**
nightjar 20, 186, **187**
— red-necked 186, **187**
Nitophyllum punctatum **60**
Nucula nucleus 102, **103**
Numenius arquata 182, **183**
nuthatch 200
— Corsican 200, **201**
— rock 200, **201**
Nycticorax nycticorax 37, 170, **171**
Nymphalis antiopa 130, **131**
— *polychloros* 130, **131**
Nymphon gracile **135**

oak, cork 10, 75
— holm 10, 75
— Kermes 17, **75**
oaks 10, 17, 75
Ocenebra erinacea 100, **101**
Ocnus planci 142, **143**
octopus, common 108, **109**
— webbed 108
Octopus vulgaris 108, **109**
octopuses 24, 45, 108–9
Odontospermum maritimum 25, **73**
Oecobius annulipes **134**
Oedipoda coerulescens 120, **121**
Oenanthe hispanica 194, **195**
— *leucura* 194, **195**
— *oenanthe* 194, **195**
Olea europea 66, **67**
— var. *oleaster* 66
olive, 66, **67**

Olios spongitarsis **134**
Ommatostrephes sagittus 108, **109**
Onobrychis caput-galli 70, **71**
Ononis spinosa 70, **71**
Ophelia bicornis 34, 90, **91**
Ophidiaster ophidianus 29, 138, **139**
Ophiocomina nigra 140, **141**
Ophiothrix fragilis 140, **141**
Ophrys speculum 15, 16, 78, **79**
Opuntia ficusindica 20, 70, **71**
orange, sea 80, **81**
orange tip 128, **129**
— Provence 128, **129**
orchid, heart-flowered tongue 78, **79**
— mirror 15, **16**, 78, **79**
— pink butterfly 78, **79**
— pyramidal 78, **79**
— Roman 78, **79**
— scarce tongue 78
orchids 15, 78–9
Orchis papilionaceae 78, **79**
Orcinus orca **210**
oriole, golden 202, **203**
Oriolus oriolus 202, **203**
ormer, common 94, **95**
Ornithogalum montanum **76**
— *nutans* 15
Oryctolagus cuniculus 208, **209**
Ostrea edulis 104, **105**
Otanthus maritimus **74**
Otus scops 20, 186, **187**
oursin *see* urchin, rock
osprey 178, **179**
Ovis ammon musimon 23, 208, **209**
owl, little 186, **187**
— 20, 186, **187**
Oxynotus centrina 150, **151**
Oxyura leucocephala 174, **175**
oyster, European *see* oyster, native
— native 104, **105**
— Portuguese 104, **105**
— saddle 104, **105**
— thorny 104, **105**
— winged 104, **105**
oystercatcher 32, 182, **183**
oysters 26, 44, 104–5

Pachygrapsus marmoratus 116, **117**
Padina pavonia 54, **55**
Paguristes oculatus 115
Pagurus arrosor **115**
Palaemon elegans **113**
— *serratus* 113
Palinurus elephas **113**
Palinurus vulgaris 43
Paliurus spinachristi 15, 64, **65**
Pallenis spinosa **73**
Palmophyllum crassum 52, **53**
palms 40
Palomena viridissima 120, **121**
Pancratium maritimum **77**
Pandion haliaetus 178, **179**
Panurus biarmicus 200, **201**
Parablennius gattorugine 160, **161**
Paracentrotus lividus 28, 140, **141**
parasite, rock-rose 14, 72, **72**
Parazoanthus axinellae 82
Parentucellia latifolia 68, **69**

parrot-fish 158, **159**
parsley, sea 64, **65**
partridge, Barbary **180**
— grey 18, **180**
— red-legged **180**
— rock **180**
Parus ater 200, **201**
— *caeruleus* 200, **201**
— *cristatus* 200, **201**
— *cristatus ultramarinus* 200
— *lugubris* 200, **201**
— *major* 200, **201**
— *palustris* 200
Passer hispaniolensis 202, **203**
Patella coerulea 94, **95**
Peachia hastata 82, **83**
pear, prickly 20, 70, **71**
pearl-fish 142, 160, **161**
pearlside 152, **153**
pea-urchin 142, **143**
Pecten jacobaeus 104, **105**
Pelagica noctiluca 82, **93**
Pelecanus crispus 168, **169**
— *onocratalus* 168, **169**
pelican, Dalmatian 168, **169**
— white 168, **169**
Pelobates cultripes 164, **165**
Penaeus trisulcatus **112**
Pennatula phosphorea **87**
perch, dusky 156, **157**
Perdix perdix 18, **180**
Peristedion cataphractum 162, **163**
periwinkle, small 96, **97**
Pernis apivorus 176, **177**
Perophora listeri **145**
petrel, storm 23, 168, **169**
Petrobius maritimus 24, 118, **119**
Petromyzon marinus 148, **149**
Petronia petronia 202, **203**
Peyssonelia squamaria 56, **57**
Phalacrocorax carbo 168, **169**
— *pygmaeus* 168, **169**
Phallusia mammillata 156, **157**
Pharus legumen **107**
Phocoena phocoena **211**
Phoenicopterus ruber 37, 170, **171**
Phoenicurus moussieri 194, **195**
— *ochruros* 194, **195**
— *phoenicurua* 194, **195**
Pholas dactylus 26, 108, **109**
phoronid **137**
Phoronis muelleri **137**
Phragmites australis 78, **79**
Phtisica marina **112**
Phyllophora nervosa **59**
Phylloscopus bonelli **199**
— *collybita* 11, **199**
— *ignicapillus* **199**
— *sibilatrix* **199**
— *trochilus* 199
Physalia physalis 44, 82, **83**
Physeter catodon **211**
Physophora hydrostatica 82, **83**
phytoplankton 42–3
Pica pica 206, **207**
Picus viridis 188, **189**
piddock, common 26, 108, **109**
— white 108

piddocks 31, 108–9
Pieris napi 128, **129**
pike, saury 152, **153**
pilchard 152, **153**
pilotfish 158, **159**
pimpernel, scarlet 66, **67**
pine, Aleppo 10, 12, 78, **79**
pines **9**, 12
pinewoods 12
Pinna nobilis 104, **105**
Pinnotheres pisum 116, **117**
Pinus halepensis 10, 78, **79**
pipefish, broad-nosed 154, **155**
— greater 154
— straight-nosed 154
pipistrelle, common 208, **209**
Pipistrellus pipistrellus 208, **209**
pipit, meadow 192, **193**
— tawny 192, **193**
— tree 192, **193**
plaice 162, **163**
plankton 42–4, **43**
plant, Spanish oyster 20
Plantago coronopus 25, 70, **71**
plantain, buckshorn *see* plantain
stag's horn
— sea 70
— stag's horn 25, 70, **71**
plants, flowering 62–79
Platalea leucrodia 170, **171**
Platychthys flesus 44, 162
Plegadis falcinellus 37, 170, **171**
Pleurobrachia pileus 87, **87**
Pleuronectes platessa 162, **163**
plover, Kentish 182, **183**
— little ringed 182, **183**
pochard 174, **175**
— red-crested 174, **175**
Podarcis muralis 166
Podiceps cristatus 168, **169**
— *nigricollis* 168, **169**
Polistes gallicus **127**
Pollachius pollachius 154, **155**
pollack 154, **155**
Polycera quadrilineatus 26, 102, **103**
Polydora ciliata 90, **91**
Polygonia c-album 130, **131**
Polynices guillemini 98, **99**
Polyprion americanus 156, **157**
Polysiphonia fruticulosa 60
— *sertularoides* 60
Pomatoceros triqueter 92, **93**
Pontobdella muricata 92, **93**
Pontonia custos 113
poppy, yellow horned 62, **63**
porbeagle 148, **149**
Porcellana platycheles **114**
Porphyra leucosticta 56, **57**
Porphyrio porphyrio 181
porpoise, common **211**
Posidonia oceanica 33, **61**
Potamilla reniformis 92, **93**
Poterium spinosum 70, **71**
pratincole, collared **181**
prawn 112, **113**
— common 113
— Dublin Bay **114**
— guardian 113

— red 112
— sea-grass 112
— snapping 112
Prionace glauca 148, **149**
Prunella modularis modularis 192,
193
Psammechinus microtuberculatus
28, 140, **141**
Psammodromus hispanicus 21, **166**
Pselaphochernes littoralis 24, **134**
Pseudolithophyllum expansum 58
pseudoscorpion 24, **134**
Pteria hirundo 104, **105**
Pterocles alchata 186, **187**
— *orientalis* 186, **187**
prey, birds of 18
Pteroides griseum 86
Pterotrachea coronata 98, **99**
Ptyonoprogne rupestris 190, **191**
Puffinus puffinus 23, 168, **169**
Punctaria latifolia 54, **55**
Pycnogonum pusillum 26, **135**
Pycnonotus barbatus 192, **193**
Pyrosoma atlanticum 146, **147**
Pyrrhocorax pyrrhocorax 22, 206,
207
Pyrrhula pyrrhula 204, **205**
Pyura microcosmus 146, **147**

quail 18, **180**
Quercus coccifera **75**
— *ilex* 10, **75**
— *suber* 10, 75
Quercusia quercus 128, **129**

rabbit 208, **209**
rabbit-fish 150, **151**
ragworm 90, **91**
ragworms 40, 90–1
ragwort 74
— silver **74**
rail, water 180, **181**
Raja asterias 150, **151**
— *clavata* 150, **151**
— *oxyrinchus* 150, **151**
Rallus aquaticus **180**
Rana ridibunda 40, 164, **165**
raven 22, 23
ray, devil 150, **151**
— edible 150, **151**
— electric 150, **151**
— starry 150, **151**
— thornback 150, **151**
rays 148–51
razor, pod 108
Recurvirostra avosetta 39, 182, **183**
redshank 182, **183**
redstart 194, **195**
— black 194, **195**
— Moussier's 194, **195**
redwing 37
reed, common 78, **79**
— giant 36, 78, **79**
Regulus ignicapillus **199**
— *regulus* **199**
Remiz pendulinus 202, **203**
remora 162, **163**
Remora remora 162, **163**

reptiles 21, 24, 164–67
Reseda lutea 62, **63**
restharrow, spiny 70, **71**
Retepora cellulosa **136**
Rhamnus alaternus 15, 64, **65**
rhinoceros 10
Rhinolophus ferrumequinum 208,
209
Rhizostoma pulmo 82, **93**
Rhopalaea neopolitana **145**
Riparia riparia 190, **191**
Rissoa variabilis 96, **97**
— *ventricosa* 96, **97**
river-lamprey 148, **149**
robin 192, **193**
— rufous bush 192, **193**
rock-borer, wrinkled 108, **109**
rockling, shore 154, **155**
— three-bearded *see* rockling, shore
rock-rose 12, 14, 17, 62, **63**
— annual 62, **63**
rock-urchin 28, 140, **141**
roller 18, 188, **189**
Romulea bulbocodium **77**
rose-garlic 15, **75**
rosemary 15, 68, **69**
Rosmarinus officinalis 15, 68, **69**
rue 15, 64, **65**
rush, sea 76
— sharp 76
— toad 76
Ruta chalepensis 15, 64, **65**

Sabella penicillus 92, **93**
Sabellaria alveolata 90, **91**
shad 158, **159**
sage 15
— three-lobed 68, **69**
sainfoin 70, **71**
salamander, fire 164, **165**
Salamandra salamandra 164, **165**
Salicornia fruticosa 40, **65**
salp 146, **147**
Salpa democratica 146, **147**
— *maxima* 146, **147**
salps 144, 146–7
Salsola kali 40, 64, **65**
saltwort 40, 64, **65**
Salvia 15
— *triloba* 68, **69**
— *verbenaca* 68
Samolus valerandi 66, **67**
samphire 74
— golden 25, **74**
— rock 25, **72**
sand-eel, Mediterranean smooth
34, 160, **161**
sandgrouse, black-bellied 186, **187**
— pin-tailed 186, **187**
sand-hopper 32, 110, **111**, **112**
sandpiper, common 182, **183**
sandracer, Spanish 166, **167**
Sardinia pilchardus 152, **153**
sardine *see* pilchard
sardines 45, 152–3
Sargassum hornschuchi 56, **57**
— *linifolium* 56
— *vulgare* 56, **57**

Sarpa salpa 156, **157**
Satureia thymbra 15, 68, **69**
Saturnia pavonia 130, **131**
— *pyri* 130, **131**
saupe 156, **157**
savory, summer 15, 68, **69**
Saxicola rubetra 194, **195**
— *torquata* **195**
Scabiosa atropurpurea var *maritima*
73
scabious 73
scale-worm **89**
scallop, queen 104, **105**
Scalpellum scalpellum 110, **111**
scampi 114
Scaphander lignarius 100, **101**
scarab, holy 124, **125**
Scarabaeus sacer 124, **125**
— *semipunctatus* 124, **125**
Sceliphron destillatorium 127
Scolia ciliata 15
— *maculata* **126**
Scolopendra cingulata 118, **119**
Scolymus hispanicus 20
Scomber japonicus 160, **161**
— *scombrus* 160, **161**
Scomberesox saurus 152, **153**
Scorpaena scrofa 162, **163**
scorpion **134**
— palpigrade micro-whip **134**
scorpion-fish, red 162, **163**
scorpion-fly 124, **125**
scorpions 17, 134
Scrobicularia plana 40, **107**
Scrupocellaria reptans 136, **136**
Scutigera coleoptrata 17, 118, **119**
Scyllarides arctus 113
— *latus* 29, **113**
Scylliorhinus stellaris 148, **149**
Scytosiphon tomentarius 56, **57**
seabirds 22, 23
seablite, common 40, 64, **65**
— herbaceous *see* seablite, common
sea-cucumber 142, **143**
sea-cucumbers 138–43
sea-egg 31, 146, **147**
sea-fan 86, **87**
sea-fir 82, **83**
sea-grass **61**
seal, Mediterranean **210**
— monk *see* seal, Mediterranean
sea-lamprey 148, **149**
sea-mat **136, 137**
sea-mouse **88, 89**
sea-pen, grey 86
— phosphorescent **87**
sea-potato *see* heart-urchin
sea-snail, purple 44, 96, **97**
sea-spider 26, **135**
sea-squirt **144, 145**, 146, **147**
— red 146, **147**
— star 146, **147**
sea-squirts 25, 26, 31, 144–7
sea-urchin 140, **141**
— black 28, 140, **141**
— long-spined 140, **141**
— Mediterranean green 28, 140, **141**
sea-urchins 28, **30**, 31, 34, 138–43

seaweed, brown 54, **55**
— green 52, **53**
— red 56, **57**, **58–61**
seaweeds 25, 26, **52–61**
— brown 54–5
— green 52–3
— red 56–61
Sedum stellatum 70, **71**
Senecio cineraria **74**
— *vernalis* 74
Sepia elegans 108
— *officinalis* 108, **109**
Serapias cordigera 78, **79**
— *parviflora* 78
serin 202, **203**
Serinus serinus 202, **203**
Serpula vermicularis 92, **93**
Serranus cabrilla 156, **157**
shark, basking 148, **149**
— blue 148, **149**
— white 148, **149**
sharks 148–51
shearwater, Cory's 23, 168, **169**
— Manx 23, 168, **169**
sheep 10
— wild 23
shelduck 172, **173**
shell, ark 102
— banded wedge 34, **107**
— bubble 100, **101**
— coat-of-mail 94, **95**
— common nut 102, **103**
— common otter **107**
— cross-cut razor **106**
— curved razor 108, **109**
— fan 104, **105**
— gaping file 104, **105**
— giant tun 34, 100, **101**
— giant worm 96, **97**
— grooved razor 108, **109**
— Hungarian cap 98, **99**
— knobbed helmet 100, **101**
— lamp **137**
— large sunset **107**
— Mediterranean cone 100, **101**
— mitre 100, **101**
— moon 98, **99**
— necklace 33, 98, **99**
— needle 96, **97**
— Noah's ark 102, **103**
— pelican's foot 98, **99**
— peppery furrow **107**
— pheasant 96, **97**
— rayed trough 34, **106**
— razor **107**
— rough star 94, **95**
— spindle 100, **101**
— tower 96, **97**
— tusk 102, **103**
— Venus **106**
— worm 96
shells, lamp 137
shipworm 108, **109**
shoveler 37, 172, **173**
shrew, Etruscan *see* shrew, Savi's pygmy
— lesser white-toothed *see* shrew, Scilly

— Savi's pygmy 208, **209**
— Scilly 208, **209**
shrike, great grey 206
— lesser grey 206, **207**
— masked 206, **207**
— red-backed 206, **207**
— woodchat 206, **207**
shrimp, burrowing **114**
— ghost **112**
— mantis 110, **111**
— oppossum 110, **111**
Silene succulenta 64
— *vulgaris* 64, **65**
Silybum marianum 25
siphonophore 82, **83**
Sipunculus nudus 92, **93**
Siriella clausi 110, **111**
Sitta europaea 200
— *neumayer* 200, **201**
— *whiteheadi* 200, **201**
skate, long-nosed 150, **151**
skink, three-toed **166**
skipper *see* pike, saury
slater, sea 24, 110, **111**
skylark 190, **191**
slug, sea 26, 102, **103**
Smerinthus ocellata 132, **133**
smew 174, **175**
snail, marine 96, **97**
— sea 98, **99**, 100, **101**
snake, grass 18, **167**
— ladder 21, **167**
— Montpelier **167**
— Southern smooth **167**
snakes 17, 167
snipe 182, **183**
snipefish *see* fish, trumpet
sole, common 162, **163**
Solea solea 162, **163**
Solen marginatus 108, **109**
solenette 162
Sonchus spinosus **74**
Sparisoma cretense 158, **159**
sparrow, hedge *see* dunnock
— rock 202, **203**
— Spanish 202, **203**
sparrowhawk 18
Sparus auratus 156, **157**
Spatangus purpureus 142, **143**
Sphinx ligustri 132, **133**
Sphyraena sphyraena 156
Sphyrna zygaena 148, **149**
spider 134, **135**
— funnel-web **135**
— 'tarantula' 17
— writing **135**
spiders 18, 134–5
— orb-web 17
Spirantes spiralis 78, **79**
spirographis spallanzanii 35, 92, **93**
Spirontocaris cranchi **112**
Spondylus gaederopus 104, **105**
sponge **80**, **81**
— bath 26, **81**
— boring **81**
— crumb-of-bread 27, **81**
— golden **81**
— leather **80**

— horse 81
— purse 26, **80**
sponges 25, 26–8, **27**, **80–1**
Spongia officinalis 27, **81**
spoonbill 170, **171**
sprat 152, **153**
springtail 24, 118, **119**
spurdog *see* dogfish, spiny
spurge, sea 62, **63**
Squalus acanthias 150, **151**
Squatina squatina 150, **151**
squid 45
— long-finned 108, **109**
— sagittal 108, **109**
squill, sea 20, **76**
Squilla mantis 110, **111**
Staphylinus caesareus **123**
star, ascidian 146, **147**
— cushion 138, **139**
— feather 29, **30**
— goose foot 138, **139**
starfish 138, **139**, 140, **141**
— blue 140, **141**
— red 138, **139**
— seven-armed 138, **139**
— spiny 138, **139**
starfishes 29
stargazer 160, **161**
starling 202, **203**
Sthenelais boa **89**
Stichopus 160
— *regalis* 142, **143**
stilt, black-winged 39, 182, **183**
stingray 150, **151**
stock 62
— sea 62, **63**
— three-pronged 62
— Virginian 62, **63**
stonechat 194, **195**
stonecrop 70, **71**
stork, white 37, 170, **171**
storksbill 64
— common 64, **65**
Streptopelia decaocto 186, **187**
— *turtur* 186, **187**
sturgeon 152, **153**
Sturnus vulgaris 202, **203**
Styela plicata 146, **147**
Suaeda maritima 40, 64, **65**
Suberites domuncula 80, **81**
sucker, Cornish 29, 162, **163**
Sula bassana 23, 168, **169**
sunfish 44, 162, **163**
Suncus etruscus 208, **209**
Sus scrofa 12, 208, **209**
swallow 190, **191**
— barn *see* swallow
— red-rumped 190, **191**
swallowtail, scarce 128, **129**
swamphen, purple *see* gallinule, purple
swift 188, **189**
— Alpine 188, **189**
— pallid 188, **189**
swordfish 45, 160, **161**
Sycon coronatum **80**
— *raphanus* 80
Sylvia atricapilla **198**

— borin 198
— cantillans 196, **197**
— communis **198**
— conspicillata 196, **197**
— hortensis **198**
— melanocephala **198**
— melanothorax **198**
— sarda 196, **197**
— undata 18, 196, **197**
Synalpheus laevimanus 112
Syngnathus acus 154
— typhle 154, **155**
Syringa 132

Tabanus borinus 124, **125**
Tachybaptus ruficollis 168, **169**
Tadorna tadorna 172, **173**
tail, peacock's 54, **55**
Talitrus saltator 32, 112
tamarisk 40, 62, **63**
Tamarix gallica 40, 62, **63**
Taonia atomaria 54, **55**
Tarentola mauritanica 164, **165**
teal 172, **173**
tellin 107
— thin **107**
Tellina balaustina 107
— tennuis **107**
Teredo navalis 108, **109**
tern, black 184, **185**
— common 184, **185**
— gull-billed 23, 184, **185**
— little 184, **185**
— Sandwich 184, **185**
— whiskered 184, **185**
terrapin, European pond 40, **166**
Testudo hermanni 18, 164, **165**
Tethya aurantium **80**
Tethys leporina 102, **103**
Tetrax tetrax **181**
Tettigonia viridissima 120, **121**
Teucrium fruticans 68, **69**
Thalassema gigas 92, **93**
thistle **74**
— carline **74**
— globe **74**
— holy see thistle, milk
— milk 25, **74**
thorn, Christ's 15, 64, **65**
thresher-shark 148, **149**
thrush, blue rock 194, **195**
— rock 194, **195**
— song 12, 194, **195**
Thunnus thynnus 45, 160, **161**
thyme 15, 68, **69**
Thymelaea hirsutum **72**
— tartonraira 72
Thymus vulgaris 15, 68, **69**, 128
Thyone fusus 142, **143**
Thysanozoon brochii **88**
Tibicina haematodes 120, **121**
Tichodroma muraria 202, **203**
tit, bearded 200, **201**
— blue 200, **201**
— coal 200, **201**
— crested 200, **201**
— great 200
— long-tailed 200, **201**

— marsh 200
— sombre 200 **201**
— penduline 202, **203**
toad, natterjack 164, **165**
— Western spadefoot 164, **165**
tope 150, **151**
topshell 94, **95**
— large 94, **95**
— painted 94, **95**
Torpedo marmorata 150, **151**
tortoise, Hermann's 18, 164, **165**
tortoises 18, 164–5
tortoiseshell, large 130, **131**
— small 130, **131**
Trachinus draco 34, 160, **161**
— radiatus 160
Trachurus trachurus 158, **159**
tree, chaste 68, **69**
— locust see carob
— strawberry 12, 66, **67**
treecreeper 202
— short-toed 202, **203**
tree-frog, common 164, **165**
trefoil 70, **71**
— birdsfoot 70, **71**
Trifolium uniflorum 70, **71**
tresses, autumn lady's 78, **79**
Trichodes apiarius **123**
Tricolia pullus 96, **97**
— speciosa 96
trigger-fish 162, **163**
Trigloporus lastoviza 162, **163**
Tringa totanus 182, **183**
Triphora perversa 96, **97**
Trisopterus minutus 154, **155**
Trivia monacha 26, 98, **99**
Troglodytes troglodytes 192, **193**
Trophon muricatus 100, **101**
Tuberaria guttata 62, **63**
tube-worm 90, **91**
tube-worms 31, 90–1
Tubularia mesembryanthemum 82, **83**
tunny 160, **161**
Turdus merula 194, **195**
— philomelos 12, 194, **195**
Turritella communis 96, **97**
— triplicata 96
Tursoips truncatus 210
turtle, green 164
— leathery 164, **165**
— loggerhead 164, **165**
Tussilago farfara 128
Typton spongicola **113**

Ulva lactuca 52, **53**
Upogebia littoralis **114**
Upupa epops 18, 188, **189**
Uranoscopus scaber 160, **161**
Urginea maritima 20, **76**
Urocerus gigas 12, **126**
Uroctea durandi **134**

Valonia utricularis 52, **53**
Vanellus vanellus 182, **183**
Vanessa atalanta 130, **131**
— cardui 128, **129**
Velella velella 44, 82, **83**

Venerupis decussata **106**
Venus verrucosa **106**
Venus, warty **106**
Verbascum undulatum 68, **69**
Veretillum cynomorum **86**
Vermetus gigas 96, **97**
— triqueter 96
Verongia aerophobia **81**
Vespa crabro **126**
vetch, horseshoe 70, **71**
— kidney 70, **71**
Vidalia volubilis 60, **61**
Vitex agnus-castus 68, **69**
Vitis vinifera 10
Vulpes vulpes 208, **209**
vulture, black 176, **177**
— cinereous see vulture, black
— Egyptian 176, **177**
— griffon 176, **177**

waders 37, 39
wagtail, grey 192, **193**
— white 192, **193**
— yellow 192, **193**
wallcreeper 202, **203**
warbler, Bonelli's **199**
— Cetti's 196, **197**
— Cyprus 198, **199**
— Dartford 18, 196, **197**
— fan-tailed 196, **197**
— garden **198**
— great reed 196, **197**
— Marmora's 196, **197**
— melodious 196, **197**
— moustached 196, **197**
— olivaceous 196, **197**
— orphean **198**
— reed 196
— Sardinian **198**
— sedge 196, **197**
— spectacled 196, **197**
— subalpine 196, **197**
— willow **199**
— wood **199**
wasp **127**
— digger 17, **127**
— scolid **126**
— spider **126**
— wood 12, **126**
water-snake, viperine 167
weever, greater 34, 160, **161**
— lesser 34, 160
weever fishes 34, 35, 160
weevil 11, 124, **125**
wendletrap, common 96, **97**
whale, blue **210**
— killer **211**
— sperm **211**
wheatear 194, **195**
— black 194, **195**
— black-eared 194, **195**
whelk, netted dog 33, 100, **101**
— thick-lipped dog 100, **101**
whinchat 194, **195**
white, green-veined 128, **129**
— marbled 130, **131**
whitethroat **198**
whiting, blue 154, **155**

wigeon 172, **173**
winkle, sting 100, **101**
— toothed 94, **95**
wolf-spider **135**
woodlark 18, 190, **191**
woodlouse 24
wood-mouse 208, **209**
woodpecker, barred *see*
  woodpecker, lesser spotted
— great spotted 11, 188, **189**
— green 188, **189**
— lesser spotted 188, **189**
— pied *see* woodpecker, great
  spotted
— Syrian 188, **189**
woodpigeon 186, **187**
worm, acorn **144**
— boring 90, **91**

— euchiurid 92, **93**
— green leaf 88, **89**
— paddle 90, **91**
— peacock 92, **93**
— pink ribbon **88**
— ribbon **88**
— sipunculid 92, **93**
worms 25, 35, 88–93, 144
— acorn 144
— echiurid 92
— polychaete 26, 34, 88–92
— ribbon 88
— sipunculid 92
wort, St John's 62, **63**
wrack, bladder 56, **57**
Wrangelia penicillata **60**
wrasse, axillary 158, **159**
— ballan 158, **159**

— corkwing 158, **159**
— rainbow 158, **159**
wreckfish 156, **157**
wren 192, **193**
wryneck 18, 188, **189**

Xiphias gladius 45, 160, **161**
Xylocopa violacea 127, **127**

yellow, clouded 128, **129**
yellowhammer 204
yellow-wort 66, **67**

Zerynthia polyxena 128, **129**
Zeus faber 154, **155**
Zostera marina 33, **61**
— *hornemanniana* 61
Zygaena carniolica 132, **133**

CONTENTS

	Acknowledgements	5
1.	Timeline of Events	7
2.	Famous Residents	13
3.	Houses and Mansions	49
4.	Churches	55
5.	Work	61
6.	Pubs, Restaurants and Hotels	97
7.	Transport	115
8.	Sport	121
9.	Ballsbridge Battles	128
10.	Crime and Mayhem	132
11.	Natural History	137

ACKNOWLEDGEMENTS

This book is dedicated to my wife Bernadette in thankful appreciation of all her help and support while I was writing it. They are also due to Mary Kenny, for her esteemed input into the book. Special thanks are also due to John Holohan of the Ballsbridge, Donnybrook and Sandymount Historical Society and to his wife, Jacqueline, for her wonderful line drawings. I'd also like to thank Grant Howie and Martin McElroy of Grant's, Upper Baggot Street, for all their help with the images for the book. I much appreciate the help in its production given by Dean Lochner of the Bondi Group and Gerard Whelan, Royal Dublin Society library, who provided the cover photo.

I would also like to thank the following: Patricia Aitchison, Trocadero restaurant; Bahá'i information centre (Eleanor Dawson); Robert Ballagh; Ballsbridge College of Further Education (Dan Bradley) Bergin family; Bobby Barden, St Bartholomew's; Ruth Barton, TCD film studies; Jonathan Beaumont; Ruth Brennan; Peter Brittain; Nigel Brophy, Ebiquity Ireland; Nicky Broughall; Paddy Byrne, Byrne's pharmacy, Merrion Road; Sean Byrne, Ballsbridge Golf Society; Aileen Chapman; Rob Clarke, CEO, Spirit Radio; Paddy Cole; Michael Cullen, Marketing.ie; Defence Forces (Commandant Denis Hanly, press officer); Department of Foreign Affairs & Trade (Bobby Smyth); Brian de Salvo; Donnybrook Fair, Upper Baggot Street (Stephen Doyle, Paddy McLoughlin) Gerry Downey; Erroll Dunne, Waterloo Garage; Peter Dunne, Mitchell and Son; Jim Eadie; First Church of Christ Scientist, Rodney Senior; Julianne Gall, Kings Inn library; German embassy, Dublin (Barbara Schmidt); Maria Gillen; Jennifer Gordon; Joanna Grimes, IPA library; Mary B. Guckian; Anthony Harrison; Bronagh Harte, Ginkgo florists; Donald Helme, RTÉ; Herbert Park Hotel, Paula Barry; *Irish Daily Mail* (Paul Henderson, Joellen Hanley); the late Paddy Kealy and his wife Chris; Irish Model Boat Club (Tom Shields); Joe Kelly, St Mary's, Haddington Road; Barry Kenny, Irish Rail; Breda Keogh, Raheny; Jenny Kingston; Kurt Kullmann; Lansdowne Hotel (Frank and Michael Quinn); Trish Laverty, FM 104; Pat Liddy; Bruce McAllaster, 7–11, Dallas, Texas; Margaret McAllister (Irish Daily Mail) and her husband, Michael; John McCarthy, McCarthy Shoes, Ranelagh; Rev Andrew McCroskery, vicar, St Bartholomew's, Clyde Road; Bob McDonagh; Deirdre McDonald, Sinead O'Carroll, Ariel House; Gerry Monaghan; National Library of Ireland, including Berni Metcalfe; National Print Museum (Carla Marrinan); Lindie Naughton; News Four; O'Brien's pub, Sussex Terrace (Tony Kelly); Breandain O'Broin, Company of Words; Hughie O'Byrne, retired deputy principal, Marian College; John O'Donnell, County Clare; Ciara O'Hara, Carlton Screen Advertising; Pembroke Library; Margaret Pfeiffer; Gráinne Ross, Dylan Hotel; Royal Botanic Gardens, Kew (Lorna Cahill); Royal Dublin Society library (Gerard Whelan); Royal Irish Academy of Music (Philip Shields); Annie Ryan; St Brigid's primary school (Annemarie Hogan, principal); St Mary's Home, Anne Kavanagh; Fiona Scott, Boys & Girls; Dick Spring; Sunshine 106. 8 FM radio (Karen Dwyer); Valerie Waters and Conor Linehan; Wellington Inn (John Gibney); Trevor White, The Little Museum of Dublin.

Margaret McAllister, a receptionist at the *Irish Daily Mail/ Irish Mail on Sunday* newspapers. She and her husband Michael live in Anglesea Road. (*Irish Daily Mail/Irish Mail on Sunday*)

1

TIMELINE OF EVENTS

2 August 1649: Baggotrath Castle (where Searson's pub and the Langkawi restaurant are now in Upper Baggot Street) was occupied by Cromwellian forces. They fought Royalist forces at what is now the junction of Upper Baggot Street and Waterloo Road before moving on to fight the Battle of Rathmines.

1659: It was revealed that three English and twenty-nine Irish families were living in the Baggotrath area, close to present day Upper Baggot Street, while Symmonscourt had twelve English families and twenty Irish.

1766: Ballsbridge and the surrounding neighbourhood had a total of forty-eight families resident, sixteen Protestant and twenty-five Catholic. Symmonscourt had five Protestant families and nine Catholic.

1 July 1870: Lansdowne Road and Ballsbridge railway station opened; within two years, Ballsbridge was dropped from its title. The DART system opened in 1984.

Leabharlanna Poibli Chathair Bhaile Átha Cliath
Dublin City Public Libraries

11 March 1878: Lansdowne Road's first rugby international was played, between Ireland and England. It wasn't until 5 February 1887 that Ireland beat England in a rugby international at Lansdowne Road.

17 March 1900: The first international soccer match was played at Lansdowne Road, between Ireland and England. England won 2–0.

25 August 1905: Serious floods on the River Dodder in Ballsbridge.

14 May 1906: First electrified No. 10 tram runs along Upper Baggot Street and Waterloo Road.

26 August 1913: The Dublin Lockout starts when tram drivers and conductors walk off the job in Ballsbridge and elsewhere in the city, shortly after 10 a.m. Their trams were left idle on the day that the Horse Show opened at the Royal Dublin Showground (RDS).

3 and 4 August 1931: More serious floods on the River Dodder, with the main Merrion Road at Ballsbridge under water and impassable.

21–26 June 1932: The Eucharistic Congress took place in Dublin. The premises of the RDS were floodlit for the duration of the event.

6 June 1940: Last No. 10 tram before it was replaced by buses.

June 1943:   Dublin Corporation built public lavatories at
                the foot of Anglesea Road, close to the bridge
                at Ballsbridge. Derelict for many years, they
                had been mooted in 2011 as a venue for a local
                museum but nothing came of the idea. As of
                the summer of 2013, Dublin City Council was
                trying to sell the block for redevelopment. It was
                recently demolished.

11 June 1963:   97.8mm of rain fell in twenty-four hours at the
                RDS.

23 May 1964:   The new US embassy in Ballsbridge is opened.

13 May 1973:   Then President of Ireland, Eamon de Valera,
                unveils a memorial at the corner of Herbert
                Park and Elgin Road, dedicated to his former
                comrades in the Dublin Brigade of the Old IRA
                during the quest for independence, beginning
                with the 1916 Easter Rising. It is the only such
                memorial in Ballsbridge.

18 July 1981:   H Block rioters turned the Merrion Road, close
                to the British embassy, into a battleground as
                they fought with gardaí, doing much damage to
                houses and gardens, and injuring many people.

19 July 1984:   Just after 8 a.m., an earthquake measuring
                5.4 on the Richter scale hit the east of Ireland,
                including Ballsbridge. The most powerful
                for decades, its epicentre was south-west of
                Caernarvon, on the Lleyn peninsula in North
                Wales. Some minor structural damage was
                caused in Ballsbridge.

Crest on the US Embassy, Ballsbridge. (Jacqueline Holohan)

23 July 1984: First DART train in public use stops at Lansdowne Road and Sydney Parade stations.

25 August 1986: Hurricane Charley hit Ballsbridge, causing severe floods beside the River Dodder and in Anglesea Road. The RDS library was flooded, destroying many books, while the main RDS arena was flooded to the depth of 1m.

March 1987: The Irish Hospitals' Sweepstakes went into voluntary liquidation, as the new national lottery was launched on 23 March 1987. The Sweepstakes' offices in Ballsbridge had opened in 1939, with 4,000 jobs, mostly female.

February 1989: The old Johnston, Mooney & O'Brien bakery at Ballsbridge closes, with the loss of 485 jobs. Subsequently, the bakery reopened in the old Downes' Butterkrust bakery in Finglas.

3 April 1996: President Mary Robinson opens the National Print Museum at what had been Beggar's Bush Barracks in Haddington Road.

31 December 2006: The old Lansdowne Road stadium, used mainly for rugby but also for soccer, closed. Subsequently, it was demolished to make way for the new Aviva stadium.

16 August 2010: Pembroke Library, run by Dublin City Council, reopened after extensive renovations. The library had originally opened in 1929 and its first librarian was Sean O'Faolain.

31 October 2010: Last bus runs on the No. 10 route along Waterloo Road and Upper Baggot Street. It was replaced by the 39A.

24 October 2011: Flash flooding caused severe damage in many parts of Ballsbridge, especially in the area close to the River Dodder.

17 June 2013: The US First Lady, Michelle Obama, made a brief visit to the US embassy in Ballsbridge. She and her two daughters, Malia (14) and Sasha (12), stayed in the Shelbourne Hotel that night, while her husband, US President Barack Obama, was at the G8 summit in County Fermanagh.

June 2014: Work is well on the way on the huge Number One Ballsbridge complex.

2

FAMOUS RESIDENTS

AILESBURY ROAD

Sir Alfred Chester Beatty was an Irish-American mining magnate and millionaire, often called the 'King of Copper'. He became a naturalised British subject in 1933. He was also an avid collector of art and books from Asia and the Middle East. In 1949, he decided to leave Britain for tax reasons and settled in Dublin, buying a twelve-room house on Ailesbury Road for IR£12,000. He moved in in May 1950, along with 35 tons of artworks.

He then bought No. 20 Shrewsbury Road and had the Chester Beatty Library and Gallery built there. It opened in 1953 and when the extension was opened in 1957, it was attended by the then President, Sean T. O'Kelly and the then Taoiseach, Eamon de Valera. The library and gallery were relocated to Dublin Castle in 2000 and subsequent attempts to redevelop the site in Shrewsbury Road have been unsuccessful. After Sir Alfred died while in Monaco in 1968, he was accorded a State funeral, one of the few occasions on which a private Irish citizen has been given such an honour.

Kevin Haugh (1891–1969) was a barrister and judge; he was Attorney General from 1940 to 1942, when he became a Supreme Court judge, a position he held until retirement in 1968 and lived on Ailesbury Road. His son, also Kevin (1944–2009), followed his father's path to the Bar and the High Court; he was also a circuit court judge. He was a popular and well-liked judge; subsequently, he became chairman of the Garda Ombudsman Commission, dealing with complaints against the force and its members, which began in 2007. One of the children from the marriage of Kevin Haugh and his wife Annette is their son Bob Haugh, who owns a well-known Dublin travel agency, The Travel Department.

J.P. McManus, a billionaire magnate with interests that include horse racing and soccer, lives permanently in Switzerland, but he has a Dublin residence.

The original house dated back to Edwardian times and became the Japanese embassy in 1970. The embassy was moved to offices beside the Merrion Centre in 1992; eventually the house was bought by Bernard McNamara, a property developer, for IR£2.95 million – a record for the road at that time.

McNamara demolished the house and built a new one on a lavish scale. In 2011 the house was sold for €10 million to J.P. McManus. He and his wife also have two mews houses at the rear, where they built an orangery in the garden of one of them.

ANGLESEA ROAD

Brendan Behan, the writer, lived all his married life at No. 5 Anglesea Road, close to the bridge at Ballsbridge. His wife was Beatrice, daughter of the painter, playwright, poet and publisher Cecil Salkeld. Behan died in 1964 but Beatrice continued to live in the house. After Behan's death, Beatrice lived with Cathal Goulding, chief of staff of the Official IRA, until 1972. Their son was Paudge. The house at No. 5 had been bought by Behan in 1961 for IR£1,600, but in 2006 Paudge reluctantly sold it.

John Byrne, a noted property developer and great friend of former Taoiseach the late Charles Haughey, lived just off Anglesea Road for many years. He was 94 years old when he died in October 2013. One of Ireland's wealthiest property developers, he was responsible for the construction of such modern architectural monstrosities as O'Connell Bridge House in central Dublin.

Neil Campbell-Sharpe, a noted photographer, lived at No. 2 Anglesea Road in the mid-1970s. He was married to Noelle Campbell-Sharpe, the one-time magazine publisher and subsequent art gallery owner, and the woman behind the Kilreilig creative arts centre in west Kerry.

Clara Dumbleton, who is in her late 80s, is one of the few residents of the area who was born in and lived in the same house all her life. Her late father, Harry, was the manager of the tar depot on Hanover Quay that belonged to the old Dublin Gas Company.

Denis O'Brien, one of Ireland's, indeed the world's, wealthiest entrepreneurs was brought up in Ballsbridge. He has extensive media interests that include radio stations in Europe and a major stake in Independent News & Media, as well as being the man behind Digicel, a world leader in mobile telephony. Before going to University College Dublin (UCD), he had started his first job at 14, at the Central Hotel in Exchequer Street in central Dublin.

Born in Cork in 1958, he is the second of four children of Denis O'Brien senior and his wife Iris. The family home was in Anglesea Road, and his parents still live in the same house there. In 2013, O'Brien was ranked by Forbes as having a net worth of around €4 billion.

BALLSBRIDGE TERRACE

Gerry Downey, a well-known men's hairdresser whose salon is in the Ballsbridge Hotel, the former Jurys Hotel, was born in Ballsbridge Terrace during the Second World War. The house he was born and brought up in is now Kite's Chinese restaurant. On occasion, he has dined in the upstairs room at Kite's that was once his bedroom. A next-door neighbour on the terrace, a member of the Presbyterian Hamill family, was an Orangeman who went north every 12 July, but when he had become too old to travel, he used to wear his Orange regalia and march around his back garden, beating his drum and playing his instruments on the big day.

BURLINGTON ROAD

Professor George O'Brien of UCD, one of Ireland's leading economists, lived in this road for many years. His dinner parties were legendary. He was wealthy enough to employ several servants at his home and he dined out frequently in Dublin.

He had an intense dislike of travel, so if any international economists wanted to meet him, they had to travel to Dublin. He was professor of economics at UCD from 1926 until 1961. In the mid-1960s, he was one of the most vociferous critics of the ESB's decision to demolish a row of Georgian houses in Lower Fitzwilliam Street to make room for their new headquarters. In his later years, he had a very fixed routine, reading the Irish morning papers at home before going to Mass in St Mary's, then collecting the English newspapers at Parsons on Baggot Street Bridge. In February 1973, on his way home from Mass, he collapsed in the street from a heart attack. He spent all that summer in Baggot Street Hospital and died on 4 January 1974.

Mary Henry, who lives at No. 12, hails from Blackrock, County Cork, where she was born in 1940. The first non-foundation scholar in medicine at Trinity College, Dublin, in 1962, she subsequently became a medical practitioner as well as a professor and she represented Trinity College graduates in the Seanad from 1993 to 2007. Her many other interests include working with Cherish, the Irish Penal Reform Trust, the Rape Crisis Centre and the Well Woman centre. She married John McEntaggart, a Dublin merchant, in 1966. Meriel, one of their three children, became a medical practitioner.

Gemma Hussey, once a Fine Gael stalwart, who was Minister for Education from 1982 to 1986, but who retired from politics in 1989, lives in Burlington Road with her husband, Derry Power. They had previously lived in Temple Road, Dartry.

Johnny Ronan, one of the most flamboyant property developers in the Celtic Tiger era, teamed up with Richard Barrett in 1989 to form Treasury Holdings, a global property development powerhouse. Ronan built a spectacular mansion in Burlington Road, nicknamed the 'Pink Palazzo'. It is now the residence of the ambassador of Qatar, whose equally spectacular embassy is in Pembroke Road.

CLYDE ROAD

Dick Spring, a former leader of the Labour Party and a former Tanaiste, now retired from politics and a director of the Fexco financial services group, was a student at Trinity College in the late 1960s, early 1970s. At one stage, he had a bedsit in Raglan Road, before sharing a flat on Clyde Road with two young women (all innocent on his part, he says) until the morality squad in the shape of the owners of the house objected and he had to move out. He also lived in the top flat of Mrs Hartigan's house at No. 12 Herbert Park for some years, before he took over a big flat in Raglan Road after his brother Donal had moved out. Since 1994, Dick Spring has kept an apartment at Beggar's Bush.

ELGIN ROAD

Robert 'Bobby' Ballagh, one of Ireland's most distinguished contemporary artists, lived as a child in the basement flat of No. 14; his father worked in the wholesale drapery firm of Ferrier Pollock, in South William Street, occupying what is now the Powerscourt Townhouse Centre. Bobby's godparents lived nearby, in Lansdowne Road, and he recalls that the Ballsbridge of the 1950s was very different to today. Elgin Road was so quiet that he and friends played tennis in the road, stretching the net across the road. From beginning to end of a game, no cars appeared!

He also recalls that in those days, the neighbourhood was very mixed. In those days, he adds, Ballsbridge wasn't posh at all, contrary to popular belief. He left Elgin Road in the early 1960s and lost track of many of the people he knew there.

Gay Byrne, the television presenter who hosted the *Late Late Show* on RTÉ until 1999, began his broadcasting career with the station in the early 1960s – the *Late Late Show* had started as a temporary summer filler in 1964. That year, he married Kathleen Watkins, the daughter of a vet, and their first home was a flat in Elgin Road.

Kevin Kelly and his wife Rose live in Elgin Road. He was a high-profile publisher, responsible for developing such magazines as *Image*.

Delia Murphy, the noted West of Ireland singer, and her husband, Tom Kiernan, came to live in this road in 1935. Delia, famous for singing such songs as 'The Spinning Wheel', and her husband stayed in Elgin Road for six years. Tom had been Director-General of Radió Éireann, but in 1941 was appointed Irish ambassador to the Vatican. In wartime Rome, Delia was one of the people who helped the Irish priest, Father Hugh O'Flaherty, known as the Vatican Pimpernel, hide Jewish people from the Nazis.

Count Plunkett (1851–1948), a biographer and Irish nationalist, a leader in 1916 and the Minister for Foreign Affairs in the first Dáil in 1919, lived at No. 40 Elgin Road. From 1907 until 1916 he had been curator of the National Museum.

Trevor White, the founder of the Little Museum of Dublin on St Stephen's Green, was the former publisher and editor of the

Dubliner magazine. He was brought up in the family home at the corner of Elgin Road and Raglan Road. Trevor's father, Peter, a former restaurateur and property developer, and his mother, Laetitia, eventually sold that house and now live in Wellington Road.

HADDINGTON ROAD

Ferdinando Caracciolo, Prince of Cursi, an old Italian family originally from Naples, came to Ireland in 1938. He became a Papal Knight and he also worked as a director of Fiat in Ireland. He lived in the penthouse apartments at No. 38 Haddington Road. He died in 1989; six months later, his son Niccolo, who was a distinguished painter, died in a car accident near Siena in Italy.

Bernadette Madden, a Dublin-born artist, has become synonymous with the creation of batiks. She had her first solo show in 1971, and since then, has had innumerable shows in Ireland and abroad. Her studio and gallery are at the foot of Haddington Road.

HERBERT PARK

John A. Costello was a staunch member of Fine Gael, Taoiseach twice, first from 1948 to 1951 when he declared this part of Ireland a Republic, and then from 1954 until 1957. Among the achievements during his first term of office was the setting up of the Industrial Development Authority and Córas Tráchtála, the export board, which is now abolished. After the defeat of the 1957 election, he returned to his career at the Bar but continued as a TD for Dublin South-East until 1969, when he succeeded in that constituency by Dr Garret FitzGerald.

Peter Dunne has long been connected with Mitchells, the Dublin wine merchants founded in 1805. He joined the firm in 1970 and was appointed a director in 1986. A man with a wry sense of humour and a great storyteller, he has tutored many Mitchell's wine courses over the years and has led many of Mitchell's wine tours abroad. He has travelled to all the major wine producing regions in the world; the oldest bottle he has tasted was an 1873 port. He and his wife Anne brought up four children, Mary-Elizabeth, Jennifer, Greta and Michael, in their Herbert Park house.

Garrett Kelleher, property developer turned film mogul, paid over €5 million for No. 32 Herbert Park, an elegant Edwardian mansion next to Herbert Park. It was sold in October 2013. Among his property projects was an enormous Spire skyscraper in Chicago, which never reached construction. Subsequently, Kelleher became a successful movie maker.

Consuelo O'Connor and her family have lived for many years in Herbert Park; she is the sister of politician Carmencita Hederman. Consuelo had been married to Brian O'Connor, a solicitor, for fifty-two years; he died in October 2013.

Former Supreme Court judge Hugh O'Flaherty, who now writes a column in the *Irish Independent* newspaper, and his wife Kay used to live in this road. They sold their house here in 2000 and moved to Sandymount.

The O'Rahilly lived in Herbert Park with his family. Born in County Kerry in 1875, he became a magistrate, but subsequently was very involved in the independence movement. He had a private income of £900 a year, which helped matters considerably.

A founding member of the Irish Volunteers, as he lay dying in the 1916 Easter Rising he penned a poignant note to his American wife, Nannie, and his family, sending 'tons and tons of love' and signing off 'goodbye darlings'.

He owned a spectacular car, a De Dion-Bouton, which ended up on a barricade in Princes Street, beside the GPO.

For many years his family owned the port of Greenore in County Louth and it was there that his grandson, Ronan O'Rahilly, had a ship fitted out to become the offshore pirate radio station, Radio Caroline.

James White was a former director of the National Gallery of Ireland from 1964 until 1980. Entirely self-taught on the subject of art, he frequently appeared on television discussing art. He had begun his working life with the Player-Wills cigarette firm in Dublin, where he had started as a clerk, eventually becoming assistant manager, before being able to move into full-time work in the art world. He also worked as an art critic and lectured on the history of art at both Trinity College and UCD.

HERBERT PARK LANE

This new apartment development was built at the same time as Embassy House and the Herbert Park Hotel, around twenty years ago, on the site of the old Johnston Mooney & O'Brien bakery. One well-known former resident here was Lucinda Creighton, a Fine Gael politician who entered politics by becoming a Dublin city councillor in 2004. In 2011, she became Minister of State for European Affairs, a position she relinquished during the 2013 abortion legislation. She is now an independent TD and has moved, not far away, to Sandymount, where she now lives with her husband, Paul Bradford, a Fine Gael senator, and their new daughter, Gwendolyn Nicola.

HERBERT ROAD

One distinguished ex-resident is the writer Mary Kenny, who was brought up in the 1950s at No. 3, subsequently sold to form part of the present-day Sandymount Hotel. She says that the nearest and most famous landmark was the Lansdowne Road stadium, now the monstrous Aviva Stadium. She also says that in Herbert Road, the gentlemen who were addressed in correspondence as 'Esquire' lived on one side of the road, while those who lived on the other side were plain 'Misters'.

She recalls that this district was markedly different in her childhood, with little traffic. One of her penchants, at about the age of 5, was to climb into unlocked parked cars and pretend to drive them. When the drivers returned, she asked them to take her for a spin and buy her sweets – all very innocent. It certainly wouldn't happen these days! Cars fascinated her and the first word in Irish that she learned was *gluaistean*, as she drew cars in her colouring book. She says that it's a measure of how safe Ballsbridge was in the 1950s cars that were not only left open, but often left with the key in the ignition in case they had to be moved.

Mary Kenny says that in the old days, Ballsbridge, like Sandymount, was a remarkably ecumenical place. Catholics and Protestants were about even in numbers and neighbourhood relations were most harmonious. Separate spheres were respected by each side. Protestant playing fields did not permit Catholic players, not only for fear of inter-marriage, but because Catholics might wish to play sports on a Sunday, which was forbidden for Protestants. Irish Protestants, in Ballsbridge as elsewhere, were strongly Sabbatarian. But they did permit Catholic visitors on weekdays and vice versa.

She remembers that the local GP, Dr Young, was known to be an atheist, which was perfectly respected, although somewhat pitied. It is said that he had had a bad experience with nuns who 'turned' him. Allegedly, an order of nuns in Gibraltar wouldn't allow him to bring a dying patient to their hospital for fear of infection. Dr Young believed his first duty was to that patient, who indeed died. After that, he would have nothing to do with religion. He was a bachelor and 'took a drink', a euphemism for excessive alcoholic consumption. But his atheism never diminished the esteem that Ballsbridge people had for him.

HEYTESBURY LANE

Geraldine and Denis Bergin have been resident in the lane for many years and run an estate agency in Upper Baggot Street. Denis began his career with Smith Griffin in 1960 and later worked at Osborne King & Megran, where he met Geraldine in 1968; she had come from Scotland to work in Ireland.

In 1972, Denis was a founding partner in Fitzgerald & Partners, which went on to merge with Sherry & Sons of Upper Baggot Street. Denis is a fellow of the Society of Chartered Surveyors in Ireland and of the Royal Institute of Chartered Surveyors, and he has long been involved with the Irish Timber Growers Association.

Denis and Geraldine founded their own estate agency in 1984; they have three daughters, Nicola, Joan and Sara. Nicola, now Nicola Williams, is particularly involved in the running of the estate agency and with the local Upper Baggot Street Traders' Association.

Olive Beaumont, who died in 2011, had lived in the lane for many years. Born in County Offaly, she was brought up in Ranelagh, Dublin, and trained in the city as a nurse before going to Guy's Hospital, London. During the Second World War, she worked as a military nurse. After the war, she returned home to Ireland and for many years was the dietician at St Mary's Home in Pembroke Park. A great lover of animals, she was also keenly interested in art; a great friend was Gordon Lambert, a former managing director of Jacobs, the biscuit firm, and a great art collector. She was a trustee of his art collection. On the day that her ashes were buried, on 16 November

2011, at Kinnity Church of Ireland Church in County Offaly, close to where she had been brought up as a child, at Pigeonstown, lots of birds settled on the graveyard.

Pauline Bewick, a distinguished contemporary painter, came to Ireland as a child in the 1930s. Her eccentric, free-thinking mother, Harry, lived a nomadic life with her daughters, including living in caravans, houseboats, a railway carriage and a Kerry farmhouse. Now in her late 70s, Pauline has been painting since she was two. Married to psychiatrist Pat Melia, she has said that while it's been a happy match. Although she continues to live in County Kerry, she has long had a Dublin residence in Heytesbury Lane.

Michael Bowles and his wife Kathleen lived at No. 34 in the lane. From Riverstown, County Sligo, where he was born in 1909, Michael joined the Army School of Music in 1932. In January, 1941, he became the first full-time director of music at Radió Éireann. Other orchestras he conducted included the BBC Symphony Orchestra. After making an immense contribution to Irish musical life, he emigrated to New Zealand in 1948 to conduct that country's national orchestra, moving on to the US in 1954. He and Kathleen returned home to Ireland in 1970 and ran a guesthouse in County Cork, before moving to County Wicklow and then finally to Heytesbury Lane. There, he and his wife were often seen taking their cat and dog, together, for walks in the evening. Kathleen's health eventually deteriorated; she predeceased Michael, who died on 6 April 1998.

Dan Breen was the head of military intelligence in Ireland during the Second World War. When he retired after the war, he continued to live in Heytesbury Lane, in a house that has long since been redeveloped. As an elderly man, he kept such a quiet demeanour that locals were bemused to find out about his wartime job. He is still remembered for driving up Heytesbury Lane in first gear, with his wife sitting in the back of their car, reading magazines.

Peter Cahill was a retired sea captain who came to live in the lane, but who died at a tragically young age from a brain haemorrhage. He used to love sitting out on the lane, having a chat with an American journalist, Jack Post, owner of a blue 2CV car, and with Richard Kingston, the artist. These chats on the lane were the beginnings of the annual barbecues. Jack Post also died early, from cancer, nearly twenty years ago, but his wife, Mary Alicia, also a writer, still lives in the lane, in one of its oldest houses.

Aileen Chapman has lived in the lane since the 1970s. She married Dr Terence Chapman, an Englishman who was a doctor at the old Baggot Street Hospital, where he set up the pulmonary unit. He became great friends with one of his patients there, Brendan Behan. The Chapman marriage didn't last and they divorced, although they continued to be friends; Dr Chapman, who married again, died in 2010.

In 1981, Aileen was on an Aer Lingus flight from Dublin to London that was hijacked, the only event of its kind in the history of Aer Lingus. An Australian monk who wanted to know the third secret of Fatima hijacked the plane, which eventually landed at Le Touquet airport in northern France.

Aileen wasn't at all put out by the events of that day, merely concerned about the fate of the leg of lamb and a smoked salmon she was taking with her to London. Aileen, who was born in Boyle, County Roscommon, moved with her family when she was 6, to the old Glasnevin in Dublin, then open country. An inveterate traveller and party goer and giver, in May 2013, she celebrated her 92nd birthday with a lively party of neighbours. Her 1992-registration car, long a feature of the lane, as of July 2014, is no longer in situ.

Brian Cleeve (1921–2003) the writer and broadcaster, lived in the lane for many years, although the site of his house, No. 60, has since been rebuilt.

Born in Southend in Essex to an Irish father and an English mother, his father was one of the Cleeve family behind the toffee-making concern in Limerick. After Brian met and married an Irishwoman, Veronica McAndie, in the space of three weeks, they went to South Africa in 1948. He ran a successful perfume business in Johannesburg, but was an outspoken critic of apartheid.

He and his wife were expelled from South Africa in 1953 and he lived for the rest of his life in Ireland. He wrote twenty-one novels, and other works, before joining the new television service Telefís Éireann when it started at the end of 1961. After his wife died in 1999, he moved to Shankill, County Dublin, and married again, to Patricia Ledwidge. Brian Cleeve was buried beneath a headstone that reads 'Servant of God'.

Two members of the Corr family, a renowned family singing group in the 1990s, lived in the lane. By 2006, they had sold over 30 million albums. After marrying her long-term boyfriend, Frank Woods, Carolyn lived there with her husband and children, while further along the lane her sister Andrea had a house at one time. In 2007, Andrea launched her solo career, alongside highly rated performances in film and theatre.

Frode Dahl and his family lived in the lane in the 1970s and 1980s. He was the Norwegian who helped Alex Findlater reopen his family business as a wine shop and restaurant in Rathmines, in 1974. Frode had married Alexandra Findlater in 1969; her father, George, had been chairman of Findlater's from 1941 to 1962, which made Frode the brother-in-law of Alex Findlater.

Eamon Dunphy, the controversial soccer pundit, lived on Heytesbury Lane about twenty years ago. More recently, he and his partner have been living in Ranelagh. Dunphy, who was born in 1945, had a successful cross-channel soccer career from 1962 until 1977, as well as making twenty-three appearances for the Republic of Ireland team. When players get too old, they often go into management, but Dunphy became a very controversial pundit on the game, in print and on radio and television. These days, Dunphy is married to Jane Gogan, commissioning editor in RTÉ.

Arran Henderson, a historian and fine art specialist, organises walking tours of Dublin under the title 'Dublin Decoded'.

George Hetherington and his wife Christine, a native of Derry, who had been the first wife of Dr Conor Cruise O'Brien, lived at No. 62. George had been very involved with Hely Thoms the printers, as owner and managing director, before becoming managing director of *The Irish Times*. In the early 1960s, he shared that job with Douglas Gageby, who later became an editor of that newspaper. George was also a poet of note. After he and Christine had died, the site of their house went through an endless phase of reconstruction that was finally completed in 2013.

Richard Kingston (1922–2003) was a distinguished painter of flowers, landscapes and still-life works. He came from a County Wicklow farming family and studied engineering at Trinity College, Dublin. He then spent a number of years working in London before

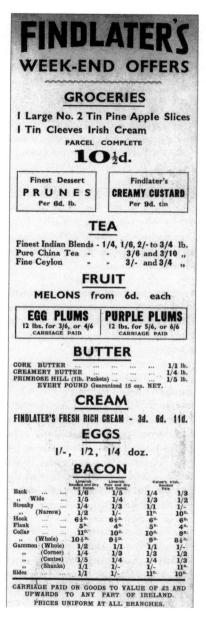

Price list for Findlater's old shop in Upper Baggot Street. (Courtesy of Alex Findlater)

returning home to become the display manager at the old Swastika Laundry. Subsequently, he became a full-time painter and had a keen interest in restoring old cars.

He and Jennifer, who became his wife and is herself an artist, met at a party in No. 16 Heytesbury Lane. Richard first exhibited at the Royal Hibernian Academy in 1962 and was a member of the board of governors of the National Gallery of Ireland from 1982 until 1989. In the early 1970s, when he and Jennifer owned No. 19 Wellington Road, they started their own gallery in the house, which they subsequently sold, moving into the mews house at the back of the garden.

Deryn Mackey, owner of the Khan boutique in Blackrock, which she opened in 1994, lived in a new house in this lane for a number of years, close on twenty years ago. She opened a branch of the boutique in Mullingar in 2007 but had to close it in 2012 because of the recession. She met her husband, Mark Fagan, a vet from the Midlands, at a ball in the Conrad Hotel.

Desmond McAvock, who lived in the lane for many years with his wife Adele, came to Dublin from his native Ballina, County Mayo. There he had been chairman of Ballina UDC three times. As a young man, he had studied art in Paris and when he came to Dublin, he became an art critic, writing for *The Irish Times* and other publications.

He and his wife also ran a language teaching business in Westland Row and the back garden for the family's two children, Jane and Peter, was Merrion Square. In the early 1970s, when a plan was mooted to build a Catholic cathedral in Merrion Square, the McAvocks moved first to Wellington Road, then to Heytesbury Lane. Over the years, he was very involved with the Upper Leeson Street Residents Association, helping campaign successfully against such projects as building a high-rise office building at the corner of Elgin Road and Raglan Road and the demolition of Litton Hall in Leeson Park. He died in February 2013, aged 95.

For many years, Ronnie Nesbitt, a long-time managing director of Arnott's department store in Dublin, lived in the lane with his wife, the vivacious Ella. The Nesbitt family had controlled Arnotts since the early twentieth century; Ronnie has joined the firm in 1937 and eventually became managing director. After he retired, in March 1979, his son Michael took over his job. Ronnie and Ella had got married in 1939. Ella was a great character in her own right; she died in 2009, aged 92, a great-grandmother, a decade after the passing of her husband.

John O'Donnell, a noted maker of documentary films, his wife Jackie, also in the film business, and their lively young daughter April, lived in the lane for thirteen years before departing to County Clare (Jackie's native county) in August 2012.

Tom Oliver, who worked for many years in the aviation business, lived in the lane with his wife Patricia, who used to work for Lisney's, the estate agents. The easy-going and genial Tom, a long-time member of Fitzwilliam Lawn Tennis Club and a keen member of the Military History Society of Ireland, always enjoyed a bit of fun and was known as 'the mayor of the lane'. He died on 20 October 2013 and is survived by his wife Patricia and daughter Melissa.

Annie Ryan, often described as one of the most innovative and dynamic people in Irish theatre, has lived in the lane with her husband, Michael West, since 1993. They have two children, Thomas and Oliver. She is Irish-American from Chicago; her grandparents had migrated to the US from Kiltimagh, County Mayo. Trained as an actress in Chicago and New York, she studied at New York University and during her third year there, came to Trinity College, Dublin, on exchange, where she met her husband. She was instrumental in founding the Corn Exchange theatre company in Dublin in 1995 and is its artistic director.

Before Thomas arrived, there had been few, if any, babies for a long time in the lane. Their house is one of the oldest in the lane; many years ago, when Annie and Michael were redecorating a bedroom, they discovered that pages from *The Irish Times* dated 1860 had been used to line the walls.

LANSDOWNE ROAD

The big house near the railway level-crossing was in the possession of the Johnston family from 1915 until 1940. Denis Johnston was a distinguished playwright and he also worked for the BBC as a war correspondent during the Second World War. His daughter is the novelist Jennifer Johnston. Later, the house formed the nucleus of the headquarters of the Institute of Public Administration, as recalled by Mary Guckian, a poet who used to work in the library.

Lord Killanin, who died in 1999 aged 84, was a journalist, author, film producer and business executive, but was best known as president of the International Olympic Committee from 1972 until 1980. The son of an officer in the Irish Guards, he was born in London and became the 3rd Baron Killanin in 1927. In 1937, working as a journalist, he covered the Japanese-Chinese war for the *Daily Mail*. In business, he was closely connected with Irish Shell and the Ulster Bank and held directorships in about fifteen companies. Later in his life, he moved from Lansdowne Road to Mountpleasant Square in Ranelagh.

Patrick McGilligan, who lived in this road for many years, had a long career in the Dáil, from 1923 to 1965 (forty-one years and five months). He held various Cabinet posts, including Minister for Industry and Commerce from 1924 to 1932; it was under his jurisdiction that the ESB was set up in 1927 and the Shannon hydro-electric scheme inaugurated. He was also responsible for setting up the Agricultural Credit Corporation in 1927. He was also Minister for External Affairs. In the 1948 Inter-Party government, he was Minister for Finance, while in the 1954–57 coalition government, he was Attorney General. He died in 1979, aged 90. His daughter, Evanne, continued to live in the house for many years after her father's passing.

Walter Starkie, the Professor of Spanish at Trinity College, after the chair was established in 1926, lived in the Botanic House at the old Trinity College Botanical Gardens in Lansdowne Road. He was also Professor of Italian and was a noted romance scholar and writer on gypsy history. His father William had been Commissioner of Education for Ireland, while Walter's sister, Enid, was a well-known literary critic at Oxford. Walter Starkie died in 1976.

Professor Michael Tierney (1894–1975), a long-time resident of this road, was Professor of Greek at UCD from 1923 until 1947, when he became president of the college, remaining in that position until he retired in 1964. He was the prime instigator of the move by UCD from Earlsfort Terrace to Belfield. His wife Eibhlín was the daughter of Eoin MacNeill, founder of the Irish Volunteers in 1913.

MERRION ROAD

Two noted residents of Merrion Road, around forty years ago, were Basil Brindley at No. 59 and Dr Michael Mulcahy at No. 73. Basil Brindley, a charming and energetic man of jockey's stature, started his own advertising agency in Dublin in 1956. Eventually, in 2005 he sold it to a British media group. Dr Mulcahy was a well-known psychiatrist. His daughter, Orna, is a senior journalist at *The Irish Times*, where she is the managing editor of features and editor of the Saturday magazine.

MESPIL ROAD

Michael Collins, one of the key figures in the fight for independence, had a number of safe houses in the Ballsbridge area. One of them was in the home of Miss Hoey, at No. 5 Mespil Road, where he had a study. On one occasion when he was due there a maid saw a posse of military personnel advancing and cycled to meet Collins on Baggot Street Bridge to warn him. He was riding his High Nelly bicycle and simply turned left instead of right, into Haddington Road, escaping capture. He also had a safe house in Heytesbury Lane, then largely undeveloped, but with plenty of gardens through which he could escape. He was assassinated in County Cork in 1922.

Percy French, the song writer, performer and watercolour artist, lived at No. 35 Mespil Road during the 1890s. He had married his first wife, Etie, in 1890, when he was 36, but the following year Etie died at the age of 20, following the death of their first-born child, Ethel. Not long after, he staged his second musical, *Strongbow*, and met a woman from the chorus called Helen Sheldon, whom he married. By the mid-1890s they were living in Mespil Road and Percy French was advising his friends that 'we are living by the canal, do drop in.' The French family left Mespil Road in 1899 when they moved to St John's Wood in London.

Iris Kellett was born in 1926, the only child of Harry and Dora Kellett. The Kellett family owned a well-known drapery store in South Great George's Street. Harry Kellett had been a veterinary surgeon in the British Army, then in 1924 he bought the old army cavalry barracks on Mespil Road and turned them into riding stables. As a child, Iris went to the nearby St Margaret's Girls' School at the corner of Mespil Road and Burlington Road (a couple of office blocks now stand on the site). In 1935, she took part in the Horse Show at the RDS for the first time, walking her pony Sparklet from Mespil Road down to the RDS.

After the Second World War, Iris developed the Mespil Road stables into renowned riding stables; among those who learned to ride there was Charles Haughey, a former Taoiseach. In 1969, after winning the European Ladies Championship at the RDS Horse Show, riding Morning Light, Iris Kellett retired from international competitions, which she had begun taking part in twenty-four years previously. In 1972, she sold the stables and riding school in Mespil Road and the site was developed into Pelican House, the then home of the Blood Bank. The Bank of Ireland headquarters now stands on the site. Iris Kellett died in 2011, after being ill for some years with dementia.

NORTHUMBERLAND ROAD

One of the great characters on the road was the late Jim Cawley, together with his loyal dog companion, Sam, who was the eccentric old caretaker of the Protestant hall,. He was a jazz enthusiast, and indeed in his earlier days had been a saxophone player in Mick Delahunty's orchestra. Jim Cawley was buried far from Northumberland Road, in Cashel, County Tipperary.

PEMBROKE LANE

John Bowman, veteran broadcaster with RTÉ, has lived in the lane for many years, having been brought up round the corner in Pembroke Road. Born in 1942, he joined the old Radió Éireann in 1962 and during the visit of President John F. Kennedy to Ireland in June 1963; he was the youngest commentator for the new television service. He presented *Questions & Answers* for twenty-one years on RTÉ television and also wrote a history of RTÉ television, 1961–2011. Another noted broadcaster, David Hanly, who was a presenter for years on the *Morning Ireland* programme on Radio 1, lived in the same lane. Long since retired, he now lives in Sandymount.

Paddy Hopkirk, the genial former racing driver, was a long-time resident of the Pembroke Lane area until about fifteen years ago, when he moved to England. He was born in Belfast in 1933 and educated at Trinity College Dublin. In the 1960s, he was a famously successful racing driver; one of the highlights of his career was winning the Monte Carlo rally in 1964. He's been married since 1967 to Jennifer, who, in 2005, was the High Sheriff of Buckinghamshire; they have three children.

Oliver Nulty and his wife Maureen were long-time residents in the lane; they were noted for the lavish parties they threw in their house there. He was born in Drogheda in 1920. Described as an old-fashioned gentleman and scholar, he set up the Oriel Gallery in Clare Street in 1968. Oliver died in 2005 and the gallery was taken over by his son, Mark.

PEMBROKE PARK

Gerry Callanan, once owner of Furlong's newsagents in Donnybrook, and one of the legendary characters of Dublin 4, lived for years with his family in a large house at the corner of Pembroke Park and Herbert Park. He also lived in an apartment in Clyde Road and in a house in Waterloo Lane, before finally settling on an apartment just off Burlington Road where his widow Máire still lives. Gerry died in November 2009.

Robert Maire Smyllie, the legendary editor of *The Irish Times* from 1934 until his death in 1954, lived at No. 23 Pembroke Park in the 1930s and through the Second World War. He lived there with his wife Kathlyn and maid Margaret; they had sussed out his lack of organisation long before anyone in *The Irish Times* and consequently took over the entire running of the household.

He often used to cycle into work, dressed in his pyjamas and an overcoat, his typewriter balanced precariously on the handlebars of the bike. Smyllie was a literally larger than life figure, weighing about 20 stone, noted for his sombrero and the fingernail of one of his little fingers shaped like a pen nib. His evenings and nights at the paper were chaotic and he could often be heard saying to one of his underlings, 'I fancy I hear the telephone machine ringing. Would you be good enough to answer it and tell whoever is on the line to f*** off.' On occasion, it was the owner of the paper.

Smyllie was also famed for singing his leader columns, in his deep baritone voice, once he had written them. He, Kathlyn and Margaret left Pembroke Park, inexplicably, in 1944, for Delgany, County Wicklow, which was much further out of town. Since Smyllie didn't drive, getting in and out of work on an infrequent bus service made his life much more difficult.

Just before the First World War, Smyllie had been working in Berlin as a tutor and managed to miss the last train out of the city. He spent the war in internment. Ironically, years later, when he lived in Pembroke Park, one of his neighbours was Robert Stumpf, the intensely pro-Nazi German doctor who worked at the hospital in Upper Baggot Street in the late 1930s.

Emily Weddall was born in 1867 into a Church of Ireland family at Edenderry, County Offaly, but spent many years in Achill, County Mayo. In 1912, she was instrumental in founding the Achill Summer School, which is now the oldest in the country. She was very friendly with the Pearse brothers, Padraig and Willie, of 1916 Easter Rising fame, and after the Rising and through the War of Independence, she worked for National Aid, helped organise Cumann na mBan and suffered imprisonment. She left Achill in the 1920s and came to live in Dublin. In the last few years of her life, she lived at St Mary's Home on Pembroke Park and died there aged 85 in 1952. Someone else in the district with strong connections to Achill is Máirtín Mac Nioclais, who went to school with John 'twin' McNamara, the renowned Achill historian. Máirtín comes from Swinford, County Mayo, while his wife, Mary, also hails from the county. They live in Heytesbury Lane.

Miriam Woodbyrne, who did much to revolutionise the Irish fashion scene with her mannequin agency, endured years of poor health before she died in 2007, aged 78. For many of those years, she had lived in St Mary's Home.

PEMBROKE PLACE

Paddy Kealy, who worked for the old Dublin Gas Company, and knew everyone in the district, died in April 2014, at the age of 89. He and his wife Chris (Christine), by whom he is survived, lived at 7 Pembroke Place for many years.

PEMBROKE ROAD

Ernest Blythe, one of Ireland's most notorious finance ministers, lived in this road for many years. In his 1924 budget, he cut a shilling from the old age pension, a move that created lifelong notoriety for him. After leaving politics, he was managing director of the Abbey Theatre, 1947 to 1967. In the years immediately after the Second World War, Blythe lived at No. 63 Pembroke Road. The road had another link with the Abbey Theatre: Éamonn Ó Gallchobhair, who was conductor of the theatre's orchestra for many years, lived at No. 92 Pembroke Road. Pembroke Road was the earliest new road in the district, opened in 1835, eleven years before Waterloo and Wellington Roads and thirty years before Clyde Road started to be built up.

Hilary Boyle, veteran protester, writer and broadcaster, lived in the road for many years. Born in Jamaica, she spent her childhood in Ireland, which she left again when she was a young married woman. She came back to Ireland, permanently, in 1934, moving to Dublin in 1962. Hilary became gardening correspondent for *Hibernia* magazine and contributed frequently to the *Sunday Miscellany* radio programme on RTÉ. She was very active on the Dublin Housing Action Committee, set up in 1967, and when the civil rights movement began in the North, she was also active there. On one occasion, she waved her umbrella defiantly at an RUC policeman who tried to stop her walking down a forbidden route.

Ursula Doyle, the wife of Jimmy O'Dea, the renowned Dublin comedian, lived separately from him in a flat at Pembroke Road. Because of that connection, after O'Dea died in 1965, he was buried from St Mary's in Haddington Road.

Dan Harrington, a great character in the district, lived in Pembroke Road for many years. From West Cork, he had worked in the construction industry for many years in England before returning home to Ireland. He and his wife lived in a flat on Pembroke Road, close to the junction with Waterloo Road; she predeceased him. Dan died in 2002, in his late 90s.

Louis le Brocquy (1916–2012), regarded as one of the most outstanding Irish painters of the twentieth century, lived in this road, at No. 61, in the mid-1930s.

Lady Sophie Mary Heath lived on this road in the 1930s, at a time when she was both poverty-stricken and an alcoholic. Born in County Limerick in 1897, she was married and had been widowed before she was 29. She went on to become a pioneering female aviator and became the first woman to fly solo from Cape Town to London in 1927/8. A book about her life by author Lindie Naughton was published in 2004. Despite the fame brought by her numerous aviation feats in the 1920s, she died destitute in London in 1939, following a fall from a tram.

Professor John O'Meara (1915–2003) was an Irish philosopher and theologian, considered one of the great scholars of St Augustine of Hippo. Born at Eyrecourt, County Galway, he graduated from UCD with an MA degree in 1939. Subsequently, he lectured at Clongowes Wood College in County Kildare, in Dublin, at Oxford, in the Sorbonne and in the US. In 1949, he married Odette Barthes de Montfort in Paris. The two of them wrote a book together, *Ordeal at Lourdes*, published in 1959. After his death, she continued to live in Pembroke Road before moving to Cork, where she died in April 2013.

Paul Walsh, SC, was a resident of this road and a former chairman of the Pembroke Road Residents Association. In 2000, when some residents succeeded in overturning an application to turn what is now the Pembroke Town House into a centre for asylum seekers, Walsh distanced himself from that campaign. But he could be a man of colourful words; in 2008, when Sean Dunne was planning to develop the Berkeley Court Hotel site in Lansdowne Road, complete with a thirty-seven-storey tower, Paul Walsh described the proposed tower as 'looking like a bent erection'.

Sheila Walsh, a former journalist with the old *Irish Press*, lived in one of the terrace houses just before the junction with Waterloo Road. When she was an active journalist, her wedding columns were legendary and she met many of the big names who came to Dublin over the years, including President Kennedy and Princess Grace of Monaco. Subsequently, she left Pembroke Road and went to live in a nursing home at Letterkenny, County Donegal, where she celebrated her 90th birthday in 2008. Sheila died in the home in Letterkenny in May 2014.

RAGLAN LANE

Two creative talents who live in this lane are Valerie Waters, a presenter on the *Nationwide* programme on RTÉ 1 television. She's particularly interested in gardening – she used to be head gardener at Annaghmakerrig, the creative artists' residence in County Monaghan – but presents segments on a vast array of subjects. Her husband is Conor Linehan, noted contemporary musician, composer and teacher at the Royal Irish Academy of Music. He has performed widely both at home and abroad. Conor's brother is Hugh Linehan, digital development editor with *The Irish Times*.

RAGLAN ROAD

Patrick Kavanagh, the poet, lived in a boarding house at No. 19 Raglan Road in 1958 and 1959; subsequently, he lived for close on twenty years at No. 62 Pembroke Road, nearby. The boarding house in Raglan Road eventually housed the headquarters of the Irish Congress of Trade Unions and is now the Mexican embassy. Kavanagh is perhaps best known for the words to the song 'Raglan Road', sung by the inimitable Luke Kelly of the Dubliners. Kavanagh had had a poem called 'Dark Haired Miriam Ran Away' published in the *Irish Press* in 1946. Over 10 years later, Kavanagh was in the old Bailey pub on Duke Street in central Dublin when he heard Luke Kelly singing with a new group, The Dubliners. Impressed, he asked Luke if he would put the poem to music, and he subsequently became renowned for his rendition of the song, set to the music of *The Dawning of the Day*. Patrick Kavanagh's last home was in the basement flat at 67 Waterloo Road. He died on 30 November 1967.

Gus Smith, who died in 2005 at the age of 74, was greatly interested in operatic music and was a long-time music critic of the *Sunday Independent* where he also worked as theatre critic and chief sub-editor. A larger than life character, he collaborated with Des Hickey on a total of twenty-seven books. His obituary for the *Sunday Independent* was written by Trevor Danker, himself a long-time columnist with that paper, who died in 2013.

SHELBOURNE ROAD

What is now a branch of Sherry FitzGerald, the estate agents and auctioneers, once housed a branch of the old First National Building Society. Carmel Skehan, sister of John Skehan, a long-time managing director of the building society, lived in a grace-and-favour apartment above the building society branch. She died nearly twenty years ago.

SHREWSBURY ROAD

Michael Maughan, one of the scions of the Irish advertising business, having long owned the Wilson Hartnell advertising agency (now Ogilvy & Mather) and also very involved in the Gowan group, has for years lived in this road with his Italian wife Gemma; they are one of Ireland's richest couples. Their Gowan group represents many leading brands as well as Honda and Peugeot cars and they also have one of Ireland's largest private stock portfolios. In 2010, Ireland's Rich List estimated the couple's worth at €180 million. In the 1987 *Thom's Directory*, he was listed as 'M. Michael Witton-Maughan' but the following year, he abandoned his double-barrelled listing.

The Kidney family bought a property called Fintragh in this road in 1965. The detached house became one of only three properties on Shrewsbury Road to have both an outdoor swimming pool and a tennis court. The house itself dates back to the early 1900s, and in the years up until 1965 it had three successive owners, the Martin, the Hogg and the Grew families. The Kidney family are very wealthy; they had close connections with the old Jurys Hotel and still have with the present-day Mespil Hotel.
    Mrs Naomi Kidney, who moved into Fintragh with her husband and family, had married a medical doctor, Dr William Kidney, and she went on to have an astonishing number of children – eleven in all. For a time, she also ran an art gallery in Upper Leeson Street. The Kidneys sold Fintragh in 1987.

The great mansion Woodside was bought in 1951 by the Pharmaceutical Society of Ireland from the then Church of Ireland Archbishop of Dublin, A.J. Barton, and was put up for sale in 2011. It was bought by an Irish venture capitalist called Seamus Fitzpatrick. Previously, in the earlier twentieth century, the house of many rooms had been the home of John C. Parkes, who owned a brass and iron foundry in the Coombe.

The grounds of the house had been bought in 1998 by Niall O'Farrell, of the Black Tie formal attire retail chain. The following year, he sold part of the site to Sean Dunne: this sale developed into a legal tussle between Dunne and O'Farrell, which Dunne eventually won. The piece of land was used for Ouragh, the home of the 'Baron and Baroness of Ballsbridge', Sean Dunne and his wife Gayle Killilea, a former journalist with the *Sunday Independent* and other newspapers.

Gayle Killilea bought another property in this road in her own name, Walford, in 2005. But it was never occupied and fell into ruin. A Cypriot-based company bought it in 2013 and announced elaborate plans for renovating and doubling the floor space of the house as well as building four very large new houses in its grounds, plans that aroused the ire of local residents. The local residents association, chaired by Michael Maughan and Carl McCann, chairman of Total Produce, has been keeping a very close eye on developments.

As for Sean Dunne himself, he had ambitious plans to redevelop the site of the former Jurys and Berkeley Court hotels in Ballsbridge, which aroused the wrath of many local residents. In the end, Sean Dunne and his family moved to the US.

Derek Quinlan, a former tax inspector turned property developer and investor, once lived in this road; he now lives in Abu Dhabi, United Arab Emirates. Another former property developer who lives here is Paddy Kelly, who bought Clancoole in the late 1990s. He built a new family home on the side gardens of the site and sold the original house to Tony Mullins, chief executive of the Barlo group.

ST MARY'S ROAD

James Dillon (1902–1986), a colourful character in the Dáil, renowned for his oratory, was a stalwart of Fine Gael in the 1940s and 1950s, and held various ministries, including that of Agriculture. He retired as party leader in 1965. Much earlier, he had been called to the Bar in 1931 and he had then run the family-owned drapery business, Monica Duff's, in his native Ballaghaderreen, County Roscommon. For many years, his Dublin home was in St Mary's Road, a comparatively new road in the district, as it only first appeared on maps in 1877.

James Larchet (1884–1967) was a composer who was also musical director of the Abbey Theatre from 1907 until 1934. As Professor of Counterpoint and Harmony at the Royal Irish Academy of Music, he taught both subjects there from 1920 to 1955. He was also Professor of Music at UCD from 1921 until 1958. Amid all his teaching duties, he found time to write many pieces of church, orchestral and vocal music. His daughter Sheila became a noted harpist.

Richard Montgomery, born in 1881, became assistant surveyor to the Pembroke Urban District Council. For most of the First World War he was a prisoner of war in Germany, but after he returned home at the end of the war, he resumed his duties with the UDC. He was promoted to surveyor in the early 1920s and carried out many important schemes in the area, including the widening of Donnybrook. He was also keenly interested in providing work for the unemployed. From 1921 until his death in 1930, he lived at No. 10 St Mary's Road.

Adelio G. Viani was considered for many years to be the most influential member of the vocal staff at the Royal Irish Academy of Music, where he was the senior professor of singing in the early twentieth century. He had obtained many outstanding musical qualifications in Milan, where he was also the music critic of *Il Tempo* newspaper. In 1932, the king of Italy made him a cavalier of the crown of Italy, but thirty years before that, he had settled in Dublin. He lived in St Mary's Road for many years; he died in 1965 and is buried at Deansgrange, together with his wife Florence, who had died in 1958. Countess Irene Viani, who had married into the family, died in Dublin in October 2013.

SYDENHAM ROAD

Anthony Hepburn-Ruston, the father of film star Audrey Hepburn, spent the last years of his life with his wife Fidelma in a flat in this small cul-de -sac opposite the RDS. During the Second World War he had been interned on the Isle of Man for what were seen as his fascist views and he came to live in Ireland after he had been released. A very tall man, always well dressed, he often took his poodle for a morning walk in Ballsbridge, where he was well known. He died in Baggot Street Hospital in 1980.

UPPER LEESON STREET

Carmencita Hederman lives on this street. Born in 1939, she had a long involvement in community politics in Dublin, becoming Lord Mayor in 1987/8, when the city celebrated its millennium. She was prominent in the founding of the Upper Leeson Street Residents Association, which is still very active in preventing unseemly development in the area. Her sister Consuelo is also well-known in the area, resident in the Herbert Park area. Carmencita has a daughter Wendy, a solicitor, who for a while became a Progressive Democrat local councillor, and a son, William, a writer.

Gerry Ryan, the 2FM presenter, lived in a flat in this street. In many ways, this idiosyncratic presenter was the mainstay of the radio station, and his tragic death in 2010 prompted widespread media coverage for many months subsequently. He had separated from his wife and at the time of his death, his partner was Melanie Verwoerd, a former South African ambassador to Ireland and a former chief executive of Unicef in Ireland.

WATERLOO LANE

John and Joan Dolan were an American couple who lived in this lane for many years; he was a writer for *Time* magazine. He died from cirrhosis of the liver while on an assignment in Asia. His wife, the heiress to an American supermarket fortune, was vice-president of a US pharmaceutical company in Cork. After his death, she used to take her chauffeured limousine down to the Shelbourne Hotel, where she enjoyed plenty of refreshments in the bar, as well as the company of young men, whom she often brought back to her house in Waterloo Lane for long-running parties. One of those parties went on for a solid ten days. After her death, the house allegedly became a brothel. After the brothel's closure the premises was used by Trinity College for language teaching to refugees and it was subsequently occupied by an accountancy practice. The building was sold again in 2014.

Lee Dunne, the writer, lived in the lane. Born in 1934 and brought up in the notorious Mountpleasant Buildings in Ranelagh, one of his most spectacular books, *Goodbye to the Hill*, was based on his childhood. Published in 1965, it sold over a million copies. He has often been described as the most banned author in Ireland until censorship was abolished, and, by his own admission, has slept with over 1,000 women.

Cecil King was a well-known sculptor, who fitted out his house in the lane with old furniture from Christchurch and St Patrick's Cathedrals. After he left, the house was bought by Nigel O'Flaherty, of Volkswagen fame, before it came into the possession of David Marshall, the hairdresser. Born in Rathdrum, County Wicklow, Cecil King became a businessman, taking up art as a part-time hobby in 1954. He held his first one-man show in 1959 and thereafter, for many years, this noted minimalist painter held one show a year for many subsequent years. He died in 1986.

Michael O'Flanagan, who played rugby and soccer for Ireland, also lived in the lane. Born in 1922 he managed the unusual sporting feat of playing for his country in both soccer and rugby. He played for such soccer clubs as Bohemian FC and Belfast Celtic, as well as being on the Ireland national soccer team in 1946 and the Irish national rugby team in 1948.

Karl Mullen, born in 1926, is a former resident of this lane. A consultant gynaecologist by profession, he captained the Irish rugby team and won twenty-five caps between 1947 and 1952. He was also captain of the British Lions on their 1950 tour of Australia and New Zealand.

WATERLOO ROAD

John Armstrong, a former journalist with *The Irish Times*, lived on this road. He had worked for the paper for almost thirty-three years, as a reporter, news editor and night editor. As news editor, he had played a key role in deciding that the newspaper should publish the story about how the then Bishop of Galway, Éamon Casey, had fathered a child with his mistress, Annie Murphy. Towards the end of his career, John Armstrong wrote extensively on antiques and fine art. He died in May 2012.

Tom Arnold is the director-general of the Institute of International and European Affairs, based in Dublin, a post he took up in November 2013 when he left his position in charge of the Constitution Commission. He is also the chairman of The Irish

ASSOCIATION FOOTBALL

International Match

IRELAND *v.* ITALY

At LANSDOWNE RD.

On Saturday, April 23, '27

KICK-OFF AT 3.30 P.M.

This match marks a decidedly progressive
step in the game in the Saorstat. It is the
first time the Free State Football Association
play as Ireland, and also is the initial representative game in which they have called on the
services of players of Free State birth assist-
ing Cross-Channel Clubs. This is the second
match between the Countries, the first, last
year at Turin, being won by the Italians by 3
goals to nil

*This Souvenir Programme is printed and presented free
by Independent Newspapers, Ltd., with the official
sanction of the Football Association of the
Irish Free State*

Notice for Ireland v Italy rugby match, 1927. (*Lansdowne Road* by
Gerard Siggins and Malachy Clerkin (O'Brien Press))

Times Trust (he had been appointed a governor of the trust in 2008) and has advised the UN on alleviating world hunger. Until 2012 he was chief executive of Concern. Before joining Concern, he had had a long career with the Department of Agriculture and Food. Married to Gillian, they have long lived in Waterloo Road; they have two children, Patrick and Laura.

Michael Colgan, who has been artistic director of the Gate Theatre since 1983, is very involved with the Dublin Theatre Festival, and has also been involved in film and TV production, lives in this road. He has been known to quip that his house there is a retirement home for actors, since well-known actors, the like of Sir Michael Gambon and John Hurt, have been known to stay there.

Polly Devlin, writer, academic and one-time features editor of *Vogue*, who is a sister of Marie, who was married to the late Seamus Heaney, owned a house in Waterloo Road from 1990 to 1999. During that decade, Polly was frequently in Dublin, and the house was her base here. She also filled it with antiques. But by 1999, she had bought a house in France and had her main house, a big country residence in Somerset with her husband, Adrian Garnett, an industrialist, so the Waterloo Road house was sold. The pre-auction reserve price on the three-bedroom terrace house with self-contained garden apartment was over IR£750,000 and the catalogue produced for the antiques sale was the size of a good-sized novel.

Desmond FitzGerald, the 29th and last Knight of Glin, who died in 2011 aged 74, had his main residence at Glin in County Limerick. But he had his townhouse in Waterloo Road. He had married Madam Olda FitzGerald, a Londoner; they moved to Glin from London in 1975. Madam FitzGerald, like her late husband, is a writer; she had written on Irish houses, gardens and parks and she enjoys her local park, Herbert Park.

Catherine Foley, a well-known Irish language writer, lived in this road during the 1990s. Once a staff journalist with *The Irish Times*, to which she still contributes, her uncle was renowned *Irish Times* journalist Donal Foley. Catherine Foley now presents programmes shown on TG4, the Irish-language TV station.

Pat Murray, historian and antiquarian, lives in the road with his family. Pat's dog Lucky, a Jack Russell terrier, was a well-known 'character' in the district until he died in 2013; Pat's new dog is a lively female of the same breed, called Skippy.

Andy Ryan, a native of County Tipperary and a legendary publican, ran the Waterloo Bar in Upper Baggot Street for forty years before selling up and retiring early in the new millennium. He and his wife Ann, a loquacious lady, live in Waterloo Road; in 2013, Andy celebrated his 92nd birthday.

Estella Solomons (1882–1968) lived for many years at No. 28 Waterloo Road. From a Jewish family, her brother Bethel became Master of the Rotunda Hospital. Estella was active in republican politics before and during the war of independence, 1919–21, and later, she and her husband ran the *Dublin Magazine* from 1923 to 1958, a renowned literary and artistic publication.

Walter Strickland (1850–1928) lived with his family for many years at No. 50 Waterloo Road. The 1911 census showed him living there, aged 60, his wife Margaret, who was 57, their daughter, Mary Harriet Alicia aged 32, George Byrne, a 52-year-old male servant and Alice Byrne, a 38-year-old female servant.

Strickland, who had been born in Cumbria and whose education included King's College, London, spent part of his youth in the West of Ireland, where his uncle was a land agent. A well-regarded art historian and antiquary, he was registrar of the National Gallery of Ireland from 1894 until 1914. His *Dictionary of Irish Artists*, published in 1913, was the culmination of twenty years of research. When Sir Hugh Lane died in 1915, Strickland was appointed temporary director of the National Gallery, before retiring in 1916. Even though he was only in charge for a short while, and despite the lack of finance due to the First World War, he managed to carry out an extensive reorganisation of the gallery.

WELLINGTON LANE

Professor Cecil Erskine lived at No. 27 in the lane for many years. He died in May 2006, at the age of 93; his wife, Peggy, otherwise Ellinore Purdon, had predeceased him by a number of years. She is still remembered for being a 'lovely lady who loved walking, despite her bad feet'. The professor had a lively medical career and was the

Trinity College Professor of Anatomy from 1947 until 1984, when he retired at the age of 71.

At the corner of Wellington Lane and Heytesbury Lane, a ramshackle collection of houses stood for many years. One of the residents there was 'Whoopy' Byrne, who had a beard like an Old Testament prophet. He had a motorbike and sidecar, in which he and his wife travelled. Many years before his death, he picked his own coffin, kept in storage locally until it was eventually needed.

Another resident in this complex was Ulrika Donnell, who had been an almoner at Baggot Street Hospital and who also had close connections with Trinity College. A dedicated cat lover, she always had several in residence.

Yet another resident here was Jimmy Young, while in the 1980s, another well-known resident here was Richard Tabuteau. Joan, Countess de Freyne, subsequently moved to Rathmines.

Next door to this complex, in a tiny house, with its entrance onto Heytesbury Lane, lived Rosamund Willoughby, once noted as an actress on the Dublin stage. She had lived here before her marriage, as Rosamund Stevens. Rosamund's husband Harold, whom she married in the mid-1970s, collapsed and died one Christmas Day, at their home, about thirty years ago. She now lives with one of their sons in Birmingham. This house remains but the rest of the complex was demolished and redeveloped in 1997.

Alan Benson, who ran the well-known Dublin travel agency Sadlier Travel, sadly died at the end of December 2013. He is buried in the Jewish cemetery in Dolphin's Barn and is survived by his wife, Susan, who continues to live in the lane.

WELLINGTON PLACE

Paddy Cole is often referred to as 'Ireland's king of jazz'. Born in Castleblayney, County Monaghan, he began his musical career over fifty years ago with the Maurice Lynch Showband in his native town. Paddy was the only boy in a family of seven children and he had quickly developed his skills as a legendary saxophonist. He's been playing the same sax since 1965. Among the other groups with

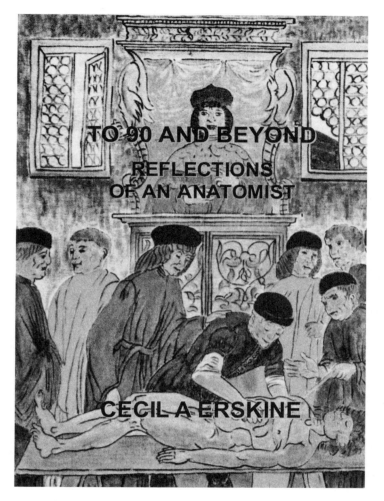

Cover of *To 90 and Beyond* by Professor Cecil Erskine, a former professor of anatomy at Trinity College, Dublin, who lived in Wellington Lane, Ballsbridge. (boox.co.uk)

which he has played was the Paddy Cole Superstars, founded in the 1970s. Paddy has played his unique blend of Dixieland jazz all over the world, and today is still going strong. When St Mary's, his parish church, held its annual barbeque in the Lansdowne Hotel in the summer of 2013, Paddy made the music contribution and the event raised €12,000 for parish funds. He repeated the exercise in July 2014. He also does a Sunday morning music show on Sunshine Radio.

Liam Lenihan was one of the district's best-known American characters. Born in New York in 1934, he had served in the US Marines during the Korean War, but subsequently lived in Ireland for many years. A marine engineer by profession, he travelled the world extensively and had family connections in Singapore, which he frequently visited. Described by Margaret Pfeiffer as one of the kindest people she has ever met, one of his earliest work stints after he came to Dublin was with Baggot Framing in Eastmoreland Place. His last residence was a flat in Wellington Place, where he died in October 2009. His funeral was at St Mary's, Haddington Road and his ashes now rest in County Galway.

Liam O'Leary, the film historian, lived here in a basement flat. Born in Youghal, County Cork, in 1910, he spent the 1950s working with the British Film Institute in London before returning to Dublin in 1966 to join RTÉ as film acceptance viewer. He was a founder of the Irish Film Society, made three films about Ireland and set up his own film archives. He died in 1992.

Michael Slazenger, connected to the Slazenger family at Powerscourt in Enniskerry, County Wicklow, lived at No. 39 Wellington Place. True to the family's exotic pastimes, until about thirty years ago, kept his light aircraft in storage in Wellington Lane, just at the back of their house in Wellington Place.

WELLINGTON ROAD

Mark Kavanagh's property company, Hardwicke, is based at No. 14, on the corner of Wellington Road and Elgin Road. Kavanagh was instrumental in the development of the International Financial Services Centre in Dublin and he also founded Captain America's restaurant in Dublin's Grafton Street, where Chris de Burgh made his musical debut. He suffered a great personal tragedy in 1988 when his wife Lynda and their children's nanny, Priscilla Clarke, went out horse riding during bad weather, near what was then the Kavanagh family home just outside Enniskerry, County Wicklow. The two women were swept away by the storm waters; Lynda's body was subsequently found but that of Priscilla has never been found.

Incongruous as it may sound, James Larkin, the great trade union leader, commemorated in a statue in O'Connell Street, spent the last few years of his life in Wellington Road. He lived with his sister Delia and her husband in their flat at No. 41; she died there in 1949, a couple of years after Larkin himself. The house that contained the flat is now the residence of the ambassador of the Republic of Cyprus.

P.J. Mara, the public relations consultant, has lived here since he bought the house in the 1990s from Richard and Jennifer Kingston. Mara was the Fianna Fáil director of elections three times and also served as government press secretary. He was the public relations maestro for Charles Haughey when the latter was Taoiseach, which led to him being lampooned in the *Scrap Saturday* programme on Radio 1.

Robert McDonagh, distinguished former diplomat, lives in Clyde Court at the junction of Wellington Road and Clyde Road. He joined what was then the Department of External Affairs as a third secretary in 1949 and subsequently became ambassador of Ireland to Germany and then Italy, before becoming Ireland's permanent representative at the United Nations. He retired from the Department of Foreign Affairs in 1989, but his two sons, Robert and Philip, continue the diplomatic tradition, both ambassadors in their own right. Philip is also a poet. When the visit to Ireland by Queen Elizabeth II was being planned for 2011, Robert, who was then the Irish ambassador in London, played a key role in the planning.

Mr Justice Murnaghan lived here for many years. He died in 1990 at the age of 83, having secured legal fame as the last judge to have sentenced someone to death in Ireland. In 1954, Michael Manning, a carter from Limerick, was hanged for the rape and murder of a nurse in the city. Murnaghan had been called to the Bar in 1930 and was appointed as a judge of the High Court in 1953. His father, in County

Tyrone, had been a solicitor, while his uncle, James Murnaghan, was a judge of the Supreme Court.

Michael O'Leary, the former politician, lived in this road twice; once in his younger days and then when he was older. He was noted for his style, his good looks and his witticisms. From Cork, he became a leader of the Irish Labour Party as well as Tanaiste; eventually, he changed from Labour to Fine Gael. After leaving politics, he became a district court judge. In May 2006, just days after he retired as a judge, he collapsed and died in the swimming pool at his holiday home in the south-west of France. He was 70 years old. His widow, the writer Mary Malony, still lives in Wellington Road.

The Hawk is the nickname used by someone who lives on this road, who describes himself as a scientist and profiler. He has one of the sharpest sets of eyes and ears in the district and little goes on without him knowing about it, the sort of person who knows what really goes on behind closed doors.

Giovanni Trappatoni, the Italian who managed the national soccer team from 2008 to 2013, was born in 1939, and before he came to Ireland, managed many top continental clubs before arriving in Ireland with his wife Paola. Denis O'Brien has helped fund the national soccer team in recent years and his funding was instrumental in encouraging Trappatoni to come to Ireland. Despite having his Irish residence at Wellington Road, Trappatoni was rarely seen in the neighbourhood.

Hugh Wells, a solicitor's clerk by profession, lived in a basement flat at No. 75 for many years before moving to Rathmines. A great character in the district, he kept a close eye on all the oddities and idiosyncrasies of Ballsbridge. He died in St James Hospital in March 2009.

3

HOUSES AND MANSIONS

ABERDEEN HOUSE

This imposing Victorian mansion once stood at the corner of Wellington Road and Clyde Road. The two-storey over-basement house was built around 1860 and was noted for its pediment gable front on one side of its three-bay elevation. The last residents were the Coyle family, who owned an insurance brokers that became Coyle Hamilton Phillips.

Geoffrey Coyle was an active member of the Gouldburn Beagles, which hunted around Dunboyne, County Meath. Aberdeen House was demolished in the early 1970s and replaced by a modern brick-façade block of apartments called Clyde Court. On the Raglan Road side of the old house was Raglan Hall, still in existence, but converted into luxury apartments. It was at Raglan Hall that John Holohan, chairman of the Ballsbridge, Sandymount and Donnybrook Historical Society, was born. At the other end of Wellington Road, close to Pembroke Road, three terraced houses that had housed the premises of Ove Arup, consulting engineers, for many years, were converted in 2013 into three private residences.

In the early 1840s, before Waterloo, Wellington and the other roads with English names had been built in the district; most of Ballsbridge was open countryside, with just six roads to its name.

NO. 36 AILESBURY ROAD

This comparatively modern house, which now houses the French embassy, was built in 1920 by Mrs Nell Humphreys, from Limerick, who then lived in it with her family and her sister Anno O'Rahilly.

The house was built by Batt O'Connor, a close friend of Michael Collins; a secret room was included in the construction, but is now just a washroom. During the War of Independence, many Irish leaders, including Eamon de Valera and Michael Collins, came to this house for meetings, but despite many raids on the house, the secret room was never discovered.

During the Civil War (1922–23), the Humprheys family were on the republican side and on 4 November 1922, the house was raided by Free State soldiers. One soldier was killed in the onslaught and Anno O'Rahilly got a bullet in the jaw. As she was being carried out on a stretcher, she whispered to the maid, 'there is money behind the curtain in my room; give it to the first person who calls.' The money ran to thousands of pounds, the entire resources of the Prisoners' Dependence Fund, of which Anno O'Rahilly was the treasurer. The first person to call was the breadman, who was on a wage of £2 a week. The money was handed to him and when the coast was clear, he handed the whole lot back without a penny missing.

While the French diplomatic service bought the big house across the road, Mytilene, in 1930, as the residence of the head of their legation to Ireland, and it has remained as the ambassador's residence ever since, the house at No. 36 only became the French embassy in 1968.

CARRISBROOK HOUSE

A fine residential mansion at the corner of Pembroke Road and Northumberland Road, it was demolished in the mid-1960s to make way for a modern office, which adopted the Carrisbrook name, adding an extra 'r'. Among its contemporary occupants is the Israeli embassy.

DE WYNDESARE

This spacious turreted building at the corner of Raglan Road and Clyde Road was once the home of Maria Georgina Eustace-Duckett, a reclusive lady who lived there with her cats and her housemaids. After she died in 1937, she left £97,000, but of that then considerable sum, a mere 1s was left to her daughter, Olive Thompson. Olive contested the will in court, arguing that her mother had been of unsound mind when she had made and signed the will. Her claim was eventually allowed and she was awarded an annual income for life from part of the estate; in time, the capital that was left was disbursed amongst various charities.

MERRION ROAD COTTAGES

Once, in a narrow laneway that once separated what is now Paddy Cullen's pub and Mary Mac's pub, a whole cluster of small cottages housed families in incredible squalor, with no running water and one communal lavatory. Similar conditions existed in the cottages beside the RDS sale grounds, where the headquarters of Allied Irish Bank is now located.

MESPIL HOUSE

Mespil House on Mespil Road, once called Gibbet Road, was demolished in 1952. For many years up until her death in 1943, the artist Sarah Purser lived in Mespil House. She had been born in what is now Dún Laoghaire, in 1848, was brought up in Dungarvan, County Waterford, and was educated in Switzerland. Part of her art education was done in Paris. She was the first female member of the Royal Hibernian Academy. She was also privately wealthy, through astute investments, primarily in Guinness. After the great house was demolished, the fine plasterwork ceilings were preserved and reinstated at Aras an Uachtárain. The Mespil flats complex was subsequently developed on the site.

RAGLAN HOUSE, SERPENTINE AVENUE

This purpose-built apartment block, right on the fringes of Ballsbridge, was ripped apart by two gas explosions on New Year's morning 1987. As a direct result of the blast, two people were killed, five rescue workers were injured and much of the structure was reduced to a 7m-high pile of rubble.

STYMIED HIGH RISE

Opposition by irate local residents and the recession scuppered the plans for the high-rise development of the Berkeley Court and Jury's Hotel. Earlier, in the 1960s, plans to develop an apartment block in Baggot Lane, that would have been six-storeys high, were demolished by local residents. In the early 1970s, not long after the Upper Leeson Street Residents Association had been founded, plans to build a skyscraper office block at the junction of Raglan Road and Clyde Road were also thrown out after concerted opposition from local residents.

TURNER'S COTTAGES

These thirty houses, built in a circle, close to the top of Shelbourne Road, dated from the mid-nineteenth century and had been built for workers at the former Turner's Ironworks on Pembroke Road. Where Turner's Cottages were situated is now the location of Hume House. People who lived elsewhere often called the cottages 'The Gut', for reasons unknown, but people who lived in Turner's Cottages never used that term.

The houses had two large downstairs rooms and two bedrooms upstairs, with a tiny boxroom. They had no separate kitchens; people cooked on open fires or sometimes on a range, while there were no bathrooms either. People had to wash in front of the fire in the main living room and use an outdoor communal toilet. Some of the families living in the cottages had five or six children. Up until the 1960s, the menfolk of the families here worked in a variety of menial jobs, including the old bottle factory in Ringsend, at coal firms in the area or in the Johnston, Mooney & O'Brien bakery at Ballsbridge.

Although the cottages were in Haddington Road parish, one of the last residents of the cottages, Breda Keogh, remembers that she and her friends went to the national school that's still in Belmont Avenue. Breda married from the cottages, when she was 23, and she and her new husband went to live in a flat at Park Avenue, Sandymount, for three years before buying a house on the northside.

Turner's Cottages were demolished in 1971/72 and the area redeveloped. The residents were moved to many other locations, with some going to new houses in Crumlin, Drimnagh and Beech Hill in Donnybrook. Despite the poverty and lack of facilities, the cottages had a strong community spirit that is now only recreated

The old Johnston, Mooney & O'Brien bakery, Ballsbridge. (Pat Liddy)

when the funeral takes place of someone who had lived there. Breda recalls that her parents were rehoused in a maisonette in Macken Street, which they hated. Her mother died not long after the move and her father only survived for a couple more years.

WELLINGTON PLACE VILLA

A house on Wellington Place that's built in the villa style, with one storey over basement, was reputedly connected with the duke of Wellington. It has long been said that the house was in fact the country residence of the Duke, in the days when this was open country, long before Waterloo Road was built. The duke was the victor of the famous Battle of Waterloo in 1815 and 30 years later, when Wellington Road and Waterloo Road were being built, they were named after the duke and the renowned battle. The house itself, the only villa on the road, doesn't resemble an eighteenth-century house, but the tall chimney stacks could indicate that a taller house once stood on the same site, and that this original house was built in the more modern Regency villa style in the early nineteenth century. However, documentation that would prove the Duke of Wellington's ownership remains elusive. One of the few references to the duke in this part of Dublin dates from 1776, when he was still the young and humble Arthur Wellesley; a newspaper report said that the boy had walked at a fast pace from Donnybrook to the South Circular Road in 20 minutes.

4

CHURCHES

BAHÁ'I CENTRE

Number 24 Burlington Road has been the national centre for the Bahá'i community of Ireland since 1984, when it left its previous centre, at No. 41 Morehampton Road. This independent world religion practices universal peace and the unity of all people. One of the first people to embrace the teachings of the Bahá'i faith in Ireland was George Townsend (1876–1957) a Church of Ireland cleric, whose father, Charles Uniacke Townsend, lived at Hatley, No. 10 Burlington Road, where George was born. Charles owned a successful land agency in Molesworth Street and at one time employed a certain George Bernard Shaw.

EPISCOPAL CHURCH, WATERLOO ROAD

The old Episcopal Church, with a mundane but high soaring façade, was a stirring sight at the Upper Baggot Street end of Waterloo Road, from the earlier nineteenth century into the early twentieth century. It was subsequently demolished and the site was used for the present-day St Martin's House, home of the National Roads Authority. The church had been built in 1835, with the cost of £6,000 raised by subscription.

The exterior was plain but the interior was described as 'exceedingly handsome' and could hold a congregation of 1,200. Demolished in the early 1920s, one of its rectors was Rt Revd Hamilton Verschoyle, who later became the Church of Ireland Bishop of Kilmore, Elphin and Ardagh. Where the church once stood, at No. 33 Upper Baggot Street, is now Eddie Rocket's diner, while next door, also on the old church site, is Helga Schworer's ladies' hairdressing salon. A neighbouring hairdresser's, Nahm's, is just along Upper Baggot Street.

FIRST CHURCH OF CHRIST, SCIENTIST

This church had been in Lower Baggot Street for many years; the church there had been designed by a firm called Millar and Symes, which specialised in bank architecture, so the new church looked like a cross between a bank headquarters and a Greek temple, complete with imposing Doric columns. The new church opened in 1928, was completed in 1931 but only lasted until 1974, when it was demolished. Subsequently, the new glass-fronted building on the site became the headquarters of Bord na Móna, then the Irish headquarters of O2, the mobile telephone company. But the old railings around the perimeter still remain in place. After the church was demolished, the local branch of the church held its meetings in a hotel, then took up residence at No. 21 Herbert Park, where it has been ever since. The congregation is small; a weekly service is held on Sundays and a weekly meeting on Wednesdays.

POOR CLARE SISTERS

This Order has been in Simmonscourt Road since 1906. In the nineteenth century, the Protestant owner of Simmonscourt Castle had the wall separating his house from St Mary's Lodge built higher. Later that century, the lodge came into the possession of the McCann

The Poor Clare's convent, Simmonscourt Road. (Jacqueline Holohan)

family and one of its members became Sister Mary Magdalene McCann. She was sent for her novitiate to the Poor Clare Monastery at Levenhulme, near Liverpool, from where she returned to their new community in Carlow in 1900. Within six years, seven sisters, and the Abbess, Mother Genevieve, came to Ballsbridge to start the new community. She remained as the Abbess in Simmonscourt Road for twenty-seven years. What is now St Damian's monastery was built between 1908 and 1912.

ST BARTHOLOMEW'S CHURCH

This church was consecrated in 1867, at a time when most of Clyde Road was still open fields. The church was designed by an English architect, Thomas Henry Wyatt. The original plans called for a spire on top of the octagonal tower, but this spire was never built because funds ran out. Next door to the church is the vast house that was opened as the vicarage and parish hall in 1872; since the 1960s, it has been the home of the Knights of Malta in Ireland but the church still has the use of the hall for functions. Andrew McCroskery, the thirteenth vicar of the church, says that over the next few years they will have to seek funding to preserve the unique interior decor of the church. Much work will be needed, too, on the exterior stonework. The church also has a distinguished musical tradition, including its choir. One member of the choir with a particularly distinguished record is Bobby Barden, who joined just over seventy years ago and has been singing with them ever since. A recent CD of the boys and men of the choir was launched in the summer of 2013.

Reverend McCroskery says that since Ballsbridge is a fairly disparate community of businesses and embassies, they want to develop the outreach to the local community. Events that help include the annual summer fair, the Bartsfest, as well as the patronal festival on the closest Sunday to St Bartholomew's Day. Ecumenical relations are also important for the parish and people from the church take part in many community events, including on Easter morning 2013 the dawn service on Sandymount Strand.

The garden of remembrance was opened a couple of years ago in the church grounds for the interment of ashes, and in 2013 a central cross was erected and dedicated, the gift of Don and Anne Cazzini. Just outside the church grounds, where Clyde Road meets Elgin Road, there used to be a postbox, now removed; the original box had been put there in late Victorian times.

St Bartholomew's church, Clyde Road. (St Bartholomew's church)

Since 1881, the church tower had been noted for its clocks and carillon. It was said that in Victorian times, the carillon would ring out 'God Save the Queen' but that particular tune has long since ceased. Since September 2013, the clocks and the carillon have been stopped, because someone complained about night-time noise pollution from the bells. Attempts to stop the mechanism between 11 p.m. and 7 a.m. didn't work, so the church had to stop the clocks and the bells that chimed every quarter of an hour rather than risk a substantial fine from Dublin City Council. In 2014, the bells and clock were restored to full working order.

ST MARY'S CHURCH, HADDINGTON ROAD

This fine church dates back to 1839 and the days when Haddington Road was called Cottage Terrace. In the years after it opened, the floor was earthen, but towards the end of the nineteenth century substantial improvements and additions were made. In 1894, the side aisles, the façade, the belfry and the tower, now illuminated at night, were added. The parish is unique as it has had a long line of bishops as parish priests. In recent years, the interior and exterior of the church have been substantially renovated. It is the only Roman Catholic church in Dublin to have memorials to parishioners who died in the First World War.

One of the innumerable stories about the church dates back over 100 years ago, to the time when two foundlings were left in the porch. They were promptly christened Joseph and Mary Haddington. The church has of course seen innumerable funerals, of the plain and the great, during its 175-year history. A State funeral held there in 1965 was of Colonel James Fitzmaurice, the aviator, who had died in the nearby hospital in Upper Baggot Street. Fitzmaurice had been made head of the Air Corps in 1927 and the following year, 1928, he was one of the crew on the *Bremen*, which made the first east-west crossing of the Atlantic.

In 2013, the church and parish suffered a great loss with the death, after a long illness, of the parish priest, Monsignor Patrick Finn, usually known simply as Father Paddy. Born in Athy, County Kildare, in 1938, the eldest of four children, he began as a priest teacher at the vocational school in Blanchardstown and chaplain to the Daughters of Charity on the Navan Road, between 1962 and 1967. Later parish appointments include Kilquade, County Wicklow; Cabra, Dublin and Clondalkin, also Dublin. In 1983, he spent a year in Kenya with the St Patrick's Missionary Society. From 1994 to 2003, he was parish priest of Dunlavin, County Wicklow, and it was from there that he transferred to St Mary's.

During his time in the parish, he oversaw the extensive renovation work on the church. Of him, Archbishop of Dublin Diarmiud Martin said that his gentleness and humanity made him a really great pastor; he loved people simply as people and was interested in them, wherever he met them. Speaking at his funeral, Dr Margaret Downes, chairperson of the parish pastoral council, said that he was welcoming and caring to all who crossed his path, especially those in difficult circumstances, and he also had a fantastic sense of humour. Fr Fachtna McCarthy was appointed administrator in January 2014.

ST MARY'S CHURCH OF IRELAND
ANGLESEA ROAD

This church dates back to 1827; it was one of the first churches in Ireland designed in the then newly fashionable Gothic style. It replaced a much smaller church on the same site that had been there since the early thirteenth century. One of the artefacts transferred from the old church to the new was the baptismal font in which W.B. Yeats had been baptised in 1865. The new church also had an imposing spire, but twelve years after it was built, in 1839, during the night of the Big Wind, it was badly damaged and had to be removed.

5
WORK

ADVERTISING

The Ballsbridge area has long been home to advertising agencies, although many of the long-established names have now gone, with the most recent disappearance being of the Leo Burnett agency on Wellington Road, which closed down in 2013.

In the 1960s, No. 46 Wellington Road had been home to Grosvenor Advertising, run by an inimitable character in the business, Johnny van Belle. In 1970, this was taken over by CDP, a London agency, which ran its Irish operations for many years subsequently. Its board of directors included Hugh O'Donnell, Bob Milne and Peter O'Keeffe. Bob Milne, who for years was its joint managing director, was a native of West Cork. He had spent years in the London advertising business before returning home to Ireland in 1962. The creative director was Breandan O'Broin, who says now that on a spring morning, with the pink flowering cherry trees in full bloom, there was no nicer place to go to work.

At its peak, CDP was one of the top five ad agencies in Dublin, employing over forty people, but inevitably time took its toll and in 2000 the Chicago-based global agency, Leo Burnett, took over and put its name on the front garden railings. But with the severity of the economic downturn in Ireland, the agency was forced to close in 2013.

Another early ad agency in the area was O'Donnell Earl which was based in Hume House on Pembroke Road.

Yet another long-time agency that no longer exists was AFA Advertising, founded by Aubrey Fogarty in Haddington Road. One of the newer agencies to start in the district was the agency founded by Brian Cronin at No. 10 Clyde Road. Cronin had lots of New York advertising experience before starting his agency in the early 1972 and it quickly won plaudits for campaigns – it did for such clients as Batchelors, the makers of canned baked beans, and Toyota cars. For the former client, he created the Barney and Beany characters, while for the latter client he ran many campaigns in Irish, very unusual at the time.

Donald Helme was another bright spark in the world of Irish advertising, having worked in big ad agencies in Dublin. He set up the Helme Partnership in 1986, and from 1988 to 2000 it was in Clyde Lane, the little lane almost beside Roly's restaurant. It then merged with an international agency and became Grey-Helme, in Serpentine Avenue, still in Ballsbridge. Donald Helme left the company he had founded in 2008; he says that the agency was 'ripped off' by a sister company within the group, which left it with insufficient business to be viable. These days, Helme is still busy presenting his jazz programmes for Lyric FM on RTÉ radio and he and his wife Dale Parry live part of their time in Italy.

Yet another high-flying agency in the old days was O'Connor O'Sullivan, which traded out of Northumberland Road. It was started in 1971 by Niall O'Sullivan and Owen O'Connor. It was eventually taken over by Helme.

Yet another was the Larkin Partnership, run by Martin Larkin in Haddington Road. Janus was a long-established ad agency that had begun as the in-house agency of Arnott's department store in Dublin. Its last port of call, before closing, was in Raglan Road; the house is now the Moroccan embassy.

But Dick Birchall, another noted figure in ad-land, set up his own agency in Waterloo Road in 1970 and it kept going for many years. Another noted figure of olden times in the ad business was Joe O'Byrne, who started his own agency in 1979. He's now in retirement, dividing his time between his Dublin home, off Burlington Road, and Spain. Adsell in Upper Leeson Street was started by Paddy Considine in 1963; in 1991, his daughter, Alice Considine O'Riordan, who also worked in the business, died tragically young.

Another long-vanished agency was Domas, once of the big names in ad-land, moved from Grafton Street to Granite House in Pembroke Road in 1958.

Frank Sheerin, a legendary advertising copywriter, had his own company at No. 31 Heytesbury Lane for many years He did the scripts for the Guinness 'Island' commercials, made in 1977, and widely considered the best Irish-made commercials of all time. Sheerin also wrote the scripts for the Harp lager 'Sally O'Brien' commercials. His personal partner is another copywriting legend, Catherine Donnelly.

One of the best-known characters in the Irish advertising business (and also the one with the sharpest elbows) was the late Peter Owens, of the eponymous ad agency. One sunny morning, just before lunch, in October 1993, this writer and his wife were driving through Ballsbridge. Their car was stopped at the lights at the top of Shelbourne Road, right opposite Roly's restaurant, which had not long opened at that stage. The present writer saw an emergency ambulance outside Roly's and said to his wife, 'I hope that's no-one I know.' Sadly, it was Peter Owens, who was just about to receive an award for his agency's advertising work in the national newspapers, when he collapsed and died from a heart attack.

Target McConnell's is a reconstruction of one of Ireland's oldest and largest advertising agencies. It is chaired by Pat Donnelly, with Geoff McGrath as CEO. Another firm, Ad Roll, a pioneer in using social media for advertising purposes, moved into Burlington Plaza on Burlington Road in July 2014. Clickworks, another digital pioneer, this time in creative design, had set up in Waterloo Lane in 2007.

New agencies have come to the fore, most notably Boys & Girls, which is close to the Upper Baggot Street end of Pembroke Road. It was founded in 2009 and by 2013 was employing around twenty-five people on a wide range of accounts. The DDFH & B agency, still going strong, was set up in Fleming's Place in 1983, but subsequently moved elsewhere, while the Billings agency, which was set up in Ballsbridge in 2003, is now in Dublin 2, renamed the Ebquity agency. For many years, The Media Bureau was in offices beside the Merrion Centre.

One newcomer to the district is Carlton Screen Advertising, which handles all cinema advertising in Ireland; now called Wide Eye Media, it moved to Fleming's Place in 2011. A number of new advertising related companies have started up in recent years, including Kinetic Advertising, an outdoor advertising agency, at Ballsbridge Terrace.

On the public relations front, one of the best-known practitioners work out of Northumberland Road, Don Hall, son of legendary TV star, Frank Hall. Terry Prone, described in a recent social media comment as 'having a finger in every hole in Dublin', was based in Northumberland Road for five years but she has now relocated to nearby Adelaide Road.

ALCOVE

Roly's restaurant was built on the site of a long-established branch of Hayes, Conyngham & Robinson, part of the chain of chemists taken over by Boots. Next door to that chemist's shop was The Alcove, a small shop that sold sweets, newspapers and other general items. The lady who ran the shop was May Martin and she was so diminutive that she had to climb stepladders to reach the jars of sweets. To customers coming in, the shop appeared to be a state of permanent chaos, but May knew exactly where everything was. The shop's site is now occupied by the Bon Espresso, which sells coffee, deli products and newspapers. On the opposite side of the road, around forty years ago, was Herbert House, another newsagents, at No. 8 Merrion Road.

BAGEL FACTORY

What is now the Bagel Factory at No. 9 Upper Baggot Street was once a store for selling fresh farm produce. Exactly 100 years ago, it was listed in the first telephone directories for Dublin; its number was 258, a slight difference from present-day phone numbers!

BAGGOT CLEANERS

Based in Upper Baggot Street, this firm of dry cleaners operated here for twenty-eight years but closed down the shop and concentrated on its Sandymount shop in June 2013. As of the summer of 2014, an Italian restaurant is due to open on the premises.

BAGGOT STREET WINES

Based at No. 17 Upper Baggot Street, this was once a branch of Oddbins but in October 2011 it reopened as Baggot Street Wines, where Gareth Connolly and Catherine Noakes are in charge. The person who charted the buyout was Gareth's father, Shay, who owns Shayz lounge bar in New York and which he runs with Gareth's brother, Jimmy. The shop is noted for its extensive range of wines, craft beers and other alcoholic drinks and has applied for planning permission to open a basement wine bar. Next door to the wine shop is Matthews' enticing Cheese Cellar, at No. 17.

BALLSBRIDGE COFFEE HOUSE

This was a grandiose plan developed but never put into effect around 1900, with the active support of prominent members of the RDS. Canon Dillon, at the time the parish priest of St Mary's, Haddington Road, was also an enthusiastic supporter. The idea was to open a coffee house together with a reading room and recreation rooms, in Ballsbridge, for the large numbers of working men in the area. The plan was that all refreshments would be non-alcoholic. Regular committee meetings were held at the RDS but this fine social idea never got off the ground.

BALLSBRIDGE AND DONNYBROOK TIMES

The area once had a local weekly newspaper of this name, launched in December 2002, but it only lasted a few months.

BALLSBRIDGE'S MAGDALENE LAUNDRY

Ballsbridge once had its very own Magdalene-style laundry, the Lamplight Laundry, mentioned in James Joyce's short stories, *Dubliners*. The Lamplight Laundry was set up in 1856, a Protestant institution for penitent females. Its inmates included women who had been working as prostitutes, or who had had children out of wedlock. The laundry employed them to provide services for many households and commercial firms in Dublin; the offices of the charity were at nearby Ballsbridge Terrace, while the location of the old laundry, which closed down in the early twentieth century, was close to the site of the present-day Herbert Park Hotel.

BALLSBRIDGE VILLAGE

This was a scheme in 2011 and 2012, designed to promote the Merrion Road end of Ballsbridge as a community entity, with the help of the RDS and the Aviva Stadium in Lansdowne Road. In Upper Baggot Street in recent years, traders have banded together in a local traders' association to market the area as a distinctive 'village'.

Leabharlanna Poibli Chathair Bhaile Átha Cliath
Dublin City Public Libraries

BANK OF IRELAND

One of the two largest Irish-based banks, the Bank of Ireland now has its headquarters on Mespil Road, where the old Pelican House of the blood transfusion service was once located. The Bank of Ireland also occupies all of Plaza Two in the Burlington Plaza development on Burlington Road. The Bank of Ireland branch at the corner of Upper Leeson Street and Sussex Road, built in the 1960s, was closed down in 2012. The three-storey building was then put on the market for letting.

BLANCHARDSTOWN MILLS

Close on a century ago, and almost beside what is now the AIB in Upper Baggot Street, was a branch of Blanchardstown Mills, which sold a wide variety of loose grocery products.

BURGER KING

What is now the Burger King fast food outlet on Upper Baggot Street was, until twenty years ago, a branch of the Dunn's fish firm. Its elegant shop on the street sold not only fresh fish but a wide range of deli items.

BURLINGTON ROAD

In the 1880s, many fine mansions were built in Burlington Road, but starting in the late 1960s a number were demolished to make way for new office buildings. In 1968, AIB opened new offices here, but these were demolished in the early twenty-first century, along with its Ark Life building, constructed in 1971. The distinctive new building of the Economic and Social Research Institute was also demolished, but the 1971 Institute for Advanced Studies building at the corner of Burlington Road and Waterloo Lane, still stands. The new building was designed in 2003 as the headquarters of the EBS building society, which is now part of AIB.

JOE BYRNE BOOKMAKERS

This was a traditional bookmakers' shop, founded in 1917 and closed down in 2013. It was one of many such bookmakers unable to survive competition from more modern bookmakers, like Paddy Power. The bookies in Mespil Road is long since closed, while in the summer of 2013 a much more modern bookies, Victor Chandler, closed down its outlet in Upper Baggot Street.

CADILLAC THAT GOT STUCK

During the visit to Ireland by US president Barak Obama in May 2011, one of the $300,000 reinforced Cadillacs used in presidential cavalcades was trying to exit the US embassy in Ballsbridge. It got stuck at the apex of the exit ramp and it took an embarrassing three hours before the vehicle could be freed.

CITY OF DUBLIN VOCATIONAL EDUCATION COMMITTEE

This august institution ceased to exist in July 2013, when the new local vocational and training boards came into being. It became the City of Dublin Education and Training Board. The CDVEC had been set up in 1951 with headquarters in the old Pembroke Town Hall at the junction of Anglesea Road and Merrion Road. In 2012/3 the organisation was appointed to run Susi, the new centralised scheme for administering third-level student grants. The scheme ran into immense trouble, with numerous students having to wait many months for their grants.

DONNYBROOK FAIR

This upmarket deli and restaurant, which also has a sub-post office, has been operated at No. 13 Upper Baggot Street since 2004, when owner of the chain, Joe Doyle, took over Murphy's newsagents. Before Murphy's, the premises had been Ryder's hardware stores.

Stephen Doyle, one of Joe Doyle's sons, was appointed manager here in 2013. One of the big recent changes to the shop has been The Grill, which provides chargrilled orders all day long. The most popular item is No. 13, a chicken takeaway. Paddy McLoughlin is a long-serving member of staff; he joined the old Murphys shop back in 2000 and is still to be found behind the counter today.

While the sub-post office is well established in Donnybrook Fair, there has been a post office in Upper Baggot Street for over 150 years. Initially, in the 1860s, it was at No. 14, on the opposite side of the street.

FÁS

The now defunct training organisation, beset by various scandals, had its headquarters in Upper Baggot Street. In 2013 the facilities offered by the organisation were subsumed into the new local education and training boards set up to replace the old vocational education committees. At one stage, Fás had plans to decentralise its headquarters to Birr, County Offaly, but these never materialised and neither did the plan for an equally spectacular development of the Fás site in Upper Baggot Street.

FENNELL PHOTOGRAPHY

Fennell Photography has long been based at No. 99 Upper Leeson Street, advertising itself as 'Ireland's premier photographic agency'. Frank Fennell, who founded the firm with his wife, Kay, is also an avid rallying enthusiast. But in 2001 he was involved in a serious crash in a rally in France that left him in a coma for thirteen days, in a hospital in Grenoble, but he made a good recovery. Frank met Kay, who has been equally enthusiastic about the photographic business over the years, at the Circuit of Ireland rally in 1973.

FILMS

Over the years, many films have been shot in Ballsbridge, including at shows in the RDS. The Horse Show was a favourite event for cameramen, going back to the 1920s. Newsreels that shot copious footage at the Horse Show over the years included Movietone News, Gaumont British News and Pathé News. Irish newsreels, too, frequently filmed at the RDS, including Amharc Éireann and Universal Irish News. Cinema newsreels lasted until the early 1970s when they were replaced by television news. But in recent years, Ballsbridge has been the location for various feature films.

Bloom (2003)

This adaptation of Joyce's *Bloomsday* featured Angelina Ball as Molly Bloom, Stephen Rea as Leopold Bloom and Hugh O'Conor, son of the pianist John O'Conor, as the young Stephen Dedalus. Many of its interior scenes were shot in a house in Elgin Road, No. 38, close to the US embassy.

Titanic: Blood and Steel (2011)

This Irish/Italian production, consisting of twelve one-hour episodes, was originally seen on the RAI network in Italy. Some of its period interior scenes were filmed in Wellington Road.

Thirteen Steps Down (2013)

This Ruth Rendell thriller for television was filmed in London and Dublin, with the former girls' secondary school on Haddington Road being used for some interior scenes.

FIRST EDITIONS

This antiquarian bookshop opened in Pembroke Lane, near its junction with Waterloo Road, in 2012. The Wee Stores had been on this site for many years, followed by other retail outlets, such as a branch of Sheridans the cheesemongers and a Parisian-style accessories shop. First Editions is run by Allan Gregory, brother-in-law of Anthony Harrison, whose mother and father ran the Wee Stores. Anthony lives just around the corner in Pembroke Road. The bookshop had an unexpected boost to trade after August 2013, following the death of Ireland's literary laureate, Seamus Heaney, when many people sought signed copies of works by the great poet. Allan Gregory is also chairman of the Irish Byron Society.

GARGOYLES

High up, at third-floor level, just below the roof, on No. 8 Upper Baggot Street, which houses the Subway/No. 8 newsagents, stand

Gargoyles above the Subway/Number 8 shop at Upper Baggot Street.
(Jacqueline Holohan)

two fine gargoyles. This block of shops was designed and built in
1890 and one of the architects involved subsequently did much work
on extending St Mary's Church just round the corner in Haddington
Road. That work included the new tower on the church, and on that
tower he designed some gargoyles. The finely carved gargoyles at
No. 8, Upper Baggot Street, mirror those on the church tower in
their intensity of detail and its possible that they were carved from
single blocks of stone at Casey's, a firm of headstone makers, on
the other side of Haddington Road. It's quite likely that the two
gargoyles at No. 8, Upper Baggot Street, were trials for the gargoyles
carved for the church tower. One of the previous occupants at No. 8
was Jennifer Gordon, an American-born homeopathic practitioner,
who has now moved to No. 15 on the opposite side of the street.

GERMAN DIPLOMATIC MISSION

The German diplomatic mission was the first to open in the new Irish Free State. It opened a consulate general at No. 58 Northumberland Road on 23 November 1923. The first head of mission was Georg von Dehn-Schimdt, from 1923 until 1934. These days, the German embassy is in Booterstown.

Soon after the German legation opened, the French followed suit, with an office at No. 32 St Stephen's Green, next to the Shelbourne Hotel. It wasn't until 1930, when the French bought the vast house called Mytilene on Ailesbury Road as the residence of their head of mission, that the long French connection began with Ballsbridge.

Diplomatic connections with Ailesbury Road were slow to develop initially. Just after the Germans and the French came to Dublin, Estonia and Romania opened legations in Ailesbury Road. But by 1930, around twenty-five countries had diplomatic representation in Dublin, and the move to make Ballsbridge the centre for foreign diplomats had begun. By 2013, around forty countries have their embassies in Ballsbridge. However, the new British embassy in Ballsbridge is comparatively recent. After their embassy in Merrion Square was burned down in 1972, it moved to premises on the Merrion Road, which had previously been used by the Agricultural Institute. The new British embassy next door didn't open until 1995 and its old embassy was turned into luxury apartments.

British Embassy, Merrion Road, Ballsbridge. (Jacqueline Holohan)

On the other hand, the US embassy, the most conspicuous, was opened in 1964. The architect who designed the embassy, John M. Johansen, inspired by Martello towers and Celtic imagery, died in October, 2012. In recent years, there was talk of the embassy relocating, but chatter on this subject has died down, while controversy raged among local residents in 2013 about the embassy's plans to heighten its surrounding railings. It wanted to heighten the railings by 2.89m, for security reasons, and to place a new cordon of bollards at street level, despite strenuous objections from An Taisce and two residents' groups. Despite all the protests, the new railings have now been put in place.

GINGKO FLORISTS

What was once a branch of the old First National Building Society in Upper Baggot Street now has a much more prepossessing occupier, Ginkgo Florists, which opened in 2013. It was opened by Bronagh Harte, who has a first-class honours degree in horticulture from Waterford Institute of Technology and who has had a decade's experience in horticulture and floriculture. She says she loves little shops with big personalities and wants to make her new shop stand out from the world of big chains and franchises. The shop provides a complete range of fresh bloom bouquets, as well as providing wedding flowers and doing corporate contracts. Bronagh also runs a flower school on the premises at weekends and in the evenings.

GRANTS PRINT AND PHOTO SHOP

This shop on Upper Baggot Street has been owned and run by New Zealander Grant Howie for the past thirty years. He says that the reason why it has lasted, while none of the other print and photo shops in the area have, is because they've always kept up-to-date with fast-changing digital and mobile phone technology. One competitor that is no longer in the area was Baggot Print & Design, run by Connie Fahy, which was directly opposite Grant's on the other side of Upper Baggot Street. Grant Howie says that in total, during the time that he's been trading in Upper Baggot Street, over twenty other quick print places and photo shops in the area have closed down. However, in 2013 Snap Printing opened a shop at Upper Leeson Street; previously it had been in Haddington Road.

HOOTER IN BALLSBRIDGE

Once a week a hooter sounds that can be heard over much of Ballsbridge. In the old days, the Swastika Laundry on Shelbourne Road had a hooter to summon its workers, but the present-day hooter, which sounds akin to an air-raid siren, is at Cathal Brugha Barracks in Rathmines. It's an alarm that's designed to alert personnel to security issues and incidents and it's tested once a week. Provided the wind is in the right direction, it can be heard clearly in Ballsbridge.

HORSESHOE CAFÉ

In Upper Baggot Street, close to the present-day TesCounty and Boots, the Horseshoe Café was a popular rendezvous in the late 1960s for workers from Bord Fáilte and even the ESB headquarters on Lower Fitzwilliam Street. The male ESB workers could always be distinguished by their customary tweed sports jackets and grey flannel trousers. One distinguished writer had a unique way of getting a seat when the place was full; Patrick Kavanagh used to stand in the middle of the floor, making disgusting noises clearing his throat. Anyone in close proximity left in a hurry, giving him a wide choice of seats. Kavanagh was renowned for spitting from one end of Baggot Street to the other.

IBM IRELAND

This noted US information technology company moved out of its extensive offices in Pembroke Road, close to Upper Baggot Street, in 2013, after thirty years' residency. The building is now being converted for a US industrial equipment group, Eaton, which plans to make the locations its global headquarters from early 2015.

INSTITUTE OF PUBLIC ADMINISTRATION

The Institute of Public Administration was founded by the late Tom Barrington to educate and train staff working in the public service and in local authorities, and is centred on the house at Lansdowne Road, beside the DART station, that was once home to the

Institute of Public Administration, Lansdowne Road. (Courtesy of
the Institute of Public Administration)

playwright Denis Johnston. He lived in the house for most of his life
and his daughter, Jennifer Johnston, the novelist, lived here until she
was 10.

By the time that Mary Guckian, now a poet, had come to work in
the IPA library, the Institute had spread over three adjoining houses,
including the former home of Denis Johnston. She remembers the
large garden at the back where all the staff sat out for coffee in
fine summer weather; it seemed to rain less in those days, she says.
Mary came to work at the IPA in 1986 and stayed for twenty-one
years, the longest time she had stayed in any job. 'As someone who
was starting to write poetry, the Johnston legacy gave me a sort of
contented feeling about the place,' she adds.

IONA TECHNOLOGIES

Once one of the high-flyers among Irish developed new technology
companies, it began life as a Trinity College company in 1991. The
software company did much to advance the use of the Internet in
Ireland and it had the state-of-the-art Iona Building on Shelbourne
Road. In 2008, the company was taken over by a US company.

IRISH CANCER SOCIETY

The society, based at Northumberland Road, has played a vital role in helping people in Ireland who are cancer sufferers. Since 1963, it has invested over €30 million in cancer research, with 95 per cent of that funding coming from the public, as well as being the national charity for cancer care. Another leading health charity, the Irish Heart Foundation, was also in Ballsbridge, at Clyde Road, but is now based in Ringsend.

IRISH COUNTRYWOMEN'S ASSOCIATION

It's had its central office at No. 58 Merrion Road since 1956. Previously, the house was the privately owned 'Cremorne'.

IRISH DAILY MAIL AND IRISH MAIL ON SUNDAY

Based in Embassy House, built in 1998 right in the heart of Ballsbridge, these two newspapers have been dramatic newcomers to the world of Irish newspaper publishing, with the daily paper selling around 50,000 copies a day and the Sunday title selling close on 100,000 copies a week. One of its recent innovations has been the opening of its own in-house TV studio – the only TV studio in Ballsbridge – which is used for making TV commercials, videos and other promotional material for the two newspapers. It is just one example of what Paul Henderson, the managing director, says is the all-important task of keeping people up to speed with the latest technology. Among the latest innovations is the evoke.ie consumer-orientated website. Alfred Harmsworth, who founded the *Daily Mail* in 1896, was born and brought up in Chapelizod, County Dublin. He became the first Lord Northcliffe.

IRISH FILM BOARD

When the original Irish Film Board was set up in 1980, it was based in Mespil Road. It was closed down in 1987 on the orders of the then Charles Haughey-led government, as a cost-saving measure. In 1993, the current President of Ireland, Michael D. Higgins, who was then culture minister, reconstituted the Film Board, which is now based in Galway.

IRISH LABOUR HISTORY MUSEUM

One of only two museums in Ballsbridge, the Irish Labour History Museum is based at Beggar's Bush, in close proximity to the National Print Museum. The Irish Labour History Society had been set up in 1973; its first president was John Swift, the head of the bakers' union, and the first deposit in its archives was the records of that union. The museum itself, together with the archives, was opened on 26 June 1990.

IRISH RED CROSS

In 1945, at the end of the Second World War, the Irish Red Cross, together with the army, set up a base on Mespil Road to help Irish families who had volunteered to look after refugee children from mainland Europe. Altogether, about 1,000 children from Austria, France and Germany came to Ireland in 1945 and 1946.

IRISH TOURIST ASSOCIATION

The forerunner of Bord Fáilte, which itself has been replaced by Fáilte Ireland and Tourism Ireland, the Association was set up in the early 1940s. It occupied part of Lea House, which was half in Pembroke Road (No. 93) and half in Elgin Road (No. 42), and which was demolished in the early 1960s to make way for the new US embassy. The other part of Lea House was occupied by a radio publicity company that made sponsored radio shows for Radió Éireann. The Red House, beside the Horse Show House pub on the Merrion Road, was once used to make the Hospitals' Sweepstakes-sponsored shows for the same station.

JOHNSTON, MOONEY & O'BRIEN

This great bakery in Ballsbridge closed down in 1989 after exactly a century on this site; it subsequently relocated to the old Downes bakery in Finglas, while it set up a bun bakery in County Meath. The firm had been formed in 1889 by the amalgamation of three bakeries: Johnston's, which had had a bakery in Ballsbridge since at least 1850; O'Brien's of Leinster Street; and John Mooney's Clonliffe

Mills on Jones Road. When it closed in Ballsbridge, it still employed nearly 500 workers and was noted for the shop, facing Ballsbridge Terrace, that sold bread and cakes that had been freshly baked inside the bakery.

When the bakery had opened, new drawplate ovens had been installed that meant a vast increase in capacity. The bread output was equivalent to 320 2lb loaves per man per day. These loaves sold for 3*d* each, but the bakery subsequently cut a farthing from the price. Tablehands were paid 34*s* a week and ovensmen 48*s* weekly. The hours were long, sixty a week. In 1904, bakers were locked out as the company tried to rewrite the terms of employment, but later that year, the bakers gave up their unequal fight and accepted the new terms.

The bakery's horse-drawn delivery vans were finally withdrawn in 1969, replaced by battery powered vans. The firm also had a chain of shops in the greater Dublin area, long since closed.

KURT KULLMANN

Kurt, a German, first came to know Sandymount in 1970 and married Catherine Donovan there in 1973. Since 1999 he and his wife have lived in the district. He also knows Ballsbridge well and is in fact a founding member of the Ballsbridge, Donnybrook and Sandymount Historical Society. Among his written works is a recently completed book on sports in the Pembroke Township.

Kurt recalls that when he first came to Dublin 4, people there who weren't born in Ireland were either tourists or diplomats. Since then, the number of foreign students has increased dramatically. Kurt says that years ago, if someone heard one's accent, they would ask, 'Where are you from?' Now, they ask, 'Where are you from originally?'

MASTERPHOTO

Today, Masterphoto, which does pre-press origination and has now diversified into printing, is one of only two business premises in Heytesbury Lane, where it has been established for over forty years. When it was starting, a variety of other tradespeople had premises in the lane, including a mattress maker and a panel beater. The latter was run for many years by a man called Foody who lived in Waterloo Road. It lasted until the early 1970s. In the 1940s, when few people lived in the lane, Paddy Harris used four mews properties as piggeries and went round in an ass and cart collecting swill.

In January 2013, Masterphoto suffered a tragedy, when one of the family that owns the company, Robert Delves (42), died on holiday in Tenerife. The hand rail of the balcony where he was standing gave way and he had a fatal fall. He lived in Rush, County Dublin, where he was very active in the local GAA club, and left his wife Ciara and three young children.

Foody's panel-beating workshop, halfway along Heytesbury Lane, traded for two decades until it closed in the mid-1970s.

MEDIA PEOPLE KILLED OUTSIDE THE RDS

Two well-known media people have been killed on the main Merrion Road outside the RDS.

Tony Butler began his newspaper career as 'Uncle Bill' on the old *Evening Press*, giving answers to readers' queries. His 'Ask the Experts' column was brilliant and widely read. In due course, he changed employers to *Independent Newspapers*. For the then *Evening Herald* – it's now *The Herald* – he wrote a similar column, then graduated to writing the nightly social diary. When he went to press conferences, he always drank milk, saying that journalists shouldn't accept hard liquor from the people they were writing about. He had a sardonic approach to life, but was immensely knowledgeable, a fund of information and a popular character in the newspaper business.

One night in 1989, when he was 69, he had been attending the launch in the RDS of a book written by his son-in-law, on the staff at the Institute of Public Administration. After the launch, Tony was making his way across the Merrion Road, on a night when the rain was teeming down, with very low visibility. Outside the Horse Show House pub, he was knocked down by a scooter. Tony remained in a coma in St Vincent's Hospital for several months and died on 10 August 1989, a much-missed journalist. His wife, who suffered from Parkinson's disease, only survived him by a year or two.

The other media person killed outside the RDS was Austin Finn, a photographer who had worked for thirty years as a press photographer, mostly with the old *Irish Press* group. For more than twenty years his iconic photos had filled the *Irish Press* and the *Evening Press*. He was also renowned for being a gentleman in an industry populated by tough guys. One of his last assignments, the evening before he was killed, was photographing the then Taoiseach, Bertie Ahern. After the *Irish Press* group closed, he worked for *Independent Newspapers*. On the day he was killed he was walking backwards at the junction of Simmonscourt Road and Merrion Road, to get a better photo angle, when he was struck by a car and died later that day in nearby St Vincent's Hospital.

MERRION CENTRE

At the corner of Nutley Lane and the Merrion Road, the Merrion Centre opened in October 1988, with Quinnsworth as its anchor tenant. Tesco took over Quinnsworth in 1997, which meant that the big supermarket here was rebranded. Before the centre was built, the land was derelict and overgrown. Next door to the centre are extensive offices, while in the centre itself, other shops include the Nutley Newsagents.

MILITARY TATTOO

This was a ground-breaking event at the RDS, staged between 28 August and 8 September 1945. It featured displays by the Army, the Air Corps, the then Marine Corps and the LDF reserves; the centrepiece of the Tattoo was a recreation of Eoin Ruadh O'Neill's victory at the Battle of Benburb in 1646. Other events included stunts on BSA motorbikes, carried out by members of the Irish Army; it also featured guns, shooting ranges and mocked-up mine fields. The event even featured a specially made film about turf production. There was also an exhibition stand on the Dublin Brigade, 1913–1921, organised by the 26th Battalion and the 5th Field Engineers.

Without a twinge of irony, the *Irish Press* newspaper noted that it had everything except the atomic bomb. The event attracted more than 200,000 visitors and was hugely popular with children; the influx of visitors to the RDS was a welcome boost for Ballsbridge at the end of the Second World War.

While several similar tattoos had been organised in the 1930s, the 1945 one was the last of its kind.

MONAGHAN'S BARBER'S SHOP

Gerry Monaghan ran a barber's shop at the start of the Merrion Road, down the little laneway close to Byrne's pharmacy. The shop ran for about forty years and Gerry's busiest time of the week, as related by his son, also Gerry, was Saturday night when many men came in to get their hair cut in readiness for Sunday Mass the next morning. The rush meant that Gerry Monaghan didn't get his dinner on Saturday nights until 11 p.m. He died about thirty-five years ago.

MONUMENT CREAMERY

Once one of the most renowned fresh food shop chains in Dublin, the Monument Creamery, was opened in the 1920s; its first shop was at Parnell Street, close to the Parnell Monument, hence the name. The founder was Seamus Ryan, who was involved in the start of Fianna Fáil in 1926. He died very young at his home in Rathgar, when he was just 37. He was given a State funeral.

One of his eight children, Patrick, served in the RAF during the Second World War and came home to manage the business, which subsequently had its head office in Camden Street, with shops all over the city. The Monument Creamery was noted for its fresh blocks of butter, in the days before refrigeration, and a stack of bakery products. In the 1940s its butter was a mere 1s 6d a pound. Its branch in Upper Baggot Street was at No. 46, now the Langkawi restaurant. The Monument Creamery went into voluntary liquidation in 1966 and closed down.

NATIONAL PRINT MUSEUM

The National Print Museum is at Beggar's Bush, where the old barracks had been built in the early nineteenth century. The first buildings were put up in 1828 on what had been slob lands on the banks of the River Liffey. In the aftermath of the formation of the Irish Free State in 1922, British forces were replaced by Free State soldiers and it was here, during the Civil War, that Erskine Childers, whose son also Erskine, and who later became a president, was shot by firing squad.

Today, the old barracks complex is used for many purposes, including sheltered accommodation for older people, the Geological

An old proofing press

Artist's sketch of the Museum

Exterior of the National Print Museum, Beggar's Bush
and an exhibit, an old printing press. (National Print
Museum)

Survey and the Irish Labour History Museum, as well as apartments.
The garrison chapel, built in 1866, was eventually converted into the
National Print Museum. The concept of such a museum went back to
1980 and it opened on a small scale in the Irish Print Union premises
in Lower Gardiner Street. Then, in 1991, the old garrison chapel was
acquired; one government minister who gave much help in this process
was Bertie Ahern, the then Minister for Labour. The new museum
was granted charitable status in 1993 and the rest is history; in the
intervening years, the museum has been substantially developed.

NUMBER ONE

This is the huge new complex under construction on the site of the old veterinary college, running from Pembroke Road through to Shelbourne Road. When completed, it will comprise offices and apartments.

O'CONNELL'S SHOE REPAIRERS

Once one of the longest surviving businesses in Upper Baggot Street, it was founded in the early twentieth century and lasted a century, until it closed down a decade ago and moved to Rathgar. The old-fashioned shoe repairer was replaced by an O2 store, which itself closed down; Grand Barbers is now on the site.

BILL O'HERLIHY

Now aged 75, this Cork native is a long time Fine Gael activist and is now chairman of the Irish Film Board. He has long had his own public relations company, set up in 1973, and based at Eastmoreland Lane, beside the Dylan Hotel. He has also been a soccer commentator and pundit on RTÉ television for over forty years.

OLDEST CHARITY

Ballsbridge is home to Dublin's oldest charity, the Sick and Indigent Roomkeepers Society, founded in 1790. For many years, it was at Palace Street, beside Dublin Castle, before moving to Lower Leeson Street. Its most recent move was to No. 74 Upper Leeson Street, at the corner with Waterloo Road. The society still looks after many needy individuals and families in Dublin and in 2012 donated €120,000 to over 200 individuals and families.

F.J. O'REILLY

This stalwart of the whiskey industry, descended from the original John Power of Power's Gold Label whiskey, did much to consolidate

Sick & Indigent Room Keepers' Society, at its most recent address, was at corner of Waterloo Road and Upper Leeson Street. (Sick & Indigent Roomkeepers' Society)

the Irish distillery industry in the 1960s into one single company, which was then taken over by Pernod Ricard, the French drinks company. O'Reilly also had long connections with the RDS, being chairman of its executive committee for many years and then president of the RDS from 1986 until 1989. He died in 2013 at the age of 90.

PASTEUR DAIRY

For years this dairy was in Pembroke Lane, opposite the end of Heytesbury Lane, and was often referred to as the 'Pasture Dairy'. It was next to the Sign Design workshops, which closed down in 2011 after a thirty-year stint in the lane. The Pasteur Dairy had been taken over about 1950 by John Cox, who took over a business founded in the city centre in 1930. It had moved to Pembroke Lane in the late 1940s. He built up a business that had many personal and retail customers all over south Dublin and at its height had up to sixteen vans painted in dark green. The slogan of the dairy was 'Rich, thick cream from the Pasteur Dairy'. The firm also sold milk and eggs, and even in the 1950s it was still using a hand churn for making butter. Cox was also noted, in the 1950s, for having a Belair Chevrolet car, a black American-made monstrosity, with huge tail fins at the rear; it was one of the first cars of its type to be seen on Irish roads.

According to Anthony Harrison, who lives in Pembroke Lane and whose parents ran the Wee Stores there, now the First Editions bookshop run by Allan Gregory, the Cox family lived in Wellington Road. It was a big family, ten children in all. John Cox used to work in the always freshly washed dairy seven days a week, but on Sundays, he treated himself and his family to lunch in the Glenview Hotel in Glen o'the Downs. His constant catchphrase was 'Cheer up, we'll soon be dead!' His second-in-command at the dairy was nicknamed 'Penny Eggs'. Cox's son eventually took over the business, but it closed down in 1970. The building was demolished and replaced by the houses that stand on the site today.

PEMBROKE FIRE BRIGADE

The old Pembroke UDC was based in the old town hall in Ballsbridge, which also housed the fire brigade. It was set up in 1881 with six firemen, who wore caps and red shirts and had two horses, four bells and 600ft of canvas hose. The following year, two telescopic ladders were bought for £4 16s each, while in May 1884 two bay geldings were purchased for £110.

RADIO AND TELEVISION

Leading commercial radio station FM 104 began life at studios in the Ballast House at O'Connell Bridge, but moved to Hume House around twenty years ago. Now owned by UTV Media in Belfast, it moved out of Hume House to its present studios in Mayor Street, near the International Financial Services Centre, in May 2010. Spirit Radio, the Christian radio station, was based in the FM 104 studios from 2009 until October 2012, when it moved to the radio centre in Bray, County Wicklow.

Ballsbridge has also had an input into the television business. RTÉ started its second television channel, known at various times as

Network Two but now RTÉ Two, in 1978. For a couple of years after its foundation, the station was based at premises in Pembroke Place, near the Herbert Park Hotel. These premises were then occupied by Cablelink, the cable TV company, which became NTL and is now UPC. Sky, the digital television provider, opened a customer service centre in Plaza One of the new Burlington Plaza development on Burlington Road. Construction of the Burlington Plaza had begun in 2007. Between 2012 and 2013, Sky created 500 new jobs at its centre there.

RAMSEY'S ROYAL NURSERIES

These extensive nurseries were sold in the late 1930s to the Irish Hospitals' Sweepstakes, which built its headquarters on the land. Those headquarters were demolished and redeveloped in the late 1980s and early 1990s as the present-day Sweepstakes' office and residential complex. As for Ramsey's Nurseries, these had started around 1860 at No. 90 Waterloo Road by Charles Ramsey; its earlier years, the firm also had a shop at Nassau Street.

As for the Sweepstakes, which began in 1930, within a few years it was so successful that its new headquarters in Ballsbridge were opened in 1939. It was an extraordinary place, a vast office complex with contemporary design that employed 4,000 people, nearly all women. The place even had its own staff canteen, a novelty for the time, where workers could enjoy soup and a roll for 3*d*, roast beef, roast mutton or fish for 5*d* and chips for 2*d*. By the beginning of 1987, the Sweepstakes was in terminal decline, about to be replaced by the National Lottery. Only 150 workers remained on the payroll and they were all made redundant in January 1987. Controversy raged for years afterwards about pension rights for those workers. The Sweepstakes itself went into voluntary liquidation in March 1987.

ROYAL CITY OF DUBLIN HOSPITAL

More popularly known as Baggot Street Hospital, it had been opened in 1832 and continued as a hospital until 1987. The present distinctive building dates from the 1890s. Since it closed as an acute hospital, it has been a community hospital. The Health Service Executive plans to close it down and convert the former offices of Hibernian Insurance in Haddington Road into the community hospital for the area.

During the Crimean War in the 1850s, forty of its nurses were present at the siege of Sebastopol. During the First World War it treated military casualties as well as casualties from the volunteers, and immediately after 1918, treated many victims of the great flu epidemic. It had many interesting people on its staff, including Helena Bewley, appointed its first lady superintendent in 1884. Just before the Second World War, one of its senior consultants was a German, Dr Strumpf. Staff were astonished to see this senior doctor giving the Nazi salute and saying 'Heil Hitler'. As soon as war broke out, he promptly disappeared back to Germany.

When it closed as an acute hospital, many services having being transferred to other Dublin hospitals during that decade, an ecumenical service was held and staff were treated to a farewell party in the old Burlington Hotel in January 1988.

RDS BLOODSTOCK SALES

For years, the RDS Bloodstock sales attracted breeders and farmers from far and wide – not just in Ireland – for the auctions of horses and cattle. Mary Kenny, who in the 1950s was living as a young girl in Herbert Road, recalls that they could hear the patter of the auctioneer over the loudspeaker system as the animals were paraded around the paddock. She says it was strangely pleasing and reassuring in its rhythmical cadences. She also says that her recollection of the Bloodstock Sales building was that it looked like an Art Deco cinema from the outside, but that could have been a trick of memory. However, she adds that, in due course, forty years ago, in metaphorical metamorphosis, the farmers and horse breeders departed and were replaced by the headquarters of AIB.

ROYAL DUBLIN SOCIETY FACELIFT

In 2004, the RDS was given the planning go-ahead for a €100 million facelift that involved the building of four giant office blocks at Anglesea Road and Simmonscourt Road. By 2013, only the two at Simmonscourt Road had been built. Michael Jacob, the RDS president at the time, said that the scheme, combined with potential income from the planned leasehold offices, would give the society significant added resources to develop further its funding of agriculture, arts, industry and science throughout Ireland.

The main RDS building in Ballsbridge is a protected structure, but the planning permission given to the society included the controversial demolition of a large number of buildings, including the Paddock Hall and the Shrewsbury Hall.

SCHOOLS

Marian College

Marian College, at the junction of Lansdowne Road and Herbert Road, is one of the leading secondary schools in the area, dating back to 1954. Its popular deputy principal, Hughie O'Byrne, retired in 2014.

The Masonic Female Orphan School

Established in 1792 for the daughters of Freemasons, the school moved to Burlington House (eventually occupied by Wesley College), close to Burlington Road. But it rapidly ran out of space and in June 1880, the Duke of Abercorn laid the foundation for the new school at the junction of what is now Merrion Road and Simmonscourt Road. The school had impressive facilities. It eventually closed down and in the 1980s the building was converted into Bewley's Hotel, which in turn was bought in 2007 by the Moran Hotel group from the Slaney Meat group headed by Wexford businessman Bert Allen.

The Pembroke School, at the corner of Waterloo Road and Pembroke Road, was established by Kathleen Meredith in 1929; for generations of schoolchildren, it was known simply as 'Miss Meredith's'. Renowned for its small classes, relaxed atmosphere and academic achievement, admission was by interview. In the senior school, preference was given to girls who had been in the junior school.

The last principal of the school was Dr Pauline O'Connell; the school closed in June 2004. The International School, Dublin, opened on the premises in 2007 but closed down five years later. The building has since been occupied by the Divine Word Missionaries, which has done extensive work on the interior.

One of the star teachers of the school in the early 1960s was the late Maeve Binchy, who taught history, Latin and religious knowledge, even though she hadn't the slightest interest in the last named subject. She simply read from the books prescribed by the diocese. If pupils were late for the first class of the day, they were locked out; on the rare occasions that Maeve Binchy was late to take a class, she was locked out and went to Searson's pub to relax for the duration of the lockout. One of Maeve's pupils at the school was the late Caroline Walsh, who, like her teacher, went on to work for *The Irish Times* and became literary editor there.

St Andrew's college, which had been founded in 1894 by members of the Protestant community in Dublin, at No. 21 St Stephen's Green, moved to Wellington Place in 1937. At that stage, it had just over 150 students. When it moved to Wellington Place, it took over the premises of what had been the Nightingale Hall Primary School. In 1938, R.M. Smyllie, then editor of *The Irish Times*, who lived in nearby Pembroke Park, was named a parent manager. Further expansions to the school took place during the 1940s and 1950s. Among the well-known teachers was John Ruddock, for sixteen years a maths teacher there, who later became even better known as a classical music promoter in Limerick. He died in 2013; he had been predeceased by his son Alan, a well-known Dublin journalist. Among noted past pupils were Denis Johnston and David Norris.

Bewley's Hotel, which was once the Masonic Girls School in Ballsbridge. The assembly hall, on the left, was built ten years after the school opened and is now an integral part of the hotel. (Jacqueline Holohan)

The college opened its new campus at Booterstown in 1973 and what had been the old premises at Nos 39 to 51 Wellington Place were demolished and replaced by apartments.

St Brigid's National School and Scoil Mhuire National School, close to St Mary's Church in Haddington Road, are due to move into what was the adjacent old St Mary's Secondary School on Haddington Road in 2015. The old building is being completely renovated and redesigned. St Brigid's, meanwhile, has a very wide variety of nationalities, over forty in all, reflecting the fact than many people from all over the world have moved into the Ballsbridge area in recent years. About half its pupils are Irish.

St Conleth's School in Clyde Road was established by Bernard Sheppard, on the eve of the Second World War. One of the teachers there after the war was a Breton nationalist called Louis Feutren, who had been in a Breton nationalist group called the Bezen Perrot, which collaborated with the Waffen SS during the German Nazi occupation of France. He fled to Ireland after the war, and from the 1950s until he retired in 1985 he was the much-respected French teacher at St Conleth's. He died towards the end of 2009.

The school has expanded much over the years and in August 2013, Donal O'Dulaing was appointed principal, following the retirement of Peter Gallagher; Donal is the son of veteran RTÉ broadcaster Donncha O'Dulaing.

St Margaret's Girls School

This Protestant school, at the corner of Burlington Road and Mespil Road, has long since been replaced by two office blocks: Burleigh House in Burlington Road and a government department in Mespil Road.

St Stephen's Schools

On Northumberland Road, these were designed by the renowned Victorian architects, Deane and Woodward, and opened in 1856. The old school buildings are now occupied by the Schoolhouse Hotel.

Wesley College

This Protestant college, for a long while on St Stephen's Green, bought its first property on Upper Leeson Street in 1918. It purchased Tullamaine, a large residence on 4 acres, for IR£3,000 and renamed it Epworth Hall. It was then used to accommodate girls and boys who were boarders, as well as a kindergarten and a preparatory school. Further purchases were Burlington House, adjacent to Embury Hall, which was bought in 1948, and in 1960 Burleigh House was bought and renamed Embury Hall. Then, in 1964, Wesley College moved to Ballinteer and Burlington House and Embury Hall were demolished; the Burlington Hotel was built on the site.

SMILES

What is now the largest private dental practice in the area if not the country has built its reputation on reasonable charges. Emmet O'Neill, one of the two men behind Smiles, is a nephew of Denis O'Brien, the mobile telephony and media billionaire. Smiles has a busy outlet in Ballsbridge, at St Martin's House. In April 2014, Smiles was sold to a British company, Oasis Healthcare.

SENTINEL VAULTS, ST MARTIN'S HOUSE, WATERLOO ROAD

The first privately owned high-security underground vaults in Ireland use the bank vault in St Martin's House, previously owned by AIB. The man who runs the company, which opened for business on 10 October 2013, is Billy Finn, formerly a senior manager with AIB.

SIGN DESIGN

A clear indication of the increasing gentrification of the lanes in the area came in 2013, when the premises of the old Sign Design Company in Pembroke Lane were sold. The craft company had traded there for thirty years but closed down in 2011 as a result of the recession. Following the sale of the site, plans were announced to turn the structure into a mews house. The same pattern is happening on all the lanes; fewer and fewer trade premises are surviving.

SPAR, UPPER BAGGOT STREET

This busy convenience store, open twenty-four hours a day, apart from Sunday night, was once a 7-Eleven shop. The 7-Eleven franchise operated in the Dublin market from 1987 until 1991; it didn't survive here, although it has a large franchise based in the US.

ST MARY'S HOME

This Church of Ireland home for elderly women started life as a school and convent named after St John the Evangelist and was run by the Anglican order of the Sisters of St Mary the Virgin. The building in Pembroke Park was built in 1891; the original entrance was in Clyde Lane, where there was also a chaplain's house. Much of the gardens were sold in the 1960s for the construction of Ardoyne House, the nearest in Ballsbridge to an apartment skyscraper. Since the 1970s, St Mary's has been actively used as a retirement home, while a few sisters of the founding order still live there.

St Mary's Home, Pembroke Park. (Alison Whittaker)

SWASTIKA LAUNDRY

Founded in 1912 by J.W. Brittain, a native of Manorhamilton, County Leitrim, it adopted the swastika motif as its emblem. In those days, the swastika was an innocent Indian sign of good luck; only later, in the early 1920s, was it adopted as the symbol of the Nazis in Germany. However, all through the Second World War and until its takeover by Spring Grove in the 1960s, it retained the swastika on its letterheads, on its chimney at the Shelbourne Road laundry and on its fleet of electric vans. Brittain's original intention had been to call it the Olympia Laundry.

Built on a greenfield site covering about 1½ hectare, the building was designed by Frederick Hayes, an architect whose offices were in Nassau Street. The laundry had stables to the rear for the horses that used to pull its vans, but in time, these gave way to battery driven vans. In its early days, the limit of its deliveries was Greystones, which meant an overnight stay for driver and horse-drawn dray.

By the 1950s, the laundry was still cleaning around 50,000 shirts a week. With such a vast turnover, customers had to have a number for every item they gave the driver. The laundry represented steady work for many people, especially women, in the locality, but the days of personal laundry for households were numbered as fashions and technology changed. However, the laundry workers were treated well; the Brittains were seen as a solid Protestant family who looked after their workers in the same way as the Bewleys.

Peter Brittain, whose father had run the laundry set up by his grandfather, has clear recollections of it. Several hundred people worked there and the employment was mostly for women, who were always referred to as 'girls' irrespective of their age. At that time, jobs for women were quite hard to come by, so a job in the laundry was sought after. Girls could start work at 14 and were called juniors, until they got to 18, when they became seniors, although always still referred to as 'girls'.

The floor space of the laundry was divided into various departments – sorting, washing, finishing and packing – and the finishing departments were further divided into ironing, flatwork, pressing and shirts. These were all referred to as 'Rooms', as with the Shirt Room or the Packing Room, although they were all in one space. On the special equipment for the shirts, each unit was manned by three girls, who could do 90 to 100 shirts an hour. Peter Brittain remembers one girl called Margaret, who was so deft at operating the shirt equipment that people were always being taken to see her.

Biddy Flood was in charge of the Shirt Room; she lived in Ringsend. In those days, there was no retirement pension and people were allowed to work on past the age of 65.

Many of the staff were second generation, their mothers having worked in the laundry before them. After twenty-five years of service, a worker would get a gold watch. But working conditions were strict. A steam whistle was operated by the boiler man and it sounded at 7.40 a.m. each working day and then at 7.57. If someone was late, they got 3 or 5 minutes grace, any later than that and they lost half-an-hour's pay.

One big change came when Richard Kingston took up the job of display manager in the late 1950s, when he had returned from London and he completely revitalised the appearance of the laundry. He invented a mechanism that enabled the special offer of the day to be posted on the side of the laundry's vans, while the laundry's shops were all redecorated in 1960s style, with bright colours. He set up all the designs in his studio and when a shop was to be transformed, it was done over a single weekend. He even designed new uniforms for the staff. Altogether, he spent fifteen years working at the Swastika Laundry, before setting out on the tortuous path of being a full-time artist, going on to become one of the most renowned artists in Ireland of his generation.

The Swastika Laundry van. (Jacqueline Holohan)

TURKISH EMBASSY

Turkey, which opened diplomatic relations with Ireland with an embassy on the Merrion Road in 1960, subsequently moved its embassy to Clyde Road. It moved from there to one of the largest embassy buildings in Ballsbridge in 2012, at the corner of Raglan Road and Elgin Road. The building had been constructed for developer Derek Quinlan. Next door is the new embassy of Belgium, relocated there at about the same time from its long time embassy in Shrewsbury Road. The Belgians paid €2.95 million for its new embassy, a building also once owned by Derek Quinlan.

TURNER'S IRONWORKS

For most of the nineteenth century, one of the biggest employers in Ballsbridge was Turner's Ironworks on Pembroke Road, where Hume House is now. Richard Turner opened his ironworks there in 1834 and they lasted there until 1876, when they were moved to North King Street. In 1892, Cramptons the builders moved its headquarters there.

The ironworks was a busy place, employing several hundred people making a vast array of ironwork, from the great palm house at the National Botanic Gardens in Glasnevin to most of the railings on front gardens across Ballsbridge. Westland Row station was one of the railway sheds built by the firm.

It also did much work outside Ireland including the Royal Botanic Gardens at Kew, near London. The great palm house here, restored in recent years, is considered the finest surviving example of Victorian ironwork and it was all made at Turner's works in Ballsbridge. It is a vast soaring space, whose design was based on a ship's hull; Turner's also supervised the changes to the heating system. Turner's, led by Richard Turner, the son of the firm's founder, also made twenty-two large vases that were part of the pond parterre in 1848. They made the ironwork for the water lily house, finished in December 1852, and they cast the 1846 Queen Elizabeth's Gate, which is now at the entrance to the lower nursery. Sadly, much of the subsequent credit for the work at Kew went to the designer involved rather than Richard Turner, who has become a rather forgotten figure.

UPPER BAGGOT STREET IN THE MID-1970S

Many people still remember some of the old shops that traded in the street in the mid-1970s, close on forty years ago. They included Roma hairdressers at No. 9, above the Kylemore Bakery shop; Ryder's hardware at No. 13; the Farm Produce Company at No. 17 and Kilmartin's the bookmakers at No. 19, which became Kilmartin's restaurant. On the other side of the street, the hospital side, the Open Till Eight boutique was at No. 20, while the Left Bank Boutique was at No. 50. Today, Upper Baggot Street has thirty-two protected properties listed by Dublin City Council.

WATERLOO GARAGE

This garage on Waterloo Lane is one of several 'lane' garages in the area – Baggot Lane also has a couple – but Erroll Dunne's establishment is probably the best known. It's been trading for close on seventy years, having been started by Erroll's father, James, who served his time at Keegan's in Ranelagh and then at the Morehampton Garage on the Morehampton Road, where Kelly's fabric shop and Terroirs food and wine shop are now located. The Waterloo Garage has been in Waterloo Lane since 1947; its first address was No. 47, but then it did a property swap with Boylan's insulation firm and moved to No. 85 where it has been ever since. In his earlier days, Erroll did a lot of motor car and bike racing and his navigator was a young man called Gerry Healy, who then started work in the Dunnes' garage. Nearly forty years later, he's still there.

Other lanes in the district, including Pembroke Lane and Baggot Lane, were once a hive of small businesses, including garages. Today, Baggot Lane still has car-related firms, the Pembroke Service Garage and Ever-Ready Panel Repairs.

WELLS CHEMISTS

Once one of the longest established chemists in Upper Baggot Street, the firm had started in Sackville Street, now O'Connell Street, in 1842, moving to Upper Baggot Street in the late 1880s. In 1888, it opened there with splendid new premises that included a laboratory;

the firm survived in the street for close on eighty years. The premises, at No. 20, are now occupied at ground-floor level by the Imsomnia coffee shop. Upper Baggot Street now has two pharmacies. One is Boots, formerly Hayes Conyngham and Robinson, and the other is Meaghers, now owned by Oonagh O'Hagan. It's part of a chain of pharmacies owned by her in the Dublin area.

WILSON'S BAKERY

In the 1930s, this renowned bakery was based in Fleming's Place, highly regarded for its celebration cakes. Wilson's had close on a dozen shops, the nearest in Upper Baggot Street and another in Rathmines. Fleming's Place also had another slightly more unusual business – a chimney sweeps. The sweep's mother kept a small office in the lane to take orders for her son while he was out sweeping the chimneys of the district.

XTRAVISION

This video rental and computer facilities shop was a well-known feature at the corner of Upper Baggot Street and Waterloo Road; it closed down in May 2013. The premises are now occupied by Hunter's, an estate agents.

6

PUBS, RESTAURANTS
AND HOTELS

HOTELS

Ariel House
This upmarket bed and breakfast establishment remains a firm favourite with many visitors from elsewhere in Ireland, indeed from all over the world, including North America. The original house at the heart of the present-day Ariel House dates back to 1850, when it

Ariel House, Lansdowne Road. (Jacqueline Holohan)

was built for a wealthy merchant shipper and his family. It became a small hotel in 1963 and in the subsequent decades it became very popular under the ownership and management of Michael O'Brien. Over the past decade, the women now running the place, Jennie McKeown, daughter of the owner, and Deirdre McDonald, have done much to restore the original Victorian décor to the three buildings that comprise the present-day Ariel House. It has thirty-seven en-suite rooms, and it provides breakfast and afternoon tea, with an emphasis on handmade, local produce. Its home baking is done daily.

Berkeley Court Hotel

This hotel on Lansdowne Road was opened by hotel magnate P.V. Doyle in 1977 as the last word in hotel luxury for Dublin, aimed at wealthy local business people and equally well-off foreign visitors. At the time of its opening, when its owner was keeping a proprietorial eye on it, a journalist at the *Irish Independent* said that Doyle, with his slicked back black hair and trim moustache, looked a little like a Mafia don greeting the rich and famous.

Many internationally known guests have stayed there over the years, including Frank Sinatra when he was giving a concert at the nearby Lansdowne Road stadium in 1989, and Helmut Kohl, who was German Chancellor from 1982 until 1998. When the former boxer Muhammed Ali was involved in the Special Olympics in Ireland in 2003, he stayed at the Berkeley Court and it was there he demonstrated a special skill – how to levitate, resting his body on just two fingers. It is now known as the Clyde Court Hotel but the lavish interior décor has been little changed. This hotel and the Ballsbridge Hotel nearby are owned by a consortium of banks and are operated by the Dalata group.

Former Burlington Hotel

What was the Burlington Hotel in Sussex Road was opened in 1972 by P.V. Doyle, who built up a chain of hotels in the Dublin area. For many years, the bulky Burlington was the largest hotel in Dublin, often called simply the 'Burlo', noted for the large servings in its restaurant and its nightclub. In recent years, the site was bought by Bernard McNamara for redevelopment, which never happened, then in 2011 the hotel was bought for €67 million by a US investment firm called Blackstone. It then announced a €15 million renovation plan and changed the name of the hotel to the Double Tree Hilton hotel.

Dylan Hotel

This luxury five-star hotel, with the latest in chic décor, has been open since 2006, with a wide range of facilities for guests. Each of the forty-four bedrooms is individually designed, equipped with the latest technology. The most elaborate room, the Dylan Signature Room, has been described as being akin to a Tim Burton set, while the cocktail bar is described as one of the finest in Dublin.

Before it became the Dylan, it had been known as the more sedate Hibernian Hotel. Originally, the building had been the nurses home for the adjacent Royal City of Dublin Hospital in Upper Baggot Street, opened at the start of the twentieth century. In recent years, the size of the Dylan Hotel has been much expanded with the addition of a major extension.

Dylan Hotel, which was once the nurses' home. (Jacqueline Holohan)

Former Jurys Hotel

Once the Intercontinental Hotel, which had been built in 1963, Jurys became an iconic hotel with such features as the Coffee Dock (open twenty-three hours a day) and the long running Jury's cabaret. It, the adjoining luxury hotel known as The Towers, and the Berkely Court had been acquired by developer Sean Dunne, who had ambitious plans to redevelop this corner of Ballsbridge; those plans were thwarted by the recession and determined local residents adamantly opposed to Dunne's grandiose scheme. As for Jurys, which has been well renovated, it's now known as the Ballsbridge Hotel.

The old Jurys is well remembered by Peter Malone, a former chief executive; Dick Bourke, a manager of the old hotel; and Jim O'Brien, who was manager of The Towers, the luxury hotel built onto the side of the old Jurys.

They remember that one of the many famous guests who stayed at Jurys was the late King Hussein of Jordan, who was able to indulge his taste for Big Macs. On one occasion, when a waiter went out to buy a toothbrush for him, he came back with something from the Jordan brand. The king was so amused that he gave the waiter a gold watch.

Well remembered from the old Jurys was the Coffee Dock. In the 1980s, it was doing 1,200 covers a day, which for the time was a tremendous throughput, making it the busiest restaurant in Ireland. For many people of all ages, the Coffee Dock was the place to see and be seen.

Another very popular attraction, especially for overseas visitors, was the Jurys Cabaret. It lasted for the best part of thirty years, with such performers as Hal Roach, whose humour was funny but clean. Singer Tony Kenny was another star of the show, which was long produced by Jimmy Potter, brother of the late comedienne, Maureen Potter.

The show generated at least one ghost story. One night, long after the show had finished, a security man at the hotel saw a man dressed in a long coat standing on the stage, asking for directions out of the place. The security man led him out of the hotel, as far as the main road, and swore that he had had a conversation with the man he was helping. But the next day, when the footage from the CCTV cameras was examined, only the security man could be seen. Hotel employees considered that the man on the stage was the ghost of someone who had worked in the show at Bunratty Castle for many years before being transferred to Jurys Cabaret. A short time later, he collapsed and died in the ballroom in the middle of a performance.

Four Seasons Hotel, Ballsbridge. (Jacqueline Holohan)

Four Seasons

The Four Seasons luxury hotel, at the corner of the Merrion Road and Simmonscourt Road, opened in February 2001. It has nearly 200 bedrooms and fourteen suites, all done out in the utmost luxury. Soon after it opened, author Robert O'Byrne wrote a condemnatory article in *The Irish Times* that created much controversy. His words were subsequently added to by another author, the late Hugh Leonard, who said that the hotel was a nightmare of non-styles, an explosion in a Lego factory. Leonard asked rhetorically if someone could not tear it down and replace it with a nice gasworks.

When Albert Reynolds, a former Taoiseach, sold his house in nearby Ailesbury road in 2007, he and his wife Kathleen moved into an apartment at the Four Seasons.

Herbert Park Hotel

This luxury hotel opened in August 1996, on part of the site of the old Johnston, Mooney & O'Brien bakery. It is Irish owned and has 153 bedrooms, four private meeting rooms, a restaurant, bar and lounge and gym. It was opened under the guidance of Paul Gallagher and since 1999 Ewan Plenderleith, from Scotland, has been the director/general manager. The hotel has retained its original contemporary style and the hotel has another priceless asset – its views of the adjacent Herbert Park.

Mespil Hotel

Once the headquarters of the old Department of Labour, Davitt House was converted into the Mespil Hotel in 1994 by Lee Kidney. The building was constructed in the mid-1960s when it was known as Annesley House. It was leased by the State from 1965 and was initially used to house the Labour Court. Kidney and his family had had a long connection with the old Jurys Hotel in Ballsbridge. The Mespil Hotel, with its 255 rooms, bar and restaurants, is a mid-range hotel that's very popular with tourists visiting Dublin, and the Mespil hotel and its sister hotel in Sligo have been consistently busy.

Pembroke Townhouse

This townhouse on Pembroke Road has comfortable facilities for guests, including close on fifty guest rooms and a breakfast room and study. Guests can also enjoy lavish breakfasts.

Sandymount Hotel

This hotel in Herbert Road was established by the Loughran family in 1955 as the Mount Herbert Hotel. For many years, it was known as the largest B&B in Ireland, but in 2011 the name was changed to the Sandymount Hotel. The hotel itself has gone more upmarket and is now being run by the second and third generation of the Loughran family. It's one of the few family-owned hotels left in Dublin.

Schoolhouse Hotel

This hotel on Northumberland Road was once the local Church of Ireland national school, opened in 1861. It closed down in 1969 and the buildings were left idle until 1997 when the Sweeney Group bought the premises and set about converting them into a hotel. The Schooolhouse Hotel, with its restaurant and bar also named after the old school, opened in 1998.

Waterloo House

This upmarket guesthouse at Nos 8 to 10 Waterloo Road, run by Evelyn Corcoran, has long been providing the utmost comfort for its guests and is highly rated. Spread over two lovely ivy-clad Georgian-style buildings, it has twenty guest rooms with facilities that include wireless Internet access. It has a four-star rating, the last word in luxury, while another guesthouse on the other side of the road, the Waterloo Lodge, is rated at three stars.

PUBS

Baggot Mooney's

This traditional pub was at the corner of Upper Baggot Street and Haddington Road. It was built in 1890 and was part of a chain of pubs founded in Dublin at that time. Inside, its décor was very much in the Victorian mode and it changed little over the years, but it closed down over thirty years ago and was replaced by a bank.

The clock on the old Baggot Mooney pub at the corner of Upper Baggot Street and Haddington Road, now a branch of Permanent TSB bank. (Jacqueline Holohan)

The pub that had been on the site before Mooney's was built and owned by a grand uncle of John Holohan, chairman of the local historical society. The premises are now occupied by a branch of the Permanent TSB Bank, although the old Mooney's clock is still in place on the exterior.

Bellamy's Pub

Like most other pubs in the district, these premises, close to the bridge in Ballsbridge, and which opened as a pub in 1859, has gone through a variety of name changes. In the early part of the twentieth century, it was owned and run by Thomas Hickey, who remained there until the 1920s. By the 1950s, the pub had become well-known as Coles, while in the 1970s it was known as the Embassy Lounge, run by Michael Haren. Sold in the spring of 2014, the pub's new owners include the noted rugby players Jamie Heaslip and Dave and Rob Kearney.

Chop House

One of the newest establishments in the district, the Chop House is at the junction of Bath Avenue and Shelbourne Road; Haddington Road, Grand Canal Street and South Lotts Road also meet here, making it one of the busiest junctions in Ballsbridge. The Chop House is at the very north-eastern tip of Ballsbridge and is owned and run by Kevin Arundel and Jillian Mulcahy. It serves traditional French cuisine with inspiration from across Asia. One of its features is a delightful small terrace for al fresco dining or drinking a cold beer. *The Michelin Eating Out in Pubs Guide 2014* lists around forty pubs across Ireland serving enticing food and included in the list is the Chop House gastro pub.

Crowe's Pub

This family owned pub, close to the bridge at Ballsbridge, and perhaps the most traditional in the area, goes back to the early years of the twentieth century. It is listed as far back as 1906 as Crowe's, but even as late as 1949 it was still billed as a 'family grocer, tea, wine and spirit merchant'. In the past two decades it has been substantially rebuilt, so the present pub bears no resemblance to the original. Going back around 130 years, one of the main features of this particular part of the Merrion Road was the Donnybrook District Dispensary; these days, the strip is a lavish dispenser of hospitality. Also at Crowe's, on the first-floor level with a separate entrance to the pub, is the Roast restaurant.

Paddy Cullen's Pub

This pub at the start of the Merrion Road has gone through a series of metamorphoses. In the 1930s and 1940s it was known as Fagan's, a grocery shop as well as a pub. By 1949, it had been taken over by Daniel Neary; while from the mid-1950s it was owned by J.J. O'Connor. By the early 1980s, it had become known simply as the Ballsbridge Inn, but in 1985 a well-known GAA player and manager, Paddy Cullen, took it over. He had been manager of the Dublin Senior Gaelic Football Team; these days, his pub is a mecca for people attending both soccer and rugby matches at the Aviva Stadium. It's packed with nostalgic sporting photographs. Beside Paddy Cullen's is the Baan Thai restaurant.

Horse Show House

Part of the Madigan group of pubs, which dates back to its original pub in Lower Abbey Street, where the group was founded in 1924. The pub here, right opposite the RDS Main Hall, goes back to the early twentieth century and at one stage, for a number of years in the 1920s, it was owned by Crowe's pub. Before Madigan's took it over, it had been run by Mrs Judith Ash and then Thomas Kavanagh. The present-day Horse Show House has a large beer garden at the back, which is called, in an excruciating pun, the Madigan Square Garden, after Madison Square Garden in New York. The interior of the pub has an interesting collection of old photographs.

Leeson Lounge

This pub is next door to O'Brien's and has been owned by Philip Morrissey since 1997. Before the present pub was established, another pub on the site was said to have sheltered two of the Invincibles responsible for the Phoenix Park murders in 1882, when the then newly appointed Secretary of State for Ireland, Lord Frederick Cavendish, and his assistant were murdered.

Mary Mac's Pub

This pub, which despite its comparative newness also has a venerable look to it, is really an extension of Paddy Cullen's next door. Until the late 1990s, Ballsbridge Travel had a shop here at No. 12 Merrion Road, but the advent of the internet made this and many other travel agents redundant. Like the next door pub, Mary Mac's is strong on sporting nostalgia.

O'Briens Pub

One of the most renowned pubs in the district, it has traded since the 1840s. In fine summer weather, crowds sit outside whiling away the time, but inside, the main bar has changed little over the years, with lots of mahogany and traditional style banquettes.

Going back to the early twentieth century, the pub was owned by someone called Morris, then a man called Hughes. In the 1940s it was run by Mick O'Brien from Moynalty, County Meath. He was succeeded in 1973 by Philip Shaffrey from Bailieborough, County Cavan; he sold O'Briens in 2003 to Tom Maguire, the present owner, while the other pub Shaffrey owned, the Stag's Head, off Dame Street, was sold in 2005. Philip Shaffrey retired to Rathgar and it was there that he died in June 2013.

Some of the staff at O'Briens have been there for many years, including barmen Tony Kelly and P.J. Malone, who've both worked there for close on forty years. The upstairs brasserie-style restaurant, The Sussex, was opened in 2007.

Ryan's

The present pub was built in 1913 and it has seen five generations of involvement by the Ryan family. The previous pub on this site had been founded in 1803; the adjoining barracks, a good source of custom, was opened in 1827. The pub was very close to the battle of Mount Street Bridge in 1916 and bullet holes could be seen in its side walls until the pub was reconstructed in 1988.

Thomas Ryan built the present pub 101 years ago, and in 1967 it was acquired by the Office of Public Works. The government of the day had grandiose plans for building a brand new concert hall at the site of the Beggar's Bush Barracks and that was why the pub was acquired. But after much shilly-shallying, the plans for the John F. Kennedy Concert Hall were abandoned. In the intervening period, the Ryans continued to lease the pub from the OPW, then the family bought the place back in 1988. Today, the pub sports many old photographs of the district on its walls.

Searson's

Searson's pub was opened in 1845 by Henry Tobin, grocer, wine and spirit merchant. He ran it until 1884 when it was taken over by William Davy, grandfather of John Holohan. The Davy family were well known and indeed were mentioned by James Joyce in his book, *Ulysses*. In 1890, William Davy carried out a major renovation of the pub and this held good for the next 100 years.

Searson's pub, Upper Baggot Street. (Jacqueline Holohan)

After Davy died in 1920, executors ran the pub until 1923, when his widow Josephine sold it to brothers Michael and William Searson. In 1926, William Searson took over the running of the place. Next door to the pub, at No. 40, was Bergin's drapery shop, well known in Victorian Dublin for its made-to-measure suits. Bergin's is one of the places featured on the long mural of old Upper Baggot Street in the Waterloo bar and café almost next door.

William Searson died in 1959 and two years later the pub was sold to the Hardy family. Eventually, it came into the ownership of a Guinness subsidiary, Murtagh Properties, but closed down in 2012. Later that year it was bought by noted Dublin publican Charlie Chawke, who had extensive renovations done. Since then, Searson's has been very busy serving drinks, meals, and providing live and onscreen entertainment.

In its earlier days, from the late 1920s onwards, it was very popular with sports journalists, while many well-known writers, such as Brendan Behan and Patrick Kavanagh, frequented the pub, but never at the same time, since they were bitter enemies.

Smyth's
Smyth's pub on Haddington Road dates back well over a century and retains its old-fashioned charm; all that it is missing is sawdust on the floor. The pub, which has a rear entrance in Percy Place, set a modern record in 1999, when it became the first pub in Ireland to be sold online.

The Pub That Got Scuppered
In 2002, Eugene Bellew, who then owned Murphys in Upper Baggot Street (now a branch of Donnybrook Fair), bought the next-door butcher's shop, Dowlings, and wanted to convert it into a pub. All the neighbouring pubs, including Smyths in Haddington Road, Searson's, the Waterloo and the Wellington Inn, joined forces in a legal battle to try and stop the pub opening. However, it did eventually open, but didn't survive all the subsequent changes to the shop.

Waterloo Bar
Established in 1840, it had a succession of owners, including John Byrne from 1866 until 1902 and Joseph Keogh from 1902 to 1923, but perhaps the best known of them all, Tipperary man Andy Ryan, took it over in 1961. In his day, the pub changed little, complete with its brown velvet banquettes, polished mahogany and stained-glass windows. In one rare interview given by Andy Ryan, he said that he considered a more mature staff the best, adding that he knew what people wanted and that in turn, they knew what they wanted. 'That is what a good pub is all about,' he added. Towards the end of 2013, Andy was photographed sitting on the bench beside the statue of a seated Patrick Kavanagh, the poet, once a 'regular' in the Waterloo. The bench with the statue is beside the Grand Canal, close to Baggot Street Bridge.

The Waterloo Bar became a great watering hole for artists from the district, in the days when it was known as 'Baggotonia'. Before he died, the newspaper columnist Con Houlihan recalled that he got to know a small group of artists, led by George Campbell, who met regularly in either the Waterloo Bar or in Searson's, almost next door. Con recalled that they didn't make a song and dance about their work, but talked about such topics as horse racing, football

The Waterloo Bar and gastro pub, Upper Baggot Street. (Jacqueline Holohan)

and boxing. One of the many well-known writers who lived in the district and who used to pop into the Waterloo for refreshments was Mary Lavin. The pub is now a gastro bar.

Andy Ryan retired from the pub business in 2002, but he and his wife Ann still live near to Waterloo Road. He sold the pub to the Quinn brothers, Frank and Michael, who also own the Lansdowne Hotel and the 51 bar in Haddington Road, among other premises. The 51 bar, almost beside St Mary's church in Haddington Road, dates to 1843, making it one of the oldest pubs in the district. Some of the stones used in the original structure came from the old Baggotrath Castle. The pub is popular with sporting fans and has a wide selection of sporting memorabilia, including photographs. The Quinns turned the Waterloo into a New York-style gastro bar, serving food as much as drink.

Wellington Inn

The Wellington Inn, at the corner of Upper Baggot Street and Mespil Road, has been in existence for the past 130 years and has traded under many different names. Around fifty years ago it was called Devine's, then it became the Crooked Bawbie and was also known as J.F. Handel's. From the mid-1980s, until it was acquired in 1998 by John Gibney, the present owner, it was called Cheers. He changed the name to its present title.

At one stage, another of its owners was Dessie Hynes, who also owned O'Donoghues in Merrion Row. The Hynes family lived in St Mary's Road and after Dessie retired, the family went to live in County Wexford. Dessie's daughter, Annette, died in Rosslare in the summer of 2013. John Gibney hasn't made too many changes to the pub; he likes to keep the old traditions, but has added a Saturday night piano bar and live sport on a big screen television.

RESTAURANTS

Asador

This restaurant was opened in 2012 by three partners, Shane Mitchell, Rebecca Murray and John Quinn, who had been inspired by Portuguese and Spanish grill-style cooking. The restaurant, in Haddington Road, serves brunch, lunch and dinner.

Bella Cuba

The Bella Cuba restaurant opened almost next door to Roly's as Ireland's only Cuban restaurant in 1999. It is still trading and in recent years has branched out with another establishment in Florida.

Bellucci's

Right opposite the RDS, this modern restaurant is in the style of a New York-Italian restaurant, complete with cocktail bar.

Bloom Brasserie

This brasserie, with French-style lunch and dinner menus, was opened in the basement of No. 11 Upper Baggot Street in July 2010, by owner and chef Pól Ó hÉannraich. The restaurant also has an outdoor terrace at the back that can be used in fine weather. It's almost next door to Donnybrook Fair and Matthews' cheese shop, making a little corner of fine foods.

Cafolla's

This Italian-owned fish and chip shop ran on Mespil Road from the late 1930s until it was sold by the Cafolla family in 2006 for €2.7 million. Annunziata or Nancy Cafolla, widow of Giovanni Cafolla, and who was often seen toiling over the deep fryers in the café, died in 2010. After it was sold, the café was converted into a more modern-style fish and chip shop, Beshoff Bros, named after Ivan Beshoff, the last survivor of the mutiny on the Russian battleship the *Potemkin* in 1905. Beshoff and his family subsequently built up a chain of fish and chip shops in Dublin. Meanwhile, this small strip of Mespil Road has built up into a small but interesting selection of take-away food shops and restaurants. The former Starbucks café on Mespil Road moved to nearby Waterloo Road; it now houses Thunder's home bakery and deli.

Embassy Grill

Situated on Pembroke Road, opposite the US embassy, it goes back to 1971; in recent years this Italian-owned café has been much refurbished. Customers can either order takeaways or enjoy a sit-down meal. In its previous existence, the premises were very popular in the 1940s as the Venetian Café, owned by an Italian man called Boni, which lasted until 1965. When he was a schoolboy Bobby Barden went to the Venetian Café, while he was still singing in the choir at St Bartholomew's in Clyde Road. He remembers that in the later 1940s it was very modern for its time and that even now, if it still existed, it wouldn't be out of place.

Expresso Bar Café

This establishment on St Mary's Road was long a popular meeting place for people well known in showbiz and the media, frequently quoted in the media, especially the *Sunday Independent*, but the owner was forced to close it down in April 2013. It has since reopened as Marcel Renard's restaurant; it's a sister restaurant to the The Green Hen restaurant in Exchequer Street.

Kilmartin's

This bistro-style restaurant ran at No. 19 Upper Baggot Street on the site of the old Kilmartin's bookies from July 1979 until April 1993. It was run by Scotsman Alan Aitchison and his wife Patricia,

KILMARTINS
WINE BAR

19 Upper Baggot St.,
Dublin 4.
Telephone: 686674

Lunch (Mon to Fri) 12 30 pm - 2 30 pm (last orders)
Dinner (Mon to Sat) 6 00 pm - 11 00 pm (last orders)

Kilmartin's restaurant and wine bar, Upper Baggot Street, which closed down in 1993.

whose family has had connections with Ballsbridge since the 1880s. In its heyday, Kilmartin's was very popular with Dublin residents, such as Mary O'Rourke, a former government minister, and the late Bernadette Greevy, an opera singer, as well as with tourists.

Kite's
This renowned Chinese restaurant has been established in two houses at Ballsbridge Terrace for over thirty years. It specialises in Cantonese cuisine, but also does Peking, Szechuan and Thai food. It is the oldest restaurant in this part of Ballsbridge, complemented by such newer arrivals as Roast, over Crowe's pub, and Bellini's, next to what was once the Toyota Centre. This part of Ballsbridge has another Chinese restaurant of equal longevity: the Orchid Szechuan on Pembroke Road. As its name implies, it specialises mainly in Szechuan dishes, but it also does some Cantonese and a few Thai dishes.

La Peniche
This is Dublin's only floating restaurant, anchored on the Grand Canal, just opposite the Mespil Hotel. It operates on a converted barge, the Riasc, and reputedly the restaurant is the only place in Dublin where the public can get a drink on Good Friday and St Patrick's Day.

Le Coq Hardi

This was the upmarket restaurant at the corner of Pembroke Road and Wellington Road set up by John Howard, a racing enthusiast, and his wife in 1977 on the site of the old Embassy Hotel.

They ran it until 2002, when they retired from the business. The building was subsequently purchased by a wine company, which still trades there today. When John Howard was in charge, the most famous and notorious frequent guest at the restaurant was a former Taoiseach Charles Haughey, who often brought his mistress, the late

The entrance to what was Le Coq Hardi restaurant on the corner of Pembroke Road/Wellington Road. (Jacqueline Holohan)

Terry Keane, to dine there. Haughey was a generous patron; in one year alone, he reputedly spent €15,000 from his Leader's Allowance at the restaurant. Once, Haughey brought his entire cabinet to dinner there. He chose beef for his main course and when the waiter asked him 'And the vegetables, sir?' Haughey allegedly replied, 'They'll have the same.'

Ravi's Kitchen

This first-floor restaurant, almost beside the Embassy Grill on Pembroke Road, opened in the summer of 2013 as an Indian establishment. It replaced a Japanese restaurant on the same level and a ground-floor Indian restaurant. Another Indian restaurant, the Jewel in the Crown, is round the corner in Shelbourne Road.

Roly's

Roly's restaurant opened in 1992 on the site of the old Hayes Conyngham and Robinson pharmacy. Its initial chef patron was Colin O'Daly, who stayed in the job until 2009. He began his cooking career as a commis chef at the restaurant in the original Dublin airport terminal, run by Johnny Oppermann. Subsequently he has become a well-known artist. Paul Cartwright, who joined in 1996, became chef de cuisine, while Hugh Hyland was appointed head chef. One of its specialities is its baking, done in the kitchens; Dave Walsh leads the bakery team. In recent years, the café adjoining the restaurant has become a popular venue for both its light meals and its takeaways, while the main restaurant remains as popular as ever. Roly Saul, who was one of the founding partners of the restaurant, gave his first name to it, and it remains even though his connection has long since ended.

The Sussex

As mentioned above, The Sussex restaurant is situated above O'Brien's pub, on the corner of Leeson Street and Sussex Terrance. Owned and operated by chef David Coffey and Damien Quinn and a favourite amongst locals and tourists alike, The Sussex has been ranked amongst the most popular restaurants in Dublin for several years.

7

TRANSPORT

RAILWAY STATIONS

The first railway station to open in the area was a temporary structure at Sydney Parade Avenue, which opened in 1835, soon after the Westland Row to Kingstown line was opened, the world's first commuter rail line. It took until 1862 for the permanent building here to be completed, with stone platforms and, in time, a brick building for the station itself and shelters on the platforms for passengers. The station was closed in 1960 during a reorganisation of railways in the Dublin area, but opened twelve years later in 1972. Today, the station generates well over 1 million journeys annually for the railway.

James Joyce immortalised both the station and the nearby road in a short story called *A Painful Case*. One of the characters in that short story, Mrs Emily Sinico, met her end at Sydney Parade. In much more recent times, a book by Ross O'Carroll Kelly highlighted the station, since its title was *Should Have Got Off at Sydney Parade*.

Ballsbridge's second railway station opened at Lansdowne Road in 1870; its full name was Lansdowne Road and Ballsbridge, but Ballsbridge was dropped from the title in 1872. It has long been a familiar stop for generations of rugby fans and soccer supporters going to matches in the nearby stadium. Since the DART service opened for public use on 23 July 1884, both these stations have become important places on the DART map.

However, when the DART system was being installed, the cost of replacing the level crossings at Lansdowne Road and Sydney Parade with tunnels was too great to be considered, so motorists and pedestrians still have to wait patiently at the barriers.

In the 1930s and '40s, a novel railway experiment was frequently seen at both stations, the battery powered Drumm trains, which started running between Amiens Street (now Connolly) station and Bray. They survived until 1949.

RDS STATION

The Ballsbridge siding was built in 1893, so that just beyond Lansdowne Road station trains could go as far as the station for the RDS, which was beside the present-day location of the Horse Show House pub. In its early days, the siding was home to an engineering facility for the railway, but this didn't last long. The special station for the RDS, opened in 1899, remained in use until 1971; it was only used when big shows were on at the RDS, especially the Horse Show and the spring. For rail travellers it was a boon because they just had to cross the Merrion Road from the station and they would be right in the RDS.

RAILWAY BRIDGES

The various railway bridges over the River Dodder, immediately beyond Lansdowne Road station, have suffered from flood damage at various times. The new railway line from Westland Row to Kingstown had no sooner opened in 1834 than the brand new bridge was destroyed in a sudden flood that had swept debris downriver from the bridges destroyed in Rathfarnham and Rathgar. This debris destroyed the new bridge but its reinstatement was swift; it was replaced within three weeks by a temporary timber bridge.

This was replaced by a second and more durable timber bridge in 1847, and then a stone bridge was built in 1851. The bridge lasted until 1934 when it was replaced again; the 1934 bridge is the one that is still in use today.

ROAD BRIDGE

In the seventeenth century, Nicholas Ball, who had a flour mill on the banks of the River Dodder, close to the present-day road bridge at Ballsbridge, built the first rudimentary bridge across the river. It replaced a ford. Ball's bridge gave the name to the district, which, in it earlier days, was called Ball's Bridge rather than Ballsbridge. Even what is now the Merrion Road outside the RDS was once called Ball's Bridge Road.

Eventually, the first stone bridge was built across the river in 1791. In the great flood of November 1834 it was swept away, but its replacement was completed the following year, 1835. In 1904 this bridge was substantially widened and strengthened and it is this bridge that still stands today, carrying five lanes of traffic. It's testament to its durability that these days, some 20,000 cars a day, not to mention buses and lorries, pass over it.

TRAMS

The first tram serving the area started on 14 March 1873, when a horse-drawn service linked Sackville Street (now O'Connell Street) to both the Phoenix Park and Donnybrook. That was a No. 9 tram. The No. 6 tram from Nelson's Pillar to Blackrock, going along Northumberland Road, opened in July 1879. By 1896 the entire line had been electrified.

The No. 10 tram, an electrified service connecting Phoenix Park with Donnybrook, via St Stephen's Green and Lower and Upper Baggot Street and Waterloo Road, opened on 14 May 1906. This was the first through service on the line. It was ended on 6 June 1940, less than a year after the start of the Second World War emergency. As the tram service came to a final halt, a makeshift band played for the crowds. The final No. 10 tram was packed with people singing 'Auld Lang Syne'. Another earlier tram service, the No. 5, from the Phoenix Park to Pembroke Road in Ballsbridge, closed down in 1930.

The No. 18 tram, from Kenilworth Road to Lansdowne Road, one of the few non-radial routes in the city, opened on 22 August 1898 and was electrified by mid-October the following year. It managed to out-last the No. 10 tram service by six months, being closed down on 1 December 1940.

One innovation on the No. 10 route didn't last long. In 1896, postboxes were installed in trams on this route so that passengers could post letters, but the uptake was poor and the boxes were withdrawn within a couple of years. Another feature of the trams was that each route had its own distinctive symbol; for the No. 10 trams, this took the form of two blue quadrangles.

Double-decker trams had been a relatively recent innovation, since they didn't start to appear until 1920. Before that, trams were single-deckers, with an open-top level so passengers who braved upstairs also had to endure the weather.

BUSES

When the trams ended, their route numbers became those of the replace bus routes, so the No. 10 tram was transformed into the No. 10 bus. Double-decker buses, built by the Dublin United Tramways Company at its Spa Works in Inchicore, and come into service on this route in 1938 and when the tram service ended in 1940, the buses took over completely.

Over the years, many different types of double-decker buses were used on the route; then, in 2001, Dublin Bus introduced Bendy buses on the route, travelling between the Phoenix Park and UCD at Belfield. However, the Bendy buses, with their two long sections connected in the middle, weren't popular with bus passengers. Neither were they suitable for the many narrow streets in Dublin, so this particular innovation was short-lived.

In 2010, Dublin Bus did a major organisation of its route network and the No. 10 bus was replaced by the 39A bus, which runs from Belfield to Ongar. The last No. 10 bus ran on 31 October 2010. A group of bus enthusiasts gathered outside Baggot Street Hospital that Saturday afternoon to take photographs of a 1970s bus with No. 10 on its destination boards.

Before Belfield had been started in the 1960s, the No. 10 bus only went as far as Donnybrook Church. On one day of the week, Sundays, the No. 10 went as far as Nutley Lane, because there were so many cars parked outside Donnybrook Church for Masses that the buses couldn't turn there.

Dublin Bus also runs the 145 bus, which stops in Upper Leeson Street and continues right through to Heuston station. These days, buses travel easily through Ballsbridge – along Waterloo Road and along Northumberland, Pembroke and Merrion roads – because of the dedicated bus lanes, which can only be used by buses and taxis.

AIRCOACH

Since 1999, the blue Aircoach buses have been a familiar sight in Ballsbridge. The company was started by John O'Sullivan, a former employee of Bus Éireann, but by 2005 it had been completely taken over by FirstCoach, a UK public transport company. After the company started, its first route linked the main hotels in Ballsbridge to Dublin airport, but after fourteen years in operation, the route was suspended in April 2013. However, vehicles on some of its other routes still ply regularly through Ballsbridge.

GREEN TRANSPORT

Up to 2013, Ballsbridge hadn't benefited from stations for the Dublin Bikes scheme; by mid-summer 2013, forty-four points were in use across the city, where people can hire bicycles. But plans to extend the scheme to bicycle stations in Ballsbridge should be in place by 2014.

Published in 2013, the draft of the greater Dublin area cycle network plan envisaged increasing the total length of cycle lanes in the area from 500km to 2,850km. Among the new cycle routes being planned are one from College Green via Merrion Square to Ballsbridge, while a second is due to run from Beresford Place via the Grand Canal and Shelbourne Road to Ballsbridge, while a third is destined to go from St Stephen's Green via Baggot Street and Northumberland Road to the Merrion Road.

Ballsbridge has also seen the introduction of a number of electric vehicle charging points, including at the Herbert Park Hotel, Bewley's Hotel and on Simmonscourt Road.

Cars belonging to the GoCar scheme, the only such car-sharing arrangement in Ireland, are increasingly seen parked in the Ballbsbridge area, awaiting collection by the next driver.

CARS

Ballsbridge and cars have long been synonymous; the first motor show in Ireland was staged in the RDS in 1908. The district was also noted, in the 1950s, for having the VW assembly plant in the former tram depot on Shebourne Road.

But during an earlier period, cars practically disappeared from the streets of the suburb. In 1939, 7,480 new cars had been licensed in the Free State, many of them to wealthy residents in Ballsbridge; by 1940, that figure had dropped dramatically to 240. Petrol rationing had been introduced in October 1939, a month after the start of the war. Cars with engines up to 10hp could get up to 8 gallons of petrol a month while larger cars were entitled to 12 gallons monthly. Only drivers of cars needed for essential services, like doctors and district nurses, could get a petrol ration. By the end of 1941, most private cars had been taken off the road.

By April 1944, petrol rationing was so severe that even doctors could no longer fill up their cars. Doctors in the country had to revert to using pony and traps to visit their patients, but in Ballsbridge doctors were within walking distance if they had to visit patients at home.

One innovation became quite popular – cars fuelled by wood gas. These cars had huge contraptions that burned wood to create gas and they worked quite efficiently. Nicky Broughall, a retired print worker with *The Irish Times*, who became prominent in the printing trade union movement, grew up in the area and recalls seeing, as a youngster, gas powered cars in Upper Baggot Street. But he remembers they were few and far between; apart from trams, then buses, and also bicycles, the streets of Ballsbridge were practically deserted during the war years.

NAME CHANGE

When the development of Upper Baggot Street started, around 1800, it was known as the Blackrock Road, while Lower Baggot Street was known simply as the road to Ball's Bridge. At the time the Irish Free State came into being in 1922, many roads and some towns across the new state were given new Irish names, but this didn't happen in Ballsbridge. All roads retained their existing names.

TRAFFIC LIGHTS

In the early 1970s, the then Dublin Corporation put up overhead traffic lights at the junction of Elgin Road and Raglan Road to try and cut down on numerous collisions here. The first morning the new lights were in operation, two motorists managed to crash into each other; one driver had been so busy looking up at the new lights that he failed to see the other car approaching.

8

SPORT

ANGLESEA TENNIS COURTS

Anglesea tennis courts, belonging to the Anglesea Tennis Club, were behind No. 95A Anglesea Road, beside the River Dodder. They were located here in the 1950s and 1960s, but by the early 1970s, were no longer in existence.

AVIVA STADIUM

Once the old stadium had been demolished and cleared, work began in 2008 on the construction of the new stadium at Lansdowne Road, named after the insurance company that is its main sponsor. In 2009,

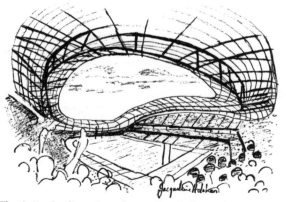

The Aviva Stadium, Lansdowne Road. (Jacqueline Holohan)

it signed a ten-year deal for the naming rights. The Aviva Stadium was opened in 2010 at a cost of €365 million and is designed as an all-weather rugby and soccer stadium. Its main tenants are the Irish rugby union team and the Republic of Ireland football team. The stadium can seat 51,700 spectators. The stadium is owned by a joint venture company that's owned by the Irish Rugby Football Union and the Football Association of Ireland on a 50/50 basis; when the sixty-year lease expires, ownership will return to the IRFU.

BALLSBRIDGE FOOTBALL CLUB

This football club played on the pitches in Herbert Park for about thirty years, before switching to Beech Hill Park. With about twenty-five older players, it plays in the Premier Sunday Amateur League for over 35s.

BALLSBRIDGE GOLF SOCIETY

This golf society has about twenty-four members, formed just over fifteen years ago. It plays on all the top courses in the greater Dublin area, including the Hermitage and the K Club. Based in the AIB Bankcentre, there is the AIB Information Technology golfing society.

CRICKET

The Ballsbridge area can claim to have had the first cricket club in Ireland. The game had been brought to Ireland by members of the British military forces in the late eighteenth century; the first comprehensive account of a game of cricket, which took place in the Phoenix Park, was published in 1792. As in England, in post-Napoleonic times, interest in the game expanded fast. In the 1820s, Trinity College Dublin was a cricketing hotbed, with many games played there during that decade.

But the first proper cricket club was set up in 1830, the Dublin Club, which was also first to have a proper pitch. To the back of Upper Baggot Street (the present-day Donnybrook Fair side) and to the east of the Grand Canal, the land was open; it hadn't been built up at all. In due course, Fleming's Place was built in this immediate area and construction took place along its length.

Elsewhere in Ballsbridge, the first mention of another cricket club didn't come until 1864, when the Merrion Club began playing at what later became the IRFU grounds at Lansdowne Road. It evolved into Merrion Wanderers and then into the Irish Land Commission Cricket Club. Finally, in 1906, it changed its name to the Merrion Cricket Club, after Upper Merrion Street, where the Land Commission had its offices.

After Lansdowne Road, the club played at various venues, at Harold's Cross, then on grounds beside the South Circular Road. Then, in 1906, the newly named Merrion Cricket Club leased grounds at Anglesea Road. The club was then reconfigured in 1950 when it bought the lands at Anglesea Road, where it has remained ever since.

In 1926 the club progressed to senior league cricket. The club's golden period was from 1940 to 1963, while the fortunes of the seniors was revived in the 1990s. Junior cricket also improved steadily during the 1990s, the same decade that women's cricket was revived.

The origins of the Pembroke Cricket Club at Sydney Parade, at the other end of Ballsbridge, are almost as far back. The club dates back to 1868 and was named after the then township of Pembroke. Currently, it has six men's teams in the league and cup competitions, while three ladies teams also play. The club is also noted for its schoolboy teams.

DUBLIN HORSE SHOW

This pivotal social and equestrian event at the RDS began in the mid-nineteenth century, when the society was located at Kildare Street in the city centre. The lawns in front of Leinster House were used for the show, which in those days, was a very modest affair. The first show was held in 1864 under the auspices of the RDS but was organised by the Royal Agricultural Society of Ireland. It had 366 entries with a total prize fund of £520; ass and mule classes were included.

The first show at Leinster House organised by the RDS took place at the end of July 1868. It wasn't until the RDS began developing in Ballsbridge in the early 1880s that the Horse Show was able to expand. The first show on the new site was staged in 1881, the year that the first viewing stand was built for 800 people, on the site of the present grandstand. In those days, horse shows were combined with sheep shows but these were all male events; women weren't allowed to ride in any jumping competitions until 1919.

In 1925, Captain Zeigler of the Swiss Army suggested an international jumping event and when the Aga Khan heard about this idea, he offered a challenge trophy. The first time that the Nations' Cup for the Aga Khan Challenge trophy was held was the following year, in 1926. Since 1868, the horse show has been a regular annual event; these days it is staged in August. The only two periods when the show wasn't held were between 1914 and 1919 and between 1940 and 1946, because of the world wars.

Today, the event is the largest equestrian event in Ireland and indeed one of the largest events of any kind staged in Ireland. The event has always been as important for its social events as for its horse riding competitions, although the days of the grand hunt balls in the Shelbourne Hotel are long gone. The show has also had various sponsors, including the Kerrygold butter brand; these days, it's sponsored by Discover Ireland. Currently, it has the third largest annual pool prize in the world for international show jumping.

One man who was particularly connected with the show was John E. Wylie, who provided the commentary on it for over forty years

Construction under way for an exhibition at the RDS. (Liam C. Martin/ National Library of Ireland)

until he retired in 1981. He had an elegant, genteel accent that was ideal for the show in those days, when the judges had to don formal wear, including bowler hats. For the highlight of the competitions, the Aga Khan Nations' Cup, the judges had to wear morning suits and top hats. Wylie's voice was the life and soul of the main arena when he was commentating and when he retired, he left a vacuum that was never quite filled.

HERBERT PARK CROQUET CLUB

Formed in 1986, it has about forty members who play on the two lawns. The first municipal bowling green in Ireland had been opened here in 1944. The bowling and tennis pavilion are currently being upgraded.

LANSDOWNE FOOTBALL CLUB

The club was founded in 1872 by Henry W.D. Dunlop, the man who developed the grounds at Lansdowne Road for sports use. The lease to the club was passed to the IRFU by Dunlop, who was president of the club from 1872 until 1904. His son, Eric, was involved with Lansdowne until his death in 2008.

Around 100 Lansdowne players have won international caps over the years, including such famous names as Michael Gibson, Moss Keane, Con Murphy, and Donal and Dick Spring. Con Murphy was the only player to have represented Ireland before and after the Second World War, and he was captain of the famous Irish team that defeated England 22–0 in the first post-war international in 1947.

LANSDOWNE ROAD STADIUM

The Lansdowne Road Stadium, used for rugby and soccer matches, dates back to the 1860s, when the grounds were opened for sports use. The stadium was named after the adjacent Lansdowne Road, which itself was named after William Petty-Fitzmaurice, the first Marquess of Lansdowne. He was also the Earl of Shelbourne, so Shelbourne Road was also named after him. It had been known as Artichoke Lane, after a French-born farmer who grew artichokes there.

The 11 March 1878, saw the first international rugby match at Lansdowne Road, when Ireland played England and lost. With the formation of the Irish Rugby Football Union, many improvements followed at the stadium, and in 1908 the first covered stand was built at Lansdowne Road, alongside the railway line. An uncovered stand was built at the north-west corner of the stadium, over the Lansdowne rugby club pavilion. In 1927, the old East Terrace was built; it was eventually replaced in 1983. The old stadium was finally demolished in 2007.

LEINSTER RUGBY

Leinster's rugby stadium at the RDS is going to be redeveloped and expanded to seat 25,000 spectators. Work is expected to start in 2016.

MARIAN COLLEGE SWIMMING

The 20m swimming pool at Marian College, at the Herbert Road end of Lansdowne Road, has been in use for over forty years. It is used by the college's water polo team, as well as by swimmers from the college and the district. The pool is also used by adults and children for swimming training. Following the floods of October 2011, the pool has been extensively refurbished. Over the years, the pool has also been used by film production companies and by firms making TV commercials.

OLD BELVEDERE

This club is based at Anglesea Road. The club was founded in 1918/19 for past pupils of Belvedere College on the north side of Dublin city. The club closed down a decade later but was reformed in 1930. It is commonly known as 'The Lodge'. Before the club acquired the lease on its Anglesea Road grounds, it played at various pitches on the north side. However, after the lease was taken on its new grounds in 1944, so much work needed to be done that they weren't ready for play until February 1949. A concrete terrace was built in 1958 and a decade later, in 1968, the present pavilion was opened. In 1993, a disastrous fire destroyed the old bar and ballroom, which were replaced two years later.

WANDERERS RUGBY CLUB

Founded in 1870, it is one of the best-known rugby clubs in the world and is the second oldest in Ireland. The club was started by members of the Dublin University Rugby club and Wanderers was one of the founding clubs of the IRFU, so that it is called Wanderers FC rather than Wanderers RFC, as were all clubs prior to the formation of the IRFU. To date, Wanderers has provided close on ninety Irish international players, as well as five captains of the Ireland team, one captain of England and Australia, as well as one captain of the Lions, Ronnie Dawson in 1959. The club has won many awards, including the Leinster Senior League on over a dozen occasions. It has a clubhouse both on the Merrion Road and at Lansdowne Road. Since 1980, it has shared Lansdowne Road with the Lansdowne Football Club. A prolonged legal case went on from 2005 to 2007 between Wanderers and the IRFU over the redevelopment of Lansdowne Road. The case was eventually settled, with Wanderers getting a corporate box and a new clubhouse.

In the earlier part of the twentieth century, three former Wanderers' players won VCs during military service: Tom Crean and Robert Johnson during the Second Boer War and Frederick Harvey, who served with the Canadian Army during the First World War. Wanderers has a close connection with Denis O'Brien, who was brought up in nearby Anglesea Road.

9

BALLSBRIDGE BATTLES

BATTLE OF BAGGOTRATH CASTLE, 1649

The Battle of Baggotrath Castle took place on 2 August 1649, at what is now the junction of Waterloo Road, Upper Baggot Street and Pembroke Road. Earlier that year, the Marquis of Ormond had created an alliance between the Irish Confederates, Lord Inchiquin's Munster Protestants, the Ulster Scots and the Royalists against the forces of the English Parliament, led by Cromwell.

By the end of July, Ormond's forces had seized the Parliamentary garrison at Rathfarnham, just south of Dublin, and seemed set to take Dublin itself. Ormond's next move was to seize Baggotrath Castle, much closer to the city of Dublin.

Parliamentary forces had demolished the castle, but Ormond believed it could be turned into a useful defensive spot. On the night of 1 August close on 2,500 Irish troops were sent to take over the castle, but many of them got lost during the short journey from their encampment at Rathmines. Meanwhile, the Parliamentary forces deployed 4,000 foot soldiers and 1,200 horse mounted soldiers close to Baggotrath Castle and on 2 August the Irish forces were quickly overwhelmed.

Parliamentary forces went on to rout the Irish troops camped in Rathmines. The defeat of the Irish alliance at Baggotrath Castle and then Rathmines had significant repercussions: a fortnight later, Cromwell's forces landed unopposed at Ringsend and thus began the Crowellian conquest of Ireland, a bloody affair that lasted for the next decade.

BATTLE OF MOUNT STREET BRIDGE, 1916

On Easter Monday morning, 24 April 1916, Patrick Pearse, the leader of the Irish Volunteers, read the proclamation of the Republic from the steps of the GPO, which the Volunteers had just taken over.

One of the strategic positions occupied that morning across Dublin was Boland's Mill, where a battalion was commanded by Eamon de Valera. At 11 a.m. that day, Lieutenant Michael Malone led sixteen Volunteers from C company, 3rd Battalion, towards Mount Street Bridge to prevent British reinforcements from entering Dublin from the south side. They occupied the schoolhouse on Northumberland Road, No. 25 Northumberland Road, the Parochial Hall on that same road and Clanwilliam House at the corner of Lower Mount Street and Clanwilliam Place. The first encounter came later that day when a unit of British soldiers, who were part of the Volunteer Training Corps, were returning from weekend exercises to Beggar's Bush Barracks. Members of the Corps, older reservists, were known as the 'Gorgeous Wrecks'.

At the junction of Northumberland Road and Haddington Road, this party came under fire, which they were unable to return, because their rifles weren't loaded. After the fire ceased, bodies littered the street and local people ran to help the wounded British soldiers. Several of the men who were killed were rugby men, members of the IRFU; one of those who died was Francis Browning, the president of the IRFU, which had its own branch of the Volunteer Training Corps at Lansdowne Road.

On 24 April mobilisation orders had been given for a division of soldiers based in England, who were sent to Dublin to take on the rebels. Early on the Wednesday morning, 26 April, they disembarked at Kingstown. Many of the young soldiers were from the Derbyshire and Nottingham areas, and were known as the Sherwood Foresters. The inexperienced soldiers marched from Kingstown, now Dún Laoghaire, to the RDS where they paused to rest. There, they learned that the schoolhouse on Northumberland Road was occupied by rebels, but they pressed on. As the soldiers moved out, one of their officers, Adjutant Captain F.C. Dietrichsen, met his wife and children on the roadside and broke ranks to greet them. He had sent them to Ireland a short while before to avoid the German Zeppelin raids in England, but when the British troops reached the junction of Northumberland Road and Haddington Road, the first shots fired by the rebels claimed the lives of ten British troops, including Adjutant Captain Dietrichsen.

The Sherwood Foresters stormed No. 25 Northumberland Road and one of those killed was Michael Malone. As the Sherwood Foresters were trying to reach their next objective, the schoolhouse, Volunteers fired on them until they ran out of ammunition. The Volunteers attempted to escape by the back of the Parochial Hall into Percy Lane, but were captured. The British soldiers then found the schoolhouse empty so they began an assault on Clanwilliam House. Three Volunteers were killed, while four British officers and 216 other ranks were killed or injured.

A total of twenty civilians were killed or injured while they attempted to help the stricken Sherwood Foresters on Mount Street Bridge. Covering fire had come from the Volunteers at Boland's Mill but this too was overrun, and Eamon de Valera was among those taken captive. He was subsequently held captive in the weighing room at the Pembroke Town Hall at the junction of Merrion Road and Anglesea Road.

1916 CIVILIAN CASUALTIES

Among the civilian casualties in Ballsbridge in the immediate aftermath of the Easter Rising was Revd Dr F.J. Watters, SM, of the Catholic University School on Lower Leeson Street. On 3 May 1916, the same day that three of the Rising's leaders, Pearse, Clarke and McDonagh, were executed, the priest, who was attached to St Mary's in Haddington Road, was coming out of St Mary's presbytery when he was shot by a British soldier. He was taken to St Vincent's Hospital on St Stephen's Green, but died on 8 May. Subsequently, he was buried at Glasnevin cemetery, where a Celtic cross was erected on his grave by his Marist confreres.

Close on a dozen civilian casualties were killed in the crossfire at Northumberland Road and Mount Street Bridge. Four of them were buried at Deans Grange cemetery.

Joseph O'Flaherty (no age given) from Northumberland Road, was buried there, as were Bridget Stewart, aged 11, who lived at No. 3 Pembroke Place (she and her family had previously lived at Turner's Cottages) and George Stewart, aged 58, who lived at No. 98 Haddington Road. The fourth victim buried at Dean's Grange was Margaret McGuinness, aged 50, From No. 3 Pembroke Cottages.

Another four casualties were buried at Glasnevin cemetery. John Byrne was a 60-year-old watchmaker who lived at No. 68 Shelbourne Road, while Richard Clarke, who was aged 73, lived at No. 61 Mespil Road. Charles Hyland was a 29-year-old dentist who lived at No. 3 Percy Place. Most tragic of all was 13-year-old Margaret Veale, who lived at No. 103 Haddington Road; she had looked out of an upstairs window with a pair of binoculars to see what was happening, when she was shot by an army sniper. She was brought to the nearby hospital in Upper Baggot Street, where she died soon afterwards.

Yet another victim from Haddington Road, 66-year-old Thomas Crowley from No. 93 Haddington Road, was buried at Mount Jerome. Two more casualties were shot dead outside Beggar's Bush Barracks, Joseph Hosford, 51, and Reginald Clery, a 22-year-old solicitor's clerk.

Two more victims of the troubles during the quest for independence were killed in the area four years later. In November 1920, Michael Collins had ordered widespread attacks on the so-called 'Cairo Gang' of British Military intelligence in Dublin, and as part of those attacks, on 21 November, two cadets with the Royal Irish Constabulary, Frank Garriss and Cecil Morris, were shot dead in the garden of No. 16 Northumberland Road.

THE MEMORIAL

The only such memorial in the Ballsbridge area was erected at the corner of Herbert Park and Elgin Road, just across from the US embassy. It commemorates the officers and men of the 3rd Battalion, Dublin Brigade, Old IRA, who died for Ireland in 1916 and afterwards. It was unveiled on 13 May 1973, by Eamon de Valera, who had been their commander in Boland's Mill in 1916. It was his last public engagement before retiring as President of Ireland.

10

CRIME AND MAYHEM

BROTHELS

Ballsbridge, surprisingly, has something a reputation for facilitating the world's oldest profession. For many years, ladies and gentlemen of the night have used Burlington Road as their strip and even today, some can still be seen plying their trade there, as well as along the banks of the Grand Canal. Over forty years ago, a Garda renowned for quelling street disorders, Jim 'Lugs' Branigan, was put in charge of a clean-up operation. When the prostitutes saw his unit's unmarked Bedford van arriving in the area with Branigan's crew, they promptly scattered. Nearby Waterloo Road was also long used by street prostitutes, but not these days. These days, most escorts operate behind closed doors.

So rampant was prostitution in the area around thirty years ago, that, on occasion, naked women were seen fleeing from altercations at the top of Wellington Lane, where it joins Waterloo Road. Wellington Lane itself has had several brothels over the years, including in the original Hamilton House. In a more recent occurrence, about five years ago, a house on the lane was rented for several months by a gang of east European women who conducted an active trade. Then, one morning, aware that they were under Garda surveillance, they fled so quickly that they even left their breakfasts untouched, leaving only a single large whip, that presumably doubled as a business card.

CURATE MURDERED

In 1826, Revd George Wogan, curate of Donnybrook, was murdered by robbers at his home in Spafield Place, described as 'near Ball's Bridge'.

JENNIFER GUINNESS

In April 1996, Jennifer Guinness, wife of merchant banker John Guinness, was kidnapped at her home in Baily, Howth, just to the north of Dublin. She was held captive for eight days in a fourth-floor flat at a house in Waterloo Road. The gang demanded a ransom of IR£2 million but five days after she was kidnapped, more than 200 gardai, many armed, surrounded the flat and eventually released her unharmed after a terrible ordeal.

LANSDOWNE ROAD RIOT

At an international soccer match between Ireland and England at the old Lansdowne Road stadium on 15 February 1995, the first 27 minutes of the game were calm, but then all hell broke loose.

David Kelly scored a goal for Ireland and that was the signal for some of the England supporters to start tearing up the seating, which was then rained down on the pitch. Some of the English rioters gave Nazi salutes. Kelly himself was hit by a flying piece of seating. At least fifty people were injured during the mayhem on and around the pitch and a supporter from Waterford, in his 60s, made it out of the stadium before collapsing and dying from a heart attack.

The match had been abandoned as soon as the mayhem started and it ended up with twenty people seriously injured and forty arrests. It turned out that members of the English National Front had come to Dublin with the specific aim of causing trouble at the match. Another eighteen years elapsed before Ireland played another friendly against England.

MURDER OUTSIDE THE BURLINGTON HOTEL

On the last day of August 2000, a group of students who had been celebrating in Anabel's nightclub in the Burlington Hotel emerged onto the roadway outside the hotel. One of them, Brian Murphy, got involved in an altercation and was tragically killed. In 2012, a film called *What Richard Did*, based loosely on the murder of Brian Murphy, was released in Ireland and went on to international release.

O'GRADY KIDNAPPING

In October 1987 a four-man criminal gang broke into the south Dublin home of John O'Grady, a dentist. The dentist and his family were terrorised throughout the night and the dentist was kidnapped against a ransom of IR£1.9 million. The gang was vicious, led by a volatile Irish National Liberation Army ex-convict called Dessie O'Hare.

John O'Grady was related through marriage to Dr Austin Darragh, a noted figure in the Irish medical world. The O'Grady family set up their headquarters in the apartment in the Cypress block in the Hazeldene complex in Anglesea Road belonging to Dr Darragh. It was there that the two little fingers of the dentist – that had been cut off by Dessie O'Hare using a hammer and chisel – were delivered. After the mutilation of his son-in-law's hands, Dr Darragh decided to pay the ransom demand.

They had arranged to collect some of the money from the Bank of Ireland in Lower Baggot Street, at 6.30 a.m., but the girl in the bank who was due to open the safe had slept in. The rest of the money, in sterling, had been flown down from Belfast by helicopter.

The whole episode was hugely discomforting for the whole family involved, but eventually the dentist was released, minus his two little figures. Not for the first time had a location in Ballsbridge played a key role in a kidnapping case.

SAVED BY THE WOMAN HE WIDOWED

In 1934, a tragic murder case happened at No. 33 Mespil Road, when Commandant Leo O'Brien, an officer in the Free State Army, shot

dead his brother-in-law, John Stokes, a Dublin civil servant. The two men had been quarrelling over an affair the army officer was having and it ended up with O'Brien shooting his brother-in-law dead. O'Brien was subsequently tried, found guilty and sentenced to death. However, O'Brien's wife and her sister, the wife of the murdered man, worked tirelessly to get the sentence commuted. A petition was organised, signed by over 60,000 people, and it was delivered to the Executive Council, as the government was then called. Various members of both the Dáil and the Seanad also campaigned for a reprieve from the death penalty. The petition was based on O'Brien's good national record and on the grounds of 'irresistible impulse'. A reprieve was announced from Government Buildings a few days before O'Brien was due to be hanged. The sentence was commuted to penal servitude for life, but he was eventually released. He ended up living a lonely life in a bedsit in Donnybrook, Dublin, with the only company offered by a few friends, since he had become totally estranged from his family.

UNSOLVED DISAPPEARANCE

One of the strangest mysteries in the district has never been solved. On 8 December 2000, a 22-year-old man, Trevor Deely, who worked for the Bank of Ireland group, disappeared without trace and has never been found. On the night in question, he had been to a pre-Christmas party and returned to his office in a building beside Leeson Street Bridge to collect an umbrella. He then walked along the Grand Canal as far as Baggot Street Bridge. At this point, images of him on CCTV were picked up and he then disappeared into the night. He had intended to continue walking down Haddington Road, then into Northumberland Road, heading for his flat in Sandymount. Despite intensive searches and enquiries over the years, no clues as to what had happened to him were ever discovered.

11

NATURAL HISTORY

CENTENARY OF HERBERT PARK

The centenary of Herbert Park was duly celebrated on 21 August 2011, when a family day out in the park that afternoon was organised by Dublin City Council. Children went for rides on a model train, as well as enjoying a carousel and a climbing wall. Chess champions invited challenges, while Tai Chi and yoga enthusiasts were also able to indulge their passions. Model boats sailed on the duck pond and some Sea Scouts demonstrated their nautical skills. Two bands, one from the army, the other the Past Times band, serenaded the bystanders, while historian and artist Pat Liddy conducted a walking tour of the area. John Holohan, chairman of the Ballsbridge, Donnybrook and Sandymount Historical Society, was one of those who dressed in suitable vintage style for the occasion.

FOXES

Foxes are often seen roaming around Ballsbridge, sometimes fed by residents. They've been seen doing such bizarre antics as climbing trees.

GERRY RYAN BENCH IN HERBERT PARK

A bench was erected in the park by Melanie Vervoerd to commemorate her partner, the 2FM radio presenter Gerry Ryan, who died in April 2010. The bench was torched by vandals in January 2012, but subsequently restored. In her tribute to Gerry Ryan engraved on the bench, Melanie Vervoerd took a line from a film, *Moulin Rouge*, which he had loved watching. It reads:

'Seasons may change from winter to spring but I love you till the end of Time.'

HERBERT PARK

Once, this area was known as Forty Acres, recorded as far back as 1200. In 1903, it was decided to stage a Dublin international exhibition and four years later, in 1907, it came into being. As part of the plans, the construction of buildings and features for the great show, including the duck pond, was carried out in 1906. But when 100 elm and oak trees were cut down to facilitate the exhibition, there was an outcry among local residents.

The exhibition itself ran for six months, from April to November 1907, attracting up to 3 million visitors. A century later, local historian Brian Siggins brought out a book, *The Great White Fair*, to commemorate the exhibition. After the exhibition site was cleared, plans went ahead to turn the space into a park. In 1909, ornamental gates were erected at both ends of the land that formed the park to denote its ownership by the Pembroke estate. In 1910, Pembroke UDC sought a gardener and an overseer for the planned new park and built a residence, No. 23 Herbert Park, which is now a training centre for the parks department of Dublin City Council.

That year, the £50 prize for designing the layout of the park went to a firm of landscape gardeners and nurserymen, Cheal and Sons, from Crawley in Sussex. On 19 August 1911 Herbert Park was opened as a public park by Lord Aberdeen, the Lord Lieutenant. That year saw the last royal visit to Dublin before independence, and the money that the Pembroke Township had left over from its celebrations was used to build a cast-iron drinking fountain in 1912 in Herbert Park.

In 1917, towards the end of the First World War, a total of forty allotment plots were created in the park. These allotments were also important during the Second World War. In recent years, allotments have been revived, just off the road that passes through the park, at the Ballsbridge end.

The year 1932 saw jurisdiction over the park pass from Pembroke UDC to Dublin Corporation. In 1997, when the Johnston, Mooney & O'Brien bakery site was being redeveloped, a new pedestrian entrance to the park was created, beside the new Herbert Park Hotel, featuring a pavilion and information panels detailing the wildlife in the park. A great variety of bird life can be found here, as well as

such species as the Great Ramshorn Snail, a common variety of snail, for whom the slow-moving waters of the pond are ideal. The park has impressive floral displays, organised by the parks department of Dublin City Council, which are changed regularly.

HERBERT PARK TREES

Between 1912 and 1916, a double row of Wheatly elm trees was planted on the edge of the footpaths beside the road running through Herbert Park. These stately trees lasted until 1986 when they had to be cut down because of Dutch elm disease. The following year, 1987, hornbeams were planted to replace them and in the intervening years, these have grown to full size.

In 1977, a Norwegian maple tree was planted in the park by Lilian Carter, mother of the then President of the United States, Jimmy Carter. The Asian Society of New York planted a specimen of the Tree of Heaven to mark its first visit to the Chester Beatty Library, then in nearby Shrewsbury Road.

In 2012, an oak tree was planted in the park and three park benches put in place dedicated to the twelve Irish businessmen killed in the Staines air crash in London in 1972 when they were on their way to Brussels for talks as part of preparations for Ireland's entry to the EEC the following year.

MODEL RAILWAY

The Dublin Society of Model and Experimental Engineers, founded in 1901, opened a railway track in Herbert Park on 27

August 1949. It ran on Saturday afternoons, giving children the chance to see the park landscape at close quarters. In 1981, the society moved the track to Marlay Park in Rathfarnham, but since then model boat enthusiasts have navigated their miniature craft in between the ducks on the park's duck pond. The Irish Model Boat Club has regular sailings on the pond of its members' crafts on Saturdays and Wednesdays all year round. About twenty people from all walks of life, including the public service and the defence forces, belong to the club, which dates back over forty years. The model boats they sail on the pond include everything from a US aircraft carrier to an icebreaker (just in case the water freezes over in winter!) The boats are battery propelled and radio controlled. On Sundays, the Dublin Radio Model Boat Club uses the pond.

RIVER DODDER

The River Dodder rises near the summit of Kippure in the Dublin mountains and wends its way through the southern suburbs of the city for 26km. After the dramatic falls at Clonskeagh, it passes beneath the bridge at Donnybrook, and then runs close to Anglesea Road. Running underneath the wide bridge at Ballsbridge, it then goes beneath the railway bridge at Lansdowne Road. It enters the River Liffey at the Grand Canal Dock in Ringsend.

In the eighteenth century, from Milltown to Ballsbridge, something like forty-five mills were located on the banks of the river, but by the early nineteenth century, all those mills had closed. One report commissioned in the earlier twentieth century was the Abercrombie Report on the development of Dublin. Many of its suggestions were never followed up, but in 1941, one of its recommendations was acted upon, the creation of a parkway strip beside the river from Ballsbridge to Old Bawn in Tallght. Dublin city and county councils decided to buy land beside rivers whenever the opportunity presented itself and develop pedestrian footpaths. Partly as a result, the Dodder, as it passes through Ballsbridge, has remained largely unspoiled, helped by the path that goes beside it as the river passes between Herbert Park and Anglesea Road. These days, virtually the whole length of the Dodder can be walked by public footpaths.

On several occasions, most notably in 1986, the river has flooded badly and, by 2013, flood prevention measures along the river were well under construction, including the section from the bridge at Ballsbridge to the Lansdowne Road railway bridge.

SPORT IN THE PARK

The Herbert Park Croquet Club was founded in 1987, while the park also has a bowling club. The first municipal bowling green in Ireland opened in the park in 1944. Today, the park also has tennis courts, with summer tennis schools for youngsters, as well as soccer pitches and a children's playground.

SWAN RIVER

Today, this river runs entirely underground through Ballsbridge. It's a tributary of the River Dodder and flows through Terenure and Rathmines, then under Ranelagh. Flowing beneath the Appian Way, it goes close to the Royal Hospital-Swan Place. Near there is a clue to its existence. Then it flows underneath Clyde Road, past the US embassy and then beneath Shelbourne Road. It empties into the Dodder at the foot of Londonbridge Road. The Swan also had a tributary of its own, where Herbert Park is now, the Muckross Stream.

WILDLIFE ON THE RIVER DODDER

The river is home to many water bird species, including mallards, moorhens and mute swans, while in recent years a small feral population of mandarin ducks has been established. The grey heron that often used to sit in the river close to the bridge at Ballsbridge was displaced by recent flood prevention work. However, it has now returned to its former habitat. Foxes are often seen along the riverbanks, while badgers and otters are sometimes spotted. Brown trout and sea trout are also present in the river but during the fishing season, from 17 March to 30 September, the best fishing locations are upriver from Ballsbridge. Local anglers restock the river every year with brown trout and these days, brown trout and even wild salmon have been caught in the lower reaches. When improvement works to the river are completed, scheduled by 2015, the whole length of the Dodder will once again become a reproducing river for salmon. For over 200 years, because of the weirs built between Donnybrook and Tallaght, salmon have only been able to get as far upriver as Donnybrook bus garage.

Leabharlanna Poibli Chathair Bhaile Atha Cliath

Dublin City Public Libraries